THE TOFFEES

ABOUT THE AUTHOR

Born in London, Graham Betts attended his first game in 1965 and has seldom been absent since, family commitments notwithstanding. Aside from a number of football books he has also written extensively on music, an industry he has worked in for the last twenty or so years. He lives in Aston Clinton in Buckinghamshire with his wife and two children.

THE TOFFEES

DAY-TO-DAY LIFE AT GOODISON PARK

GRAHAM BETTS

MAINSTREAM
PUBLISHING

EDINBURGH AND LONDON

First published in Great Britain in 1998 by
MAINSTREAM PUBLISHING COMPANY (EDINBURGH) LTD
7 Albany Street
Edinburgh EH1 3UG

ISBN 1 84018 036 6

A catalogue record for this book is available from the British Library

Typeset in 9½ on 12pt Times
Printed and bound in Great Britain by Butler & Tanner Ltd, Frome

Like many of the game's great clubs, the roots of Everton Football Club lie intertwined with the church and cricket. In 1878 a group of youths connected with St Domingo's Church had formed a cricket club and adopted football in order to enjoy some form of recreation during the winter months, changing their name to Everton to reflect the district in November 1879.

Everton made great strides over the next ten years, rising to become one of the most famous clubs in the country and founder members of the Football League in 1888. Whilst Preston won the League in the first two seasons it was in operation, Everton ended their domination and by the turn of the new century were vying with the likes of Aston Villa for the game's top honours.

The division between Everton and their former mentor John Houlding ultimately led to the club moving out of Anfield Road and into a new purpose built ground at Goodison Park. It quickly became one of the best in the country, hosting the FA Cup final two years after it first opened its gates and later staging international, World Cup and representative matches during the course of the next hundred years or so.

Fortunately, Everton have been blessed with sides worthy of such a fine stadium during that time. Everton has welcomed the League title on no fewer than nine occasions, the FA Cup five times and the European Cup-Winners' Cup in 1985. More importantly, there is a certain style about Everton that has been handed down from generation to generation; Ted Sagar and Neville Southall were the epitome of loyalty to the Everton cause and Dixie Dean and Gary Lineker expert strikers operating in different eras.

Whilst countless Everton books before have tended to start with the club's humble beginnings and work their way through to the present day, this book tells the story day by day and enables the reader to follow the landing of the first League title, the run that led to the European Cup-Winners' Cup and the ending of the championship barren spell in 1985. There is the joy of winning countless trophies and honours, tempered with relegation to the Second Division on two occasions.

I have also included details of the goals Dixie Dean scored during that record breaking season of 1927–28. Even 60 years on it still seems a wonderful achievement never likely to be bettered, but at the time Dean's goalscoring attracted little attention until almost the final weeks of the season. This was chiefly because interest was focused on the exploits of Huddersfield, who at the start of April headed the First Division and were through to the final of the FA Cup, and most pundits were convinced they would lift the double. Everton's sudden appearance at the death took everyone by surprise, with the press focusing only on Dean's achievements at the end of the season, so Dixie Dean didn't get the attention he deserved until he'd already accomplished the feat. I hope this book goes some way to redressing the situation; those who want to follow it week by week should turn straight to August 27th!

A book of this kind could not have been written without the invaluable help and assistance from numerous others, and I am therefore indebted to the following people for the part they have played in getting this project off the ground: Brian and Jube Watts, who spent many an hour checking over results, Brian and Frankie Renfrey, who've known the best of times and worst of times following Everton over the years, John Betambeau and John Roberts for their material help. Thanks also to Phil Robinson and Richard Lerman for their encouragement along the way, and to Bill Campbell at Mainstream.

I would also like to thank my family, Caroline, Jo and Steven, who can now move around the house without fear of treading on football books and programmes!

The photographs in this book have been supplied by Wellard Huxley Promotions, Bob Bond and John Allen (proprietor of *The Football Card Collector* magazine).

| 1891 | Aston Villa | H | Football League | 5–0 |

Everton brushed aside the challenge of Aston Villa with a 5–0 win at home as they closed in on their first ever League title. Goals from Brady (two), Chadwick, Geary and Milward left Everton just needing a victory over Notts County in their next match to confirm themselves as champions.

| 1894 | Darwen | A | First Division | 3–3 |
| 1895 | Sheffield Wednesday | A | First Division | 0–3 |

After winning their opening eight games of the season Everton had suffered something of a change in fortune, losing once and then drawing their next three games. They had then got back on the winning trail with four straight victories, a run that was brought to an end with the 3–0 reverse at Sheffield Wednesday. The defeat was enough to knock Everton off top spot and down to third; from having the title seemingly sown up Everton went into freefall, winning only five of their remaining 13 games and finishing the campaign in second position.

| 1896 | Blackburn Rovers | A | First Division | 3–2 |

The New Year opened with a 3–2 win at Ewood Park against Blackburn Rovers thanks to goals from Bell, Chadwick and an own goal.

| 1897 | Sheffield United | A | First Division | 2–1 |

Jack Taylor scored twice for Everton as they won 2–1 at Sheffield United. It would be almost a hundred years before Everton again won away from home on New Year's Day – the heralding in of each New Year was obviously well celebrated at Goodison!

1898	Blackburn Rovers	A	First Division	1–1
1900	Preston North End	H	First Division	1–0
1901	Bury	A	First Division	0–3
1903	Bury	A	First Division	2–4
1906	Manchester City	A	First Division	0–1
1907	Bury	H	First Division	1–0
1909	Newcastle United	H	First Division	0–1
1910	Bury	A	First Division	2–2
1913	Tottenham Hotspur	H	First Division	1–2
1914	Oldham Athletic	A	First Division	0–2
1915	Tottenham Hotspur	H	First Division	1–1
1918	Liverpool	A	Lancashire Subsidiary Tournament	1–4
1919	Liverpool	H	Lancashire Section Subsidiary Tournament	1–2
1921	West Bromwich Albion	H	First Division	2–2
1923	Tottenham Hotspur	H	First Division	3–1
1924	Sunderland	A	First Division	0–3
1925	Burnley	H	First Division	3–2
1926	Bury	A	First Division	0–1
1927	Burnley	H	First Division	3–2
1929	Derby County	H	First Division	4–0
1931	Bury	H	Second Division	3–2
1934	Derby County	H	First Division	0–3
1935	Derby County	H	First Division	2–2
1937	Preston North End	H	First Division	2–2
1938	Arsenal	A	First Division	1–2

| 1944 | Chester | H | Football League North (Second Championship) 7–0 |

Alex Stevenson scored four of Everton's goals in the 7–0 rout of Chester.

1946	Bury	H	Football League North	3–1
1947	Aston Villa	H	First Division	2–0
1949	Middlesbrough	H	First Division	3–1
1953	Barnsley	H	Second Division	2–1
1955	Preston North End	A	First Division	0–0
1959	Newcastle United	A	First Division	0–4
1966	Tottenham Hotspur	A	First Division	2–2
1972	Arsenal	A	First Division	1–1
1974	Ipswich Town	A	First Division	0–3
1980	Nottingham Forest	H	First Division	1–0
1983	West Bromwich Albion	A	First Division	2–2
1985	Luton Town	H	First Division	2–1
1986	Newcastle United	A	First Division	2–2
1987	Aston Villa	H	First Division	3–0
1988	Sheffield Wednesday	A	First Division	0–1
1990	Luton Town	H	First Division	2–1
1991	Chelsea	A	First Division	2–1

A visit to Stamford Bridge hardly seemed the ideal way to start the New Year, but Everton were keen to maintain a run that had taken them out of the bottom half of the table and into the top half. And so it proved, Graeme Sharp and an own goal from Jason Cundy were enough to give Everton a 2–1 win over Chelsea. It was the first time Everton had won away from home on New Year's Day since 1897 when they won at Sheffield United.

| 1992 | Southampton | A | First Division | 2–1 |

An Everton win away from home on New Year's Day turned out to be like the buses – you wait nearly a hundred years and then two come along almost at once – a trip to the south coast and Southampton was rewarded with a 2–1 victory. Mark Ward gave Everton the lead in the first half and Peter Beardsley wrapped up the points in the second.

1994	West Ham United	H	FA Premier League	0–1
1996	Wimbledon	A	FA Premier League	3–2
1997	Blackburn Rovers	H	FA Premier League	0–2

JANUARY 2ND

1892	Burnley	H	Football League	1–1
1897	Stoke City	A	First Division	3–2
1899	Nottingham Forest	H	First Division	1–3
1904	Notts County	A	First Division	3–0
1909	Bristol City	H	First Division	5–2
1911	Newcastle United	H	First Division	1–5

Everton slumped to their heaviest defeat of the season, home or away, with this 5–1 victory for Newcastle United.

1915	Newcastle United	H	First Division	3–0
1922	Sunderland	H	First Division	3–0
1926	Sheffield United	A	First Division	1–1
1928	Blackburn Rovers	A	First Division	2–4

Although Everton lost 4–2, Dixie Dean started the New Year as he had finished the old, scoring both Everton's goals to take his tally to 37 for the season. Whilst Everton were making steady progress up the table, Dean was beginning to whittle away at Camsell's record.

1932	Birmingham City	A	First Division	0–4
1937	Brentford	A	First Division	2–2
1943	Tranmere Rovers	H	Football League North (Second Championship)	4–0
1960	Bolton Wanderers	H	First Division	0–1
1965	Burnley	H	First Division	2–1
1971	Blackburn Rovers	H	FA Cup 3rd Round	2–0

Everton got off to a winning start in the FA Cup with a 2–0 home win over Blackburn Rovers. Jimmy Husband got both of the goals for the home side and earned Everton another home tie in the next round against Middlesbrough.

1978	Nottingham Forest	A	First Division	1–1
1982	West Ham United	A	FA Cup 3rd Round	1–2
1984	Birmingham City	A	First Division	2–0
1989	Nottingham Forest	A	First Division	0–2
1993	Wimbledon	A	FA Cup 3rd Round	0–0

Wimbledon away in the FA Cup third round was probably one of the hardest ties Everton could have drawn, but a solid defensive performance enabled them to earn a replay at Goodison Park thanks to a 0–0 draw at Selhurst Park.

| 1995 | Wimbledon | A | FA Premier League | 1–2 |

Another trip to Selhurst Park and Wimbledon but this time for League points. Despite a goal from Paul Rideout Everton were 2–1 behind at half-time and Wimbledon withstood all that Everton could throw at them in the second half to hold on for their win.

JANUARY 3RD

| 1891 | Notts County | H | Football League | 4–2 |

A 5–0 win over Notts County at Anfield Road ensured Everton would replace Preston North End as League Champions at the end of the third season of League football. Everton still had two games to play (both of which were lost) but still managed to finish two points ahead of the reigning champions.

1893	Sunderland	A	First Division	3–4
1900	Glasgow Rangers	A	Friendly	4–2
1903	Middlesbrough	H	First Division	3–0

Robert Balmer made his debut for Everton in the 3–0 home win over Middlesbrough. The younger brother of Walter, who was also on Everton's books at the time, Robert finally broke into the side on a regular basis in 1905–06 and was initially linked at full-back with his brother. Following Walter's departure he formed a partnership with John Maconnachie and made his final appearance during the 1911–12 season.

| 1914 | Newcastle United | H | First Division | 2–0 |
| 1920 | Sheffield Wednesday | H | First Division | 1–1 |

Charlie Brewster made his debut for Everton in the 1–1 home draw with Sheffield Wednesday. Born in Culsalmond he began his professional career with Aberdeen in 1913 and cost Everton £1,500 when he signed shortly before making his debut. An extremely dependable centre-half (he was capped by Scotland whilst with Everton) he could never be sure of a regular place in the club side and in November 1922 moved on to Wolverhampton Wanderers, later playing for Lovells' Athletic and Wallasey United, had a spell coaching in America and finishing his career as player-manager of Inverness.

1925	West Bromwich Albion	A	First Division	0–3
1931	Swansea Town	A	Second Division	5–2
1942	Sheffield Wednesday	H	Football League North (Second Championship)	2–0
1948	Blackpool	A	First Division	0–5

On the same day John McLaughlan was born in Stirling. Signed by Everton from Falkirk in October 1971 he spent four years with the club, making 61 appearances at full-back, scoring one goal.

1953	Blackburn Rovers	H	Second Division	0–3
1970	Sheffield United	A	FA Cup 3rd Round	1–2
1976	Derby County	A	FA Cup 3rd Round	1–2

More cup woe for Everton, with Derby County ending their interest in the competition at the first hurdle 2–1 at the Baseball Ground, Everton's goal coming from Gary Jones.

1981	Arsenal	H	FA Cup 3rd Round	2–0
1983	Tottenham Hotspur	A	First Division	1–2
1987	Queens Park Rangers	A	First Division	1–0
1988	Nottingham Forest	H	First Division	1–0
1994	Chelsea	A	FA Premier League	2–4

JANUARY 4TH

1890	Aston Villa	H	Football League	7–0

Everton began the New Year in cavalier fashion, spanking Aston Villa to the tune of 7–0 thanks to goals from Brady (two), Chadwick (two), Geary (two) and Latta.

1897	Glasgow Rangers	A	Friendly	4–4
1898	Glasgow Rangers	A	Friendly	3–5
1908	Manchester City	A	First Division	2–4
1913	Notts County	A	First Division	1–0
1919	Blackburn Rovers	H	Lancashire Section Principal Tournament	9–0

Everton were destined to win the Lancashire Section Principal Tournament, dropping only seven out of a possible 76 points. Their cause was somewhat helped with a 9–0 win over Blackburn Rovers at Goodison Park, Gault leading the scoring with five goals.

1930	Liverpool	H	First Division	3–3
1936	Liverpool	H	First Division	0–0

On the same day Jimmy Fell was born in Grimsby. A winger who began his playing career with Waltham FC, he arrived at Goodison via Grimsby where he made more than 150 League appearances for the Blundell Park club before switching to Everton. He spent a year with the club, making 27 League appearances before moving on to Newcastle United, later playing for Walsall before finishing his career with Lincoln.

1941	Liverpool	A	North Regional League	2–1
1947	Blackburn Rovers	H	First Division	1–0

1949 Roger Kenyon born in Blackpool. He signed with Everton in September 1966 and made his debut in the 1967–68 season, although he did not break into the side on a regular basis until 1970–71. A car accident in 1974 halted his career somewhat, but he eventually recovered and remained at Goodison until 1978 when he went to play in Canada for Vancouver Whitecaps. He later returned to England and played for Bristol City.

1958	Sunderland	A	FA Cup 3rd Round	2–2
1964	Hull City	A	FA Cup 3rd Round	1–1
1969	Ipswich Town	H	FA Cup 3rd Round	2–1

1972 Bill Shankly attacked the Everton management for failing to attend a disciplinary hearing for Alan Ball, the player who had transferred to Arsenal two weeks previously! The appeal against his caution, incurred whilst he was an Everton player, was unsuccessful.

1975 Altrincham   H   FA Cup 3rd Round   1–1
Altrincham pulled off one of the shocks of the FA Cup third round with a 1–1 draw at Goodison Park, Dave Clements scoring Everton's goal.

| 1992 | Southend United | H | FA Cup 3rd Round | 1–0 |
| 1998 | Newcastle United | H | FA Cup 3rd Round | 0–1 |

JANUARY 5TH

1894	Newton Heath	H	First Division	2–0
1895	Wolverhampton Wanderers	A	First Division	0–1
1901	Wolverhampton Wanderers	A	First Division	1–1
1907	Preston North End	A	First Division	1–1

1913 Walter Boyes born in Sheffield. Despite having one leg longer than the other Wally excelled at football whilst at school and represented Sheffield Schoolboys. He later joined West Bromwich Albion and scored in the FA Cup final of 1935 against Sheffield Wednesday! He joined Everton in February 1938 and won a League championship medal in 1939. He remained at Goodison until 1949 when he joined Notts County, but having made only three appearances for the Magpies joined Scunthorpe United where he finished his League career. He later went into management and coaching and died in September 1960 at the comparatively young age of 47.

1918	Blackpool	A	Lancashire Section Principal Tournament	0–1
1924	Bolton Wanderers	H	First Division	2–2
1929	Portsmouth	A	First Division	0–3
1935	Preston North End	A	First Division	2–2
1946	Preston North End	A	FA Cup 3rd Round 1st Leg	1–2

With normal League football still to resume after the end of the Second World War, it was decided to make the early rounds of the FA Cup decided over two legs. Everton took on Preston North End at Deepdale in the third round first leg and were beaten 2–1.

1951 Gary Jones born in Liverpool. An extremely talented yet controversial character, he made his debut for the club in the 1970–71 season and went on to make nearly 100 appearances for the first team during the next six seasons. However, a series of bust-ups with manager Billy Bingham led to him handing in a transfer request and subsequently being sold to Birmingham City for £110,000. After one season there he went to play in North America for Fort Lauderdale.

1952	Rotherham United	A	Second Division	1–1
1957	Blackburn Rovers	H	FA Cup 3rd Round	1–0
1962	King's Lynn	H	FA Cup 3rd Round	4–0

Non-League King's Lynn were the visitors in the FA Cup third round and gave a good account of themselves in a 4–0 win for Everton, the goals coming from Billy Bingham, Bobby Collins, Jimmy Fell and Roy Vernon.

1972   Everton's Chairman George Watts defended the club after Bill Shankly's outburst, stating 'We did not know about the date of the hearing, and Mr Mee [Arsenal manager] informed me he does not wish Mr Catterick to attend.' Bill Shankly then consulted with the Arsenal management team and, never lost for words, withdrew his earlier statement!

1974	Blackburn Rovers	H	FA Cup 3rd Round	3–0
1980	Aldershot	H	FA Cup 3rd Round	4–1
1985	Leeds United	A	FA Cup 3rd Round	2–0
1986	Exeter City	H	FA Cup 3rd Round	1–0
1991	Charlton Athletic	A	FA Cup 3rd Round	2–1
1997	Swindon Town	H	FA Cup 3rd Round	3–0

Richard Dunne became the youngest player to have played for Everton when he was selected for the FA Cup third round cup-tie against Swindon at Goodison Park. He was only 17 years and 106 days old. Everton won the match 3–0.

JANUARY 6TH

1894	Newton Heath	H	First Division	2–0
1900	Newcastle United	H	First Division	3–2
1906	Preston North End	H	First Division	1–0
1912	Manchester United	H	First Division	4–0
1917	Blackburn Rovers	A	Lancashire Section Principal Tournament	5–1
1923	Huddersfield Town	A	First Division	0–1
1934	Birmingham City	H	First Division	2–0
1940	Manchester United	H	War Regional League, Western Division	3–2
1945	Bolton Wanderers	H	Football League North (Second Championship)	2–1
1951	Hull City	A	FA Cup 3rd Round	0–2

With the League campaign already turning into a struggle, the FA Cup offered Everton the chance of rescuing a disastrous season, although Second Division Hull City would be no pushovers. Sadly, any thoughts of going one better than the previous season's semi-final placing were dashed with a 2–0 defeat at Boothferry Park.

1968	Wolverhampton Wanderers	A	First Division	3–1
1973	Stoke City	H	First Division	2–0
1982	Manchester United	A	First Division	1–1
1984	Stoke City	A	FA Cup 3rd Round	2–0

The start of Everton's run to Wembley in the FA Cup began with a 2–0 win at Stoke City thanks to goals from Andy Gray and Alan Irvine. It would take Everton another six games before they strode out beneath the twin towers to face Watford.

| 1990 | Middlesbrough | A | FA Cup 3rd Round | 0–0 |

JANUARY 7TH

1893	Notts County	H	First Division	6–0
1895	Stoke City	H	First Division	3–0
1899	Newcastle United	A	First Division	2–2
1905	Sheffield United	A	First Division	0–1
1911	Preston North End	A	First Division	2–0
1922	Crystal Palace	H	FA Cup 1st Round	0–6

Everton were drawn away at Crystal Palace, then a mid-table Second Division club, in the third round of the FA Cup. Their preparations for the tie weren't helped by an injury to goalkeeper Tom Fern, for he had to struggle through the match with a damaged hand, something an outfield player might have got away with but which was a vital part of the goalkeeper's armoury! Palace made the most of his misery, winning the game 6–0 as Fern tried to stem the flow. Despite his injury it would be unfair to attach all of the blame to the defence, for Palace goalkeeper Jack Alderson had so little to do during the game that he could be seen eating oranges handed to him by the crowd!

| 1928 | Middlesbrough | H | First Division | 3–1 |

For the third consecutive game Dixie Dean scored twice to reach 39 goals for the season, with Irvine netting the other in the 3–1 win.

1933	Birmingham City	A	First Division	0–4
1939	Derby County	A	FA Cup 3rd Round	1–0
1950	Queens Park Rangers	A	FA Cup 3rd Round	2–0
1956	Bristol City	H	FA Cup 3rd Round	3–1
1961	Sheffield United	H	FA Cup 3rd Round	0–1
1964	Hull City	H	FA Cup 3rd Round Replay	2–1
1967	Stoke City	A	First Division	1–2
1975	Altrincham	A	FA Cup 3rd Round Replay	2–0

Altrincham's shock draw at Goodison Park in the FA Cup ignited considerable interest in the North West, so much so the non-League side were forced to switch the replay to Old Trafford in order to accommodate all of those who wished to attend. In the event a crowd of 35,530 were present to see Bob Latchford and Mick Lyons score once in each half to end Altrincham's run.

| 1978 | Aston Villa | H | FA Cup 3rd Round | 4–1 |

1982 Everton paid a then record fee of £700,000 to Stoke City for Adrian Heath. Heath remained at the club for the next seven years, winning two League titles and the FA Cup.

| 1989 | West Bromwich Albion | A | FA Cup 3rd Round | 1–1 |

1994 After almost a month without a manager, Everton appointed Mike Walker to the position. The move for the Norwich City manager had been rumoured for some time but Everton had been refused permission by Norwich City to talk to him. Walker then resigned and moved on to Goodison Park, with the Football League later asking Everton to explain their actions.

| 1995 | Derby County | H | FA Cup 3rd Round | 1–0 |
| 1996 | Stockport County | H | FA Cup 3rd Round | 2–2 |

With Liverpool also being drawn at home in the third round of the FA Cup, Everton's tie with Stockport was switched to the Sunday. Everton were once again shocked, Helliwell scoring a deserved equaliser after Gary Ablett and Graham Stuart had seemingly put Everton into the next round. Stockport's first goal was scored by Alun Armstrong.

JANUARY 8TH

1898	Sheffield Wednesday	H	First Division	1–0
1910	Tottenham Hotspur	A	First Division	0–3
1916	Rochdale	H	Lancashire Section Principal Tournament	3–2
1921	Stockport County	H	FA Cup 1st Round	1–0

Everton were made to suffer in the FA Cup first round match with Stockport County at Goodison Park, only going through 1–0 thanks to the benefit of an own goal.

| 1927 | Poole Town | H | FA Cup 3rd Round | 3–1 |

Non-League Poole Town were the visitors in the FA Cup third round having beaten Newport County and Nunhead in the previous rounds. Goals from Dixie Dean, Bobby Irvine and Alec Troup took Everton through to the next round with a 3–1 win.

1938	Chelsea	A	FA Cup 3rd Round	1–0

A trip to Stamford Bridge for the FA Cup third round was a potential nightmare for Everton, but they countered anything that Chelsea could throw at them and won the game with Alex Stevenson's strike.

1944	Crewe Alexandra	H	Football League North (Second Championship)	9–1

Everton registered a 9–1 win over Crewe Alexandra in the League North (Second Championship), with McIntosh getting a hat-trick. Everton were to score nine again in the competition, against Chester in a 9–2 win in March.

1949	Manchester City	H	FA Cup 3rd Round	1–0
1955	Southend United	H	FA Cup 3rd Round	3–1
1958	Sunderland	H	FA Cup 3rd Round Replay	3–1
1966	Aston Villa	H	First Division	2–0
1972	West Ham United	H	First Division	2–1
1977	Stoke City	H	FA Cup 3rd Round	2–0
1983	Newport County	A	FA Cup 3rd Round	1–1
1994	Bolton Wanderers	A	FA Cup 3rd Round	1–1

JANUARY 9TH

1892	Notts County	A	Football League	3–1
1897	Nottingham Forest	H	First Division	3–1
1904	Sheffield United	H	First Division	2–0
1909	Preston North End	A	First Division	3–3
1915	Barnsley	H	FA Cup 1st Round	3–0
1926	Fulham	H	FA Cup 3rd Round	1–1
1937	Bolton Wanderers	H	First Division	3–2
1943	Liverpool	H	Football League North (Second Championship)	1–3
1946	Preston North End	H	FA Cup 3rd Round 2nd Leg	2–2

Preston came to Goodison Park for the FA Cup third round second leg and fought out a 2–2 draw, thus ensuring progress into the next round 4–3 on aggregate.

1954	Notts County	H	FA Cup 3rd Round	2–1

1959   Former Everton player John Kirwan died. Brought into English football from Ireland by Southport he soon became the subject of much attention by the bigger clubs and Everton finally won a dispute with Blackburn Rovers in order to sign him, where he was expected to replace the Spurs-bound John Cameron. After 24 appearances for the club he was persuaded to join Spurs where Cameron had taken over as player-manager, and he later played for Chelsea, Clyde and Leyton before turning to coaching.

1960	Bradford City	A	FA Cup 3rd Round	0–3
1965	Sheffield Wednesday	H	FA Cup 3rd Round	2–2
1971	Burnley	A	First Division	2–2
1988	Sheffield Wednesday	A	FA Cup 3rd Round	1–1

When Everton took to the field at Hillsborough for the FA Cup third round clash with Sheffield Wednesday, they would have been unaware how familiar they were to become with the opposition, for it would take four games before one side finally gained the upper hand. Everton had begun the New Year at the very same venue, going down 1–0 in the League, but the cup was always a different matter, with players raising their game. So it proved today, with Peter Reid scoring the goal that ensured a replay back at Goodison Park.

1993   Crystal Palace   A   FA Premier League   2–0

JANUARY 10TH

1891   Preston North End   H   Football League   0–1

The new played host to the old; despite a win for Preston at Anfield Road Everton were already crowned as League champions for the first time in their history, replacing Preston who had been champions for the previous two seasons.

1914   Glossop   A   FA Cup 1st Round   1–2
1920   Birmingham City   A   FA Cup 1st Round   0–2
1925   Burnley   H   FA Cup 1st Round   2–1
1931   Plymouth Argyle   A   FA Cup 3rd Round   2–0
1942   Blackburn Rovers   H   Football League North (Second Championship) 0–0
1948   Grimsby Town   A   FA Cup 3rd Round   4–1

On the same day Mike Bernard was born in Shrewsbury. He started his career with Stoke City in 1965 and was a member of the side that won the League Cup in 1972 before joining Everton for £140,000 in May of that year. Although he had made his name as a midfield player prior to his arrival at Goodison, he was successfully converted to defence and made over 100 appearances for Everton's League side in this position. When he lost his place in 1977 there was considerable speculation that he would return to Stoke, but instead chose to join Oldham Athletic, with whom he finished his career owing to injury on 1979.

1953   Ipswich Town   H   FA Cup 3rd Round   3–2
1954   John Gidman born in Liverpool. Although he was signed as an apprentice by Liverpool he began his League career with Aston Villa, signing at Villa Park in August 1971. He cost Everton £650,000 in October 1979, by which time he had won his only cap for England. He spent less than two years at Goodison Park before Ron Atkinson made him his first signing for Manchester United, and he remained at Old Trafford until 1986. He moved across the city to Manchester City and later played for Stoke.

1959   Sunderland   H   FA Cup 3rd Round   4–0
1970   Ipswich Town   H   First Division   3–0
1976   Newcastle United   A   First Division   0–5
1977   Billy Bingham was sacked as manager of Everton having been in the post since May 1973. With the club having slumped in the League and in need of a fresh approach, Bingham paid the price for lack of success at Goodison Park, with coach Steve Burtenshaw taking over as caretaker until an adequate replacement could be found.

1979   Sunderland   A   FA Cup 3rd Round   1–2
1981   Arsenal   H   First Division   1–2
1987   Southampton   H   FA Cup 3rd Round   2–1
1990   Middlesbrough   H   FA Cup 3rd Round Replay   1–1
1998   Crystal Palace   A   FA Premier League   3–1

JANUARY 11TH

1896   Bury   A   First Division   1–1
1902   Liverpool   H   First Division   4–0

1908	Tottenham Hotspur	H	FA Cup 1st Round	1–0
1919	Oldham Athletic	A	Lancashire Section Principal Tournament	3–0
1930	Carlisle United	A	FA Cup 3rd Round	4–2
1936	Preston North End	H	FA Cup 3rd Round	1–3
1941	Liverpool	H	North Regional League	4–1
1947	Southend United	H	FA Cup 3rd Round	4–2

1948 Joe Harper born in Greenock. He began his career with Morton and was first brought down to England by Huddersfield Town in 1966 but failed to settle and returned to Scotland with Aberdeen. In 1972 he was bought by Everton for £180,000 as a ready made replacement for the injured Joe Royle, but less than two years later he returned back to Scotland with Hibernian, later rejoining Aberdeen.

1955 Ken McNaught born in Kirkcaldy. The son of a former professional footballer with Raith Rovers, Ken was signed by Everton as an apprentice after completing his school exams. He made his debut for the club during the 1974–75 season and made 84 appearances for the first team before a £200,000 move to Aston Villa in August 1977. He remained at Villa Park for six seasons, helping them win the League and European Cup before moving on to West Bromwich Albion, finishing his career through injury with Sheffield United, his playing days brought to an end by injury.

1958	Chelsea	A	First Division	1–3

1961 Adrian Heath born in Stoke. He began his career with his local side and spent three years at the Victoria Ground before a £700,000 move to Everton in 1982. Over the next seven years he helped Everton win the League title in 1985 and 1987, the FA Cup in 1984 and the FA Charity Shield for four consecutive seasons. Unfortunately severely damaged knee ligaments ruled him out of the European Cup-Winners' Cup side. He was sold to Aston Villa for £360,000 in 1989 and later played for Manchester City, Stoke, Burnley, Sheffield United and a second spell at Burnley, where he was later manager. He also returned to Goodison as assistant to Howard Kendal during his third spell in charge at the club.

1964	Burnley	A	First Division	3–2
1966	West Ham United	H	First Division	2–2
1969	Sunderland	A	First Division	3–1
1975	Leicester City	H	First Division	3–0
1983	Newport County	H	FA Cup 3rd Round Replay	2–1
1986	Queens Park Rangers	H	First Division	4–3
1989	West Bromwich Albion	H	FA Cup 3rd Round Replay	1–0
1992	Manchester United	A	First Division	0–1
1997	Sheffield Wednesday	A	FA Premier League	1–2

JANUARY 12TH

1889	Stoke City	H	Football League	2–1
1893	Nottingham Forest	A	First Division	1–2
1895	Derby County	A	First Division	2–2
1901	Aston Villa	H	First Division	2–1
1907	Sheffield United	H	FA Cup 1st Round	1–0
1918	Blackpool	H	Lancashire Section Principal Tournament	7–2
1924	Preston North End	H	FA Cup 1st Round	3–1
1929	Chelsea	A	FA Cup 3rd Round	0–2
1935	Grimsby Town	H	FA Cup 3rd Round	6–3

A high scoring game in the third round of the FA Cup saw Everton see off Grimsby Town 6–3 at Goodison Park thanks to goals from Albert Geldard, who scored a hat-trick, Alex Stevenson (two) and Jimmy Cunliffe.

1946	Blackburn Rovers	A	Football League North	1–2
1952	Leyton Orient	A	FA Cup 3rd Round	0–0
1957	Aston Villa	A	First Division	1–5
1974	Queens Park Rangers	A	First Division	0–1
1980	Aston Villa	A	First Division	1–2
1985	Newcastle United	H	First Division	4–0

A 4–0 win over Newcastle United at Goodison Park took Everton back to the top of the table over Spurs, who were held to a draw by QPR. Goals from Derek Mountfield, Graeme Sharp and a brace from Kevin Sheedy earned Everton top spot; they were not to be headed for the rest of the season.

| 1993 | Wimbeldon | H | FA Cup 3rd Round Replay | 1–2 |

Having secured a 0–0 draw at Wimbledon in the first clash Everton had high hopes of winning through to the fourth round of the FA Cup in the replay at Goodison, but in front of just 15,293 Everton went down 2–1 to exit the competition.

JANUARY 13TH

1894	Preston North End	A	First Division	4–2
1900	Aston Villa	A	First Division	1–1
1906	West Bromwich Albion	H	FA Cup 1st Round	3–1

Everton's run to the FA Cup final at Crystal Palace began with a 3–1 home win over West Bromwich Albion thanks to goals from Harold Hardman, Harry Makepeace and Jack Sharp.

| 1912 | Clapton Orient | A | FA Cup 1st Round | 2–1 |
| 1917 | Manchester City | H | Lancashire Section Principal Tournament | 0–2 |

1920 John Humphreys born in Llandudno. He joined Everton from Llandudno in 1942 and made a number of appearances during war time, although his League debut had to wait until the end of hostilities. He made 53 League appearances and won one cap for Wales.

1923	Bradford Park Avenue	H	FA Cup 1st Round	1–1
1934	Tottenham Hotspur	A	FA Cup 3rd Round	0–3
1945	Bolton Wanderers	A	Football League North (Second Championship)	3–1
1951	Stoke City	H	First Division	0–3
1962	Sheffield Wednesday	A	First Division	1–3
1965	Sheffield Wednesday	A	FA Cup 3rd Round Replay	3–0
1973	Aston Villa	H	FA Cup 3rd Round	3–2
1988	Sheffield Wednesday	H	FA Cup 3rd Round Replay	1–1

Having secured a draw at Hillsborough in their first cup meeting Everton were confident of completing the task in front of their own fans at Goodison against Sheffield Wednesday. The visitors, however, had other ideas and silenced the crowd with a first half goal from Chapman. The Everton fans in the 32,935 crowd did much to lift the spirit of the players and were ecstatic when Graeme Sharp equalised. Extra time brought no further goals and the toss of a coin dictated that the second replay would be at Goodison.

1990	Southampton	A	First Division	2–2
1991	Manchester City	H	First Division	2–0
1996	Chelsea	H	FA Premier League	1–1

JANUARY 14TH

1893	West Bromwich Albion	H	First Division	1–0
1899	Preston North end	H	First Division	2–0
1905	Newcastle United	H	First Division	2–1
1911	Crystal Palace	A	FA Cup 1st Round	4–0

1911 On the same day George Jackson was born in Liverpool. After making his debut for Everton in the 1934–35 season he seemed assured of a lengthy career at Goodison Park. In terms of years it was, for he did not leave the club until 1949, but unfortunately the Second World War cut right across his career and he was able to make only 79 appearances for the first team. He was known as Stonewall by the fans and when his career at Goodison ended joined Caernavon Town.

1922 Bolton Wanderers   A   First Division   0–1

Hunter Hart came straight into the Everton side after his transfer from Airdrie, making his debut in the match at Bolton which ended in a 1–0 defeat for Everton. Initially used as a half-back he later switched to centre-half and shored up the defence, making exactly 300 appearances for the first team during his time at Goodison Park. He retired in 1930.

1926	Fulham	A	FA Cup 3rd Round Replay	0–1
1928	Preston North End	A	FA Cup 3rd Round	3–0
1933	Leicester City	A	FA Cup 3rd Round	3–2
1939	Arsenal	H	First Division	2–0
1950	Portsmouth	H	First Division	1–2
1956	Charlton Athletic	H	First Division	3–2
1967	Sheffield United	H	First Division	4–1

1971 Fourteen months after joining the club from Blackburn Rovers, Keith Newton handed in a transfer request. This was subsequently turned down.

1978	Aston Villa	H	First Division	1–0
1984	Stoke City	A	First Division	1–1
1989	Arsenal	H	First Division	1–3
1995	Arsenal	A	FA Premier League	1–1

JANUARY 15TH

1898	Notts County	A	First Division	2–3
1910	Middlesbrough	A	FA Cup 1st Round	1–1
1913	Stockport County	H	FA Cup 1st Round	5–1
1916	Bolton Wanderers	H	Lancashire Section Principal Tournament	2–1
1921	Aston Villa	A	First Division	3–1

1923 Tom Eglington born in Dublin. He and Peter Farrell both played for Shamrock Rovers and were snapped up by Everton in 1946 for a joint fee of £10,000. Tom went on to make over 400 appearances for Everton over the next ten years or so, making the left wing berth his own during that time. As well as being an extremely creative player, he was also adept at finishing, scoring five in one match against Doncaster Rovers. He finished his playing career with Tranmere Rovers and then returned to Ireland. He won a total of 24 caps for the Republic of Ireland and six for Northern Ireland whilst with Everton.

1927	Tottenham Hotspur	H	First Division	1–2
1938	Blackpool	H	First Division	3–1
1944	Crewe Alexandra	A	Football League North (Second Championship)	6–2

1955	Burnley	H	First Division	1–1
1963	Barnsley	A	FA Cup 3rd Round	3–0
1966	Blackpool	A	First Division	0–2
1972	Crystal Palace	A	FA Cup 3rd Round	2–2

The FA Cup third round match between Crystal Palace and Everton produced five bookings, a sending-off, four goals, frequent pitch invasions and considerable controversy. The goals were evenly shared, Alan Whittle and Colin Harvey netting for Everton, although Palace had Tommy Dawes sent off and the game was in danger of being abandoned owing to the pitch invasions before the police finally managed to retain control. After the game Palace chairman Arthur Wait blamed Everton and the referee for the problems, stating 'It was a diabolical game, and Everton were the culprits. Dawes had a real stinker; at one stage I thought he was going to book the corner flag.' The replay promised to be exciting!

1977	Ipswich Town	A	First Division	0–2
1983	Watford	H	First Division	1–0
1994	Swindon Town	H	FA Premier League	6–2

Tony Cottee scored a hat-trick, one of the goals coming from the penalty spot, as Everton hit Premier League strugglers Swindon for six. The other goals for Everton came from John Ebrell, Gary Ablett and Peter Beagrie, whilst Swindon finished the season being relegated back into the First division after conceding 100 goals in the top flight.

JANUARY 16TH

1892	Burnley	H	FA Cup 1st Round	2–4
1897	West Bromwich Albion	A	First Division	4–1
1904	Newcastle United	A	First Division	0–1
1909	Burnley	H	FA Cup 1st Round	3–1
1915	Middlesbrough	A	First Division	1–5
1926	Cardiff City	H	First Division	1–1
1932	Sunderland	H	First Division	4–2
1937	Bournemouth	H	FA Cup 3rd Round	5–0

Bournemouth visited Goodison in the FA Cup third round and were despatched 5–0, with Everton's goals coming from Torry Gillick (two), Alex Stevenson (two) and Jimmy Cunliffe.

1943	Liverpool	A	Football League North (Second Championship)	1–2
1952	Leyton Orient	H	FA Cup 3rd Round Replay	1–3
1954	Bury	H	Second Division	0–0

1957 Trevor Ross born in Ashton-under-Lyme. Initially introduced to League football by Arsenal he was sold to Everton for £180,000 in November 1977 and went on to make 146 appearances for the first team. After loan spells with Portsmouth and Sheffield United and a disastrous six months in Greece he joined Sheffield United on a permanent basis.

1960	Fulham	A	First Division	0–2
1965	Sheffield United	A	First Division	0–0
1971	Chelsea	H	First Division	3–0
1988	Norwich City	A	First Division	3–0
1993	Leeds United	H	FA Premier League	2–0

JANUARY 17TH

| 1891 | Sunderland | A | FA Cup 1st Round | 0–1 |
| 1895 | Aston Villa | H | First Division | 4–2 |

A 4–2 win over Aston Villa at home enabled Everton to maintain third position in the League thanks to goals from Jack Milward (two), John Bell and Fred Geary.

1898	Stoke City	H	First Division	1–1
1903	Wolverhampton Wanderers	H	First Division	2–1
1914	Liverpool	A	First Division	2–1
1920	Sheffield Wednesday	A	First Division	0–1

Joe Peacock made his debut in the 1–0 defeat at Hillsborough. Born in Wigan in 1900 he joined Everton from non-League Atherton in the summer of 1919 and went on to make 161 appearances for the club, scoring 12 goals during his eight seasons with the club. He left for Middlesbrough in 1927 and helped them to the Second Division championship in 1928–29 as well as earning international recognition, collecting three caps for England. He finished his playing career with Sheffield Wednesday and Clapton Orient before turning to coaching.

| 1923 | Bradford Park Avenue | A | FA Cup 1st Round Replay | 0–1 |
| 1925 | Tottenham Hotspur | H | First Division | 1–0 |

Albert Virr made his debut in the 1–0 home win over Spurs. During the course of six seasons he made a total of 126 first-team outings, scoring three goals and helped the team to the League title in 1927–28, but a serious knee injury sustained in 1929 effectively brought his career to an end, although he did make five appearances following the campaign with little success. Upon his retirement he became a schoolteacher and died in July 1959 at the age of 57.

1931	West Bromwich Albion	H	Second Division	2–1
1942	Blackburn Rovers	A	Football League North (Second Championship)	0–0
1948	Derby County	H	First Division	1–3
1953	Nottingham Forest	A	Second Division	3–3
1959	Arsenal	A	First Division	1–3
1970	Southampton	A	First Division	1–2
1976	Norwich City	H	First Division	1–1
1981	Ipswich Town	H	First Division	0–0
1987	Sheffield Wednesday	H	First Division	2–0
1990	Middlesbrough	A	FA Cup 3rd Round 2nd Replay	1–0

Everton finally overcame Middlesbrough in the FA Cup third round, winning 1–0 at Ayresome Park thanks to a goal from Norman Whiteside. The tie had already produced two draws, 0–0 and 1–1, before Everton won.

| 1996 | Stockport County | A | FA Cup 3rd Round Replay | 3–2 |

Stockport County had almost pulled off a shock win at Goodison Park in the FA Cup third round, drawing 2–2 to force a replay. Everton had to live on their nerves in the replay, finally winning 3–2 at Edgeley Park thanks to goals from Duncan Ferguson, Graham Stuart and David Ebbrell.

JANUARY 18TH

| 1890 | Derby County | H | FA Cup 1st Round | 11–2 |

The FA Cup first round match with Derby County saw Everton score 11 times at

Anfield, with Derby responding with two goals of their own. Not surprisingly, the 11–2 scoreline represents Everton's biggest ever win, with Brady, Geary and Millward all scoring hat-tricks, Holt and Doyle getting the goals for Everton.

1894	Nottingham Forest	A	First Division	2–3
1902	Newcastle United	A	First Division	1–1
1908	Bury	A	First Division	0–3
1913	Manchester United	H	First Division	4–1
1919	Oldham Athletic	H	Lancashire Section Principal Tournament	3–1
1930	Derby County	H	First Division	4–0

Ben Williams made his debut in the Everton defence as they shut out the Derby attack. Born in Penhriwceiber in Wales he considered a career as a professional boxer before being persuaded to pursue football by Swansea Town in 1923. He made nearly 100 appearances for the Swans before joining Everton in December 1929 and was made captain as the side won the Second Division championship in 1931. In January 1933 he underwent a serious cartilage operation and was forced to sit out as the club won the FA Cup at the end of the campaign. Indeed, his career never fully recovered and in 1936 he was transferred to Newport County, subsequently becoming coach to the club.

1947	Portsmouth	A	First Division	1–2

1951   Bob Latchford born in Birmingham. Along with his brother Dave he began his career with Birmingham City, making over 150 League appearances before a £350,000 move to Everton in 1974. He was top goalscorer in each of his first four full seasons at Goodison and in 1977–78 became the first player in six years to reach 30 League goals in a season. In 1981 he was transferred to Swansea and later played in Holland, returning to England and signing for Coventry. He finished his League career with Lincoln City.

1958	Sunderland	A	First Division	1–1

1961   Peter Beardsley born in Newcastle. He began his career with Carlisle and then went to Canada to play for Vancouver Whitecaps, subsequently being recommended to Manchester United. After one substitute appearance he was released on a free transfer, returning to Canada and then trying in England once again with Newcastle United. Here he developed into an exceptional player, being capped by England and prompting a £1.9 million move to Liverpool in 1987. He was sold to Everton for £1 million in 1991 and showed that Liverpool might have been hasty in letting him go so soon. In 1993 he returned to Newcastle for £1.4 million, later playing for Sheffield United and Fulham.

1964	Ipswich Town	H	First Division	1–1
1969	Ipswich Town	H	First Division	2–2
1972	Crystal Palace	H	FA Cup 3rd Round Replay	3–2
1975	Birmingham City	A	First Division	3–0
1977	Bolton Wanderers	H	League Cup Semi-Final 1st Leg	1–1

Everton had already gone further in the competition than ever before, their quarter-final appearance in the competition's inaugural season of 1960–61 their previous best showing. Duncan McKenzie gave them a dream start against Bolton in front of a crowd of 48,000, but Neil Whatmore equalised for Bolton to leave Everton's hopes of reaching the final hanging by a thread.

1978	Leeds United	A	League Cup 5th Round	1–4
1984	Oxford United	A	Milk Cup 5th Round	1–1

The match that effectively brought Howard Kendall a change of fortune as manager of

Everton – 1–0 down at Oxford United in the Milk Cup fifth round, a bad back pass was seized upon by Adrian Heath for a late equaliser and a replay at Goodison Park.

| 1986 | Birmingham City | A | First Division | 2–0 |
| 1989 | Wimbledon | A | Simod Cup Quarter-Final | 2–1 |

Everton won through to the semi-finals of the Simod Cup with a 2–1 win at Wimbledon in front of 2,477 fans, both their goals coming from Wayne Clarke.

| 1998 | Chelsea | H | FA Premier League | 3–1 |

JANUARY 19TH

| 1889 | Preston North End | H | Football League | 0–2 |

Bob Kelson made his only appearance of the season in the 2–0 defeat at home to eventual champions Preston North End. He actually joined Preston at the end of the season and helped them to win the League title for a second consecutive season before returning to Everton in 1891. Originally used as a half-back he converted to full-back and was a member of the side that reached the 1893 FA Cup final and left the club in 1896 to return to his native Scotland, signing with Dundee. He won eight caps for Scotland over the course of 13 years, although all of them were awarded whilst he was playing in Scotland, the selectors refusing to pick any player with English clubs.

1901	Liverpool	A	First Division	2–1
1907	Newcastle United	H	First Division	3–0
1910	Middlesbrough	H	FA Cup 1st Round Replay	5–3

Everton won a thrilling FA Cup third round replay with Middlesbrough 5–3. The first game at Ayresome Park had finished 1–1, but at Goodison Park both teams opened up and gave an exhibition of attacking football. Everton's goals came from Freeman, Makepeace, Taylor, White and Young.

1918	Manchester City	A	Lancashire Section Principal Tournament	2–0
1924	Middlesbrough	H	First Division	1–0
1929	Birmingham City	H	First Division	0–2
1932	Liverpool	H	FA Cup 3rd Round	1–2
1935	Grimsby Town	H	First Division	3–1

1941 Fred Pickering born in Blackburn. Introduced to League football by his home town team, he was transferred to Everton for £85,000 in 1964 and quickly established himself as an exceptional striker, earning a call-up for England the same year. He made 115 appearances for Everton, scoring 70 goals, but was left out of the side for the 1966 FA Cup final. He was sold to Birmingham City in 1967 for £50,000 and later played for Blackpool, Blackburn for a second time and Brighton.

1946	Blackburn Rovers	H	Football League North	4–1
1952	Cardiff City	H	Second Division	3–0
1957	Luton Town	H	First Division	2–1

1972 Dixie Dean was taken to hospital after suffering a heart attack.

1974	Leeds United	H	First Division	0–0
1982	Southampton	H	First Division	1–1
1991	Arsenal	A	First Division	0–1
1992	Nottingham Forest	H	First Division	1–1
1994	Bolton Wanderers	H	FA Cup 3rd Round Replay	2–3
1997	Arsenal	A	FA Premier League	1–3

JANUARY 20TH

1900	Liverpool	H	First Division	3–1
1906	Newcastle United	A	First Division	2–4
1912	Liverpool	A	First Division	3–1
1917	Blackpool	A	Lancashire Section Principal Tournament	1–1
1923	Stoke City	H	First Division	4–0

1923 Jack Cock made his debut for the club in the 4–0 home win over Stoke City, scoring once. He began his career with Brentford and then Huddersfield Town before the outbreak of the First World War, during which he was mistakenly reported to have been killed. Very much alive he resumed his career with Chelsea and was transferred to Everton in January 1923, remaining at Goodison until March 1925 when he joined Plymouth. He later played for Millwall, a club he also managed between 1944 and 1948, and also appeared in numerous films. He won two England caps during his career, one apiece whilst on the books of Huddersfield and Chelsea.

1934	Sheffield Wednesday	A	First Division	0–0
1940	Wrexham	A	War Regional League, Western Division	0–0
1945	Stockport County	A	Football League North (Second Championship)	3–0
1951	Liverpool	A	First Division	2–0
1962	Leicester City	H	First Division	3–2
1965	Manchester United	A	Inter-Cities Fairs Cup 3rd Round 1st Leg	1–1

In the second round of the Inter-Cities Fairs Cup, considered to be Europe's third major competition, Everton had disposed of Scottish opposition in the shape of Kilmarnock. Their reward for progressing into the third round was a trip to Manchester to face United! Thankfully it was still some time before UEFA insisted that clubs be in the city 24 hours before a match (in 1990, when United returned to Europe and were drawn to face Wrexham, UEFA insisted they be in Wrexham 24 hours before the game, even though the journey took only 40 minutes!) and so Everton were able to travel on the day of the game to Old Trafford. With United having got the better of Everton in the two League meetings between the sides, Everton were keen to exact some form of revenge, and a goal from Fred Pickering was enough to secure a 1–1 draw.

1968	Leeds United	A	First Division	0–2
1988	Manchester City	H	Littlewoods Cup 5th Round	2–0

Adrian Heath and Graeme Sharp scored either side of the half-time break to take Everton into the semi-finals of the Littlewoods Cup to face Arsenal over two legs in front of a crowd of 40,014.

1990	Sheffield Wednesday	H	First Division	2–0
1996	Arsenal	A	FA Premier League	2–1

JANUARY 21ST

1893	West Bromwich Albion	H	FA Cup 1st Round	4–1
1899	Liverpool	A	First Division	0–2
1905	Preston North End	A	First Division	1–1
1911	Notts County	H	First Division	5–0
1922	Aston Villa	H	First Division	3–2
1928	Birmingham City	A	First Division	2–2
1933	Sunderland	H	First Division	6–1

Everton hammered six goals past Sunderland at Goodison Park, with Dixie Dean scoring twice and Dunn, Stein and Thomson all getting one apiece.

1939	Doncaster Rovers	H	FA Cup 4th Round	8–0

Tommy Lawton scored four times in Everton's 8–0 win over Doncaster Rovers in the FA Cup fourth round at Goodison Park. The other goals came from Wally Boyes (two), Torry Gillick and Alex Stevenson, and with Everton on their way to winning the League, thoughts were beginning to turn to a possible double.

1950	Wolverhampton Wanderers	A	First Division	1–1
1956	Tottenham Hotspur	A	First Division	1–1
1961	Wolverhampton Wanderers	A	First Division	1–4
1967	West Bromwich Albion	A	First Division	0–1
1978	Wolverhampton Wanderers	A	First Division	1–3
1984	Tottenham Hotspur	H	First Division	2–1
1987	Liverpool	H	Littlewoods Cup 5th Round	0–1

Having met in the FA Cup final the previous season, Everton were paired with Liverpool again in the Littlewoods Cup fifth round at Goodison Park. A crowd of 53,323 (the last time Goodison Park witnessed a crowd above 50,000 for the visit of Liverpool) saw a bruising game in which little quarter was expected or given. A clash between Gary Stevens and Jim Beglin left the Liverpool player with a broken leg, but the incident affected Stevens for the rest of the game. With seven minutes left and a replay looking the likeliest outcome, Ian Rush struck to win the tie for Liverpool.

1989	Luton Town	A	First Division	0–1
1995	Crystal Palace	H	FA Premier League	3–1

JANUARY 22ND

1907 William 'Dixie' Dean born in Birkenhead. One of the greatest goalscorers who ever played, Dean is perhaps best known for his exploits in one season – 1927–28. The previous season George Camsell had hit 59 goals for Middlesbrough in the Second Division, a record many said would never be beaten. On the last day of the 1927–28 season, with Dean on 57 goals, his Everton side were faced by Arsenal, but Dean managed to score a hat-trick (he scored his third goal some eight minutes before the end of the 3–3 draw) and take the record. He began his career with Tranmere before moving to Everton and won 16 England caps. He scored a then record 379 goals in League matches and won a League Championship medal and FA Cup winners' medal. He finished his League career with Notts County and went to Sligo Rovers just before the Second World War. He was captured and taken prisoner in the western desert and after the war ran a pub in Chester. Such was the regard with which he was held, 36,000 turned up at Everton for a testimonial held in 1964. Acknowledged throughout the game, a story is told of a chance meeting with Liverpool goalkeeper Elisha Scott. Dean nodded to acknowledge Scott, whereupon the goalkeeper dived across the pavement as though trying to save a header! A football man through and through, Dean died while watching a Liverpool and Everton derby match in 1980.

1910	Preston North End	H	First Division	2–1
1916	Manchester City	A	Lancashire Section Principal Tournament	1–2

1921	Aston Villa	H	First Division	1–1
1927	West Ham United	A	First Division	1–2
1936	Bolton Wanderers	H	First Division	3–3
1938	Sunderland	H	FA Cup 4th Round	0–1
1944	Liverpool	A	Football League North (Second Championship)	4–1
1949	Chelsea	H	First Division	2–1
1966	Sunderland	H	FA Cup 3rd Round	3–0
1972	West Bromwich Albion	H	First Division	2–1

1973 Paul Gerrard born in Heywood. He began his career with Oldham Athletic and gave five years' good service, prompting a £1 million move to Everton in 1996. Signed as cover for Neville Southall, he made his debut in November 1996, coming on at half-time against Southampton in a match Everton were winning 5–1 at Southall's instigation. Everton went on to win 7–1.

1977	Queens Park Rangers	H	First Division	1–3
1983	Norwich City	A	First Division	1–0
1991	Sunderland	H	Zenith Data Systems Cup Northern Quarter-Final	4–1
1994	Manchester United	A	FA Premier League	0–1

Following the recent death of Sir Matt Busby, former manager of Manchester United, the match at Old Trafford between United and Everton was turned into something of a tribute to one of the finest manager's in the British game. A lone Scottish piper led both teams out on to the pitch, with a black ribbon draped over Sir Matt's usual seat in the ground. The two teams then put on a performance to grace the occasion, with United finally winning 1–0 with a goal from Ryan Giggs.

JANUARY 23RD

1904	Aston Villa	H	First Division	1–0
1909	Middlesbrough	H	First Division	1–1
1915	Sheffield United	H	First Division	0–0
1926	Tottenham Hotspur	A	First Division	1–1
1937	Liverpool	A	First Division	2–3

1940 Brian Labone born in Liverpool. One of the greatest players to have played for the club, he spent his entire career at Goodison Park, making over 500 appearances for the first team during his time. He was signed as a junior and joined the professional ranks in 1957, making his debut in the 1957–58 seasons. By 1959–60 he was a regular in the side and helped them win the League title in 1963 and 1970 and the FA Cup in 1966, also playing in the FA Cup final in 1968. He was a full England international player, collecting six caps and going to the 1970 World Cup finals in Mexico. He might have gone on to better Ted Sagar's record for the number of League appearances for Everton but for an injury which forced him to retire in 1972.

1943	Manchester United	A	Football League North (Second Championship)	4–1
1954	Doncaster Rovers	A	Second Division	2–2
1960	Nottingham Forest	H	First Division	5–1

1969 Andrei Kanchelskis born in Kirovograd. He was first introduced to English football with Manchester United, signing for them 1991 for £650,000 from Shakhtyor Donetsk. Four years later he cost Everton £5 million and turned in superb performances during season 1995–96. Unfortunately he was unable to settle and was sold to Fiorentina for an Everton record fee of £8 million in January 1997. In the summer of 1998 he returned to British football, signing for Glasgow Rangers.

| 1971 | Middlesbrough | H | FA Cup 4th Round | 3–0 |
| 1982 | Wolverhampton Wanderers | A | First Division | 3–0 |

JANUARY 24TH

1880 Everton met St Peter's for the second match since their formation and won 4–0. Although the local paper reported the score but omitted the scorers, it did give Everton's line-up, which was: W. Jones, T. Evans, J. Douglas, C. Chiles, S. Chalk, R.W. Morris, A. White, F. Brettle, A. Wade, Smith and W. Williams.

| 1914 | Aston Villa | H | First Division | 1–4 |

Joe Clennell made his debut for Everton in the 4–1 defeat at home to Aston Villa, although he scored Everton's lone goal. He began his career with Blackburn Rovers and proved an instant hit with the supporters and team-mates alike, settling into the side for the rest of the season and then helping them lift the title in 1914–15. He scored 128 goals for the club during the First World War when football was organised on a regional basis, and netted 12 in 18 appearances in 1919–20 when the normal League was resumed. Unfortunately he then succumbed to injury and made just two appearances in two seasons, joining Cardiff City in October 1921.

1920	Newcastle United	H	First Division	3–0
1925	Bolton Wanderers	A	First Division	0–1
1931	Crystal Palace	A	FA Cup 4th Round	6–0

Everton got their revenge for their FA Cup defeat of 1921–22, beating Crystal Palace by the same 6–0 scoreline that Palace had inflicted on them nine years previously. Four of the goals were scored by Dixie Dean, Tommy Johnson and own goals providing the other two.

1948	Wolverhampton Wanderers	A	FA Cup 4th Round	1–1
1953	Southampton	H	Second Division	2–2
1959	Charlton Athletic	A	FA Cup 4th Round	2–2
1970	Newcastle United	H	First Division	0–0
1973	Manchester United	A	First Division	0–0
1981	Liverpool	H	FA Cup 4th Round	2–1
1984	Oxford United	H	Milk Cup 5th Round Replay	4–1

Kevin Richardson, Kevin Sheedy, Adrian Heath and Graeme Sharp scored the goals that finally ended the challenge from Oxford United in the Milk Cup and took the club to a semi-final clash with Aston Villa over two legs.

| 1995 | Liverpool | A | FA Premier League | 0–0 |

JANUARY 25TH

1892 A special general meeting of the club was held to express disenchantment by the members with the rent they were being charged by John Houlding, owner of Anfield Road and therefore Everton's landlord. A Mr George Mahon, an organist at St Domingo's church and a leading accountant, announced to the assembled crowd that he already had another ground in mind, an option he held on Mere Green Field. Although there were those who felt it might be better to stay at Anfield Road (although many were known to be unhappy with the fact that the club's dressing-rooms were at licensed premises, the Sandon Hotel, also owned by John Houlding), the meeting passed the motion 'The club be formed into a limited company under the name of The Everton Football Club Limited, with a capital of £500 in £1 shares, each member to be allowed one share, ten shillings to be called up in monthly instalments of two shillings and sixpence. Such shares as are not taken up to be allotted as the directors may determine.' Not surprisingly, the news when it reached John Houlding was not well received, with him claiming ownership of the name Everton. This was held to be untrue, since the club had existed before his initial involvement, and he therefore remained at Anfield Road and formed a new club, Liverpool AFC (he had wanted to call the club Liverpool FC but was forced to change after objections from the local rugby club!).

1896	Preston North End	A	First Division	1–1
1902	Liverpool	A	FA Cup 1st Round	2–2

The very first FA Cup meeting between Everton and Liverpool, with Everton emerging from Anfield with a 2–2 draw thanks to goals from Sharp and Young.

1908	Aston Villa	H	First Division	1–0
1913	Aston Villa	A	First Division	1–1
1919	Manchester City	A	Lancashire Section Principal Tournament	0–1
1930	Blackburn Rovers	A	FA Cup 4th Round	1–4
1941	Burnley	A	North Regional League	3–2
1947	Sheffield Wednesday	A	FA Cup 4th Round	1–2

1950 Mike Pejic born in Chesterton. Initially introduced to League football by Stoke City he was sold to Everton for £150,000 in February 1977 and went on to make nearly 100 appearances for the first team. He suffered a pelvic disorder in 1978 and was ruled out for the rest of the season and then sold to Aston Villa for £250,000 in September 1979, subsequently retiring through his earlier injury in 1981.

1964	Leeds United	A	FA Cup 4th Round	1–1
1969	Coventry City	H	FA Cup 4th Round	2–0
1975	Plymouth Argyle	A	FA Cup 4th Round	3–1
1986	Blackburn Rovers	H	FA Cup 4th Round	3–1
1987	Nottingham Forest	A	First Division	0–1
1988	Sheffield Wednesday	H	FA Cup 3rd Round 2nd Replay	1–1

Everton and Sheffield Wednesday tried for a third time to settle their FA Cup third round match, with the second replay at Goodison Park attracting 37,414; interest in the battle was growing. Everton looked to have won the game thanks to a goal from Trevor Steven, but a late equaliser from Lee Chapman meant there would be a fourth game in the series.

1997 Bradford City   H   FA Cup 4th Round   2–3

After a goalless first half the cup-tie with Bradford City exploded into life five minutes after the break, with Dreyer and Waddle firing City into a two-goal lead within two minutes. An own goal by O'Brien pulled Everton back into the game, but City extended their lead just before the hour and seldom looked like giving away their advantage for a second time. Gary Speed scored in the final minute for Everton but there was insufficient time left for an equaliser.

JANUARY 26TH

1889	Wolverhampton Wanderers	A	Football League	0–4

1895	Sheffield United	H	First Division	1–1
1907	Aston Villa	A	First Division	1–2
1918	Manchester City	H	Lancashire Section Principal Tournament	0–0
1924	Middlesbrough	A	First Division	1–1
1929	Manchester City	A	First Division	1–5
1931	Port Vale	A	Second Division	3–1

Although Everton had played Port Vale throughout the First World War in the various regional Leagues that were organised, this was the first time they had visited Vale Park in the Football League. The win for Everton made it a worthwhile visit too.

1935	Sunderland	A	FA Cup 4th Round	1–1
1938	Brentford	A	First Division	0–3
1952	Birmingham City	A	Second Division	2–1
1957	West Ham United	H	FA Cup 4th Round	2–1
1980	Wigan Athletic	H	FA Cup 4th Round	3–0
1985	Doncaster Rovers	H	FA Cup 4th Round	2–0

Trevor Steven and Gary Stevens scored in the first half to end the game as a competition and keep Everton on track for a possible treble of League, FA Cup and European Cup-Winners' Cup.

1992	Chelsea	A	FA Cup 4th Round	0–1
1993	Wimbledon	A	FA Premier League	3–1

Wimbledon and Everton attracted the Premier League's lowest attendance when only 3,039 passed through the turnstiles at Selhurst Park to see Everton win 3–1 thanks to goals from Tony Cottee (two) and Ian Snodin.

JANUARY 27TH

1872   Jack Taylor born in Dumbarton. He was signed by Everton from St Mirren in 1896 and went on to establish a record 100 consecutive League appearances after making his debut. He remained with the club until July 1912 when he signed for South Liverpool and was killed in a motor accident in 1949.

1894	Stoke City	A	FA Cup 1st Round	0–1
1900	Southampton	A	FA Cup 1st Round	0–3
1906	Aston Villa	H	First Division	4–2
1912	Aston Villa	H	First Division	1–1
1917	Rochdale	A	Lancashire Section Principal Tournament	1–2
1923	Stoke City	A	First Division	1–4

Alec Troup made his debut on the wing for Everton. It was the subsequent emergence of Dixie Dean that was the making of Alec, for he supplied many of the crosses and passes from which Dean blasted his goals, particularly in the 1927–28 season. Born in Forfar in 1895 he played for Forfar Athletic and Dundee before Everton bought him in January 1923, even though he was known to have a weak collarbone and needed heavy strapping before each game. He made 259 appearances for the first team, scoring 35 goals and won five caps for Scotland before returning to Dundee in 1930. He retired three years later and opened a clothes shop in his home town of Forfar where he died in 1953.

1932	Manchester City	A	First Division	0–1
1945	Stockport County	H	Football League North (Second Championship)	9–2

Tommy Lawton scored four of Everton's goals as they swamped Stockport in the regional war League. The other goals were scored by Bentham (two), McIntosh, Rawlings and Stevenson.

1962	Manchester City	H	FA Cup 4th Round	2–0

1965   Mike Newell born in Liverpool. He began his career in the lower Leagues with Crewe and then Wigan before moving to Luton in 1986. The following year he joined Leicester City and had developed into a feared striker, prompting a scramble among the bigger clubs for his signature. He was sold to Everton for £850,000 in 1989 but a little over two years later was sold to Blackburn for £1.1 million. After helping them win the League title in 1995 he was sold to Birmingham City and later played for West Ham and Bradford City.

1968	Southport	A	FA Cup 3rd Round	1–0
1973	Leicester City	H	First Division	0–1
1974	West Bromwich Albion	H	FA Cup 4th Round	0–0
1988	Sheffield Wednesday	A	FA Cup 3rd Round 3rd Replay	5–0

Anyone who saw the three previous FA Cup third round clashes between Everton and Sheffield Wednesday would attest that they were two evenly matched and balanced sides, with perhaps the draws the fairest result on each occasion. Everton's chance of progressing had seemingly gone by their inability to beat Wednesday at Goodison, but during the first half at Hillsborough tore into the home side at every opportunity. By half-time the score was just unbelievable; Everton were 5–0 ahead! Graeme Sharp had scored a hat-trick and Adrian Heath and Ian Snodin one apiece, and if the second half failed to live up to similar expectations (how could it!), then the job had been done. The four matches had lasted over seven hours of play and attracted 142,606 fans along the way, although such a marathon would now be impossible given that penalty kicks are used in the first replay. Having got past Sheffield Wednesday at the fourth attempt, Everton could now look forward to entertaining Middlesbrough in the fourth round – this would run to three matches!

1991	Woking	A	FA Cup 4th Round	1–0
1996	Port Vale	H	FA Cup 4th Round	2–2

JANUARY 28TH

1893	Stoke City	A	First Division	1–0
1899	Jarrow	H	FA Cup 1st Round	3–1

Non-League Jarrow were the visitors to Goodison in the first round of the FA Cup, Everton winning rather more easily than the 3–1 scoreline suggested.

1905	Middlesbrough	H	First Division	1–0
1911	Manchester United	A	First Division	2–2
1928	Arsenal	A	FA Cup 4th Round	3–4
1933	Bury	H	FA Cup 4th Round	3–1

1938   Former Everton player Jack Sharp died. After finishing his playing careers in football and cricket, he opened a sports goods shop in Whitechapel in Liverpool and continued to serve Everton in the capacity of director.

1939	Huddersfield Town	H	First Division	3–2
1950	West Ham United	A	FA Cup 4th Round	2–1
1956	Port Vale	A	FA Cup 4th Round	3–2
1959	Charlton Athletic	H	FA Cup 4th Round Replay	4–1
1964	Leeds United	H	FA Cup 4th Round Replay	2–0

1967	Burnley	A	FA Cup 3rd Round	0–0
1969	Wolverhampton Wanderers	H	First Division	4–0
1978	Middlesbrough	A	FA Cup 4th Round	2–3
1984	Gillingham	H	FA Cup 4th Round	0–0
1989	Plymouth Argyle	A	FA Cup 4th Round	1–1

Everton survived a difficult trip to Home Park to face Plymouth Argyle in the fourth round of the FA Cup, Kevin Sheedy scoring from the penalty spot to earn a replay at Goodison Park.

| 1990 | Sheffield Wednesday | A | FA Cup 4th Round | 2–1 |

JANUARY 29TH

1898	Blackburn Rovers	H	FA Cup 1st Round	1–0
1916	Stoke City	H	Lancashire Section Principal Tournament	4–1
1921	Sheffield Wednesday	H	FA Cup 2nd Round	1–1
1927	Hull City	A	FA Cup 4th Round	1–1

1929 Jimmy Tansey born in Liverpool. He joined Everton in May 1948 and made 133 appearances at full-back for the club during 12 years at Goodison Park. He left for Crewe during the close season of 1960 but made only one appearance for the Gresty Road club. His younger brother Gerald was also on Everton's books for a while but failed to make the first team, subsequently joining Tranmere.

1930 George Rankin born in Liverpool. He joined Everton as a junior and signed professional forms in August 1948. In eight years with the club he made only 36 League appearances before being sold to Southport in July 1956, going on to play 144 League games for the Haig Avenue outfit.

1936	Huddersfield Town	A	First Division	1–2
1938	Bolton Wanderers	H	First Division	4–1
1944	Liverpool	H	Football League North (Second Championship)	2–3
1947	Liverpool	H	First Division	1–0
1949	Chelsea	A	FA Cup 4th Round	0–2
1955	Liverpool	H	FA Cup 4th Round	0–4
1958	Blackburn Rovers	H	FA Cup 4th Round	1–2
1963	Swindon Town	A	FA Cup 4th Round	5–1

Swindon were battling for promotion from the Third Division when they were drawn against Everton in the FA Cup, with their home form in particular responsible for their placing in the upper reaches of the table. Everton meanwhile were at the top end of the First Division and in a good run of form. Two goals from Roy Vernon and single strikes from Billy Bingham, Jimmy Gabriel and John Morrissey emphasised the gulf between the two sides as Everton won 5–1 at the County Ground.

| 1966 | Northampton Town | A | First Division | 2–0 |

Everton visited Northampton Town's County Ground for the only time in a League match and returned home with both points thanks to a 2–0 win. The goals were scored by Derek Temple and Alex Scott.

1966	Nottingham Forest	A	First Division	2–0
1972	Chelsea	A	First Division	0–4
1977	Swindon Town	A	FA Cup 4th Round	2–2
1995	Bristol City	A	FA Cup 4th Round	1–0

1997   Newcastle United   A   FA Premier League   1–4
On the same day Andrei Kanchelskis was sold to Italian Serie A club Fiorentina for an Everton record transfer fee of £8 million. He had asked for a transfer for some time, claiming he wished to try his luck on the continent, a wish that was granted following Everton's recent exit from the FA Cup.

JANUARY 30TH

1897   Burton Wanderers   H   FA Cup 1st Round   5–2
1902   Liverpool   H   FA Cup 1st Round Replay   0–2
Liverpool won 2–0 in the FA Cup first round replay at Goodison and thus won the very first clash between the two clubs in the competition.
1904   Middlesbrough   A   First Division   0–3
1909   Manchester City   A   First Division   0–4
1915   Bristol City   H   FA Cup 2nd Round   4–0
1926   Leicester City   H   First Division   1–0
1932   Liverpool   H   First Division   2–1
1935   Sunderland   H   FA Cup 4th Round Replay   6–4
One of the greatest games ever seen at Goodison Park resulted in a 6–4 win for Everton against Sunderland in the FA Cup fourth round replay. The two sides had drawn 1–1 at Roker Park four days previously and another close game was predicted, but few could have realised the classic they were about to witness. Jackie Coulter opened the scoring for Everton after 14 minutes and increased the lead to 2–0 on half an hour. Although Sunderland pulled one back before half-time it did not take Alex Stevenson long to restore the two goal advantage. Sunderland then launched a comeback that saw them force extra time, hitting the vital equaliser with only seconds left on the clock. Coulter completed his hat-trick in the first period of extra time only for Sunderland to equalise once again, and a second replay started looking increasingly likely. That was until Albert Geldard took over, scoring twice in the final nine minutes of the game to finally settle the match in Everton's favour.
1937   Sheffield Wednesday   H   FA Cup 4th Round   3–0
1943   Manchester United   H   Football League North (Second Championship) 0–5
1954   Swansea Town   H   FA Cup 4th Round   3–0
1965   Leeds United   A   FA Cup 4th Round   1–1
1971   Tottenham Hotspur   A   First Division   1–2
1974   West Bromwich Albion   A   FA Cup 4th Round Replay   0–1
1977   Everton appointed Gordon Lee as manager in place of Billy Bingham who had departed earlier in the month. Lee had been manager at Newcastle United and announced that the Everton move was a good one as it would be beneficial to be nearer to his children who were being educated in Lancashire! He remained in the post until May 1981.
1982   Tottenham Hotspur   H   First Division   1–1
1983   Shrewsbury Town   H   FA Cup 4th Round   2–1
1988   Middlesbrough   H   FA Cup 4th Round   1–1
1993   Norwich City   H   FA Premier League   0–1

JANUARY 31ST

1903   Sheffield United   H   First Division   1–0
1925   Sunderland   A   FA Cup 2nd Round   0–0

| 1931 | Bradford City | H | Second Division | 4–2 |

1934 Alan Sanders born in Salford. He began his professional career with Manchester City but left the Maine Road club in July 1956 having failed to appear in the first team. He had better luck at Goodison Park, making 56 appearances in the League and then left in 1959 to join Swansea. He finished his career with Brighton in 1965.

1942	Wolverhampton Wanderers	H	Football League North (Second Championship)	2–1
1948	Wolverhampton Wanderers	H	FA Cup 4th Round Replay	3–2
1953	Nottingham Forest	H	FA Cup 4th Round	4–1
1959	Manchester City	H	First Division	3–1
1967	Burnley	H	FA Cup 3rd Round Replay	2–1
1970	Wolverhampton Wanderers	H	First Division	1–0
1976	Burnley	H	First Division	2–3
1979	Aston Villa	H	First Division	1–1
1981	Nottingham Forest	A	First Division	0–1
1984	Gillingham	A	FA Cup 4th Round Replay	0–0
1987	Bradford City	A	FA Cup 4th Round	1–0
1989	Plymouth Argyle	H	FA Cup 4th Round Replay	4–0

Two goals in either half saw Everton through to the fifth round to face Barnsley at Oakwell, with Graeme Sharp scoring twice and Pat Nevin and Kevin Sheedy netting the other goals.

| 1998 | West Ham United | A | FA Premier League | 2–2 |

FEBRUARY 1ST

1896	Nottingham Forest	A	FA Cup 1st Round	2–0
1902	Sheffield United	A	First Division	0–0
1908	Oldham Athletic	A	FA Cup 2nd Round	0–0
1913	Brighton & Hove Albion	A	FA Cup 2nd Round	0–0
1919	Manchester City	H	Lancashire Section Principal Tournament	3–0
1930	Portsmouth	H	First Division	1–1
1933	Manchester City	A	First Division	0–3
1936	Middlesbrough	H	First Division	5–2

Dixie Dean netted two more goals as Middlesbrough were beaten 5–2. Everton's other goals were scored by Jimmy Cunliffe, Albert Geldard and Torry Gillick, but despite the result Middlesbrough still finished the season ahead of Everton in the League table.

1939	Portsmouth	A	First Division	1–0
1941	Barnsley	H	North Regional League	3–1
1947	Huddersfield Town	H	First Division	1–0
1958	Luton Town	H	First Division	0–2
1964	Sheffield Wednesday	A	First Division	3–0
1969	Queens Park Rangers	A	First Division	1–0
1975	Tottenham Hotspur	H	First Division	1–0
1977	Swindon Town	H	FA Cup 4th Round Replay	2–1

Everton's twin assault on Wembley kept on track with a 2–1 replay win over Swindon in the FA Cup thanks to goals from Martin Dobson and David Jones. The win meant Everton now faced a difficult trip to Ninian Park to face Cardiff City in the fifth round.

1986	Tottenham Hotspur	H	First Division	1–0
1995	Newcastle United	A	FA Premier League	0–2
1997	Nottingham Forest	H	FA Premier League	2–0

FEBRUARY 2ND

1895	Southport	A	FA Cup 1st Round	3–0
1905	Liverpool	A	FA Cup 1st Round	1–1
1907	West Ham United	A	FA Cup 2nd Round	2–1
1918	Rochdale	A	Lancashire Section Principal Tournament	2–2
1924	Brighton & Hove Albion	A	FA Cup 2nd Round	2–5
1927	Hull City	H	FA Cup 4th Round Replay	2–2
1929	Huddersfield Town	H	First Division	0–3
1946	Bradford Park Avenue	H	Football League North	0–0
1957	Sunderland	A	First Division	1–1
1965	Leeds United	H	FA Cup 4th Round Replay	1–2

Having drawn 1–1 at Elland Road thanks to a goal from Fred Pickering in the first meeting Everton could have been forgiven for thinking they had done the difficult part of the job against the League leaders. At Goodison Park, however, Leeds responded to the challenge and scored twice, with Everton managing a consolation effort from Pickering. Leeds were destined to finish runners-up in both the cup and League that year, beaten in the cup by Liverpool and pipped to the title on goal average by Manchester United. Everton, however, had a little over a year to wait before getting their hands on the cup.

1974	Sheffield United	A	First Division	1–1
1980	Wolverhampton Wanderers	A	First Division	0–0
1985	Watford	H	First Division	4–0

Bad weather across the country during January meant this was the first match Everton had played for three points since their 4–0 win over Newcastle on January 12th. Two goals from Kevin Sheedy and efforts from Derek Mountfield and Graeme Sharp repeated the 4–0 success, Everton's fifth successive League victory.

| 1991 | Sunderland | H | First Division | 2–0 |
| 1992 | Aston Villa | A | First Division | 0–0 |

FEBRUARY 3RD

1890	Stoke City	A	FA Cup 2nd Round	2–4
1894	West Bromwich Albion	A	First Division	1–3
1896	Small Heath	H	First Division	3–0
1900	Burnley	A	First Division	1–3
1906	Chesterfield	H	FA Cup 2nd Round	3–0

Chesterfield had been drawn out of the bag first for the FA Cup second round match with Everton but chose to forgo home advantage in order to earn a share of higher receipts from playing the match at Goodison Park. There Everton had little trouble in obtaining a 3–0 win thanks to goals from Settle, Taylor and Young on their way to winning the cup at the Crystal Palace.

| 1912 | Bury | H | FA Cup 2nd Round | 1–1 |
| 1917 | Bolton Wanderers | H | Lancashire Section Principal Tournament | 1–0 |

1921	Sheffield Wednesday	A	FA Cup 2nd Round Replay	1–0
1934	Arsenal	A	First Division	2–1

On the same day Alan Shackleton was born in Padham. The centre-forward began his career with Burnley and hit 18 goals in 31 League appearances before moving to Leeds. Everton signed him from the Elland Road club in 1959 and he scored 10 goals in 26 outings before moving on to Oldham.

1936	Sheffield Wednesday	A	First Division	3–3
1937	Huddersfield Town	A	First Division	3–0

On the same day Alex Young was born in Loanhead. He arrived at Goodison Park from Hearts and was an instant hit with the fans, earning the nickname The Golden Vision (which subsequently became the title of a television play based on Young) and inspiring the team to the League title in 1963. Three years later he helped the club win the FA Cup and remained with Everton until 1968 when he went to become player-manager of Glentoran. A few weeks later he was back in England playing for Stockport County, but after only 23 games was forced to retire owing to injury. He won eight caps for Scotland during his career.

1945	Liverpool	H	Football League North (Second Championship)	4–1
1951	Portsmouth	A	First Division	3–6
1962	Ipswich Town	A	First Division	2–4
1968	Liverpool	H	First Division	1–0
1973	Millwall	H	FA Cup 4th Round	0–2
1979	Wolverhampton Wanderers	A	First Division	0–1
1988	Middlesbrough	A	FA Cup 4th Round Replay	2–2
1990	Liverpool	A	First Division	1–2
1996	Southampton	A	FA Premier League	2–2

FEBRUARY 4TH

1893	Nottingham Forest	H	FA Cup 2nd Round	4–2

Everton were destined to reach the final for the first time at the end of the season, with Milward (two), Chadwick and Geary scoring the goals that saw off Nottingham Forest at Goodison Park.

1911	Liverpool	H	FA Cup 2nd Round	2–1

This was the fourth time Everton and Liverpool had been paired in the FA Cup, with 50,000 packing into Goodison for the derby game with extra flavour. Alex Young scored twice for Everton, with Parkinson netting for Liverpool, but Everton's run came to an end in the next round against Derby.

1925	Sunderland	H	FA Cup 2nd Round Replay	2–1
1928	Huddersfield Town	A	First Division	1–4

Despite the 4–1 defeat Dixie Dean got on the scoresheet again to register his 40th goal of the season in just 26 appearances.

1933	Arsenal	H	First Division	1–1
1939	Liverpool	A	First Division	3–0
1950	Aston Villa	H	First Division	1–1
1956	Portsmouth	H	First Division	0–2
1961	Bolton Wanderers	H	First Division	1–2
1967	Leeds United	H	First Division	2–0

1978	Leicester City	H	First Division		2–0
1984	Notts County	H	First Division		4–1

Adrian Heath scored a hat-trick as Everton's revival continued, with Kevin Sheedy netting the other goal from the penalty spot. Although Everton were beginning to climb up the table and make progress in both cup competitions, just 13,016 were at Goodison Park for the game. Twelve months later 'sold out' notices were posted all around the ground.

1989	Wimbledon	H	First Division		1–1
1995	Norwich City	H	FA Premier League		2–1

FEBRUARY 5TH

1898	Sheffield Wednesday	A	First Division		1–2
1908	Oldham Athletic	H	FA Cup 2nd Round Replay		6–1
1910	Woolwich Arsenal	H	FA Cup 2nd Round		5–0
1913	Brighton & Hove Albion	H	FA Cup 2nd Round Replay		1–0
1916	Burnley	A	Lancashire Section Principal Tournament		1–2
1921	Manchester City	H	First Division		3–0
1927	Leicester City	A	First Division		2–6

Warney Cresswell made his first appearance for the club in the 6–2 defeat at Filbert Street against Leicester City. An extremely accomplished defender he had cost Sunderland a then record fee of £5,500 when he moved to Roker Park from South Shields in 1922, and five years later moved on to Goodison. He was to remain with the club until 1936, making over 300 appearances for the club and later went into management with Port Vale and Southampton. He won nine caps for England during his career.

1930	Manchester City	A	First Division		2–1
1938	Huddersfield Town	A	First Division		3–1
1944	Wrexham	H	Football League North (Second Championship)	2–3
1949	Liverpool	A	First Division		0–0
1955	Chelsea	H	First Division		1–1
1966	Stoke City	H	First Division		2–1

1969 Andy Hinchcliffe born in Manchester. A product of the Manchester City youth scheme he made over 100 appearances for the club before an £800,000 move to Everton in 1990. He then became a permanent fixture in the defence, winning an FA Cup winners' medal in 1995 and also collecting three caps for England. He was sold to Sheffield Wednesday midway through the 1997–98 season.

1972	Walsall	H	FA Cup 4th Round		2–1
1977	Aston Villa	A	First Division		0–2
1983	Notts County	H	First Division		3–0
1986	Tottenham Hotspur	A	Screen Sport Super Cup Semi-Final 1st Leg	0–0

The semi-final first leg of the Super Cup against Spurs at White Hart Lane was for true die-hards only, for a snow storm during the game made conditions farcical and a goalless draw was always going to be the likeliest result.

1994	Chelsea	H	FA Premier League		4–2

FEBRUARY 6TH

1894	Sunderland	A	First Division		0–1
1897	Preston North End	H	First Division		3–4

1904	Tottenham Hotspur	H	FA Cup 1st Round	1–2
1909	Manchester United	A	FA Cup 2nd Round	0–1
1915	Liverpool	H	First Division	1–3
1924	Preston North End	H	First Division	1–1
1926	Liverpool	H	First Division	3–3
1932	Arsenal	H	First Division	1–3

The visit of reigning champions Arsenal to Goodison Park attracted a crowd of 56,698, the biggest of the season. Arsenal were also Everton's biggest threat to their own title aspirations, but after the visitors had recorded a 3–1 win, many felt the trophy was destined to remain at Highbury for a second consecutive season. Everton, however, were to have the last word, winning the League by two points.

| 1937 | Sunderland | H | First Division | 3–0 |
| 1943 | Chester | H | Football League North (Second Championship) 4–5 |

1947 John Hurst born in Blackpool. A schoolboy international when he joined the club, Hurst signed professional forms with Everton in October 1964 and made his debut in 1965. He went on to make nearly 400 appearances for the first team, helping them win the League in 1970. In June 1976 he was released by Everton and joined Oldham where he finished his playing career.

1954	Blackburn Rovers	H	Second Division	1–1
1960	Sheffield Wednesday	A	First Division	2–2
1965	Birmingham City	H	First Division	1–1
1971	Huddersfield Town	H	First Division	2–1
1982	Brighton & Hove Albion	A	First Division	1–3
1984	Gillingham	A	FA Cup 4th Round 2nd Replay	3–0

After two goalless games with Gillingham Everton lost the toss for venue and had to return to the Priestfield Stadium for a third meeting. At last Everton made their pedigree tell, with Kevin Sheedy scoring twice and Adrian Heath the other as the team finally moved into the next round to face Shrewsbury Town.

| 1993 | Sheffield Wednesday | A | FA Premier League | 1–3 |

FEBRUARY 7TH

| 1903 | Portsmouth | H | FA Cup 1st Round | 5–0 |

1910 Ted Sagar born in Moorend. Although initially spotted by Hull City and given a trial at Boothferry Park, Everton nipped in to offer him professional forms first. He signed in 1929 and went on to remain with the club for an astonishing 24 years and one month, the longest spell any player has spent with one club and a record unlikely to be broken. In that time he made 495 appearances for the first team, a figure that would have been much higher but for the Second World War. One of the greatest goalkeepers in the game he was unfortunate not to have won more than four caps for England, but whilst with Everton he did collect two League titles and the FA Cup. He died in October 1986.

1914	Middlesbrough	A	First Division	0–2
1920	Aston Villa	H	First Division	1–1
1925	Liverpool	A	First Division	1–3
1927	Hull City	Villa Park	FA Cup 4th Round 2nd Replay	2–3

After two draws (1–1 at Boothferry Park and 2–2 at Goodison Park) Hull City and Everton elected to try again at neutral Villa Park for their third meeting. There Hull won 3–2 despite Everton goals from Dean and Dominy.

1931   Charlton Athletic   A   Second Division   7–0
Dixie Dean scored a hat-trick as Everton registered their biggest away win of the season at the Valley. The other goals were scored by Critchley, Dunn, Johnson and Stein, meaning that all five Everton forwards scored and in an 18 minute spell. Charlton must have been glad to see the back of Everton that season, for in October Everton had won 7–1 at Goodison!

1934   Manchester City   H   First Division   2–0
1935   Huddersfield Town   A   First Division   1–1
1942   Burnley   H   Football League North (Second Championship) 3–2
1948   Fulham   A   FA Cup 5th Round   1–1
1953   Brentford   H   Second Division   5–0
1959   Leeds United   A   First Division   0–1
1976   Sheffield United   A   First Division   0–0
1981   Aston Villa   H   First Division   1–3
1987   Coventry City   H   First Division   3–1
1988   Arsenal   H   Littlewoods Cup Semi-Final 1st Leg   0–1
Everton had played eight cup-ties in a month by the time they faced Arsenal in the Littlewoods Cup semi-final first leg at Goodison, with the visit of Middlesbrough in the FA Cup fourth round second replay due in two days' time. Perhaps their minds were already on that fixture, for Perry Groves gave Arsenal the lead after ten minutes and Trevor Steven missed a penalty to give Everton an almighty task for the second leg.

1992   Oldham Athletic   H   First Division   2–1
1998   Barnsley   A   FA Premier League   2–2

FEBRUARY 8TH

1890   Burnley   A   Football League   1–0
1905   Liverpool   H   FA Cup 1st Round Replay   2–1
1908   Middlesbrough   H   First Division   2–1
1912   Bury   H   FA Cup 2nd Round Replay   6–0
Everton had already drawn at home with Bury five days earlier 1–1, but Bury agreed to staging the replay at Goodison Park in order to take a share in bigger receipts. Everton made no mistake second time around, with Browell scoring four and Davidson and Jefferis adding the others in a one-sided 6–0 win.

1913   Liverpool   H   First Division   0–2
1919   Port Vale   A   Lancashire Section Principal Tournament   1–0
1922   Aston Villa   A   First Division   1–2
1930   Arsenal   A   First Division   0–4
1936   Aston Villa   A   First Division   1–1
1941   Liverpool   A   North Regional League   3–1
1964   Liverpool   H   First Division   3–1
With Liverpool on their way to winning the title held by Everton, a crowd of 66,515 were drawn to Goodison for the season's second meeting between the two rivals. Everton were looking to avenge a 2–1 defeat at Anfield, and goals from Jimmy Gabriel and two from Roy Vernon enabled them to bring Liverpool's charge to a halt.

1969   Tottenham Hotspur   A   First Division   1–1
1975   Manchester City   A   First Division   1–2
1992   Queens Park Rangers   H   First Division   0–0

FEBRUARY 9TH

1889	Wolverhampton Wanderers	H	Football League	1–2
1901	Southampton	A	FA Cup 1st Round	3–1

The death of Queen Victoria had caused the opening round of the FA Cup to be delayed, with Everton finally getting to travel to Southampton in early February. Southampton were then a Southern League side but the previous season had reached the FA Cup final, only to lose 4–0 to Bury. Everton on the other hand were lying in mid-table of the First Division and turned in a superb performance in winning at The Dell, scoring through Settle, Taylor and Turner.

1907	Bristol City	A	First Division	1–2
1918	Rochdale	H	Lancashire Section Principal Tournament	2–2
1924	Preston North End	A	First Division	1–0
1929	Liverpool	A	First Division	2–1
1935	Wolverhampton Wanderers	H	First Division	5–2
1946	Manchester City	H	Football League North	4–1
1952	Leicester City	H	Second Division	2–0
1957	Charlton Athletic	H	First Division	5–0
1965	Manchester United	H	Inter-Cities Fairs Cup 3rd Round 2nd Leg	1–2

Everton's Inter-Cities Fairs Cup tie with Manchester United was delicately poised after the first leg, with the 1–1 draw leaving everything to play for in the second leg at Goodison Park. There United were to find something extra in their reserves and scored twice, Everton's lone reply coming from Fred Pickering, his sixth in the competition.

1974	Wolverhampton Wanderers	H	First Division	2–1
1980	Ipswich Town	H	First Division	0–4
1988	Middlesbrough	H	FA Cup 4th Round 2nd Replay	2–1

It normally takes six games to win the FA Cup; Everton had now completed seven and had only just made it to the fifth round! After taking four games to dispose of Sheffield Wednesday in the third round, Middlesbrough had required three games before Everton finally won 2–1 at Goodison, Graeme Sharp and an own goal taking them through to face rivals Liverpool in the next round.

1991	Liverpool	A	First Division	1–3

FEBRUARY 10TH

1906	Sheffield United	H	First Division	3–2
1912	Sheffield United	H	First Division	3–2
1915	Aston Villa	A	First Division	5–1

Bobby Parker scored a hat-trick as Everton brushed aside Aston Villa at Villa Park, thus taking another step closer to the League title. Their other goals were scored by Galt and Kirsopp, and brought to an end a run of three games in which only one point had been gained.

1917	Port Vale	A	Lancashire Section Principal Tournament	1–1
1923	Chelsea	H	First Division	3–1
1926	Manchester City	H	First Division	1–1

1934	Liverpool	H	First Division	0–0
1940	Stoke City	A	War Regional League, Western Division	0–1
1945	Liverpool	A	Football League North (Second Championship)	1–3
1962	Burnley	H	First Division	2–2
1973	Southampton	A	First Division	0–0
1979	Bristol City	H	First Division	4–1
1990	Charlton Athletic	H	First Division	2–1
1993	Tottenham Hotspur	H	FA Premier League	1–2
1996	Manchester City	H	FA Premier League	2–0

FEBRUARY 11TH

1893	Preston North End	H	First Division	6–0
1899	Nottingham Forest	H	FA Cup 2nd Round	0–1
1905	Bury	H	First Division	2–0
1911	Bury	A	First Division	0–0
1920	Newcastle United	A	First Division	3–3

On the same day George Burnett was born in Liverpool. He joined Everton as a junior during the Second World War and had to wait for the end of hostilities before making his first-team debut. He made 47 appearances in goal for the club before leaving for Oldham in October 1951, another victim of Ted Sagar's remarkable record of consistency and longevity.

1922	Middlesbrough	A	First Division	1–3
1928	Tottenham Hotspur	H	First Division	2–5
1933	Liverpool	A	First Division	4–7

Liverpool sprung a surprise before the game, selecting a side that relied on youth as opposed to the seasoned professionals Everton had expected to be up against. A crowd of 50,000 were at Anfield for the game, with Everton taking the lead after eight minutes through Dixie Dean. It didn't take Liverpool long to equalise or then take the lead, with Everton's defence unable to cope with the speed of the Liverpool wingers, and Cresswell inadvertently helped on a free-kick that led to Liverpool's third shortly before half-time. Everton got back into the game through Albert Geldard soon after the break, but that only seemed to inspire Liverpool to pull away again, scoring twice in a short spell. Everton were still not finished and Dean scored his second of the game with a header to bring the score to 5–3, but Liverpool scored two more before Stein scored in the last minute to make the final result 7–4.

1939	Birmingham City	A	FA Cup 5th Round	2–2

The visit of Everton in the FA Cup attracted St Andrews' biggest ever crowd, with 66,844 present for the 2–2 draw. Goals from Wally Boyes and Alex Stevenson earned Everton a replay which they subsequently won.

1950	Tottenham Hotspur	H	FA Cup 5th Round	1–0
1956	Newcastle United	H	First Division	0–0
1961	West Ham United	A	First Division	0–4
1967	Newcastle United	A	First Division	3–0

1974 Nick Barmby born in Hull. He started his career with Spurs despite the interest of just about every major club in the country and proved one of the brightest young talents in the game, breaking into the England side whilst still at White Hart Lane. Moved on to Middlesbrough for a fee of £5.25 million in 1995 but a little over a year later was on the move again, this time to Everton, for £5.75 million. Although he had since lost his place in the England side, time is still on his side for return.

1984	West Bromwich Albion	A	First Division	1–1
1986	Manchester City	H	First Division	4–0
1989	Southampton	A	First Division	1–1

FEBRUARY 12TH

1898	Stoke City	A	FA Cup 2nd Round	0–0
1910	Liverpool	A	First Division	1–0
1916	Preston North End	H	Lancashire Section Principal Tournament	2–0
1921	Manchester United	A	First Division	2–1
1927	Liverpool	A	First Division	0–1
1944	Wrexham	A	Football League North (Second Championship)	1–2
1949	Birmingham City	A	First Division	0–0
1955	Cardiff City	A	First Division	3–4
1963	Leicester City	A	First Division	1–3
1966	Bedford Town	A	FA Cup 4th Round	3–0

Non-League Bedford Town were a surprise qualifier for the FA Cup fourth round, although their route had not been too taxing, involving Exeter City and Brighton in the first two rounds and fellow non-Leaguers Hereford in the third round. They resisted the temptation of switching the tie with Everton to Goodison, preferring to try to cause an upset on their own ground. Everton were in no mood to be the victims of a giant-killing, scoring through Derek Temple (two) and Fred Pickering on their way to winning the cup that season.

1969	Bristol City	H	FA Cup 5th Round	1–0

Joe Royle scored the only goal of the game that earned Everton a quarter-final clash with Manchester United at Old Trafford.

1972	Leeds United	H	First Division	0–0
1977	Leicester City	H	First Division	1–2
1983	Aston Villa	A	First Division	0–2
1994	Ipswich Town	H	FA Premier League	0–0

FEBRUARY 13TH

1892	Burnley	A	Football League	0–1
1893	Sheffield Wednesday	A	First Division	2–0
1897	Bury	H	FA Cup 2nd Round	3–0
1904	Bury	A	First Division	0–0
1909	Bury	A	First Division	2–2
1926	Huddersfield Town	A	First Division	0–3
1932	Blackpool	A	First Division	0–2
1937	Wolverhampton Wanderers	A	First Division	2–7

Despite the 7–2 defeat against Wolves, the game saw the first goal scored for Everton by Tommy Lawton. He went on to find the net 65 times during his 87 League matches for the club and would probably have got close to Dixie Dean's record had it not been for the outbreak of the Second World War.

1943	Chester	A	Football League North (Second Championship)	1–0

1949 Geoff Nulty born in Prescot. Although he was initially signed by Stoke City he joined Burnley in July 1968 having failed to play for the Potteries club. At Burnley he developed into a highly skilful defender and in 1974 he was snapped up by Newcastle, having made 123 League appearances for the club. After a further 100 appearances for the St James' Park club he was sold to Everton for £40,000, his career coming to an end following a tackle by Jimmy Case in 1980.

1954 Derby County   A   Second Division   6–2

The start of a spell of exemplary goalscoring from Everton, with Eddie Wainwright grabbing a hat-trick and Dave Hickson, Jack Lindsay and John Willie Parker getting the others in a 6–2 win at the Baseball Ground. In the next five games Everton scored a total of 21 goals, firing them up the table on their way to promotion.

Year	Opponent	H/A	Competition	Score
1960	Wolverhampton Wanderers	H	First Division	0–2
1965	West Ham United	A	First Division	1–0
1971	Derby County	H	FA Cup 5th Round	1–0
1982	Stoke City	H	First Division	0–0
1988	Queens Park Rangers	H	First Division	2–0
1995	West Ham United	A	FA Premier League	2–2

FEBRUARY 14TH

1903 J Sheridan was capped by Ireland for the match against England at Wolverhampton, the first Everton player to represent the country. England won the match 4–0.

Year	Opponent	H/A	Competition	Score
1903	Aston Villa	H	First Division	0–1
1914	Sheffield United	H	First Division	5–0
1920	Aston Villa	A	First Division	2–2
1923	Chelsea	A	First Division	1–3
1925	Sunderland	A	First Division	1–4
1931	Grimsby Town	H	FA Cup 5th Round	5–3
1942	Burnley	A	Football League North (Second Championship)	0–1
1948	Fulham	H	FA Cup 5th Round Replay	0–1

On the same day Martin Dobson was born in Blackburn. Although initially on Bolton Wanderers' books, Martin moved to Burnley before he had made a first-team appearance for Bolton. He spent seven years at Turf Moor and was then sold to Everton for a then record fee of £300,000 in August 1974. After making 230 appearances for Everton he returned to Burnley for £100,000 in August 1979, and later had a spell as manager of Bury.

Year	Opponent	H/A	Competition	Score
1953	Manchester United	H	FA Cup 5th Round	2–1
1959	Aston Villa	H	FA Cup 5th Round	1–4
1970	Arsenal	H	First Division	2–2
1981	Southampton	A	FA Cup 5th Round	0–0
1987	Oxford United	A	First Division	1–1
1989	Aston Villa	H	First Division	1–1
1996	Port Vale	A	FA Cup 4th Round Replay	1–2
1998	Derby County	H	FA Premier League	1–2

FEBRUARY 15TH

1878 Jack Sharp born in Hereford. He began his League career with Aston Villa, joining them from Hereford Thistle. He switched to Everton in 1899 and went on to make 300 League appearances before retiring in 1910 to concentrate on his other passion, cricket (although he maintained his connection with Everton, serving the club as a director). Having won two caps for England at football, he was then awarded three at the summer sport. His brother was also a notable player (and indeed played for Hereford Thistle, Aston Villa and Everton!) whilst his son was a director of Everton at one time.

| 1890 | Glasgow Rangers | H | Friendly | 8–1 |

Glasgow Rangers visited Anfield for a friendly and were beaten 8–1. The two clubs also agreed to a meeting at Ibrox later in the year.

1896	Sheffield United	H	FA Cup 2nd Round	3–0
1902	Bury	A	First Division	0–1
1908	Sheffield United	A	First Division	0–2
1913	Bolton Wanderers	A	First Division	0–0
1919	Port Vale	H	Lancashire Section Principal Tournament	3–1
1936	Wolverhampton Wanderers	H	First Division	4–1
1939	Birmingham City	H	FA Cup 5th Round Replay	2–1
1941	Manchester United	A	League War Cup	2–2
1947	Sunderland	H	First Division	4–2
1958	Leicester City	H	First Division	2–2
1961	Shrewsbury Town	A	League Cup 5th Round	1–2

After disposing of Accrington Stanley, Walsall, Bury and Tranmere Rovers in the League Cup Everton had hopes of winning the competition, given that perhaps the strongest team they could expect to face were Aston Villa. Indeed, Villa went on to win the cup in its very first season, but it was Shrewsbury who ended the Everton dream, winning 2–1 at Gay Meadow in the quarter-final.

1964	Sunderland	A	FA Cup 5th Round	1–3
1975	Fulham	H	FA Cup 5th Round	1–2
1977	Bolton Wanderers	A	League Cup Semi-Final 2nd Leg	1–0

The first leg at Goodison had ended in a 1–1 draw, passing the advantage to Bolton in the race to make the final. But Everton responded well at Burnden Park, silencing the home supporters in the 50,413 crowd with a first half goal from Bob Latchford and holding out to make the League Cup final for the first time in their history.

| 1984 | Aston Villa | H | Milk Cup Semi-Final 1st Leg | 2–0 |

With Liverpool having been avoided in the semi-final draw (they were paired with Walsall) a first Merseyside final was still a possibility, but Everton were required to overcome experienced League Cup campaigners Aston Villa over two legs in order to reach Wembley. Such was the backlog of fixtures being experienced by Everton, Liverpool had already made it to the final by the time Everton kicked off at Goodison against Villa, with a crowd of 40,006 present for an intriguing battle. Everton scored in each half through Kevin Sheedy and Kevin Richardson to send the fans home happy.

FEBRUARY 16TH

1895	Blackburn Rovers	H	FA Cup 2nd Round	1–1
1901	Manchester City	H	First Division	5–2
1918	Blackburn Rovers	A	Lancashire Section Principal Tournament	6–0
1924	Chelsea	H	First Division	2–0

1931 Bobby Collins born in Glasgow. He initially joined Everton from Scottish junior football but soon after declared he was homesick and returned to Glasgow to sign for Celtic. Seven years later he cost Everton £39,000 and made his debut in 1958. He spent four seasons with Everton before moving to Elland Road for £30,000, helping Leeds United out of the Second Division and to the very top of the English game. A broken thigh sustained in a European match effectively ended his Leeds career and he moved to Bury in February 1967, later playing for Oldham Athletic. When his playing career ended he turned to management, serving Hull City, Huddersfield Town and Barnsley as well as coaching at Blackpool.

1935	Derby County	H	FA Cup 5th Round	3–1
1938	Liverpool	H	First Division	1–3
1946	Manchester City	A	Football League North	3–1
1952	Blackburn Rovers	A	Second Division	0–1
1957	Manchester United	A	FA Cup 5th Round	0–1
1971	Southampton	A	First Division	2–2
1974	West Ham United	A	First Division	3–4
1980	Wrexham	H	FA Cup 5th Round	5–2
1985	Telford United	H	FA Cup 5th Round	3–0

Telford had accounted for Lincoln City, Preston, Bradford City and Darlington on their way to the fifth round, where they got a plum draw away at Everton. A crowd of 47,402 ensured Telford would receive a £50,000 share of the gate receipts, although it was Everton who went into the next round courtesy of goals from Peter Reid, a Kevin Sheedy penalty and Gary Stevens.

1988 Luton Town   H   Simod Cup Quarter-Final   1–2
The Simod Cup, a sponsored version of the Full Member's Cup which had run for the two previous seasons, remains probably the most shambolic of all competitions Everton have ever entered, for without even kicking a ball in anger they had made their way through to the quarter-finals! Their only match in the competition this season saw them lose 2–1 at home to Luton (who went on to reach the final at Wembley, the day out enjoyed by the fans being the only remotely good thing to emerge) in front of just 5,204 fans.

FEBRUARY 17TH

1898	Stoke City	H	FA Cup 2nd Round Replay	5–1
1900	Nottingham Forest	A	First Division	2–4
1906	Notts County	A	First Division	0–0

Joe Donachie made his debut for the club in the 0–0 draw at Notts County. He went on to make 40 League appearances in his first spell at Everton, which ended in 1908, but after the First World War he returned to the club from Rangers and played a further 16 matches.

1912	Oldham Athletic	A	First Division	0–3
1917	Oldham Athletic	H	Lancashire Section Principal Tournament	2–0
1923	Middlesbrough	A	First Division	4–2
1934	Middlesbrough	H	First Division	1–1

1935 Ken Rea born in Liverpool. He joined the club as a junior and signed professional forms in June 1956 but made only 46 appearances before retiring in 1958.

1945 Southport   H   Football League North (Second Championship) 6–0

1951	Chelsea	H	First Division	3–0
1962	Burnley	A	FA Cup 5th Round	1–3
1968	Carlisle United	A	FA Cup 4th Round	2–0
1979	Southampton	A	First Division	0–3

Virtually the entire football programme was decimated by bad weather, with all of the FA Cup ties cancelled and only five League games played, with Everton's visit to Southampton the only game to survive in the First Division. Everton must have wished it hadn't: they lost 3–0.

1981	Southampton	H	FA Cup 5th Round Replay	1–0
1990	Oldham Athletic	A	FA Cup 5th Round	2–2
1991	Liverpool	A	FA Cup 5th Round	0–0

One of the more forgettable Merseyside clashes saw both sides cancelling each other out, clear cut chances few and far between and Everton fully worth their second chance at Goodison Park. That game eventually entered folklore, although it would have been the furthest thing from the minds of those in the 38,323 who made their way home after the first meeting.

FEBRUARY 18TH

1893	Sheffield Wednesday	H	FA Cup 3rd Round	3–0
1896	Sheffield Wednesday	A	First Division	1–3
1905	Stoke City	A	FA Cup 2nd Round	4–0
1911	Sheffield United	H	First Division	1–0
1920	Oldham Athletic	H	First Division	0–2
1931	Barnsley	H	Second Division	5–2
1933	Leeds United	H	FA Cup 5th Round	2–0
1939	Bolton Wanderers	H	First Division	2–1

1944 Henry Newton born in Nottingham. Signed by Nottingham Forest in June 1961 he made nearly 300 League appearances for the club before being transferred to Everton, choosing Goodison in preference to Derby County who were also after his signature. His arrival in October 1970 cost the club £150,000, but a series of injuries restricted him to only 83 first-team appearances in four seasons. He was sold to Derby in September 1973 for £110,000, helping them win the League title in 1975. He finished his playing career with Walsall.

1950	Charlton Athletic	A	First Division	0–2
1953	Doncaster Rovers	A	Second Division	0–3
1956	Chelsea	H	FA Cup 5th Round	1–0
1959	West Bromwich Albion	H	First Division	3–3
1961	Chelsea	H	First Division	1–1
1964	Birmingham City	H	First Division	3–0
1967	Wolverhampton Wanderers	A	FA Cup 4th Round	1–1
1978	West Ham United	H	First Division	2–1
1984	Shrewsbury Town	H	FA Cup 5th Round	3–0
1989	Barnsley	A	FA Cup 5th Round	1–0
1995	Norwich City	H	FA Cup 5th Round	5–0

Everton's revival under Joe Royle continued with an emphatic 5–0 win over Norwich in the fifth round of the FA Cup on their way to winning the trophy. Anders Limpar and

Joe Parkinson gave Everton a 2–0 lead in the first half, and with Norwich committed to attack in the second half to try and rescue the tie, additional goals from Paul Rideout, Duncan Ferguson and Graham Stuart rounded off the scoring.

FEBRUARY 19TH

| 1910 | Sunderland | H | FA Cup 3rd Round | 2–0 |

Harry Makepeace and Alex Young scored the goals that took Everton past Sunderland and into the FA Cup quarter-finals to face Coventry City at Highfield Road.

1916	Stockport County	A	Lancashire Section Principal Tournament	1–3
1921	Newcastle United	H	FA Cup 3rd Round	3–0
1927	Blackburn Rovers	H	First Division	1–0
1938	Wolverhampton Wanderers	H	First Division	0–1
1944	Tranmere Rovers	A	Football League North (Second Championship)	1–0
1949	Preston North End	A	First Division	1–3
1966	Burnley	A	First Division	1–1
1972	Newcastle United	A	First Division	0–0
1977	Stoke City	A	First Division	1–0
1980	Bristol City	A	First Division	1–2
1983	Tottenham Hotspur	H	FA Cup 5th Round	2–0

Everton brought to an end a Spurs run of 18 FA Cup ties without defeat, during which they had won the trophy on two consecutive seasons. Andy King and Graeme Sharp scored the goals that took Everton through to the quarter-finals to face Manchester United at Old Trafford.

| 1994 | Arsenal | H | FA Premier League | 1–1 |

FEBRUARY 20TH

1895	Blackburn Rovers	A	FA Cup 2nd Round Replay	3–2
1909	Sheffield United	H	First Division	5–1
1915	Queens Park Rangers	A	FA Cup 3rd Round	2–1
1932	Sheffield United	H	First Division	5–1
1935	Chelsea	A	First Division	0–3
1937	Tottenham Hotspur	H	FA Cup 5th Round	1–1
1943	Southport	A	Football League North (Second Championship)	8–3
1954	Sheffield Wednesday	A	FA Cup 5th Round	1–3
1960	Arsenal	A	First Division	1–2
1965	Sheffield Wednesday	A	First Division	1–0

1967 Mike Milligan born in Manchester. He began his career with Oldham Athletic and joined Everton for £1 million in 1990 but after only a season at Goodison was sold back to Oldham for £600,000. He later moved to Norwich City.

1971	Liverpool	H	First Division	0–0
1982	West Bromwich Albion	A	First Division	0–0
1991	Liverpool	H	FA Cup 5th Round Replay	4–4

Everton and Liverpool put the uninspiring 0–0 draw of the first clash behind them with an unforgettable 4–4 draw that ebbed and flowed throughout. A crowd of 37,766 created a unique atmosphere that was more than matched by the play, with Liverpool taking the lead through Peter Beardsley but Everton equalising two minutes after the break. Twenty minutes from time an already exciting match moved up a gear, with Beardsley restoring Liverpool's lead only for Sharp to capitalise on a clash between Bruce Grobbelaar and Steve Nichol for a simple tap in. Ian Rush put Liverpool ahead for a third time; Tony Cottee equalised. John Barnes curled in a free-kick to seemingly put Liverpool into the sixth round, but Tony Cottee popped up again to bring Everton level for a fourth time with three minutes left on the clock. Despite the draw Everton were the happiest side at the final whistle, having broken Liverpool's spirit with their refusal to lie down and die, and soon after the game Kenny Dalglish stunned football with his resignation from the manager's job at Anfield.

| 1993 | Aston Villa | A | FA Premier League | 1–2 |

FEBRUARY 21ST

| 1903 | Manchester United | H | FA Cup 2nd Round | 3–1 |
| 1914 | Derby County | A | First Division | 0–1 |

1924 Gordon Dugdale born in Liverpool. Gordon seemed assured of a lengthy and successful career at Goodison until a heart complaint forced him to give up playing after only three seasons. He had made 63 first-team appearances for Everton and was on the verge of selection for the England side going to the 1950 World Cup when the problem, which had affected him during the Second World War whilst on service, suddenly recurred, forcing him to retire.

1925	Sheffield United	A	FA Cup 3rd Round	0–1
1931	Nottingham Forest	H	Second Division	2–0
1942	Oldham Athletic	A	Football League North (Second Championship)	0–1
1948	Wolverhampton Wanderers	A	First Division	4–2

1949 Former Everton player Jack Taylor was killed in a motor accident. He had played for the club between 1896 and 1912, his career with the club being brought to an end after he had been hit in the throat by a shot.

1953	Swansea Town	H	Second Division	0–0
1956	Arsenal	A	First Division	2–3
1959	Birmingham City	A	First Division	1–2
1967	Wolverhampton Wanderers	H	FA Cup 4th Round Replay	3–1
1970	Coventry City	H	First Division	0–0
1976	Manchester City	A	First Division	0–3
1981	Coventry City	H	First Division	3–0
1988	Liverpool	H	FA Cup 5th Round	0–1

Liverpool arrived at Goodison Park top of the table and seemingly on their way to a second double of League and FA Cup within two years. Ray Houghton scored the only goal of the game in front of a crowd of 48,270 to put Liverpool into the quarter-finals. Although they went on to win the League, Wimbledon tripped them up in the FA Cup final.

| 1990 | Oldham Athletic | H | FA Cup 5th Round Replay | 1–1 |
| 1996 | Manchester United | A | FA Premier League | 0–2 |

FEBRUARY 22ND

| 1890 | Accrington | A | Football League | 3–5 |
| 1896 | Sunderland | A | First Division | 0–3 |

1898	Sheffield United	A	First Division	0–0
1902	Blackburn Rovers	H	First Division	0–2
1908	Bolton Wanderers	A	FA Cup 3rd Round	3–3
1913	Bristol Rovers	A	FA Cup 3rd Round	4–0
1919	Bolton Wanderers	H	Lancashire Section Principal Tournament	4–1
1930	Middlesbrough	A	First Division	2–1
1933	Blackpool	A	First Division	1–2
1936	Chelsea	A	First Division	2–2
1937	Tottenham Hotspur	A	FA Cup 5th Round Replay	3–4

One of the greatest cup-ties Everton took part in, although they were the ones feeling aggrieved at the end of the game. Everton quickly settled into their stride, with the 17-year-old Tommy Lawton giving them the lead after just two minutes. Dixie Dean extended the lead on 20 minutes whilst Everton were still dominating, although Morrison pulled one back seven minutes later and the score remained at 2–1 until half-time. Early in the second half Joe Mercer took a throw in, the ball was worked upfield to Dixie Dean and he headed towards the goal before being brought down in the penalty area. As the referee pointed to the spot he noticed a linesman waving furiously and went over to consult, only to decide there had been a foul throw by Joe Mercer! Everton did get a third just after the hour and that appeared to wrap up the game, but Spurs scored two minutes later to set up a frantic final 25 minutes. The equaliser came five minutes from time, and the crowd had hardly settled down again when Spurs scored the winner. After the game the Everton team looked stunned, with Joe Mercer claiming it to be the finest match he'd ever taken part in, but that the game had changed on the throw-in decision.

1939	Wolverhampton Wanderers	A	First Division	0–7

Everton were destined to win the League title at the end of the season but finished up on the wrong end of a 7–0 hammering from Wolves at Molineux. It was the only game goalkeeper Ted Sagar missed all season; perhaps he had an idea things were going to go wrong!

1941	Manchester United	H	League War Cup	2–1
1947	Bolton Wanderers	A	First Division	2–0
1958	Newcastle United	H	First Division	1–2
1964	Sheffield United	A	First Division	0–0
1975	Liverpool	A	First Division	0–0
1984	Aston Villa	A	Milk Cup Semi-Final 2nd Leg	0–1
1986	Liverpool	A	First Division	2–0

Everton had gone to the top of the table at the beginning of the month and consolidated their position with an excellent 2–0 win at Anfield. Kevin Ratcliffe scored the first when a speculative header from 25 yards eluded goalkeeper Bruce Grobbelaar after 73 minutes, but Everton were well worth their lead. Gary Lineker added a second 12 minutes from time, lobbing the keeper with what had been his only worthwhile chance of the game. Unfortunately, it was Liverpool who used the result as a launch pad, going on to win 11 and draw the other of their final 12 matches and lift the title at Everton's expense.

1987	Wimbledon	A	FA Cup 5th Round	1–3
1995	Leeds United	A	FA Premier League	0–1
1997	Coventry City	A	FA Premier League	0–0

FEBRUARY 23RD

1889	West Bromwich Albion	H	Football League	0–1
1895	Preston North End	H	First Division	4–2
1901	Sheffield United	A	FA Cup 2nd Round	0–2
1907	Bolton Wanderers	H	FA Cup 3rd Round	0–0
1918	Blackburn Rovers	H	Lancashire Section Principal Tournament	2–1

1919 Johnny Carey born in Dublin. As a player he made his name with Manchester United, captaining them to the FA Cup in 1948 and subsequently the League title before going on to management with Blackburn Rovers. He was appointed manager at Goodison Park in October 1958 with the team languishing near the bottom of the table and with a brief to stave off relegation. That he succeeded in doing, but thereafter Everton needed to be challenging for honours, which he could not, and at the end of 1960–61 he was dismissed, going on to manage Orient and Nottingham Forest.

1921	Manchester City	A	First Division	0–2
1924	Chelsea	A	First Division	1–1
1929	Blackburn Rovers	H	First Division	5–2
1935	Aston Villa	H	First Division	2–2
1946	Newcastle United	A	Football League North	3–1
1955	Manchester City	H	First Division	1–0
1957	Arsenal	A	First Division	0–2
1963	Wolverhampton Wanderers	H	First Division	0–0
1971	Manchester United	H	First Division	1–0
1974	Coventry City	H	First Division	1–0
1980	Crystal Palace	A	First Division	1–1
1985	Leicester City	A	First Division	2–1
1991	Sheffield United	H	First Division	1–2
1992	Leeds United	H	First Division	1–1
1998	Liverpool	A	FA Premier League	1–1

FEBRUARY 24TH

1894 Smart Arridge collected his first Welsh cap as an Everton player, having already earned two caps whilst playing for Bootle, in the 4–1 win over Ireland. He had joined Everton in 1893 but despite his international calling had to wait until 1895–96 before becoming a permanent fixture in the League side, although he subsequently lost his place from the side that went on to reach the FA Cup final and at the end of the season went to join New Brighton Tower. He won three caps for Wales whilst with Everton and eight in total during his career.

1906	Bradford City	H	FA Cup 3rd Round	1–0
1912	Oldham Athletic	A	FA Cup 3rd Round	2–0
1917	Preston North End	A	Lancashire Section Principal Tournament	2–2

1920 Cyril Lello born in Ludlow. He began his playing career with Lincoln City during the Second World War as an inside-forward, coming to Everton via Shrewsbury. At Goodison he was converted to half-back and made over 250 appearances for the first team, helping them win promotion back into the First Division in 1953–54. In November 1956 he was transferred to Rochdale, where he finished his career.

| 1934 | Blackburn Rovers | A | First Division | 1–1 |

1940	New Brighton	H	War Regional League, Western Division	3–0
1945	Southport	A	Football League North (Second Championship)	5–3
1954	Brentford	H	Second Division	6–1

Everton scored six for the second consecutive League match, with Brentford the luckless victims this time around. Dave Hickson (two), John Willie Parker (two), Wally Fielding and Eddie Wainwright scored the goals as 23,145 fans roared their approval.

1962	Nottingham Forest	A	First Division	1–2
1973	Tottenham Hotspur	A	First Division	0–3
1976	Tottenham Hotspur	H	First Division	1–0
1979	Ipswich Town	H	First Division	0–1
1988	Arsenal	A	Littlewoods Cup Semi-Final 2nd Leg	1–3

Everton were eliminated from the second cup competition in a week, with their defeat by Liverpool in the FA Cup being followed by a 3–1 reverse at Highbury in the semi-final second leg of the Littlewoods Cup. In truth the tie had been lost at home where Everton lost 1–0, but a 4–1 aggregate defeat was a bitter pill to swallow.

| 1996 | Nottingham Forest | H | FA Premier League | 3–0 |

FEBRUARY 25TH

1893	Accrington	A	First Division	3–0
1899	Bolton Wanderers	A	First Division	4–2
1905	Blackburn Rovers	H	First Division	1–0
1911	Derby County	A	FA Cup 3rd Round	0–5
1922	Tottenham Hotspur	A	First Division	0–2
1925	Cardiff City	H	First Division	1–2
1928	Liverpool	A	First Division	3–3

In what was his 100th appearance for the club, Dixie Dean ended with double cause for celebration. In front of a crowd of 56,447 at Anfield Liverpool took a fifth minute lead but Dean equalised after 17 minutes and fired Everton ahead five minutes before half-time. He completed his hat-trick on the hour and with Liverpool forced to reshuffle their side owing to injury to full-back Lucas, the two points seemed to be there for the taking by Everton. Liverpool pulled a goal back on 79 minutes to set up a frantic finale to the game with Hodgson being credited with the equalising goal. Despite dropping a point to their great rivals Everton remained on top of the First Division on goal average and with Dean having netted 43 goals thus far. It would be another five games before he increased the tally.

1933	Derby County	H	First Division	4–2
1939	Leeds United	A	First Division	2–1
1950	Arsenal	H	First Division	0–1
1956	Bolton Wanderers	H	First Division	1–0
1961	Preston North End	A	First Division	0–1
1967	West Ham United	H	First Division	4–0
1975	Luton Town	H	First Division	3–1
1978	Manchester City	A	First Division	0–1
1984	Watford	A	First Division	4–4

A second half goal feast between the two sides destined to meet in the end of season FA Cup final saw seven goals fired home, with Everton recovering from a 1–0 deficit at half-time to claim a point. Everton's goals were scored by Graeme Sharp (two), Andy Gray and Adrian Heath.

| 1989 | Derby County | A | First Division | 2–3 |
| 1995 | Manchester United | H | FA Premier League | 1–0 |

Something of a trial run for the FA Cup final at the end of the season, even down to Everton winning by the only goal of the game, this time scored by Duncan Ferguson in front of Goodison's biggest League crowd of the season, 40,011.

FEBRUARY 26TH

| 1895 | Sheffield United | A | First Division | 2–4 |
| 1898 | Burnley | A | FA Cup 3rd Round | 3–1 |

Everton made the semi-finals of the FA Cup for the third time with Jack Taylor (two) and John Bell scoring the goals that saw off Burnley at Turf Moor.

1908	Bolton Wanderers	H	FA Cup 3rd Round Replay	3–1
1910	Sheffield United	A	First Division	0–3
1916	Liverpool	H	Lancashire Section Principal Tournament	0–1
1921	Chelsea	A	First Division	1–0

1924 William Higgins born in Tranmere. He began his career as an amateur with Tranmere Rovers and signed for Everton during the Second World War, finishing his career at Goodison in 1949.

1927	Huddersfield Town	A	First Division	0–0
1938	Leeds United	A	First Division	4–4
1944	Tranmere Rovers	H	Football League North (Second Championship)	5–1
1949	Burnley	H	First Division	2–1

1957 Alan Biley born in Leighton Buzzard. He began his career on the books of Luton but failed to make the grade, subsequently joining Cambridge United. He came to prominence following United's cup exploits and was transferred to Derby County in January 1980, subsequently switching to Everton in July 1981. He made just 19 appearances for the club during his first season, subsequently going on loan to Stoke.

1966	Chelsea	H	First Division	2–1
1968	Southampton	A	First Division	2–3
1972	Tottenham Hotspur	H	FA Cup 5th Round	0–2
1977	Cardiff City	A	FA Cup 5th Round	2–1

Bob Latchford and Duncan McKenzie both scored to ease Everton into the sixth round of the FA Cup at the expense of Cardiff City.

| 1983 | Swansea City | H | First Division | 2–2 |

FEBRUARY 27TH

1897	Blackburn Rovers	H	FA Cup 3rd Round	2–0
1904	Nottingham Forest	A	First Division	4–0
1907	Bolton Wanderers	A	FA Cup 3rd Round Replay	3–0
1909	Aston Villa	A	First Division	1–3
1915	Manchester United	A	First Division	2–1
1926	Burnley	H	First Division	1–1
1932	Sheffield Wednesday	A	First Division	3–1
1937	Birmingham City	A	First Division	0–2
1943	Southport	H	Football League North (Second Championship)	10–2

A week previously Everton had scored eight goals at Haig Avenue in the same competition. This time around Tommy Lawton scored four, George Mutch two and Cook, Fowler, Stevenson and an own goal completed the rout.

1954	Plymouth Argyle	H	Second Division	8–4

John Willie Parker scored four times as Everton took their tally to 20 goals in just three games with an 8–4 blitz of Plymouth. Dave Hickson scored twice and Cyril Lello and Jack Lindsay got the others in front of 44,496 spectators.

1957	Preston North End	H	First Division	1–4
1960	Preston North End	H	First Division	4–0
1965	Blackpool	H	First Division	0–0
1971	West Bromwich Albion	H	First Division	3–3
1982	West Ham United	H	First Division	0–0
1988	Southampton	H	First Division	1–0
1991	Liverpool	H	FA Cup 5th Round 2nd Replay	1–0

After the drama of a week previously the action would be hard pressed to match it, but with Dalglish gone from Anfield the Liverpool side was in something of turmoil, and Dave Watson scored the only goal of the game to heap further misery on Everton's greatest rivals.

1993	Oldham Athletic	H	FA Premier League	2–2

FEBRUARY 28TH

1903	Bury	H	First Division	3–0
1912	Bolton Wanderers	H	First Division	1–0
1914	Manchester City	H	First Division	1–0
1920	Oldham Athletic	A	First Division	1–4
1923	Middlesbrough	H	First Division	5–3
1925	Nottingham Forest	H	First Division	3–1
1931	Southport	H	FA Cup 6th Round	9–1

Everton beat Southport 9–1 in the FA Cup quarter-final with Dixie Dean getting four of the goals. His daughter was born on the same day and named Nina in recognition of the score!

1942	Oldham Athletic	H	Football League North (Second Championship)	4–0
1948	Middlesbrough	H	First Division	2–1
1951	Fulham	H	First Division	1–0
1953	Aston Villa	A	FA Cup 6th Round	1–0

Dave Hickson scored the only goal of the game at Villa Park as Everton moved into the FA Cup semi-final to meet Bolton Wanderers at Maine Road.

1959	Tottenham Hotspur	H	First Division	2–1
1964	Aston Villa	H	First Division	4–2
1970	Nottingham Forest	A	First Division	1–1
1976	Wolverhampton Wanderers	H	First Division	3–0
1981	Crystal Palace	A	First Division	3–2
1987	Manchester United	A	First Division	0–0
1989	Queens Park Rangers	H	Simod Cup Semi-Final	1–0

A single goal from Pat Nevin enabled Everton to beat Queens Park Rangers 1–0 in the semi-final of the Simod Cup at Goodison Park. Although there was a place at Wembley at stake for the winners, just 7,072 saw the match.

1998	Newcastle United	H	FA Premier League	0–0

FEBRUARY 29TH

1896	Sheffield Wednesday	A	FA Cup 3rd Round	0–4
1908	Nottingham Forest	A	First Division	2–5
1936	Manchester City	H	First Division	2–2
1992	West Ham United	A	First Division	2–0

Maurice Johnston and Gary Ablett both scored to ensure an Everton win at Upton Park and retain ninth place in the First Division. Whilst it was Ablett's only goal of the season, Johnston netted seven in 21 League appearances that term following his arrival from Glasgow Rangers.

MARCH 1ST

| 1902 | Stoke City | A | First Division | 2–1 |
| 1913 | Newcastle United | A | First Division | 0–2 |

1914 Tommy Watson born in Wolsingham. Known throughout his career as Gordon, he joined Everton in January 1933 and made his debut during the 1936–37 season. He played enough games in 1938–39 to earn a medal when the team won the League, but the outbreak of the Second World War completely wrecked his career, and by the time he retired in 1949 he had made just 66 appearances for the first team. He was then appointed first-team trainer and in 1968 joined the club's promotions department.

1918 George Saunders born in Birkenhead. Recommended to Everton by none other than Dixie Dean, George signed professional forms in February 1939 but had to wait until the resumption of League football after the Second World War before making his debut. He went on to make 140 appearances for the club, the war having cut right across his career, and he retired at the end of the 1951–52 season.

1919	Bolton Wanderers	A	Lancashire Section Principal Tournament	6–3
1922	Middlesbrough	H	First Division	4–1
1924	Newcastle United	H	First Division	2–2
1930	Blackburn Rovers	H	First Division	2–2

1937 John Bramwell born in Ashton. He joined Everton from the then non-League Wigan Athletic in April 1958 and made 52 appearances as a full-back before being transferred to Luton in October 1960 where he made a further 188 appearances.

1941	Southport	H	League War Cup	5–0
1952	Queens Park Rangers	H	Second Division	3–0
1958	Burnley	A	First Division	2–0
1969	Manchester United	A	FA Cup 6th Round	1–0
1972	Tottenham Hotspur	H	First Division	1–1
1975	Arsenal	A	First Division	2–0
1977	Arsenal	H	First Division	2–1
1980	Liverpool	H	First Division	1–2

Liverpool dominated the first half of the Merseyside derby, taking a two goal lead through David Johnson and a Phil Neal penalty. Everton fought back in the second half, pulling one goal back from Peter Eastoe but were unable to force the equaliser. The 53,108 crowd included former Everton great Dixie Dean who sadly died soon after the final whistle.

| 1986 | Aston Villa | H | First Division | 2–0 |
| 1997 | Arsenal · | H | FA Premier League | 0–2 |

MARCH 2ND

1889 Everton hosted the international match between England and Ireland, with England winning at Anfield 6–1. There were already rumblings that Everton were not happy at Anfield, for the rent at the ground was costing the club £250 a year and landlord John Houlding held sole right to sell refreshments at the ground, but the FA's decision to award them the international was instrumental in ensuring Everton would remain at Anfield at least until 1892.

1895	Sheffield Wednesday	A	FA Cup 3rd Round	0–2
1897	Bury	A	First Division	1–3
1901	Nottingham Forest	H	First Division	4–1
1907	Bolton Wanderers	H	First Division	1–0
1912	Bradford City	A	First Division	0–1
1918	Port Vale	A	Lancashire Section Principal Tournament	1–0
1927	Sheffield Wednesday	H	First Division	2–1
1935	Bolton Wanderers	H	FA Cup 6th Round	1–2
1946	Newcastle United	H	Football League North	4–1
1968	Coventry City	H	First Division	3–1
1974	Leicester City	A	First Division	1–2
1983	Manchester City	A	First Division	0–0
1985	Manchester United	A	First Division	1–1
1991	Manchester United	A	First Division	2–0
1996	Middlesbrough	A	FA Premier League	2–0

Everton moved up to sixth place in the Premier League with a 2–0 win at the Riverside Stadium thanks to goals from Tony Grant and an Andy Hinchcliffe penalty. With a possible European place still in sight the win was a vital one.

MARCH 3RD

| 1894 | Stoke City | A | First Division | 1–3 |

1902 Walter Abbott collected his only cap for England in the 0–0 draw against Wales at Wrexham. He had joined Everton in 1899 from Small Heath as an inside-forward but was switched to wing half during his time with the club, making nearly 300 appearances for the first team. He left Everton for Burnley in 1908 and later returned to Small Heath, by now known as Birmingham where his career was ended by injury. Although he played extremely well in his only international for his country, he was overlooked for further honours.

1905	Southampton	H	FA Cup 3rd Round	4–0
1906	Bolton Wanderers	A	First Division	2–3
1917	Burnley	H	Lancashire Section Principal Tournament	5–0
1923	Oldham Athletic	A	First Division	0–1
1928	West Ham United	A	First Division	0–0
1933	Luton Town	H	FA Cup 6th Round	6–0
1934	Tottenham Hotspur	A	First Division	0–3
1937	Leeds United	H	First Division	7–1

Dixie Dean and Alex Stevenson both scored twice as Everton swamped Leeds United at Goodison Park. The other goals were netted by Albert Geldard, Torry Gillick and Tommy Lawton.

| 1945 | Chester | H | Football League North (Second Championship) | 4–1 |

1951	Bolton Wanderers	A	First Division	0–2
1956	Manchester City	A	FA Cup 6th Round	1–2
1962	Wolverhampton Wanderers	H	First Division	4–0
1966	Coventry City	H	FA Cup 5th Round	3–0
1973	Liverpool	H	First Division	0–2
1979	Queens Park Rangers	H	First Division	2–1
1984	Liverpool	H	First Division	1–1
1987	Charlton Athletic	H	Full Members Cup	2–2

Everton were eliminated from the Full Member's Cup, drawing 2–2 with Charlton Athletic at Goodison and then losing 6–4 on penalties. Even though Everton were just one step away from the semi-final stage of the competition, just 7,914 souls ventured out for the evening to watch the game.

1990	Wimbledon	A	First Division	1–3
1993	Blackburn Rovers	H	FA Premier League	2–1

MARCH 4TH

1893	Preston North End	Bramall Lane	FA Cup Semi-Final	2–2

Everton's very first appearance in the FA Cup semi-final saw them at Sheffield's Bramall Lane facing Preston North End, one of the most consistent sides of the era. Indeed, they had won the League in both of its first two seasons and then finished second for the next three years (behind Everton themselves in 1891) and would prove to be a tough hurdle for Everton to overcome if they were to make the final for the first time. Goals from Edgar Chadwick and Gordon earned Everton a second bite of the cherry at Ewood Park.

1899	Sheffield Wednesday	A	First Division	2–1
1907	Sheffield United	A	First Division	1–4
1911	Sunderland	H	First Division	2–2
1916	Manchester United	A	Lancashire Section Southern Division Supplementary Tournament	2–0
1922	Bradford City	H	First Division	2–0
1939	Wolverhampton Wanderers	A	FA Cup 6th Round	0–2
1944	Blackpool	A	Football League North (Second Championship)	1–7
1950	Derby County	A	FA Cup 6th Round	2–1

Goals by Ted Buckle and Eddie Wainwright set up a Merseyside clash with Liverpool in the semi-final at Maine Road, although both clubs would rather have met in the final!

1961	Fulham	H	First Division	1–0
1967	Leicester City	A	First Division	2–2
1972	Liverpool	A	First Division	0–4
1978	Queens Park Rangers	H	First Division	3–3
1986	Tottenham Hotspur	A	FA Cup 5th Round	2–1

Having wrecked Spurs' chances of winning the League the previous year Everton completed the 'double', knocking them out of the FA Cup at White Hart Lane. The tie had been earlier postponed because of bad weather, but on a cold Wednesday night

Adrian Heath and Gary Lineker warmed the Everton supporters in the 23,338 crowd as Everton survived a frantic Spurs push for the equaliser.

| 1995 | Leicester City | A | FA Premier League | 2–2 |

MARCH 5TH

1892	Stoke City	H	Football League	1–0
1898	Bury	H	First Division	4–2
1910	Coventry City	A	FA Cup 4th Round	2–0
1921	Wolverhampton Wanderers	H	FA Cup 4th Round	0–1
1927	Newcastle United	A	First Division	3–7

A crowd of 40,202 were at St James' Park for the clash between the League leaders Newcastle and strugglers Everton. The game went according to form with Newcastle inflicting a 7–3 defeat on Everton despite two goals from Dominy and one from Forshaw. Everton recovered from the setback to finish the season third from bottom in the First Division and thus avoided relegation, whilst Newcastle went on to win the title.

1930	Aston Villa	H	First Division	3–4
1932	Aston Villa	H	First Division	4–2
1938	Grimsby Town	H	First Division	3–2
1949	Blackpool	H	First Division	5–0

Eddie Wainwright scored four of Everton's goals as Blackpool were demolished at Goodison Park in front of a crowd of 25,548. Jimmy McIntosh scored Everton's other goal.

1953	Notts County	A	Second Division	2–2
1955	Sheffield Wednesday	A	First Division	2–2
1960	West Ham United	A	First Division	2–2
1977	Bristol City	A	First Division	2–1
1983	Sunderland	A	First Division	1–2
1988	Newcastle United	H	First Division	1–0
1994	Oldham Athletic	H	FA Premier League	2–1
1997	Southampton	A	FA Premier League	2–2

MARCH 6TH

1897	Blackburn Rovers	A	First Division	2–4
1915	Bradford City	A	FA Cup 4th Round	2–0
1920	Manchester United	A	First Division	2–1
1926	Leeds United	A	First Division	1–1
1935	Leeds United	H	First Division	4–4
1937	Middlesbrough	H	First Division	2–3
1943	Blackpool	A	Football League North (Second Championship)	1–4
1948	Charlton Athletic	A	First Division	3–2
1954	Swansea Town	A	Second Division	2–0
1957	Manchester United	H	First Division	1–2
1965	Blackburn Rovers	A	First Division	2–0
1971	Colchester United	H	FA Cup 6th Round	5–0

Colchester United had beaten Leeds United in the fifth round of the FA Cup and then drawn Everton away. The tie certainly captured the imagination of the folk of

Colchester, for they filled three Trident jets, two special trains and 21 coaches for the trip to Goodison Park! A crowd of 53,028 were present to see United's cup runneth over, beaten 5–0 by goals from Howard Kendall (two), Joe Royle, Jimmy Husband and Alan Ball. Compensation for United came in the form of their share of the receipts of £26,000.

1976	Leicester City	A	First Division	0–1
1979	Middlesbrough	A	First Division	2–1
1982	Ipswich Town	A	First Division	0–3
1985	Fortuna Sittard	H	European Cup-Winners' Cup 3rd Round 1st Leg	3–0

Dutch club Feyenoord had won the domestic double in 1983–84, the third time they had accomplished such a feat and which handed beaten cup finalists Fortuna Sittard entry into the European Cup-Winners' Cup. They had already beaten KB Copenhagen and Wisla Krakow in the competition and arrived at Goodison for the first leg of the third round in upbeat and confident mood of halting Everton's own progress. A crowd of 25,782 were to witness one of Andy Gray's finest performances in the blue shirt of Everton, scoring a hat-trick that gave them a 3–0 win and almost certain qualification for the semi-finals.

MARCH 7TH

1891 Charlie Parry was selected for the Wales side to face England at Sunderland, the first Everton player to represent the country. England won the match 4–1. Parry had been spotted by Everton playing junior football in Wales and made his debut in the opening game of the 1889–90 season, scoring from his position of wing half. He went on to win six caps for his country whilst at Everton and a further seven with Newtown, having been successfully converted to full-back during his later career with Everton.

1896	Preston North End	H	First Division	3–2
1903	Millwall	A	FA Cup 3rd Round	0–1
1908	Southampton	H	FA Cup 4th Round	0–0
1910	Woolwich Arsenal	H	First Division	1–0
1914	Bradford City	A	First Division	1–0
1925	Bury	A	First Division	0–1
1931	Reading	H	Second Division	3–2
1936	Sunderland	A	First Division	3–3
1942	Wolverhampton W	A	Football League North (Second Championship)	1–11

Everton showed only four changes from the side that had beaten Oldham 4–0 a week previously, with Burnett replacing Ted Sagar in goal perhaps the key. Everton were simply swamped on the day, managing a consolation effort by Anderson. But for the fact that the regional war Leagues are considered unofficial, this would have been Everton's worst-ever defeat.

1953	Leicester City	H	Second Division	2–2
1956	Manchester City	A	First Division	0–3
1959	Manchester United	A	First Division	1–2
1964	Tottenham Hotspur	A	First Division	4–2
1970	Burnley	A	First Division	2–1
1981	Manchester City	H	FA Cup 6th Round	2–2
1993	Coventry City	A	FA Premier League	1–0
1998	Southampton	A	FA Premier League	1–2

MARCH 8TH

1890	West Bromwich Albion	H	Football League	5–1
1902	Grimsby Town	H	First Division	0–1
1913	Oldham Athletic	H	FA Cup 4th Round	0–1
1919	Preston North End	H	Lancashire Section Principal Tournament	3–2
1930	Newcastle United	A	First Division	0–1

1930 Tommy Johnson made his debut for the club in the 1–0 defeat at Newcastle. Born near Barrow he began his League career with Manchester City, appearing in the 1926 FA Cup final and was transferred to Everton in March 1930 having scored 158 League goals. He made 159 appearances for Everton, scoring 64 goals and won a winners' medal in the FA Cup in 1933, against Manchester City, before finishing his career with Liverpool.

1933	Leicester City	H	First Division	6–3
1939	Leicester City	H	First Division	4–0
1941	Southport	A	League War Cup	5–0
1947	Grimsby Town	A	First Division	2–2
1950	Bolton Wanderers	A	First Division	2–1
1952	Notts County	A	Second Division	0–0
1958	Preston North End	H	First Division	4–2
1972	Manchester United	A	First Division	0–0
1975	Queens Park Rangers	H	First Division	2–1
1980	Ipswich Town	H	FA Cup 6th Round	2–1

1980 Goals from Brian Kidd and Bob Latchford took Everton past Ipswich in the FA Cup sixth round and into the semi-final to face West Ham United. It was the 18th time Everton had reached the semi-final stage of the country's premier cup competition, a record.

1986	Luton Town	A	FA Cup 6th Round	2–2
1987	Watford	A	First Division	1–2
1995	Nottingham Forest	A	FA Premier League	1–2
1997	Leeds United	A	FA Premier League	0–1

MARCH 9TH

1901	Blackburn Rovers	A	First Division	1–2
1907	Crystal Palace	A	FA Cup 4th Round	1–1
1912	Swindon Town	A	FA Cup 4th Round	1–2
1918	Port Vale	H	Lancashire Section Principal Tournament	7–0
1921	Manchester United	H	First Division	2–0
1929	Leeds United	A	First Division	1–3
1935	West Bromwich Albion	A	First Division	1–0
1940	Manchester City	A	War Regional League, Western Division	2–2
1946	Sheffield Wednesday	H	Football League North	2–2
1957	Birmingham City	A	First Division	3–1
1963	Nottingham Forest	H	First Division	2–0
1968	Tranmere Rovers	H	FA Cup 5th Round	2–0
1971	Panathinaikos	H	European Cup 3rd Round 1st Leg	1–1

1971 A crowd of 46,047 squeezed into Goodison Park for the eagerly awaited European Cup match with Greek champions Panathinaikos, confident that little stood between their team and a place in the semi-finals and perhaps an all British final thereafter, for Celtic were also making steady progress in the competition. Panathinaikos had other ideas of course, and the Greeks were out to prove something of a surprise package in the tournament being expertly managed by the great Ferenc Puskas. Despite almost constant pressure from Everton, Panathinaikos refused to crumble, and all Everton had to show for their efforts was a goal from David Johnson. Unfortunately they had also been hit on the break by Antoniadis, a goal that was to prove extremely costly to Everton.

| 1974 | Birmingham City | H | First Division | 4–1 |
| 1985 | Ipswich Town | H | FA Cup 6th Round | 2–2 |

Former Everton manager Harry Catterick died shortly after the FA Cup sixth round match with Ipswich Town which ended in a 2–2 draw. He had been appointed manager in 1961, replacing Johnny Carey, having previously played for the club shortly after the Second World War. Born in Cheadle Heath on 26th November 1919 he had signed with Everton during the war and went on to make 59 League appearances for the team before being transferred to Crewe Alexandra where he finished his playing career. Upon returning to Everton he restored the club to its former fortunes, guiding them to two League titles and the FA Cup and signing a host of big name players, including Howard Kendall, Alan Ball and Gordon West. The beginning of the end of his managerial reign came in January 1972 when he suffered a heart attack, being moved into an executive role in April, which paved the way for the return of Billy Bingham as manager.

| 1988 | Tottenham Hotspur | A | First Division | 1–2 |
| 1996 | Coventry City | H | FA Premier League | 2–2 |

MARCH 10TH

1897	Nottingham Forest	A	First Division	0–3
1900	Sunderland	H	First Division	1–0
1906	Sheffield Wednesday	H	FA Cup 4th Round	4–3
1917	Manchester United	A	Lancashire Section Principal Tournament	2–0
1923	Oldham Athletic	H	First Division	0–0
1928	Portsmouth	H	First Division	0–0
1934	Leicester City	H	First Division	1–1
1945	Chester	A	Football League North (Second Championship)	4–6

1950 Alan Whittle born in Liverpool. An exceptionally talented forward he was expected to set the game alight when first introduced to the Everton side in 1968, but sadly he never quite matched the expectations. He made 86 appearances for the first team before being transferred to Crystal Palace in 1972 for £100,000, later playing for Orient and Bournemouth before retiring.

1951	Charlton Athletic	H	First Division	0–0
1956	Sunderland	H	First Division	1–2
1969	Manchester United	H	First Division	0–0
1973	Leeds United	A	First Division	1–2
1979	Nottingham Forest	H	First Division	1–1
1984	Notts County	A	FA Cup 6th Round	2–1

A crowd of 19,534 were at Meadow Lane for the sixth-round clash between Notts County and Everton, with the visitors looking to make the semi-final stage for the 19th time in their history. John Chiedozie scored for County and Kevin Richardson for

Everton in the first half to leave the tie nicely poised for the second period, and Andy Gray hit the winner to set up a clash with Southampton at Highbury.

1990	Oldham Athletic	H	FA Cup 5th Round 2nd Replay	1–2
1992	Wimbledon	A	First Division	0–0
1993	Chelsea	A	FA Premier League	1–2

MARCH 11TH

| 1899 | Sunderland | H | First Division | 0–0 |
| 1905 | Sheffield Wednesday | H | First Division | 5–2 |

Everton maintained their position at the top of the First Division with a fine 5–2 win over Sheffield Wednesday thanks to goals from Alex Young (two), Harry Makepeace, Jack Sharp and Jack Taylor. Earlier in the season the two sides had fought out a 5–5 draw at Hillsborough.

1908	Southampton	A	FA Cup 4th Round Replay	2–3
1911	Woolwich Arsenal	A	First Division	0–1
1916	Stockport County	H	Lancashire Section Southern Division Supplementary Tournament	2–0
1922	Bradford City	A	First Division	1–3
1933	Portsmouth	A	First Division	2–2
1939	Middlesbrough	A	First Division	4–4
1944	Blackpool	H	Football League North (Second Championship)	1–3
1950	Chelsea	H	First Division	1–1
1961	Manchester City	A	First Division	1–2
1967	Liverpool	H	FA Cup 5th Round	1–0

Such was the interest generated by the FA Cup fifth round paring between Everton and Liverpool it was decided to screen the match on closed circuit television. Whilst 64,318 watched the action live at Goodison, a further 40,169 were at Anfield, an aggregate crowd of 104,487! A goal from Alan Ball was enough to win the game for Everton.

1970	Tottenham Hotspur	A	First Division	1–0
1972	Manchester City	H	First Division	1–2
1978	Bristol City	A	First Division	1–0
1981	Manchester City	A	FA Cup 6th Round Replay	1–3
1989	Sheffield Wednesday	H	First Division	1–0
1991	West Ham United	A	FA Cup 6th Round	1–2

MARCH 12TH

1892	Stoke City	A	Football League	1–0
1898	Nottingham Forest	A	First Division	2–2
1904	Sunderland	A	First Division	0–2
1910	Bolton Wanderers	A	First Division	1–0
1913	Sheffield United	H	First Division	0–1
1921	Tottenham Hotspur	A	First Division	0–2
1927	Leeds United	H	First Division	2–1
1938	Preston North End	A	First Division	1–2
1949	Derby County	A	First Division	2–3
1960	Chelsea	H	First Division	6–1

Tommy Ring scored the first goals of his Everton career, netting twice in the League clash with Chelsea. The other goals were grabbed by Bobby Collins, Jimmy Harris, Micky Lill and Roy Vernon.

1966	Arsenal	A	First Division	1–0
1977	Aston Villa		Wembley League Cup Final	0–0

Everton were through to the League Cup final for the first time in their history and facing Aston Villa at Wembley. Manager Gordon Lee, only in charge since January led the side out for their first appearance at the grand old stadium since 1968 in the FA Cup final. The game itself was something of a tame affair, the two sides cancelling each other out and ending 0–0, with Hillsborough scheduled for the replay.

1980	Manchester United	A	First Division	0–0
1983	Manchester United	A	FA Cup 6th Round	0–1
1986	Luton Town	H	FA Cup 6th Round Replay	1–0

Luton were beaten in the FA Cup for the second consecutive season, this time at the sixth-round stage, thanks to a goal from Gary Lineker in the replay at Goodison Park. It was his fourth goal in the cup that season.

1988	Chelsea	A	First Division	0–0
1995	Newcastle United	H	FA Cup 6th Round	1–0

MARCH 13TH

1897	Blackburn Rovers	H	First Division	0–3
1907	Crystal Palace	H	FA Cup 4th Round Replay	4–0
1909	Sunderland	A	First Division	0–2
1915	Blackburn Rovers	A	First Division	1–2
1920	Manchester United	H	First Division	0–0
1926	Arsenal	H	First Division	2–3
1937	West Bromwich Albion	A	First Division	1–2
1943	Blackpool	H	Football League North (Second Championship)	4–3
1948	Arsenal	H	First Division	0–2
1954	Rotherham United	H	Second Division	3–0
1965	Aston Villa	H	First Division	3–1
1971	Stoke City	H	First Division	2–0
1976	Queens Park Rangers	H	First Division	0–2
1979	Liverpool	A	First Division	1–1
1982	Middlesbrough	H	First Division	2–0
1984	Nottingham Forest	A	First Division	0–1
1985	Ipswich Town	A	FA Cup 6th Round Replay	1–0

FA Cup holders Everton had been held to a 2–2 draw at Goodison by Ipswich in the first meeting between the two sides, but showed little sign of wanting to relinquish the trophy with a controlled performance at Portman Road. A Graeme Sharp penalty after 76 minutes was enough to take them through, although the evening was overshadowed by the events at Kenilworth Road in the cup meeting between Luton and Millwall. Everton would meet Luton in the semi-final at Villa Park.

1991	Barnsley	A	Zenith Data Systems Cup Northern Semi-Final	1–0

A first half goal from Tony Cottee in front of a crowd of just 10,287 was enough to see off Barnsley and set up a Northern Final between Everton and Leeds United over two legs.

1993	Nottingham Forest	H	FA Premier League	3–0
1994	Liverpool	A	FA Premier League	1–2

MARCH 14TH

1891	Burnley	A	Football League	2–3

Despite two goals from Fred Geary Everton lost their final League match of the season at Burnley 3–2. Everton had actually played their previous League match on January 10th, when they had been presented with the championship trophy, and had then had to wait a little over two months before wrapping up the campaign. Geary had ended the season as top League scorer for Everton with 20 to his credit.

1903	Sunderland	H	First Division	0–3
1908	Blackburn Rovers	A	First Division	0–2
1910	Aston Villa	H	First Division	0–0
1914	Blackburn Rovers	H	First Division	0–0
1928	Manchester United	A	First Division	0–1
1931	West Bromwich Albion	Old Trafford	FA Cup Semi-Final	0–1

The FA Cup semi-final draw brought together the two Second Division survivors, Everton and Albion, whilst Sunderland and Birmingham City of the First Division met in the other tie. Everton and Albion were evenly matched, occupying the top two positions of their division, but on the day Albion had all of the luck and won through to the final at Wembley to meet local rivals Birmingham City, eventually winning the cup. They were denied a 'double' however, for Everton were to win the Second Division title by seven points.

1936	Blackburn Rovers	H	First Division	4–0
1942	Blackpool	H	Football League North (Second Championship)	2–2
1953	West Ham United	A	Second Division	1–3
1959	Blackpool	H	First Division	3–1
1962	Sheffield United	A	First Division	1–1
1964	Nottingham Forest	H	First Division	2–1
1970	Tottenham Hotspur	H	First Division	3–2
1981	Leeds United	H	First Division	1–2
1987	Southampton	H	First Division	3–0
1990	Manchester United	A	First Division	0–0
1992	Luton Town	H	First Division	1–1
1998	Blackburn Rovers	H	FA Premier League	1–0

MARCH 15TH

1890	Derby County	H	Football League	3–0

On the same day Johnny Holt was selected for England for the international against Wales at Wrexham, the first Everton player to represent the country, with England winning the match 3–1. Holt had joined Everton in 1888 from Bootle and was a regular at centre-half for the next ten years before moving on to Reading. Known as the 'Little Everton Devil' among the supporters of the time, he won nine England caps whilst with the club and a further one with Reading.

1902	Sunderland	H	First Division	2–0
1913	Chelsea	A	First Division	3–1
1919	Preston North End	A	Lancashire Section Principal Tournament	3–2

1920   Dicky Downs won his only cap for England when they were beaten 2–1 by Wales at Highbury, barely days after signing for the club from Barnsley for £3,000. He was to remain at Everton for the next three years, moving on to Brighton in 1923 but was forced to retire the following year owing to injury.

1922	Tottenham Hotspur	H	First Division	0–0
1924	West Ham United	A	First Division	1–2
1930	West Ham United	H	First Division	1–2
1941	Manchester City	H	League War Cup	1–1
1952	Luton Town	H	Second Division	1–3
1958	West Bromwich Albion	A	First Division	0–4
1966	Nottingham Forest	H	First Division	3–0
1975	Leeds United	A	First Division	0–0
1978	Norwich City	A	First Division	0–0
1980	Coventry City	H	First Division	1–1
1983	Southampton	H	First Division	2–0
1995	Manchester City	H	FA Premier League	1–1
1997	Derby County	H	FA Premier League	1–0

MARCH 16TH

1893	Preston North End	Ewood Park	FA Cup Semi-Final Replay	0–0

That Everton and Preston North End were two evenly matched sides was borne out at Ewood Park where a goalless draw in their FA Cup semi-final replay meant a third match to try and decide who Wolverhampton Wanderers' opponents in the final would be.

1895	Burnley	A	First Division	4–2
1901	Stoke City	H	First Division	3–0
1907	Stoke City	H	First Division	3–0
1912	Manchester City	A	First Division	0–4
1918	Bolton Wanderers	A	Lancashire Section Principal Tournament	3–2

1925 Dixie Dean was signed from Tranmere Rovers for a fee of £3,000. This remains probably the most important purchase Everton have ever made.

1929	Burnley	H	First Division	2–0
1931	Tottenham Hotspur	A	Second Division	0–1
1935	Arsenal	H	First Division	0–2
1940	Chester	H	War Regional League, Western Division	5–0
1946	Sheffield Wednesday	A	Football League North	0–0
1957	West Bromwich Albion	H	First Division	0–1
1963	West Ham United	A	FA Cup 5th Round	0–1

1967 Terry Phelan born in Manchester. After being rejected as a youngster by Leeds United he resurrected his career with Swansea before earning a transfer to Wimbledon in 1987, costing the club £100,000. A member of the side which won the FA Cup in 1988 he was then sold to Manchester City for £2.5 million in 1992, returning to London with Chelsea in 1995 for £900,000. Joe Royle signed him for Everton for £850,000 in 1997. A full international for Eire, he has over 30 caps to his credit.

1968	West Bromwich Albion	A	First Division	6–2
1974	Burnley	A	First Division	1–3
1977	Aston Villa	Hillsborough	League Cup Final Replay	1–1

Everton and Aston Villa tried again in the League Cup final replay at Hillsborough, where 55,000 were packed into the ground. Once again it was stalemate, with a Roger Kenyon netting an own goal and Bob Latchford scoring for Everton, extra time failing to separate the two sides. The League Cup final would therefore go to a third match for the very first time.

1985	Aston Villa	A	First Division	1–1
1986	Chelsea	H	First Division	1–1
1991	Southampton	A	First Division	4–3

MARCH 17TH

1900	Wolverhampton Wanderers	A	First Division	1–2
1902	Manchester City	A	First Division	0–2
1906	Blackburn Rovers	A	First Division	2–1
1915	Oldham Athletic	H	First Division	3–4

On the same day Stanley Bentham was born in Leigh. He began his career with Bolton Wanderers but turned professional with Wigan Athletic in December 1933. An immediate hit he quickly attracted interest from other clubs and signed with Everton in February 1934. He finished his playing career at Goodison in 1949, by which time he had a League championship medal in his possession, and then served on the backroom staff until 1962 when he joined Luton Town.

1917	Liverpool	H	Lancashire Section Principal Tournament	2–2
1923	Sheffield United	H	First Division	5–1
1926	Sunderland	H	First Division	2–1
1928	Leicester City	A	First Division	0–1

George Martin made his debut in the 1–0 defeat at Filbert Street. He had begun his professional career with Bo'Ness in Scotland, transferring to Hull City in 1922, although the deal earned Hull a £50 fine for improper conduct. He joined Everton in March 1928 and went on to make 86 appearances for the club, scoring 32 goals and helping them win the League title twice, although on both occasions he made insufficient appearances to qualify for a medal. He left Everton for Luton in 1933 where he finished his playing career, later becoming manager. He then switched to Newcastle United in 1947 and later spent two years in charge at Aston Villa.

| 1932 | Huddersfield Town | H | First Division | 4–1 |
| 1943 | Ernie Hunt born in Swindon. He joined Swindon in March 1960 and made over 200 | | | |

appearances for the club before joining Wolves in 1965. He signed for Everton in September 1967 but made only 14 League appearances before being sold to Coventry. It was his spell at Highfield Road that effectively made his name, especially a carefully worked free-kick goal that was televised. He later played for Doncaster Rovers and Bristol City before finishing his career.

1945	Preston North End	H	Football League North (Second Championship)	3–0
1951	Manchester United	A	First Division	0–3
1956	Huddersfield Town	A	First Division	0–1
1962	Chelsea	H	First Division	4–0
1971	Newcastle United	A	First Division	1–2
1973	Sheffield United	H	First Division	2–1
1981	Southampton	A	First Division	0–3

1984	Ipswich Town	H	First Division	1–0
1990	Crystal Palace	H	First Division	4–0
1992	Notts County	A	First Division	0–0
1996	Leeds United	A	FA Premier League	2–2

MARCH 18TH

1893	Wolverhampton Wanderers	A	First Division	4–2
1899	Bury	A	First Division	1–3
1905	Sunderland	A	First Division	3–2
1908	Birmingham City	H	First Division	4–1
1911	Bradford City	H	First Division	0–0

Tom Fleetwood made his debut for Everton in the 0–0 draw with Bradford City at Goodison Park. He joined the club from Rochdale as a forward but was adaptable enough to turn out at half-back, centre-half or at centre-forward, and spent 12 years with the club before signing for Oldham Athletic in August 1923. The closest he came to international recognition was two appearances for England in the Victory Internationals against Scotland in 1919, but there were no caps awarded for either of these.

1916	Manchester City	H	Lancashire Section Southern Division Supplementary Tournament	1–1
1922	Preston North End	A	First Division	0–1
1925	Notts County	H	First Division	1–0
1933	West Ham United	Molineux	FA Cup Semi-Final	2–1

Everton's second semi-final inside three years saw them make amends for their previous elimination, scoring through Ted Critchley and Jimmy Dunn to deny West Ham at Molineux and reach their fifth final.

1939	Birmingham City	H	First Division	4–2
1944	Chester	H	Football League North (Second Championship)	5–2
1950	Stoke City	A	First Division	0–1
1961	Nottingham Forest	H	First Division	1–0
1972	Sheffield United	A	First Division	1–1
1975	Middlesbrough	A	First Division	0–2
1980	Stoke City	H	First Division	2–0
1995	Queens Park Rangers	A	FA Premier League	3–2

MARCH 19TH

| 1892 | Accrington | H | Football League | 3–0 |
| 1898 | Derby County | Molineux | FA Cup Semi-Final | 1–3 |

Everton had been beaten finalists the previous season and hoped to go one better this time around, but at Molineux they came up against a Derby side in general and Steve Bloomer in particular out to stop them, especially as Everton had beaten Derby at the same stage the previous season. Everton managed one goal from Edgar Chadwick on the day but were overwhelmed by a rampant Derby side.

1910	Chelsea	H	First Division	2–2
1927	Arsenal	A	First Division	2–1
1938	Middlesbrough	H	First Division	2–2
1949	Aston Villa	H	First Division	1–3

1955	Manchester United	A	First Division	2–1
1960	West Bromwich Albion	A	First Division	2–6

Derek Kevan scored five of Albion's goals, only the second time an opposing player had scored as many as five goals against Everton and equalling a record set in 1928 by Johnson of Manchester City.

1963	Ipswich Town	A	First Division	3–0
1966	Liverpool	H	First Division	0–0
1977	Derby County	H	FA Cup 6th Round	2–0
1983	Liverpool	A	First Division	0–0
1986	Tottenham Hotspur	H	Screen Sport Super Cup Semi-Final 2nd Leg	3–1

An extra-time victory over Spurs in the semi-final second leg of the Super Cup took Everton into the final, where they would face Liverpool. Spurs had scored first through Mark Falco but an equaliser by Adrian Heath necessitated an extra half-hour, during which Derek Mountfield and Graeme Sharp scored the goals that booked a place in the final. Unfortunately, the fact the competition had been unappreciated by the fans tended to be mirrored by the organisers, for there had been no dates booked for the final, irrespective of whether it was to be a single game or played over two legs, and no trophy yet commissioned. In the event, the final was held over to the following season.

1989	Wimbledon	H	FA Cup 6th Round	1–0
1991	Leeds United	A	Zenith Data Systems Cup Northern Final 1st Leg	3–3

Peter Beagrie, Robert Warzycha and Mike Milligan scored the goals that seemingly put Everton in the driving seat in the Zenith Data Systems Cup, although Lee Chapman scored an equaliser in the second half to leave the tie still evenly balanced.

MARCH 20TH

1893	Preston North End	Trent Bridge	FA Cup Semi-Final 2nd Replay	2–1

At the third attempt, Everton overcame Preston North End and booked their place in the FA Cup final for the very first time. The third meeting between the clubs, at Trent Bridge in Nottingham, was almost as close as the first two, Everton finally winning 2–1 thanks to goals from Gordon and Newell.

1897	Derby County	Victoria Ground	FA Cup Semi-Final	3–2

Everton finally squeezed past Derby to make the final of the FA Cup for the second time in their history. Goals from Edgar Chadwick, Alfred Milward and Hartley to set up a clash with League champions Aston Villa at the Crystal Palace.

1909	Chelsea	H	First Division	3–2
1915	Notts County	H	First Division	4–0
1920	Sheffield United	A	First Division	2–1
1926	Manchester United	A	First Division	0–0
1935	Liverpool	A	First Division	1–2
1937	Manchester City	H	First Division	1–1
1943	Southport	A	Football League North (Second Championship)	1–4
1948	Sheffield United	A	First Division	1–2
1954	Leicester City	A	Second Division	2–2

1965	Leeds United	A	First Division	1–4

1966   Ian Marshall born in Liverpool. After only a handful of appearances for Everton, he was sold to Oldham in 1988 for £100,000 and developed into an exceptional striker, later playing for Ipswich and Leicester City.

1971	Nottingham Forest	A	First Division	2–3
1976	Leeds United	H	First Division	1–3
1982	Manchester City	A	First Division	1–1
1984	Leicester City	H	First Division	1–1
1985	Fortuna Sittard	A	European Cup-Winners' Cup 3rd Round 2nd Leg	2–0

With a 3–0 lead from the first leg of their European Cup-Winners' Cup third round tie against Fortuna Sittard, Everton were expected to be in little danger of going through to the next round of the competition, but it was vital that they didn't concede an early goal or give the home supporters in the crowd of 20,000 anything to cheer. Everton put in possibly their most controlled performance of the campaign on the evening, scoring in each half through Graeme Sharp and Peter Reid, and wrapped up the tie 5–0 on aggregate.

1988	Liverpool	H	First Division	1–0
1993	Liverpool	A	FA Premier League	0–1

MARCH 21ST

1895	Burnley	H	First Division	3–2
1898	Preston North End	H	First Division	1–1
1903	Stoke City	A	First Division	0–2
1906	Woolwich Arsenal	H	First Division	0–1
1908	Bolton Wanderers	H	First Division	2–1
1913	Derby County	H	First Division	2–2
1914	Sunderland	A	First Division	2–5
1925	Arsenal	A	First Division	1–3

The Everton team sheet contained the name William Ralph Dean for the first time in the 3–1 defeat at Highbury against Arsenal. Known universally as Dixie (a nickname he hated), he went on to make 399 appearances for the League side.

1931	Millwall	H	Second Division	2–0
1942	Southport	H	Football League North (Second Championship)	3–1
1953	Bolton Wanderers	Maine Road	FA Cup Semi-Final	3–4

Not for the first time, nor the last, Everton were favourites when the FA Cup semi-final draw paired them with Bolton Wanderers at Maine Road. Unfortunately, Bolton paid no attention to the odds and by half-time had raced into a four-goal lead, with Nat Lofthouse leading the charge. Everton's cause was not helped by losing Dave Hickson for a 15-minute spell with a head injury, but Bolton looked capable of going on to register the biggest ever semi-final defeat. That they didn't said much about Everton's powers of recovery, for in an emotion-packed second half they dug deep into their reserves and clawed their way back into the game, scoring three times through Parker, Farrell and Hickson. With six minutes left Bolton were on the ropes and Everton had hopes of taking the game into extra time, but despite throwing everything at Bolton in a desperate attempt to complete the comeback, the equalising goal just wouldn't come, although Everton also missed a penalty just before half-time. Of course, come the final against Blackpool it would be Bolton's turn to be on the receiving end of a 4–3 scoreline, achieved with one of the finest comebacks ever seen at Wembley.

| 1959 | Blackburn Rovers | A | First Division | 1–2 |
| 1964 | Blackburn Rovers | A | First Division | 6–1 |

Fred Pickering scored a hat-trick, Dennis Stevens got two and Roy Vernon the other in an exemplary performance at Ewood Park.

1970	Liverpool	A	First Division	2–0
1972	Crystal Palace	H	First Division	0–0
1981	Liverpool	A	First Division	0–1
1984	Southampton	H	First Division	1–0
1987	Charlton Athletic	H	First Division	2–1
1990	Millwall	A	First Division	2–1
1991	Leeds United	H	Zenith Data Systems Cup Northern Final	3–1

Mel Sterland gave Leeds the lead in the first half at Goodison Park but Tony Cottee equalised to send the game into extra time. There goals from Cottee again and John Ebbrell earned Everton an appearance at Wembley for the final, although the crowd at Goodison was just 12,603.

| 1992 | Norwich City | A | First Division | 3–4 |
| 1994 | Norwich City | A | FA Premier League | 0–3 |

MARCH 22ND

| 1890 | West Bromwich Albion | A | Football League | 1–4 |

Everton lost 4–1 at West Bromwich Albion in the final League match of the season. However, Fred Geary's goal for Everton enabled them to become, along with Bolton Wanderers, the only side to have scored in every League match during the course of a season.

1902	Small Heath	A	First Division	1–0
1913	Woolwich Arsenal	H	First Division	3–0
1919	Rochdale	H	Lancashire Section Principal Tournament	3–1
1924	West Ham United	H	First Division	2–1
1941	Manchester City	A	League War Cup	0–2
1947	Manchester United	A	First Division	0–3
1952	Bury	A	Second Division	0–1
1958	Portsmouth	H	First Division	4–2
1961	Aston Villa	H	First Division	1–2
1969	Manchester City	Villa Park	FA Cup Semi-Final	0–1

Everton had lost the cup final the previous season and were anxious to make amends this time around, having seen off the challenge of Ipswich, Coventry, Bristol City and Manchester United in the earlier rounds. The semi-final draw paired them with United's rivals City at Villa Park (in 1966 they had similarly met both Manchester clubs!), but Joe Royle was unable to better his goalscoring exploits of previous rounds, with Everton going down to the only goal of the game from Neil Young.

1975	Ipswich Town	H	First Division	1–1
1977	Liverpool	H	First Division	0–0
1980	Middlesbrough	A	First Division	1–2
1986	Luton Town	A	First Division	1–2

| 1989 | Newcastle United | A | First Division | 0–2 |
| 1997 | Manchester United | H | FA Premier League | 0–2 |

MARCH 23RD

1912	Preston North End	H	First Division	1–0
1918	Bolton Wanderers	H	Lancashire Section Principal Tournament	2–3
1929	Cardiff City	A	First Division	2–0
1935	Portsmouth	A	First Division	1–5
1940	Crewe Alexandra	A	War Regional League, Western Division	1–2
1946	Huddersfield Town	A	Football League North	1–0
1955	Huddersfield Town	H	First Division	4–0
1957	Portsmouth	A	First Division	2–3
1963	Manchester City	H	First Division	2–1
1965	West Bromwich Albion	A	First Division	0–4
1968	Newcastle United	H	First Division	1–0
1974	Chelsea	H	First Division	1–1
1985	Arsenal	H	First Division	2–0

Everton beat Arsenal 2–0 at Goodison thanks to goals from Andy Gray and Graeme Sharp. They went on to win the next nine League matches and created a new record of ten consecutive League wins in a single season.

| 1991 | Nottingham Forest | H | First Division | 0–0 |
| 1996 | Wimbledon | H | FA Premier League | 2–4 |

MARCH 24TH

1894	Wolverhampton Wanderers	H	First Division	3–0
1900	Wolverhampton Wanderers	H	First Division	0–1
1906	Sunderland	H	First Division	3–1
1909	Nottingham Forest	H	First Division	3–3
1915	Bolton Wanderers	H	First Division	5–3
1917	Stockport County	A	Lancashire Section Principal Tournament	1–5
1928	Derby County	H	First Division	2–2

Dixie Dean had gone through something of lean spell, having not netted since the match against Liverpool on February 25th (although he missed one of these games through injury). In the following five games neither he nor Everton scored (proof of his worth to the club), but he hit two in the match against Derby at Goodison to get back on track to challenge George Camsell's record. The match finished 2–2.

| 1934 | Sheffield United | H | First Division | 4–0 |

1939 Alex 'Sandy' Brown born in Glasgow. Sandy began his career with Partick Thistle and was snapped up by Everton for £38,000 in September 1963. He went on to make over 200 appearances for the first team, winning a League championship medal in 1970. Unfortunately, he had to miss the 1966 FA Cup final owing to injury. He left Everton for Shrewsbury in 1971 and finished his League career with Southport.

| 1945 | Liverpool | A | Football League North (Second Championship) | 0–1 |
| 1951 | Blackpool | H | First Division | 0–2 |

1953 Jim Pearson born in Falkirk. As a striker he made his name with St Johnstone, scoring

39 goals in 96 appearances and prompting a £100,000 move to Everton in July 1974. Unfortunately, the goals dried up at Goodison and in August 1978 he was allowed to go to Newcastle for £70,000.

1956	Cardiff City	H	First Division	2–0
1962	Tottenham Hotspur	A	First Division	1–3
1971	Panathinaikos	A	European Cup 3rd Round 2nd Leg	0–0

Everton slipped out of the European Cup despite a goalless draw in Athens against Panathinaikos, for the Greek's 1–1 draw at Goodison Park enabled them to go through on the away goals rule. The Greek side, highly unfancied outside their own country, went on to reach the final (the same away goal rule taking them past Red Star Belgrade in the semi-final) where they lost 2–0 to Ajax of Amsterdam at Wembley. With English clubs banned from Europe in 1985, Everton were unable to enter the competition in either 1985–86 and 1987–88, making this the club's last appearance in the European Cup.

1973	Ipswich Town	A	First Division	1–0
1978	Newcastle United	A	First Division	2–0
1979	Derby County	A	First Division	0–0
1990	Norwich City	H	First Division	3–1
1993	Ipswich Town	H	FA Premier League	3–0

MARCH 25TH

1893	Wolverhampton Wanderers	Fallow-field	FA Cup Final	0–1

Everton played in the FA Cup final for the first time, meeting Wolverhampton Wanderers at the Athletic Grounds at Fallowfield in Manchester. This was the first time the final had been played outside London (with the exception of the 1886 replay at the Racecourse Ground in Derby), and although 45,000 (paying receipts of £2,300) were packed into the ground, it was a totally unsuitable venue for such a prestigious match. Many in the crowd could not see the action, prompting numerous occasions when spectators encroached on to the playing field, and it had even seemed at one stage unlikely that the game would begin. It did however, and a speculative shot from Wolves centre-forward Allen was lost against the sun by Everton's goalkeeper Williams and sailed into the net for the only goal of the game.

1905	Aston Villa	Victoria Ground	FA Cup Semi-Final	1–1

A repeat of the 1897 final as Everton took on Aston Villa at the Victoria Ground in Stoke. With Everton also sitting on top of the First Division the coincidences were even greater, for in 1897 it was Villa who had completed the double, now both Everton and Newcastle (second in the League and playing in the other semi-final) stood a chance of emulating that feat. A crowd of 35,000 were at the first clash between the two sides, with Jack Sharp scoring the Everton goal that ensured a second chance at Trent Bridge in Nottingham.

1907	West Bromwich Albion	Burnden Park	FA Semi-Final	2–1

Everton had taken six games to get to the semi-final with Albion, with Sheffield United and West Ham being disposed of first time around and Bolton and Crystal Palace requiring a replay. Jack Sharp and G Wilson scored the goals that overcame Albion and took Everton into the final to meet Sheffield Wednesday.

1916	Oldham Athletic	A	Lancashire Section Southern Division Supplementary Tournament	2–1
1921	Bolton Wanderers	A	First Division	2–4
1931	Wolverhampton Wanderers	A	Second Division	1–3
1932	West Bromwich Albion	H	First Division	2–1
1933	Aston Villa	A	First Division	1–2
1936	Arsenal	A	First Division	1–1
1944	Chester	A	Football League North (Second Championship)	9–2
1950	Liverpool	Maine Road	FA Cup Semi-Final	0–2

Although Everton dominated for much of the game, the lack of a proven goalscorer in the side proved their undoing, with countless chances being created but nobody on hand to turn them into goals. Liverpool on the other hand were able to take advantage of the few chances they carved out, scoring through Bob Paisley and Billy Liddell and having another chance cleared off the line. Paisley was to be dropped for the final, whilst Everton would have to wait 16 years before winning through to Wembley again.

1953	Fulham	H	Second Division	3–3
1960	Newcastle United	H	First Division	1–2
1961	West Bromwich Albion	A	First Division	0–3
1972	Wolverhampton Wanderers	H	First Division	2–2
1978	Leeds United	H	First Division	2–0
1984	Liverpool	Wembley	Milk Cup Final	0–0

Liverpool and Everton had been two of the country's top sides for over 90 years, with an abundance of trophies having resided at either Anfield or Goodison Park during that time. However, for all their domination, the two rivals had never met in a major cup final. That was until the Milk Cup final of 1984, with ticket demand far outweighing supply and the city of Liverpool supplanting itself in London for the day. The match was hardly a classic, not surprisingly given what was at stake, but the behaviour of the fans drew praise from the police and Everton matched their rivals in every department and showed that the balance of power in Liverpool was beginning to swing in their favour.

1989	Millwall	H	First Division	1–1

MARCH 26TH

1894	Bolton Wanderers	H	First Division	3–2
1898	Bolton Wanderers	A	First Division	0–1
1904	Small Heath	A	First Division	1–1
1910	Barnsley	Elland Road	FA Cup Semi-Final	0–0

Everton had scored 15 goals on their way to the semi-final but found them hard to come by against a Barnsley side making their first appearance in the FA Cup semi-final. Barnsley themselves were unable to find a way through a resilient Everton defence, necessitating a replay in five days time at Old Trafford.

1921	Oldham Athletic	H	First Division	5–2
1927	Sheffield United	H	First Division	2–0
1932	Chelsea	A	First Division	0–0

1937	Manchester United	A	First Division	1–2
1938	Chelsea	A	First Division	0–2
1948	Grimsby Town	A	First Division	0–3
1949	Sunderland	A	First Division	1–1
1951	Sheffield Wednesday	H	First Division	0–0
1955	Portsmouth	H	First Division	2–3
1963	Arsenal	A	First Division	3–4
1966	Manchester City	A	FA Cup 6th Round	0–0
1977	Tottenham Hotspur	H	First Division	4–0
1983	Arsenal	H	First Division	2–3
1988	Watford	A	First Division	2–1
1994	Tottenham Hotspur	H	FA Premier League	0–1

MARCH 27TH

1909	Blackburn Rovers	A	First Division	0–0
1911	Aston Villa	A	First Division	1–2
1912	Woolwich Arsenal	H	First Division	1–0
1915	Chelsea	Villa Park	FA Cup Semi-Final	0–2

Chelsea had only been in existence for ten years, Mr H.A. Mears forming the club after Fulham had turned down his offer of moving into Stamford Bridge. They could boast the likes of the great Vivian Woodward in their line-up, but he was not available for the semi-final at Villa Park, but if Everton thought this would nullify the threat for Chelsea they were mistaken, for Bob Thomson was in fine form and had been inspirational in getting Chelsea to the semi-final. He was man of the match again in the semi-final clash as Chelsea overcame Everton 2–0 and denied them a possible double. Incidentally, Woodward was available for the final against Sheffield United but refused to play, for he would have had to replace Bob Thomson in the side and felt Thomson deserved his chance; Chelsea lost 3–0 in the Khaki Final.

1920	Sheffield United	H	First Division	5–0
1926	Notts County	H	First Division	3–0
1937	Portsmouth	A	First Division	2–2
1943	Southport	H	Football League North (Second Championship)	2–1
1948	Stoke City	H	First Division	0–1
1954	West Ham United	H	Second Division	1–2
1959	Luton Town	A	First Division	1–0

1963 Gary Stevens born in Barrow. Signed by Everton as a schoolboy he graduated through the ranks and became an integral part of the side that lifted the FA Cup in 1984 and the League and European Cup-Winners' Cup the following year. He added a second League title in 1987 before joining Glasgow Rangers for £1 million in 1988, adding to his collection of honours north of the border. Indeed, in 1992 he became only the second Englishman to have won winners' medals in both the FA Cup and Scottish Cup and at the same time only the second player to have won both League and Cup medals on both sides of the border, Dave Mackay having been the first. He returned to England to play for Tranmere Rovers for £350,000 in September 1994. A full England international he won 46 caps for his country.

1964	West Bromwich Albion	H	First Division	1–1
1971	Liverpool	Old Trafford	FA Cup Semi-Final	1–2

Everton and Liverpool were paired in the FA Cup semi-final at Old Trafford, where a capacity crowd of 63,000 paid £75,000 receipts. Alan Ball gave Everton an early lead, Alan Whittle having put him through after excellent combination work by Joe Royle and Johnny Morrissey. Whittle missed a chance to settle the game soon afterwards, shooting wide when an unmarked Alan Ball was screaming for the ball at the far post, but Everton were still in command of the game. Liverpool's equaliser through Steve Heighway seemed to knock Everton out of their stride, and with Howard Kendall and Colin Harvey starting to fade Liverpool struck the winner 15 minutes from time to win the game, Brian Hall firing home the goal to set up a final clash with Arsenal.

1976	Ipswich Town	A	First Division	0–1
1978	Manchester United	A	First Division	2–1
1982	Liverpool	H	First Division	1–3
1989	Middlesbrough	A	First Division	3–3

1997 After reported clashes with chairman Peter Johnson over transfer deals, Everton manager Joe Royle left the club by mutual consent. He had been in charge since November 1994 and had taken the club to the FA Cup at the end of his first season. For the rest of the current season Dave Watson would be caretaker player-manager.

MARCH 28TH

1903	Derby County	A	First Division	1–0
1908	Birmingham City	A	First Division	1–2
1910	Bury	H	First Division	3–0
1914	Tottenham Hotspur	H	First Division	1–1
1921	Bolton Wanderers	H	First Division	2–3
1925	Aston Villa	H	First Division	2–0

Dixie Dean got on the score sheet for the first time in what was only his second match for the club in the 2–0 home win over Aston Villa. He went on to score another 348 League goals whilst with Everton.

1931	Stoke City	A	Second Division	0–2
1932	West Bromwich Albion	A	First Division	1–1
1936	Grimsby Town	H	First Division	4–0
1942	Oldham Athletic	A	Football League North (Second Championship)	2–1
1953	Rotherham United	A	Second Division	2–2
1959	Aston Villa	H	First Division	2–1
1964	Blackpool	H	First Division	3–1
1970	Chelsea	H	First Division	5–2
1980	Arsenal	H	First Division	0–1
1981	Manchester United	H	First Division	0–1
1984	Liverpool	Maine Road	Milk Cup Final Replay	0–1

The Milk Cup final replay was held at Maine Road between Everton and Liverpool. Following the goalless draw at Wembley another close game was expected, and sure enough there was only one goal in it, with Graeme Souness's volley enough to ensure Liverpool won the League/Milk Cup for the fourth consecutive season.

| 1987 | Arsenal | A | First Division | 1–0 |
| 1998 | Aston Villa | H | FA Premier League | 1–4 |

MARCH 29TH

1884   Everton won their very first cup, beating Earlestown 1–0 in the final of the Liverpool
Cup at Bootle. The trophy was presented to club president John Houlding, who
although relatively new to the post was already known as King John of Everton.

1902	Derby County	H	First Division	2–0
1905	Aston Villa	Trent Bridge	FA Cup Semi-Final Replay	1–2

The selected venue for the FA Cup semi-final replay was Trent Bridge in Nottingham,
then the home of Notts County, although they shared the round with the county cricket
side. Whether Villa found the turf cultivated for the summer game to their particular
liking is not known but they were well worth their 2–1 win on the day. Worse was to
follow for Everton, for they also missed out on the League, pipped at the last moment
by Newcastle United, who were to face Villa in the FA Cup final.

1907	Liverpool	H	First Division	0–0
1913	Bradford City	A	First Division	1–4
1918	Liverpool	H	Lancashire Section Subsidiary Tournament	3–2
1919	Rochdale	A	Lancashire Section Principal Tournament	3–1
1924	Cardiff City	A	First Division	0–0
1929	Sunderland	A	First Division	2–2
1930	Birmingham City	H	First Division	2–4
1937	Manchester United	H	First Division	2–3
1939	Manchester United	A	First Division	2–0
1941	Chesterfield	H	North Regional League	0–1
1947	Stoke City	H	First Division	2–2
1948	Grimsby Town	H	First Division	3–1
1950	West Bromwich Albion	H	First Division	1–2
1952	Swansea Town	H	Second Division	2–1
1958	Birmingham City	A	First Division	1–2
1966	Manchester City	H	FA Cup 6th Round Replay	0–0

The first meeting between the two sides had produced plenty of action but no goals, and
there was more of the same at Goodison Park, with even an extra thirty minutes failing
to separate the two sides. With another goalless match behind them, the second replay
would now be held at Molineux.

1969	Chelsea	H	First Division	1–2
1975	Carlisle United	A	First Division	0–3

The only occasion Everton have visited Brunton Park, the home of Carlisle United, in
the League saw the home side win 3–0, although at the end of the season they were
relegated.

1986	Newcastle United	H	First Division	1–0
1988	Wimbledon	H	First Division	2–2
1994	Aston Villa	A	FA Premier League	0–0

MARCH 30TH

1889	Blackburn Rovers	H	Football League	3–1
1901	Sheffield Wednesday	A	First Division	1–3
1907	Sunderland	H	First Division	4–1

Five days after winning through to the FA Cup final Everton kept the double in sight with a 4–1 win over Sunderland to keep the pressure on Manchester United at the top of the table. Unfortunately this was followed by something of a collapse, for only one more League match out of six was won and Everton faded to finish in third place, six points behind United and three behind Bristol City.

1918	Stockport County	H	Lancashire Section Subsidiary Tournament	4–0
1923	Bolton Wanderers	A	First Division	2–0
1929	Sheffield United	H	First Division	1–3
1934	Leeds United	A	First Division	2–2
1935	Stoke City	H	First Division	5–0
1940	Liverpool	H	War Regional League, Western Division	1–3
1946	Huddersfield Town	H	Football League North	5–2
1956	Sheffield United	H	First Division	1–4
1957	Newcastle United	H	First Division	2–1
1959	Luton Town	H	First Division	3–1
1962	Blackpool	H	First Division	2–2
1963	Sheffield United	A	First Division	1–2
1968	Leicester City	A	FA Cup 6th Round	3–1

Everton turned in one of their best performances in the cup that season with a 3–1 win at Filbert Street to make the semi-final for the 14th time in their history. Two goals from Jimmy Husband and one from Howard Kendall put paid to a spirited fight from Leicester.

1970	Stoke City	A	First Division	1–0
1971	West Ham United	H	First Division	0–1
1974	Tottenham Hotspur	A	First Division	2–0
1979	Norwich City	H	First Division	2–2
1985	Southampton	A	First Division	2–1
1991	Aston Villa	A	First Division	2–2
1996	Blackburn Rovers	A	FA Premier League	3–0

MARCH 31ST

1894   Goodison Park hosted the FA Cup final between Notts County and Bolton Wanderers, with a crowd of 37,000 present to see County win 4–1.

1900   Blackburn Rovers   H   First Division   0–0

Jack Crelley made his debut for the club in the goalless draw at home to Blackburn Rovers. Born in Liverpool he actually made his name down in the south with Millwall Athletic, returning to Merseyside in 1899 upon signing for Everton. He remained at Goodison until 1907 when he joined Exeter City, having helped the club win the FA Cup in 1906. His place at full-back in the final the following year was taken by Robert Balmer.

1902   Nottingham Forest   H   First Division   1–0

1906   Liverpool   Villa Park FA Cup Semi-Final   2–0

With both Liverpool and Everton making steady progress in the FA Cup there was a hope that the two might meet in the final for the first time. Sadly, they were paired in the semi-final which did at least mean a day out for both sets of supporters when Villa Park was chosen as the venue. Whilst Liverpool stayed overnight in Tamworth, Everton travelled down on the day and ran out to loud cheers from the 50,000 crowd. Everton's goalkeeper Billy Scott (the brother of Elisha Scott, who was later recommended to

Liverpool by Billy!) was the busiest of the two custodians in the opening exchanges, but gradually Everton began to exert control and had a number of chances in the first half to take the lead. The second half followed much the same pattern, but the deadlock was finally broken when Abbott shot home a low drive from the edge of the area. A second from Harold Hardman, later to become a director of Manchester United, sealed the game for Everton and took them into the final to meet Newcastle United.

1910	Barnsley	Old Trafford	FA Cup Semi-Final Replay	0–3

A disappointing display from Everton brought an effective end to their season with elimination from the FA Cup semi-final by Barnsley in a replay. Everton fans did get to see the final however, for after Newcastle and Barnsley had drawn at the Crystal Palace, the replay was held at Goodison Park.

1917	Southport	H	Lancashire Section Subsidiary Tournament	4–2
1923	Burnley	H	First Division	1–0
1928	Sunderland	A	First Division	2–0
1934	Wolverhampton Wanderers	A	First Division	0–2
1945	Liverpool	H	Football League North (Second Championship)	0–1
1951	Tottenham Hotspur	A	First Division	0–3
1956	Aston Villa	A	First Division	0–2
1961	Blackburn Rovers	A	First Division	3–1
1964	West Bromwich Albion	A	First Division	2–4
1965	Chelsea	H	First Division	1–1
1973	West Ham United	A	First Division	0–2
1975	Coventry City	H	First Division	1–0
1981	West Bromwich Albion	A	First Division	0–2
1986	Manchester United	A	First Division	0–0
1990	Arsenal	A	First Division	0–1

APRIL 1ST

1893	Blackburn Rovers	H	First Division	4–0
1899	Notts County	H	First Division	1–2
1903	Newcastle United	A	First Division	0–3
1904	Liverpool	H	First Division	5–2
1908	Chelsea	H	First Division	0–3
1916	Liverpool	H	Lancashire Section Southern Division Supplementary Tournament	1–0
1922	Chelsea	A	First Division	0–1
1933	Middlesbrough	H	First Division	0–0
1939	Stoke City	H	First Division	1–1
1944	Tranmere Rovers	A	Football League North (Second Championship)	5–0

1948   Dai Davies born in Ammanford. After just nine appearances for Swansea City Dai was signed by Everton in December 1970, initially as understudy to Gordon West. His inability to break into the first team prompted a loan spell back at Swansea, a move that would have been permanent had the Swans been able to afford the transfer fee, but he subsequently returned to Goodison and made 94 first-team appearances before being sold to Wrexham in 1977 for £8,000. He won a total of 52 caps for Wales, a record for a goalkeeper.

| 1950 | Manchester United | A | First Division | 1–1 |

1957 John Bailey born in Liverpool. He began his professional career with Blackburn Rovers in 1975 and went on to make over 100 League appearances for the Ewood Park club before a £300,000 move brought him to Goodison in July 1979. He was a regular at full-back until the arrival of Pat Van den Hauwe and had forced himself into the England set-up, winning a B international cap. He won an FA Cup winners' medal in 1984 but then lost his place and was transferred to Newcastle in 1985 for £80,000.

1961	Birmingham City	H	First Division	1–0
1963	Aston Villa	A	First Division	2–0
1967	Aston Villa	H	First Division	3–1
1969	West Ham United	H	First Division	1–0
1970	West Bromwich Albion	H	First Division	2–0

Everton's third win over Easter, this time 2–0 at home to West Bromwich Albion thanks to goals from Colin Harvey and Alan Whittle, clinched the League title from Leeds United, the reigning champions.

1972	Huddersfield town	A	First Division	0–0
1978	Derby County	H	First Division	2–1
1989	Queens Park Rangers	H	First Division	4–1
1991	Norwich City	H	First Division	1–0
1992	Southampton	H	First Division	0–1
1995	Blackburn Rovers	H	FA Premier League	1–2

APRIL 2ND

| 1892 | Glasgow Rangers | H | Friendly | 0–2 |

On the same day Edgar Chadwick scored for England after just 30 seconds in the clash with Scotland at Ibrox in only his second game for his country. Born in Blackburn Chadwick was already something of a star when he joined Everton from Blackburn Olympic in 1888, making his debut in the very first League match the club ever played. He remained at Everton until 1899, winning a League championship medal and two runners-up medals in the FA Cup, going on to play for Southampton (he collected another losers' medal in the FA Cup in 1900), where he helped the club win the Southern League before going on to coach overseas. He later returned to Blackburn to become a baker and died in February 1942 at the age of 73. He won a total of seven caps for England whilst with Everton.

1898	Nottingham Forest	H	First Division	2–0
1904	Wolverhampton Wanderers	H	First Division	2–0
1910	Nottingham Forest	H	First Division	0–4
1913	Oldham Athletic	H	First Division	2–3
1915	Burnley	H	First Division	0–2
1920	Derby County	H	First Division	2–0
1921	Oldham Athletic	A	First Division	1–0
1923	Bolton Wanderers	H	First Division	1–1
1924	Newcastle United	A	First Division	1–3
1926	Bury	H	First Division	1–1
1927	Derby County	A	First Division	0–0
1929	Derby County	A	First Division	0–3

| 1932 | Grimsby Town | H | First Division | 4–2 |
| 1934 | Leeds United | H | First Division | 2–0 |

Jack Jones made his debut for the club following his recent arrival from Ellesmere Port Town. He had begun his career as a centre-forward but was successfully converted to full-back, going on to make 108 appearances for the club before moving on to Sunderland in 1938.

1938	West Bromwich Albion	H	First Division	5–3
1945	Liverpool	A	Football League North (Second Championship)	3–1
1949	Charlton Athletic	A	First Division	1–3
1955	Blackpool	A	First Division	0–4
1956	Sheffield United	A	First Division	1–1
1960	Birmingham City	A	First Division	2–2
1974	Manchester City	A	First Division	1–1
1977	West Ham United	A	First Division	2–2
1980	Manchester City	A	First Division	1–1
1983	Nottingham Forest	A	First Division	0–2
1994	Sheffield Wednesday	A	FA Premier League	1–5

APRIL 3RD

1893	Bolton Wanderers	H	First Division	3–0
1896	Derby County	H	First Division	2–2
1897	Preston North End	A	First Division	1–4
1899	Derby County	H	First Division	1–2
1906	Stoke City	H	First Division	0–3
1909	Bradford City	H	First Division	0–1
1915	Sheffield Wednesday	H	First Division	0–1
1920	Middlesbrough	A	First Division	1–1
1926	Aston Villa	A	First Division	1–3
1931	Bristol City	A	Second Division	1–0
1937	Chelsea	H	First Division	0–0
1940	Stockport County	H	War Regional League, Western Division	7–0

Alex Stevenson scored four times as Stockport were brushed aside 7–0 at Goodison. The other goals were scored by Tommy Lawton, who scored twice and Tom Wyles.

1943	Wrexham	A	Football League North (Second Championship)	1–4
1946	Bradford Park Avenue	A	Football League North	2–1
1948	Burnley	A	First Division	1–0
1954	Leeds United	A	Second Division	1–3
1961	Blackburn Rovers	H	First Division	2–2
1965	Leicester City	A	First Division	1–2
1971	Manchester City	A	First Division	0–3
1973	Norwich City	H	First Division	2–2
1976	Liverpool	A	First Division	0–1
1979	Bolton Wanderers	A	First Division	1–3
1982	Nottingham Forest	A	First Division	1–0
1985	Tottenham Hotspur	A	First Division	2–1

Everton travelled to White Hart Lane in confident mood for the League match with Spurs in what had already been billed as the title decider. Everton were in the middle of an eighteen match unbeaten run, having already secured 26 out of a possible 30 points, a run that had taken them to the top of the table ahead of their London rivals. Spurs were beginning to falter; at the start of the year they had been favourites, but whilst they were capable of great results on their travels (they had recently won at Anfield for the first time in 70 odd years) they were unpredictable at home. It was an action packed evening at White Hart Lane, with Andy Gray opening the scoring for Everton and Trevor Steven seemingly making the game safe with a second. Spurs fought back, scoring through Mark Falco and laying siege to the Everton goal. Ultimately they were to be denied by Neville Southall who had one of the games of his life and produced a string of world class saves. With a 2–1 win to their credit, Everton were on their way to the title.

APRIL 4TH

1896　John Bell was selected for the Scotland side to face England in Glasgow, the first Everton player to represent the country. Scotland won the match 2–1. Bell had joined Everton from Dumbarton after helping them to the Scottish League title in its inaugural season and already an international player, having first been picked in 1890. He won three caps whilst with Everton, all against England, and a total of ten throughout his career, later playing for Spurs, Celtic (where he collected the last of his caps) and New Brighton Tower before returning to Goodison for a second spell. He finished his playing career with Preston, eventually becoming player-coach.

1903	Sheffield Wednesday	H	First Division	1–1
1904	Sheffield Wednesday	H	First Division	2–0
1908	Newcastle United	H	First Division	2–0
1914	West Bromwich Albion	H	First Division	2–0
1925	Huddersfield Town	A	First Division	0–2
1931	Bradford Park Avenue	H	Second Division	4–2
1936	Stoke City	A	First Division	1–2
1942	Preston North End	H	Football League North (Second Championship)	2–2
1947	Blackpool	H	First Division	1–1
1953	Plymouth Argyle	H	Second Division	2–0
1958	Leeds United	H	First Division	0–1
1959	West Ham United	A	First Division	2–3
1962	Bolton Wanderers	A	First Division	1–1
1964	Stoke City	A	First Division	2–3
1970	Sheffield United	A	First Division	1–0
1972	Coventry City	A	First Division	1–4
1975	Burnley	H	First Division	1–1
1981	Tottenham Hotspur	A	First Division	2–2
1983	Stoke City	H	First Division	3–1
1987	Chelsea	A	First Division	2–1

A 2–1 win at Stamford Bridge against Chelsea enabled Everton to take over at the top of the table once again, climbing above rivals Liverpool. Joe McLaughlin put past his own goalkeeper to give Everton the lead in the first half, and Alan Harper scored in the second half to secure the points. Everton were not to be headed again in the race for the title.

1988	West Ham United	A	First Division	0–0

1990	Nottingham Forest	H	First Division	4–0
1992	Crystal Palace	A	First Division	0–2
1994	Blackburn Rovers	H	FA Premier League	0–3
1998	Tottenham Hotspur	A	FA Premier League	1–1

APRIL 5TH

1902	Sheffield Wednesday	A	First Division	1–1
1905	Woolwich Arsenal	H	First Division	1–0
1912	Notts County	A	First Division	1–0
1913	Manchester City	H	First Division	0–0

1918 Jimmy McIntosh born in Dumfries. He joined Everton in March 1949 from Blackpool having previously played for Preston and Blackpool during the war. He made 58 appearances at centre-forward for the club before moving into non-League football.

1919	Stockport County	A	Lancashire Section Subsidiary Tournament	1–0
1920	Derby County	A	First Division	5–2
1924	Cardiff City	H	First Division	0–0
1930	Leicester City	A	First Division	4–5
1933	Newcastle United	H	First Division	0–0
1941	Southport	A	North Regional League	5–3
1947	Middlesbrough	A	First Division	0–4
1952	Coventry City	A	Second Division	1–2
1958	Tottenham Hotspur	H	First Division	3–4
1966	Manchester City		Molineux FA Cup 6th Round 2nd Replay	2–0

Fred Pickering and Derek Temple scored the goals that finally broke the deadlock between Everton and Manchester City after 230 minutes of goalless action. After this win at neutral Molineux Everton were to face Manchester United in the semi-final at Burnden Park.

1969	West Bromwich Albion	A	First Division	1–1
1977	Manchester United	H	First Division	1–2
1978	Liverpool	H	First Division	0–1
1980	Bolton Wanderers	H	First Division	3–1
1986	Sheffield Wednesday		Villa Park FA Cup Semi-Final	2–1

Everton were looking to reach the final for the third consecutive season, a feat previously achieved by Arsenal between 1978 and 1980. With Liverpool in the other semi-final there was a distinct possibility of an all-Merseyside final, and both Everton and Liverpool were still in the hunt for a double; the stakes therefore could not have been higher. Everton responded magnificently, especially as they were missing Gary Lineker, and goals from Alan Harper and Graeme Sharp finally saw off Wednesday in front of a crowd of 47,711. At the final whistle came through the news that Liverpool had beaten Southampton in their semi-final; the two Merseyside rivals would now meet at Wembley.

| 1997 | Aston Villa | A | FA Premier League | 1–3 |

APRIL 6TH

1896	Bolton Wanderers	H	First Division	1–1
1901	Sunderland	H	First Division	1–0
1907	Birmingham City	A	First Division	0–1

1910	Manchester United	A	First Division	2–3
1911	Blackburn Rovers	A	First Division	1–0

Frank Jefferis made his debut for the club in the 1–0 win at Blackburn Rovers. Born in Hampshire in 1887 he started his career with Southampton in 1905 and joined Everton in March 1911. He went on to become an important member of the side that won the League championship in 1914–15, although he missed much of the end of the season through injury. He moved to Preston in 1920 and three years later joined Southport as player-coach, retiring from playing in 1925, although he returned to play two further games in 1927 when they were short of players. In 1936 he joined Millwall as trainer and died whilst still in the position two years later.

1912	Sunderland	A	First Division	0–4
1915	Sunderland	A	First Division	3–0
1918	Stockport County	A	Lancashire Section Subsidiary Tournament	1–0
1921	Chelsea	H	First Division	5–1
1928	Blackburn Rovers	H	First Division	4–1

Another two goals for Dixie Dean took his tally to 47 for the season, with Hart and Martin scoring the others in the 4–1 win.

1929	Bury	A	First Division	2–1
1931	Bristol City	H	Second Division	1–3
1935	Manchester City	A	First Division	2–2
1940	Port Vale	A	War Regional League, Western Division	1–2
1942	Preston North End	A	Football League North (Second Championship)	2–1
1946	Chesterfield	H	Football League North	4–0
1953	Huddersfield Town	H	Second Division	2–1
1957	Sheffield Wednesday	A	First Division	2–2
1963	Blackburn Rovers	H	First Division	0–0
1968	Arsenal	H	First Division	2–0
1971	Ipswich Town	A	First Division	0–0
1974	Newcastle United	A	First Division	1–2
1982	Birmingham City	A	First Division	2–0
1985	Sunderland	H	First Division	4–1
1996	Bolton Wanderers	H	FA Premier League	3–0

APRIL 7TH

1894	Stoke City	H	First Division	6–2
1896	Derby County	A	First Division	1–2
1900	Derby County	A	First Division	1–2
1906	Wolverhampton Wanderers	H	First Division	2–2
1917	Liverpool	A	Lancashire Section Subsidiary Tournament	4–0
1923	Burnley	A	First Division	1–0
1928	Bury	H	First Division	1–1

Everton's goal in the 1–1 draw was netted by Dixie Dean, his 48th goal of the season. His goals had come from 32 appearances, having missed three games through injury.

1934	Stoke City	H	First Division	2–2
1939	Sunderland	A	First Division	2–1
1945	Wrexham	A	Football League North (Second Championship)	2–1

1947	Blackpool	A	First Division	3–0
1950	Blackpool	H	First Division	2–0
1951	Wolverhampton Wanderers	H	First Division	1–1
1953	Huddersfield Town	A	Second Division	2–8

A day after beating Huddersfield Town at Goodison Park 2–1, Everton travelled to Leeds Road to face the same opposition. Quite what Huddersfield had seen that they could turn to their advantage is not known, but they won 8–2 as Everton continued their tumble down the Second Division.

1956	Wolverhampton Wanderers	H	First Division	2–1
1958	Leeds United	A	First Division	0–1
1962	Blackburn Rovers	A	First Division	1–1
1973	Coventry City	H	First Division	2–0
1976	Stoke City	H	First Division	2–1
1979	West Bromwich Albion	A	First Division	0–1
1984	Luton Town	A	First Division	3–0
1990	Queens Park Rangers	H	First Division	1–0
1991	Crystal Palace	Wembley	Zenith Data Systems Cup Final	1–4

Everton met Crystal Palace in the final of the Zenith Data Systems Cup at Wembley, with Palace winning 4–1 after extra time. Everton goal was scored by Robert Warzycha in front of a crowd of 52,460.

APRIL 8TH

1893	Burnley	A	First Division	0–3
1895	Wolverhampton Wanderers	H	First Division	2–1
1898	Derby County	H	First Division	3–0
1899	Stoke City	A	First Division	1–2
1901	Newcastle United	H	First Division	0–1
1905	Stoke City	A	First Division	2–2
1907	Blackburn Rovers	A	First Division	1–2
1908	Manchester United	H	First Division	1–3
1911	Manchester City	A	First Division	1–2
1912	Notts County	H	First Division	1–1
1916	Manchester United	H	Lancashire Section Southern Division Supplementary Tournament	3–1
1922	Chelsea	H	First Division	2–3
1933	Bolton Wanderers	A	First Division	4–2
1939	Chelsea	A	First Division	2–0
1944	Tranmere Rovers	H	Football League North (Second Championship)	4–0

1949   Joe Royle born in Liverpool. One of the finest centre-forwards to have played for the club Joe signed professional forms with Everton in August 1966, although he actually made his debut in the previous season when aged only 16. He went on to make 272 appearances for the first team before joining Manchester City in December 1974. He later played for Bristol City and Norwich City before having to retire owing to injury and then turned to management. He spent 12 years in charge at Oldham, turning down overtures from other clubs (including Everton) during that time, but in 1994 accepted the offer of taking over at Goodison Park following the sacking of Mike Walker. He left in 1997 after a series of disagreements with the directors and accepted an offer to take over at Manchester City towards the end of the season, although he as unable to prevent them being relegated to the Second Division at the end of the campaign.

1950	Birmingham City	H	First Division	0–0
1955	Newcastle United	H	First Division	1–2
1961	Newcastle United	A	First Division	4–0
1963	Liverpool	A	First Division	0–0
1966	Newcastle United	A	First Division	0–0
1967	Notts Forest	A	FA Cup 6th Round	2–3
1969	Burnley	A	First Division	2–1
1970	Sunderland	A	First Division	0–0

With the season ending early owing to the forthcoming World Cup in Mexico, Everton completed their campaign with a goalless draw at Roker Park to take their points tally for the season to 66, a new record for the club under the old two points for a win system. Everton were already confirmed as champions, finishing nine points ahead of Leeds United in second place. It was United's misfortune to finish the season second in both League and FA Cup, for Chelsea were to beat them in a cup after a replay at Old Trafford.

1972	Southampton	A	First Division	1–0
1978	Coventry City	A	First Division	2–3
1989	Arsenal	A	First Division	0–2
1996	Queens Park Rangers	A	FA Premier League	1–3

APRIL 9TH

1898	Stoke City	A	First Division	0–2
1901	Notts County	A	First Division	2–3
1904	Stoke City	H	First Division	0–1
1906	Birmingham City	A	First Division	0–1
1909	Liverpool	H	First Division	5–0

Everton recorded their biggest win to date over their great rivals with a 5–0 demolition at Goodison Park. Sam Hardy chose this game of all games to look jaded, but Everton were in no mood to give him an easy ride after a long season, creating countless chances and keeping pressure on the Liverpool defence throughout. Tim Coleman gave Everton the lead after only eight minutes with a weak shot that Hardy should have saved and that seemed to set the tone for the rest of the afternoon. Liverpool wasted two chances to get back on level terms, and Everton then took advantage of a defensive lapse, Bertie Freeman firing home another weak shot that Hardy would have saved on any other day. There was to be no respite in the second half; Wattie White made it 3–0 with a long range drive, a later shot from White was only half cleared by Hardy and R.F. Turner pounced for a tap in, and Coleman added his second of the game near the end. The game saw Turner making his debut for Everton, not long after he had been fined by the Football Association following his arrival from Leicester Fosse. At the time he joined Everton, the maximum allowable signing-on fee was £10 (a figure that remained in force until 1960, and even then it was only payable if the player had not asked for a transfer), but Turner asked Everton for £100 and was promptly reported to the FA by the club. The FA let him off lightly with a fine, but he hit the news again a year later concerning his wedding. His former club Leicester lost 12–0 in a League match against Nottingham Forest, a result that was vital to Forest's battle against relegation. As the score equalled the then record for the First Division, a Football League commission was set up to investigate. They found that the Leicester players, resigned to relegation anyway, had enjoyed a two-day drinking binge to help Turner celebrate his wedding and the matter was allowed to drop!

1910	Sunderland	A	First Division	1–0
1913	Sunderland	A	First Division	1–3
1917	Stockport County	H	Lancashire Section Subsidiary Tournament	1–1
1921	Preston North End	H	First Division	0–1
1927	Manchester United	H	First Division	0–0
1932	Leicester City	A	First Division	1–0
1938	Stoke City	A	First Division	1–1
1949	Sheffield United	A	First Division	1–1
1955	Tottenham Hotspur	H	First Division	1–0
1960	Tottenham Hotspur	H	First Division	2–1
1966	Sheffield United	H	First Division	1–3
1968	Leicester City	H	First Division	2–1
1975	Luton Town	A	First Division	1–2
1977	Middlesbrough	A	First Division	2–2
1983	Brighton & Hove Albion	A	First Division	2–1
1984	Arsenal	H	First Division	0–0
1988	Portsmouth	H	First Division	2–1
1994	West Ham United	A	FA Premier League	1–0
1995	Tottenham Hotspur	Elland Road	FA Cup Semi-Final	4–1

Elland Road was not a popular choice for either Everton or Spurs as a venue for an FA Cup semi-final, even more so given a 1 p.m. kick-off. Whilst Spurs might have been forgiven for thinking their name was on the cup, having been re-admitted to the competition after being banned for financial irregularities at the beginning of the season, Everton had enjoyed a revival under Joe Royle. On the day it was Everton who played with greater urgency, taking a two goal lead through Matt Jackson and Graham Stuart. A disputed penalty put Spurs back in the game, but two late strikes from Daniel Amokachi settled it for Everton, 4–1 and a trip to Wembley for the final.

| 1997 | Leicester City | H | FA Premier League | 1–1 |

APRIL 10TH

| 1897 | Aston Villa | Crystal Palace | FA Cup Final | 2–3 |

A record crowd of 65,891 were at the Crystal Palace to see if Aston Villa could pull off only the second double of League and FA Cup, although there were a considerable number of Everton supporters in attendance who hoped they wouldn't. The match itself was one of the best seen in the final, with Everton's John Bell being named man of the match and the five goals all coming in a 25-minute spell in the first half. Villa scored first through Campbell, but John Bell levelled soon after and then inspired Everton to take the lead through Richard Boyle within ten minutes. Villa responded equally, scoring twice themselves before half-time and dominated much of the second half, finally holding on to win the cup to go with the League already secured. Lord Rosebery handed over the trophy, the last time it would be presented to a winning captain, for Villa contrived to lose it when it was stolen from a shop display in September!

1903	Liverpool	A	First Division	0–0
1907	Woolwich Arsenal	H	First Division	2–1
1909	Manchester United	A	First Division	2–2
1914	Burnley	A	First Division	0–2
1915	West Bromwich Albion	A	First Division	2–1
1920	Middlesbrough	H	First Division	0–2
1922	Preston North End	H	First Division	0–0
1925	Preston North End	A	First Division	1–1
1929	West Ham United	H	First Division	0–4
1936	Brentford	H	First Division	1–2
1937	Stoke City	A	First Division	1–2
1939	Sunderland	H	First Division	6–2
1943	Tranmere Rovers	H	Football League North (Second Championship)	4–1
1944	Liverpool	H	Football League North (Second Championship)	3–0
1948	Manchester United	H	First Division	2–0
1950	Blackpool	A	First Division	1–0
1954	Stoke City	H	Second Division	1–1
1965	Sunderland	H	First Division	1–1
1971	Wolverhampton Wanderers	H	First Division	1–2
1976	Arsenal	H	First Division	0–0
1979	Coventry City	H	First Division	3–3
1982	Manchester United	H	First Division	3–3
1985	Bayern Munich	A	European Cup-Winners' Cup Semi-Final 1st Leg	0–0

The 1972 Olympics are mostly remembered for the murder of Israeli athletes by Arab terrorists, but once the games were over Bayern Munich moved into what is one of the most modern stadiums in the world. Freed of the expense of building their own ground, they had invested their resources in building a succession of powerful teams, winning the League title five times between 1972 and 1984 and the cup twice in the same period. They had also won the European Cup three times and been beaten finalists on one occasion. They, like Everton, were on their way to winning their domestic League title, and so would prove the sternest of tests in the European Cup-Winners' Cup semi-final. The first leg was scheduled for Munich where, in front of 78,000, Everton were forced to defend for much of the time, the Germans intent on building a convincing lead to take to England for the second leg. But they found Neville Southall in superb form, even if they managed to get past Gary Stevens, Pat Van den Hauwe, Kevin Ratcliffe and Derek Mountfield, and for once in the season it was the defenders who claimed most of the plaudits in a fine 0–0 draw.

1989	Charlton Athletic	H	First Division	3–2
1991	Wimbledon	H	First Division	1–2
1993	Middlesbrough	A	FA Premier League	2–1

APRIL 11TH

1896	Stoke City	A	First Division	2–1
1898	Sunderland	H	First Division	2–0
1908	Sunderland	H	First Division	0–3
1910	Blackburn Rovers	A	First Division	1–2
1914	Sheffield Wednesday	A	First Division	2–2

On the same day Albert Geldard was born in Bradford. He joined the local Park Avenue club as a youngster and achieved a slice of history that may never be equalled; he made his League debut at the age of 15 years and 156 days, the youngest player to have played in a League match in peacetime. By the time he joined Everton in 1932 he was an old hand at 18! He helped Everton win the FA Cup in 1933, and won four caps whilst at Goodison. In 1938 he was sold to Bolton for £4,500 and remained at Burnden Park until 1946 when he finished his career.

1925	Blackburn Rovers	H	First Division	1–0

| 1930 | Tommy E. Jones born in Liverpool. He signed professional forms for Everton in |

January 1948 and made his debut in 1950, going on to become first choice centre-half for the next ten seasons. He made over 400 appearances for Everton until an injury sustained in a reserve match brought his career to a halt.

1931	Oldham Athletic	A	Second Division	3–3
1936	West Bromwich Albion	H	First Division	5–3
1942	Liverpool	A	Football League North (Second Championship)	2–0
1952	Hull City	H	Second Division	5–0
1953	Leeds United	A	Second Division	0–2
1955	Newcastle United	A	First Division	0–4
1959	Nottingham Forest	H	First Division	1–3
1964	Wolverhampton Wanderers	H	First Division	3–3
1966	Newcastle United	H	First Division	1–0
1973	West Bromwich Albion	A	First Division	1–4
1981	Norwich City	H	First Division	0–2

An hour after Everton had been beaten 2–0 at home by Norwich City chairman Philip Carter announced that the position of the manager and his staff were under review. Nearly a month later manager Gordon Lee was sacked.

1987	West Ham United	H	First Division	4–0
1992	Sheffield United	H	First Division	0–2
1998	Leeds United	H	FA Premier League	2–0

APRIL 12TH

1895	Glasgow Rangers	H	Friendly	0–4
1902	Notts County	H	First Division	0–1
1909	Newcastle United	A	First Division	0–3
1913	West Bromwich Albion	A	First Division	0–0
1919	Stockport County	H	Lancashire Section Subsidiary Tournament	0–1
1924	Tottenham Hotspur	A	First Division	5–2

Midway during the game Everton winger Sam Chedgzov took a corner and proceeded to dribble the ball towards the goal. As both attackers and defenders watched in amusement and disbelief, Chedgzov took the ball into the area and promptly scored.

The referee allowed the goal to stand since the new rule about corner kicks did not stipulate that the player taking the kick could only touch the ball once before it needed to be played by another player (not surprisingly, this rule was amended at the end of the season!).

1930 Grimsby Town H First Division 2–4

It was not apparent at the time, but the 4–2 home defeat by Grimsby was ultimately to cost Everton their place in the First Division, for at the end of the season they finished bottom of the table, one point behind both Burnley and Sheffield United. Everton had given a debut to goalkeeper Billy Coggins, newly arrived from Bristol City, but with precious little time to organise the defence to his satisfaction, it was a baptism of fire. He recovered to help the club race through the Second division the following season and made 56 appearances for the club before he was ousted by Ted Sagar. Coggins remained at Goodison until 1934 when he left to join Queens Park Rangers. He died in July 1958 at the age of 56.

1941 Manchester United H North Regional League 1–2
1947 Chelsea H First Division 2–0
1952 West Ham United H Second Division 2–0
1958 Sheffield Wednesday A First Division 1–2
1964 Under the headline THE BIGGEST SPORTS SCANDAL OF THE CENTURY the *Sunday People* revealed that a First Division match played on December 1st 1962, Ipswich versus Sheffield Wednesday, had been fixed by three Wednesday players prior to the game. The players had arranged the fix for gambling purposes, and Wednesday had lost 2–0. The three players were named as Peter Swan, David 'Bronco' Layne and Tony Kay, with Kay now playing for Everton. All three players were immediately suspended by their clubs and were ultimately jailed and banned for life from football. Whilst Everton lost the £55,000 they had spent on buying him, Tony Kay probably suffered more than any other player involved in the coup, for he lost his playing career, had to leave his Everton club house and give up his part-time jobs as a steward and coach. The FA ban even forbade him from turning out for the Thorp Arch Open Prison team! Although the ringleader of the betting ring was an ex-Everton player in Jimmy Gauld, his initial contact at Wednesday had been Layne, a former colleague at Swindon.

1965 Liverpool H First Division 2–1
1969 Coventry City H First Division 3–0
1971 Coventry City H First Division 3–0
1973 Harry Catterick was appointed general manager of Everton whilst the club advertised for a 'track suit' team manager following Catterick's recent heart attack. The club eventually appointed former player Billy Bingham to the role.
1975 Newcastle United A First Division 1–0
1980 West Ham United Villa Park FA Cup Semi-Final 1–1
Two London and both Merseyside clubs had reached the semi-finals of the FA Cup, with Liverpool taking on Arsenal at Hillsborough and Everton clashing with Second Division West Ham at Villa Park. A crowd of 47,685 were at Villa Park for the meeting with the London side belying their status, but Brian Kidd gave Everton the lead in the first half thanks to a hotly disputed penalty. Kidd did not have such a good time of it in the second half, becoming only the third player to have been sent off in an FA Cup semi-final, and West Ham equalised through Pearson to earn a replay.
1986 Arsenal A First Division 1–0

1993	Queens Park Rangers	H	FA Premier League	3–5
1997	Tottenham Hotspur	H	FA Premier League	1–0

APRIL 13TH

1872 John Cameron born in Ayr. He began his career with Ayr Parkhouse and then Queen's Park, signing amateur forms with Everton in 1895, even though he carried on playing for Queen's Park at the same time. Indeed, when he was awarded his first Scottish cap in March 1896, he was listed as a Queen's Park player. Persuaded to become a professional in 1896 he made 46 appearances in the League before being transferred to Spurs in May 1898, becoming player-manager-secretary a year later. Despite the three roles he found the strength to guide them to the FA Cup in 1901, the only time a non-League club has won the cup since the introduction of the Football League in 1888 (Spurs were members of the Southern League at the time and did not join the Football League until 1908). He later managed Ayr United before concentrating on journalism.

1895	Derby County	H	First Division	2–3

Everton fell to their only home defeat of the season, beaten 3–2 by Derby despite goals from Geary and Milward.

1901	Derby County	A	First Division	1–0
1903	Blackburn Rovers	H	First Division	0–3
1906	Liverpool	A	First Division	1–1
1907	Derby County	A	First Division	2–5
1910	Notts County	A	First Division	3–2
1912	Blackburn Rovers	H	First Division	1–3

The First Division's match of the day brought League leaders Blackburn Rovers to Goodison Park, where Everton lay in third place. Everton desperately needed a win to keep their championship hopes alive, but despite a goal from Davidson went down to their only home defeat of the season. Despite collecting five points out of six in their final three games, Everton finished the season in second place, three points behind Blackburn at the final reckoning.

1914	Oldham Athletic	H	First Division	0–2
1918	Southport	H	Lancashire Section Subsidiary Tournament	6–1
1925	Preston North End	H	First Division	0–0

1926 Tommy Clinton born in Dublin. He began his career with Dundalk, from whom Everton signed him in March 1948. His actual signature was secured under unusual circumstances; secretary Theo Kelly had arrived in Ireland to persuade him to come to Goodison and was chatting to him on the platform at Dundalk station. Then Clinton's train began to leave and he put pen to paper whilst leaning out of a carriage! He went on to serve Everton until 1955 when he joined Blackburn Rovers, but after only a handful of appearances joined Tranmere Rovers where he finished his career.

1929	Aston Villa	H	First Division	0–1
1935	Middlesbrough	H	First Division	1–1
1936	Brentford	A	First Division	1–4
1946	Chesterfield	A	Football League North	1–1
1957	Cardiff City	H	First Division	0–0
1963	Blackburn Rovers	A	First Division	2–1
1968	Sheffield United	A	First Division	1–0
1974	Norwich City	H	First Division	4–1

1977	Aston Villa	Old Trafford	League Cup Final 2nd Replay	2–3

After two draws at Wembley and Hillsborough Everton and Aston Villa met for the third time in the League Cup final at Old Trafford. The crowd of 54,749 knew they were see the matter finished on the night, for it had already been decided that in the event of another draw after extra time, the match would be settled on penalties. In the event there was no need for such an ending, for both clubs played a more open and attacking game than had been seen in the two previous encounters. Bob Latchford gave Everton the lead in the 38th minute and that seemed for some time to be enough to win the cup, but Aston Villa equalised through Chris Nicholl ten minutes from time and then took the lead a minute later through Brian Little. Everton had little option but to go straight on to the offensive in an attempt to rescue the game, and with time running out were rewarded when Mick Lyons headed home from a corner. That meant energy sapping extra time again, with Everton looking the more tired of the two teams, especially as they were also involved in a marathon FA Cup run at the time. In the closing minutes Brian Little skipped through the Everton defence to convert a centre to deny them the prize, the only domestic trophy to have so far eluded them.

1982	Coventry City	A	First Division	0–1
1985	Luton Town	Villa Park	FA Cup Semi-Final	2–1

Once again Everton and Liverpool had avoided each other in the FA Cup semi-final, with Liverpool taking on Manchester United at Goodison whilst Everton played a spirited if modest Luton side at Villa Park. Just as countless opponents had done in the past, Luton raised their game against the League leaders, taking the lead in the first half through Ricky Hill and throwing a defensive cordon around Les Sealey. With time running out and the double disappearing, Kevin Sheedy popped up to equalise five minutes from time. Thus reprieved Everton took control and Derek Mountfield headed home the winner in extra time to book a return to Wembley.

1991	Chelsea	H	First Division	2–2
1998	Wimbledon	A	FA Premier League	0–0

APRIL 14TH

1900	Bury	H	First Division	2–0
1906	Derby County	H	First Division	2–1
1911	Nottingham Forest	H	First Division	2–1

Alan Grenyer made his League debut for Everton, deputising for Harry Makepeace at left half in the 2–1 home win over Nottingham Forest. Grenyer had been signed from South Shields but found Makepeace a difficult player to shift from the side, making only four appearances in two seasons and finally getting an extended run in 1912–13. He made enough appearances in 1914–15 to collect a championship medal but like many of his generation found the First World War cut right across his career. After 148 appearances for the club he was sold to North Shields in November 1924.

1915	Bradford Park Avenue	A	First Division	2–1
1917	Southport	A	Lancashire Section Subsidiary Tournament	1–0
1922	Huddersfield Town	H	First Division	6–2
1923	Aston Villa	H	First Division	2–1
1928	Sheffield United	A	First Division	3–1

Two goals for Dixie Dean took him to the magical 50 mark for the season, but with just four games of the campaign left, the 59 goal target set the previous season by George Camsell was still looking safe.

1934	Chelsea	A	First Division	0–2
1937	Preston North End	A	First Division	0–1

On the same day Roy Vernon was born in Hollywell. He began his career with Blackburn Rovers and made over 100 appearances for their League side before a £27,000 transfer to Everton that saw Eddie Thomas make the opposite journey in part-exchange. He was made captain at Goodison and guided the team to the League title in 1963 before moving on to Stoke in 1965 for £40,000. He finished his playing career with a brief stint at Halifax and South Africa.

1941	Blackpool	H	North Regional League	2–2
1945	Wrexham	H	Football League North (Second Championship)	5–3
1948	Chelsea	H	First Division	2–3
1951	Sunderland	A	First Division	0–4
1952	Hull City	A	Second Division	0–1
1956	Chelsea	A	First Division	1–6
1962	West Ham United	H	First Division	3–0
1969	Newcastle United	H	First Division	1–1
1973	Wolverhampton Wanderers	A	First Division	2–4
1979	Manchester City	A	First Division	0–0
1984	Southampton		Highbury FA Cup Semi-Final	1–0

Having missed out on the Milk Cup Everton booked an immediate return to Wembley in the FA Cup final, only the third side to have reached the final of both major domestic cup competitions in the same season. An extra time goal from Adrian Heath in front of a crowd of 46,587 at Highbury was enough to settle the tie with Southampton.

1990	Luton Town	A	First Division	2–2
1995	Newcastle United	H	FA Premier League	2–0

APRIL 15TH

1892	Derby County	H	Football League	1–2
1893	Derby County	H	First Division	5–0
1899	Aston Villa	H	First Division	1–1
1905	Small Heath	H	First Division	2–1
1911	Oldham Athletic	A	First Division	0–2
1916	Stockport County	A	Lancashire Section Southern Division Supplementary Tournament	2–1
1922	Sheffield United	A	First Division	0–1
1933	Chelsea	H	First Division	3–2
1938	Sunderland	H	First Division	3–3

On the same day John King was born in Marylebone. He joined Everton in March 1956 and spent over three years with the club, making 48 League appearances before leaving for Bournemouth in July 1960. He later returned to Merseyside to sign for Tranmere, finishing his career with Port Vale.

1939	Preston North End	H	First Division	0–0
1944	Liverpool	A	Football League North (Second Championship)	0–3
1950	Derby County	A	First Division	0–2

| 1953 | Bury | H | Second Division | 3–0 |

A 3–0 win at home to Bury just about made Everton safe from relegation into the Third Division, but two defeats and a draw in their final three matches left Everton barely five points away from the trapdoor. Indeed, 1952–53 must rank as one of the poorest in the club's history, for despite reaching the FA Cup semi-final, they won only five League matches after the New Year and finished in 16th place in the League, their lowest ever placing.

1959	Portsmouth	A	First Division	3–2
1960	Blackpool	H	First Division	4–0
1961	Cardiff City	H	First Division	5–1
1963	Birmingham City	H	First Division	2–2
1968	Sheffield Wednesday	H	First Division	1–0
1972	Leicester City	H	First Division	0–0
1974	Manchester United	A	First Division	0–3
1978	Ipswich Town	H	First Division	1–0
1986	Watford	A	First Division	2–0
1989	Norwich City	Villa Park	FA Cup Semi-Final	1–0

Pat Nevin scored the goal that won a place at Wembley for Everton, but the joy expressed at the final whistle was soon tempered with the news from the other semi-final where Liverpool and Nottingham Forest had met at Hillsborough. Whilst the whole of Merseyside had wanted to see a clash between Liverpool and Everton at Wembley, the deaths of 96 fans at Hillsborough plunged the entire city into mourning.

APRIL 16TH

1892	Notts County	H	Football League	4–0
1894	Bolton Wanderers	A	First Division	1–0
1897	Derby County	H	First Division	5–2
1900	Glossop	H	First Division	4–1
1904	Derby County	A	First Division	1–0
1906	Manchester City	H	First Division	0–3
1910	Middlesbrough	H	First Division	1–1
1921	Preston North End	A	First Division	0–1
1923	Sheffield United	A	First Division	1–0
1927	Bolton Wanderers	A	First Division	0–5
1932	West Ham United	H	First Division	6–1

Dixie Dean scored a hat-trick as West Ham were brushed aside 6–1 at Goodison Park. Everton's other goals were scored by Tommy Johnson (two) and Jimmy Stein as Everton moved closer to the League title. Although Everton were to score only one more goal in the final four games of the campaign, it was enough to win the League.

1938	Charlton Athletic	H	First Division	3–0
1949	Arsenal	H	First Division	0–0
1954	Lincoln City	H	Second Division	3–1
1955	Bolton Wanderers	A	First Division	0–2
1960	Leicester City	A	First Division	3–3
1963	Birmingham City	A	First Division	1–0
1965	Fulham	H	First Division	2–0
1966	Leeds United	A	First Division	1–4

The Everton side showed eight changes from the previous League match, but the FA Cup semi-final was due to be played the following week. This subsequently cost Everton a then record fine of £2,000 from the Football League Management Committee for fielding a weakened side.

1968	Sheffield Wednesday	A	First Division	0–0
1977	Derby County	A	First Division	3–2
1979	Bolton Wanderers	H	First Division	1–0
1980	West Ham United	Elland Road	FA Cup Semi-Final Replay	1–2

After the controversy surrounding the first clash between the two sides four days earlier, the real drama of the semi-final replay came in extra time. With the 90 minutes having failed to separate the two sides, an extra half-hour was required, with Alan Devonshire giving West Ham the lead. Bob Latchford equalised with just seven minutes to go and the game looked to be heading for a third meeting before Frank Lampard headed home a late winner two minutes from time. It was a cruel blow for Everton, but West Ham went on to win the cup, beating Arsenal at Wembley.

1985	West Bromwich Albion	H	First Division	4–1
1990	Derby County	H	First Division	2–1
1994	Queens Park Rangers	A	FA Premier League	1–2
1996	Liverpool	H	FA Premier League	1–1

A 40,120 crowd at Goodison Park for the match between Everton and Liverpool produced record receipts of £450,000. The game finished all square at 1–1, with Andrei Kanchelskis netting for Everton.

1997	Liverpool	H	FA Premier League	1–1

APRIL 17TH

1888 Representatives of Aston Villa, Blackburn Rovers, Bolton Wanderers, Burnley, Derby County, Everton, Notts County, Preston North End, Stoke, West Bromwich Albion and Wolverhampton Wanderers met at the Royal Hotel in Manchester and agreed to the formation of the Football League (since the original Football League comprised 12 clubs we can only assume that Accrington were present at the meeting but not listed in the minutes). The move followed concerns that too many friendly games are being cancelled thereby depriving clubs of gate money, and playing a set number of matches home and away should offset any losses derived from losing friendly matches. Membership was set at £2 2s a year, clubs would be obliged to pay their full-strength team in all matches and William McGregor, the proposer of the Football League, was duly named as chairman, Harry Lockett of Stoke secretary and William Suddell of Preston North End treasurer. There was much discussion concerning the name of the League – McGregor's suggestion of 'Association Football Union' was rejected because of a possible confusion with the Rugby Football Union. McGregor's objections to 'Football League' because he thought it might be confused with the extreme political organisation 'Irish Home Rule League and the Land League' were overruled. The title was also adopted because it did not limit the competition to English teams; it was believed that Scottish teams might like to take part.

1897	West Bromwich Albion	H	First Division	6–3
1908	Liverpool	A	First Division	0–0

Bertie Freeman was introduced to the League side for the first time in the Merseyside derby at Anfield which ultimately finished goalless. He had joined Everton after playing for Aston Villa and Arsenal and went on to make 94 first-team appearances before moving to Burnley in 1911, later winning a winners' medal in the FA Cup whilst at Turf Moor. In 1908–09 he led the goalscoring charts in the First Division with 36 goals.

1909	Sheffield Wednesday	A	First Division	0–2
1911	Tottenham Hotspur	A	First Division	1–0
1915	Manchester City	A	First Division	1–0
1920	Burnley	A	First Division	0–5
1926	West Ham United	A	First Division	0–1
1933	Leeds United	H	First Division	0–1
1937	Charlton Athletic	H	First Division	2–2
1940	Tranmere Rovers	H	War Regional League, Western Division	5–3
1943	Tranmere Rovers	A	Football League North (Second Championship)	2–1
1948	Preston North End	A	First Division	0–3
1954	Fulham	A	Second Division	0–0
1965	Wolverhampton Wanderers	A	First Division	4–2
1971	Derby County	A	First Division	1–3
1973	Chelsea	H	First Division	1–0
1976	Manchester United	A	First Division	1–2
1982	Sunderland	A	First Division	1–3
1984	Southampton	A	First Division	1–3
1993	Southampton	A	FA Premier League	0–0
1995	Sheffield Wednesday	A	FA Premier League	0–0

APRIL 18TH

1892	Bolton Wanderers	H	Football League	2–5
1903	Notts County	H	First Division	2–0
1904	West Bromwich Albion	H	First Division	4–0
1908	Woolwich Arsenal	A	First Division	1–2

Everton took the opportunity to introduce Val Harris into the side for the first time in the 2–1 defeat at Woolwich Arsenal in the League. Born in Dublin he had joined the club from Shelbourne, having already established himself in the Irish national side. By 1914 he had made 214 appearances for the club and 20 for his country and then returned to Shelbourne the same year.

1914	Bolton Wanderers	H	First Division	1–1
1919	Liverpool	A	Lancashire Section Subsidiary Tournament	1–1
1922	Huddersfield Town	A	First Division	2–1
1924	Arsenal	H	First Division	3–1
1925	West Ham United	A	First Division	1–4
1927	Birmingham City	H	First Division	3–1
1928	Newcastle United	H	First Division	3–0

Whilst the goals scored by Critchley and Weldon helped take Everton another step closer to the title, it was Dixie Dean's goal that set the game alight, for it was his 51st goal of the season.

1930	Burnley	H	First Division	3–0
1931	Burnley	H	Second Division	3–2

1933	Leeds United	A	First Division	0–1
1936	Leeds United	A	First Division	1–3
1938	Sunderland	A	First Division	0–2

1940 John Morrissey born in Liverpool. A product of Liverpool's youth scheme he made 36 appearances in three seasons for the Anfield outfit before moving across Stanley Park for a cut-price fee of £10,000 in 1962. He was a key member of the side that won the League title in 1963 and 1970, but after this latter success found his place in the side under threat and moved to Oldham Athletic in 1972. Six months later he was forced to retire through injury.

1942	Liverpool	H	Football League North (Second Championship)	0–1
1949	Charlton Athletic	H	First Division	1–1
1953	Luton Town	H	Second Division	1–1
1959	Chelsea	A	First Division	1–3
1960	Blackpool	A	First Division	0–0
1964	Chelsea	A	First Division	0–1
1967	Southampton	H	First Division	0–1
1981	Middlesbrough	H	First Division	4–1
1987	Aston Villa	A	First Division	1–0

Alongside Dixie Dean Kevin Sheedy has probably scored more vital goals for Everton than any other player in their history. His goal against Aston Villa was enough to collect another three points in their quest for the League title, although there were still a couple more twists and turns before the trophy was landed.

1992	Coventry City	⮞ A	First Division	1–0
1998	Leicester City	H	FA Premier League	1–1

APRIL 19TH

1890 Glasgow Rangers A Friendly 6–2

Everton paid their first visit to Ibrox for a friendly match with Glasgow Rangers, putting in a superb performance that brushed aside the Scottish team 6–2.

1902 Bolton Wanderers A First Division 3–1

1918 Aubrey Powell born in Swansea. A full Welsh international with eight caps to his credit, he joined Everton from Leeds United and made 35 League appearances for the club before joining Birmingham City in August 1950.

1919 Southport A Lancashire Section Subsidiary Tournament 1–4

1924 Tottenham Hotspur H First Division 4–2

Although Huddersfield Town were to win the League title (on goal average from Cardiff City) with Everton languishing in seventh place, a hat-trick from Bill Chadwick in the penultimate match of the season against Spurs enabled him to finish the First Division's top goalscorer with 28 to his credit. Everton won the game 4–2 and Chadwick went on to register 50 goals in 102 League appearances for the club before joining Leeds United in November 1925.

1930	Manchester United	A	First Division	3–3
1941	Chesterfield	A	North Regional League	1–4
1946	Barnsley	A	Football League North	0–2
1947	Sheffield United	A	First Division	0–2
1952	Sheffield United	A	Second Division	2–1
1954	Lincoln City	A	Second Division	1–1

1957	Manchester City	A	First Division	4–2
1958	Manchester City	H	First Division	2–5
1965	Fulham	A	First Division	1–1
1967	Chelsea	H	First Division	3–1
1969	Sheffield Wednesday	A	First Division	2–2
1975	Sheffield United	H	First Division	2–3
1976	Middlesbrough	H	First Division	3–1
1977	Norwich City	H	First Division	3–1
1980	Tottenham Hotspur	A	First Division	0–3
1983	Manchester United	H	First Division	2–0
1986	Ipswich Town	H	First Division	1–0

The League title race had become a three way battle between Liverpool, Everton and West Ham, with Everton and Liverpool level on points but with the Anfield club in the middle of what would become a run of 12 games without defeat, during which time only one game was drawn. Against this Everton could point to a run of only one defeat since the turn of the year, but they were still left relying on a possible Liverpool slip. As the end came in sight the nerves got tighter, but a goal from Graeme Sharp in the second half would keep the pressure on the other two sides – Liverpool won at West Bromwich Albion and West Ham won at Watford.

1988	Coventry City	A	First Division	2–1
1997	West Ham United	A	FA Premier League	2–2

APRIL 20TH

1895	Sunderland	A	First Division	1–2
1897	Derby County	A	First Division	1–0
1901	Bolton Wanderers	H	First Division	2–3
1907	Sheffield Wednesday	Crystal Palace	FA Cup Final	1–2

Everton were back at the Crystal Palace in the FA Cup final, this time facing Sheffield Wednesday. The cup run had begun against Sheffield United, Everton winning 1–0 thanks to an own goal and now it was to come to an end against the other side from the steel city. It was not a memorable final, indeed perhaps one of the poorest of many years, with Stewart giving Wednesday the lead after 21 minutes and Jack Sharp equalising shortly before half-time. The two sides cancelled each other out during the second half, with Simpson scoring the winner in the very last minute. Apart from Wednesday it was a bad day all round for those connected with the final, for the referee Nat Whittaker had been fined the day before for delaying a League match (he missed a train connection!). At the final whistle the cup was presented by Lord Alverstone with a 84,594 crowd looking on.

1908	Notts County	H	First Division	1–0
1912	Sheffield Wednesday	A	First Division	3–1

1915 Frederick Wall of the Football Association announced that following the end of the current season, professional football would be abandoned until after the First World War. Everton were still battling with Oldham for the League title at the time and were thus to hold on to the trophy for five years.

1918	Southport	A	Lancashire Section Subsidiary Tournament	4–0
1929	Leicester City	A	First Division	1–4

1935	Blackburn Rovers	A	First Division	2–6
1940	Preston North End	H	War League Cup	3–1
1946	Burnley	H	Football League North	2–0
1955	Leicester City	A	First Division	2–2
1957	Chelsea	A	First Division	1–5
1962	Birmingham City	H	First Division	4–1
1963	Tottenham Hotspur	H	First Division	1–0

The arrival of Spurs at Goodison Park had been eagerly awaited by players and supporters alike, for along with Leicester City Spurs remained Everton's chief challengers for the title. Both Spurs and Leicester had their minds on other things, with Leicester progressing though to the FA Cup final and Spurs the European Cup-Winners' Cup final, while for Everton the League remained the main objective. A crowd of 67,650, the second biggest of the season (Liverpool's visit in September had been bigger) packed into the ground confident that Everton could see off the Spurs and a goal from Alex Young was enough to maintain Everton's unbeaten home record and secure both points. When the League table was drawn up, Everton were top on goal average; they were to retain that position for the rest of the season.

1968	Chelsea	H	First Division	2–1
1974	Liverpool	A	First Division	0–0
1981	Manchester City	A	First Division	1–3
1982	Nottingham Forest	H	First Division	2–1
1985	Stoke City	A	First Division	2–0
1987	Newcastle United	H	First Division	3–0
1991	Crystal Palace	A	First Division	0–0
1992	Manchester City	H	First Division	1–2

APRIL 21ST

1900	Notts County	A	First Division	2–2
1905	Manchester City	A	First Division	0–2

Everton were battling for the League title along with Newcastle United and Manchester City, and at first it appeared as though the tension of the race for the title had boiled over in a particularly bitter meeting between City and Everton at Hyde Road, with Tom Booth of Everton and Frank Booth of City being involved in a number of unsavoury incidents. The matter might have rested there had it not been for an even worse meeting between City and Aston Villa the following week which led to accusations that City's Sandy Turnbull had been punched off the ball by Alec Leake and then been attacked in the tunnel after the game. Villa for their part claimed that the City players had made numerous approaches during the game offering bribes, all of which guaranteed the Football Association would look into the matter, finally announcing their findings on 4th August 1905.

1906	Newcastle United	Crystal Palace	FA Cup Final	1–0

Newcastle United were firm favourites to win the FA Cup final against Everton, just as they had been 12 months earlier when facing Aston Villa. Then Villa had won 2–0 to deny Newcastle the double but, just as importantly, had planted the seeds of doubt into Newcastle's mind whenever they played at The Crystal Palace. Newcastle were to reach the final four times in the space of seven years but could not win even one at Crystal

Palace; their only success coming in 1910 in a replay at Goodison Park! So it proved in 1906 in front of a crowd of 75,609, with Newcastle having perhaps the better of what was a tedious match but unable to score. Early in the second half Sandy Young appeared to have opened the scoring for Everton when he turned the ball home after a fumble by Newcastle's goalkeeper, but this was ruled out for offside. The let off seemed to inspire Newcastle for a period, but they had little to show for their efforts apart from a stern lecture from the referee for ungentlemanly conduct. Then, with only 13 minutes left, Sandy Young was at the end of a cross from Sharp to hit the ball home. This effort was adjudged legitimate and Everton had won the FA Cup for the first time in their history. Although we now know the phrase as 'third time lucky', a contemporary saying of the early 20th century was 'the third time counts for all'; it certainly did for Everton in their third appearance in the final.

1916	Liverpool	A	Lancashire Section Southern Division Supplementary Tournament	2–5
1917	Liverpool	H	Lancashire Section Subsidiary Tournament	5–0
1923	Aston Villa	A	First Division	0–3
1924	Arsenal	A	First Division	1–0
1928	Aston Villa	H	First Division	3–2

Everton completed the 'double' over Villa, having already won by the same score at Villa Park earlier in the campaign. Then Dixie Dean had hit a hat-trick; this time he had to settle for two goals to take him to 53 for the season with just two games left to play.

1932   Albert Dunlop born in Liverpool. Although he joined Everton at the age of 17 in 1949, he had to wait until the 1956–57 season before making his debut. After a slow start he went on to make 231 first-team appearances before joining Wrexham in 1963, making 15 appearances before retiring.

| 1934 | Portsmouth | H | First Division | 1–1 |

Jackie Coulter made his debut in the 1–1 home draw with Portsmouth. He had joined Everton for a fee of £3,000 from Belfast Celtic earlier in the year and immediately linked well with Dixie Dean and Billy Cook and seemed set to become an influential member of the side until a broken leg sustained whilst representing Northern Ireland brought his career to a temporary halt. Unable to completely recover from its effects he was sold to Grimsby Town in 1937 after just 58 appearances for Everton. He eventually retired to Belfast where he died in January 1981.

1945	Southport	A	Football League North (Second Championship)	5–0
1948	Liverpool	A	First Division	0–4
1951	Aston Villa	H	First Division	1–2
1956	Blackpool	H	First Division	1–0
1962	Manchester United	A	First Division	1–1
1973	Arsenal	H	First Division	0–0
1976	Derby County	A	First Division	3–1
1979	Leeds United	A	First Division	0–1
1984	Sunderland	A	First Division	1–2
1990	Manchester City	A	First Division	0–1

APRIL 22ND

| 1899 | Burnley | A | First Division | 0–0 |

Jimmy Settle made his only appearance of the season in the goalless draw at Turf Moor.

CLOCKWISE FROM TOP LEFT: Everton picture card, cigarette cards of Jack Taylor, John Macconachie and Cliff Britton

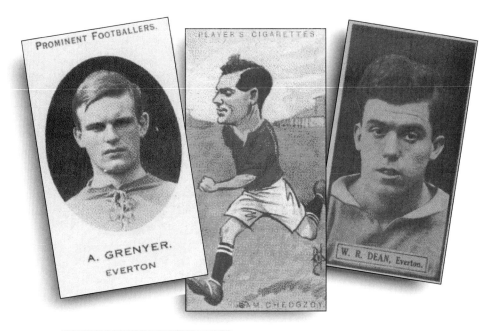

CLOCKWISE FROM TOP LEFT: Cigarette cards of Alan Grenyer, Sam Chedgzoy, Dixie Dean and Colin Harvey

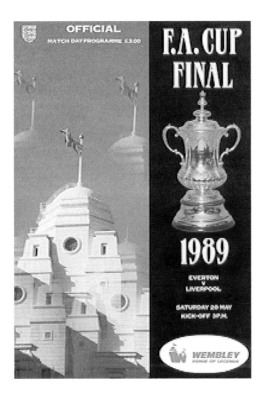

TOP: Programme from the 1989 FA Cup final between Liverpool and Everton, which Liverpool won 3–2 after extra time

RIGHT: Programme from the 1986 FA Cup final between Liverpool and Everton, which Liverpool won 3–1

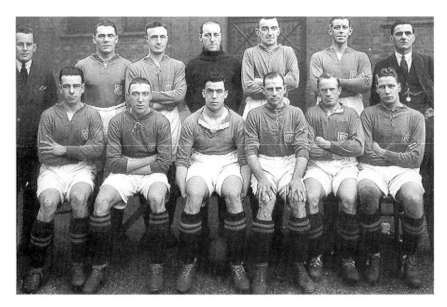

The 1927–28 League champions

Action from the 1933 FA Cup final between Everton and Manchester City, which Everton won 3–0

Ted Sagar, who between 1929 and 1953 made 465 League appearances, is chaired off the field after his final game for the club

Everton draw level in the 1966 FA Cup final against Sheffield Wednesday. The final score was 3–2 to the Toffees

The 1984–85 championship-winning side with the League trophy

Howard Kendall and Kenny Dalglish lead their teams out for the 1986 FA Cup
final. Liverpool won 3–1 to complete the double

TOP: Neville Southall, an Everton and Wales legend

RIGHT: Gary Lineker, one of England's greatest-ever strikers, was a Goodison Park hero

TOP: Walter Smith, who took over as manager in the summer of 1998 after a very successful reign at Rangers

RIGHT: During his first spell in charge, Howard Kendall guided the club to two League titles, the FA Cup and the European Cup-Winners' Cup

He went on to make 269 appearances for the club, scoring 97 goals and won medals in the FA Cup finals of 1906 and 1907, collecting a winners' medal in the first. He also won six caps for England and left Everton to join Stockport County in the summer of 1908, retiring a year later.

1901	West Bromwich Albion	A	First Division	2–1
1905	Woolwich Arsenal	A	First Division	1–2

Everton travelled down to Woolwich Arsenal, the club then playing at the Manor Ground in Plumstead, to replay the League match which had been abandoned owing to fog in November. Then Everton had been leading 3–1; this time they lost 2–1 and surrendered the League title to Newcastle United, who were to win the title by a single point.

1907	Manchester United	A	First Division	0–3
1911	Sheffield Wednesday	H	First Division	1–1
1912	West Bromwich Albion	H	First Division	3–0
1916	Manchester City	A	Lancashire Section Southern Division Supplementary Tournament	4–5
1922	Sheffield United	H	First Division	1–1
1929	Arsenal	A	First Division	0–2
1933	Huddersfield Town	A	First Division	0–0
1935	Derby County	A	First Division	1–4
1939	Charlton Athletic	A	First Division	1–2
1944	Liverpool	A	Football League North (Second Championship)	2–4
1946	Barnsley	H	Football League North	0–4
1950	Burnley	H	First Division	1–1
1953	Lincoln City	H	Second Division	0–3
1957	Manchester City	H	First Division	1–1
1961	Sheffield Wednesday	A	First Division	2–1
1967	Blackpool	A	First Division	1–0
1967	Tottenham Hotspur	H	First Division	0–1
1968	Nottingham Forest	A	First Division	0–1
1969	Leeds United	H	First Division	0–0
1972	Stoke City	A	First Division	1–1
1978	Middlesbrough	A	First Division	0–0
1989	Tottenham Hotspur	A	First Division	1–2

Immediately following the Hillsborough disaster the Football League gave Liverpool, Everton and Tranmere Rovers permission to postpone their matches for as long as they liked as the city was still in mourning following the huge death toll (and there were a number of other clubs who similarly postponed their matches as a mark of respect, such as Arsenal and QPR, the former in defiance of the League). Everton returned to the fray with a visit to a White Hart Lane ground that bore little relation to the one they had come to the previous season, for the 15–foot fences had been removed. Before the game the Spurs fans presented a wreath for the Everton fans to take back to Merseyside, the minute's silence was immaculately observed and the game, like all others played on the day, kicked off at 3.06 p.m., the exact time the Liverpool and Forest semi-final had been abandoned. Given the circumstances the game itself was played with all the enthusiasm of a testimonial, with Spurs winning 2–1.

APRIL 23RD

1906	Sheffield Wednesday	A	First Division	1–3
1910	Manchester United	H	First Division	3–3
1919	Southport	H	Lancashire Section Subsidiary Tournament	1–2
1921	Burnley	H	First Division	1–1
1927	Aston Villa	H	First Division	2–2
1932	Middlesbrough	A	First Division	0–1
1938	Birmingham City	A	First Division	3–0
1949	Huddersfield Town	A	First Division	1–1
1955	Charlton Athletic	H	First Division	2–2
1958	Blackpool	A	First Division	1–0
1960	Leeds United	H	First Division	1–0
1966	Manchester United	Burnden Park	FA Cup Semi-Final	1–0

A single goal from Colin Harvey earned Everton their first appearance in the FA Cup final for 33 years and kept Merseyside on track for another sweep of the two major honours; FA Cup and League championship, the latter destined for Liverpool as Leeds United's challenge faltered. Whilst Everton had been inconsistent in the League, hovering around mid-table, they had managed to raise their game whenever the cup came around, none more so than a tense tie with Manchester United.

1974	Manchester United	H	First Division	1–0
1977	Liverpool	Maine Road	FA Cup Semi-Final	2–2

Everton and Liverpool contested the FA Cup semi-final at Maine Road, with the match finishing a 2–2 draw and therefore requiring a replay. However, in an incident that is still talked about by those who were present, referee Clive Thomas sensationally disallowed what appeared to have been a perfectly legitimate winner for Everton when Bryan Hamilton netted in the very last seconds. There has never been an adequate explanation as to why the goal was disallowed, but Liverpool were given an unexpected reprieve and were to win the replay 3–0.

1983	Birmingham City	A	First Division	0–1
1984	Wolverhampton Wanderers	H	First Division	2–0
1988	Oxford United	A	First Division	1–1
1994	Coventry City	H	FA Premier League	0–0

APRIL 24TH

1895	Aston Villa	A	First Division	2–2
1897	Bury	H	First Division	1–2
1905	Nottingham Forest	A	First Division	2–0
1909	Leicester City	H	First Division	4–2
1920	Burnley	H	First Division	1–2
1926	Newcastle United	H	First Division	3–0
1937	Grimsby Town	A	First Division	0–1

1943 Gordon West born in Barnsley. After making his name with Blackpool he cost Everton a then record fee for a goalkeeper, £27,000 to come to Goodison Park. He immediately replaced Albert Dunlop and went on to win two League titles and the FA Cup, as well as representing England on three occasions. That figure might have been higher but he chose to opt out of the squad for the 1970 World Cup finals in Mexico, preferring to remain at home with his family. The arrival of David Lawson effectively brought his Everton career to an end, having made 399 appearances for the first team. Astonishingly, he played for Tranmere Rovers almost three years after having played his last game for Everton.

1948	Portsmouth	H	First Division	0–2
1954	Birmingham City	H	Second Division	1–0
1962	Birmingham City	A	First Division	0–0
1963	Arsenal	H	First Division	1–1
1965	Arsenal	H	First Division	1–0
1971	Blackpool	H	First Division	0–0
1976	West Ham United	H	First Division	2–0
1982	Arsenal	H	First Division	2–1
1985	Bayern Munich	H	European Cup-Winners' Cup	3–1
			Semi-Final 2nd Leg	

One of the greatest European nights ever witnessed at Goodison Park saw the crack German side Bayern Munich arrive for the European Cup-Winners' Cup semi-final second leg. The first leg had finished goalless but Everton were not taking anything for granted, for the Germans were known to be an extremely well organised side particularly good at catching teams on the breakaway. Indeed, in the first half they did just that, scoring through Hoeness for what many believed would be a vital away goal. Everton now needed to score at least twice to make the final. It was a feature of Everton's play during the season that they never knew when they were beaten, and with a crowd of 49,476 crowd willing them on, anything was possible. Graeme Sharp levelled the scores on the night and then Andy Gray, perhaps the player to have turned Everton's fortunes around since he arrived at the club, gave them the lead. Mindful that a Bayern equaliser would send the Germans through on away goals, Everton continued to push forward in an effort to put the game firmly beyond reach, and Gary Stevens, one of the heroes of the first leg, scored the final goal in a thrilling 3–1 win. Everton were thus through to their very first European final and still on course for an unprecedented treble of League, FA Cup and European Cup-Winners' Cup.

| 1991 | Tottenham Hotspur | A | First Division | 3–3 |

APRIL 25TH

1904	Manchester City	H	First Division	1–0
1908	Sheffield Wednesday	H	First Division	0–0
1914	Chelsea	A	First Division	0–1
1931	Southampton	A	Second Division	1–2
1934	Huddersfield Town	A	First Division	0–1
1936	Birmingham City	H	First Division	4–3
1942	West Bromwich Albion	A	Football League North (Second Championship)	1–3
1953	Birmingham City	A	Second Division	2–4

Everton's twelfth defeat away from home, this time at Birmingham City, brought a depressing season to a depressing end. For manager Cliff Britton the season could not end quickly enough, the 4–2 defeat on par with the kind of performances the team had turned in throughout the campaign. On their day, they could be brilliant, as a 7–1 win over Doncaster Rovers and a run to the FA Cup semi-finals showed, but were also prone to self destruction, as an 8–2 defeat at Huddersfield proved. He would need more performances of the former rather than the latter to get the club back into the First Division.

1959	Wolverhampton Wanderers	H	First Division	0–1
1964	West Ham United	H	First Division	2–0
1966	Manchester United	H	First Division	0–0
1967	Arsenal	A	First Division	1–3
1967	Sunderland	A	First Division	2–0
1969	Nottingham Forest	A	First Division	0–1
1973	Newcastle United	A	First Division	0–0
1978	West Bromwich Albion	A	First Division	1–3
1981	Stoke City	H	First Division	0–1
1987	Liverpool	A	First Division	1–3

The top two in the League clashed at Anfield, with Liverpool in greater need of the points if they were to catch their great rivals. Everton arrived having won their previous seven games, whilst Liverpool were beginning to falter in their challenge. Despite this, a crowd of 44,827 expected as full-blooded a Merseyside derby as of right, and they were not to be disappointed. Liverpool took the lead after just nine minutes, ex-Everton player Steve McMahon latching on to an Ian Rush pass to fire past Neville Southall. Everton were level soon after when Wayne Clarke, a deadline day arrival and playing in place of the injured Graeme Sharp, was fouled and Kevin Sheedy curled home the free-kick from 25 yards. Rush restored Liverpool's lead right on the stroke of half-time and forced Southall into a number of saves in the second period, finally scoring some six minutes from time with a delicate chip. Everton, however, were to have the last laugh, for Liverpool's challenge ran out of steam before the end of the season and brought the title back to Goodison.

| 1992 | Tottenham Hotspur | A | First Division | 3–3 |
| 1998 | Sheffield Wednesday | H | FA Premier League | 1–3 |

APRIL 26TH

| 1913 | Sheffield Wednesday | H | First Division | 3–1 |
| 1915 | Chelsea | H | First Division | 2–2 |

A 2–2 home draw with Chelsea enabled Everton to win the League title for the second time in their history, finishing just one point ahead of Oldham Athletic. It had been a quite astonishing finish to the season, for at the turn of the month the League seemed most likely to go to either Manchester City, who were top, or Oldham, who were fourth. City had lost form at the most crucial of times, whilst Oldham's cause had not been helped by the furore surrounding their match against Middlesbrough over Easter, 4–1 down they had a man sent off ten minutes after half-time who refused to go, leaving the referee little option but to take both sides off the field. Everton, meanwhile, quietly went about their business, winning four straight matches to put themselves in pole position. Goals from Tom Fleetwood and Bobby Parker clinched the required point, whilst Parker's strike enabled him to finish the season as the division's top goalscorer with 35. This was to be the last League action at Goodison or anywhere else for four years, for it had already been decided to suspend the Football League whilst the First World War

was being fought and would not resume until the 1919–20 season, although regional
football was maintained during the interim period.

1920	Preston North End	A	First Division	0–1
1930	Sheffield United	H	First Division	3–2
1941	New Brighton	A	North Regional League	4–0
1943	Liverpool	A	Football League North (Second Championship)	1–4
1947	Preston North End	H	First Division	2–0
1952	Barnsley	H	Second Division	1–1
1958	Nottingham Forest	A	First Division	3–0
1975	Chelsea	A	First Division	1–1
1980	Southampton	H	First Division	2–0
1986	Nottingham Forest	A	First Division	0–0

Gary Lineker returned to the side having missed the match against Ipswich, although
he was unable to find the net in the game with Forest. Unfortunately, neither was
anyone else on the Everton side, allowing Liverpool to take a two point advantage at the
top of the table, the first time in the month there had been anything between the two at
the top of the table.

APRIL 27TH

1901	Goodison Park had staged the FA Cup final in 1893 and would later play host to the replay in 1910, but it should also have staged the replay between Spurs and Sheffield United, for it was the FA's first choice. Unfortunately, Liverpool successfully complained that as they were at home on the same day (against Nottingham Forest) their gate would be affected and the game was switched to Bolton's Burnden Park. The result was the lowest cup final crowd this century, 20,447.			

1907	Sheffield Wednesday	A	First Division	1–1
1912	Bury	H	First Division	1–1
1921	Tottenham Hotspur	H	First Division	0–0
1925	Sheffield United	H	First Division	1–1
1929	Manchester United	H	First Division	2–4
1938	Blackpool	A	First Division	2–0
1940	Preston North End	A	War League Cup	2–2
1946	Burnley	A	Football League North	0–1
1949	Leeds United	H	First Division	2–0
1957	Bolton Wanderers	A	First Division	1–1
1963	West Ham United	A	First Division	2–1
1967	Tottenham Hotspur	A	First Division	0–2
1968	Leeds United	Old Trafford	FA Cup Semi-Final	1–0

1972 Brian Labone announced his retirement after more than 400 games for the club owing
to injury. He had suffered an Achilles tendon injury during a reserve team match the
previous September.

1974	Southampton	H	First Division	0–3
1977	Liverpool	Maine Road	FA Cup Semi-Final Replay	0–3

Everton played as though they were still aggrieved by the events at the first meeting
four days earlier, allowing Liverpool to take the initiative right from the off. Having

been seen as the villain of the peace in the first match, referee Clive Thomas did little to further enamour himself to the Everton fans by awarding a penalty to Liverpool after adjudging Mike Pejic had pushed David Johnson; Phil Neal put Liverpool ahead from the spot. Everton were themselves denied a penalty, Clemence catching Duncan McKenzie with a raised foot but all they got was an indirect free-kick which was subsequently cleared. A goal by Jimmy Case goal drained the fight out of Everton and it was with no surprise when Ray Kennedy added a third. In truth, Everton were undone as much by refereeing decisions over the two games as they were by Liverpool, even if their rivals were going for an unprecedented treble.

| 1985 | Norwich City | H | First Division | 3–0 |
| 1996 | Sheffield Wednesday | A | FA Premier League | 5–2 |

APRIL 28TH

| 1900 | Manchester City | H | First Division | 4–0 |
| 1906 | Nottingham Forest | H | First Division | 4–1 |

1910 With the FA Cup final at Crystal Palace between Newcastle United and Barnsley having been drawn 1–1, Goodison Park was chosen to stage the replay. A crowd of 69,000 were present to see Newcastle win 2–0 to lift the cup.

1914	Glasgow Rangers	A	James Wilson Benefit Match	2–6
1917	Stockport County	A	Lancashire Section Subsidiary Tournament	1–2
1923	Preston North End	H	First Division	1–0
1928	Burnley	A	First Division	5–3

At the beginning of April 1928, the only story that interested the media was the impending double of Huddersfield Town. They were five points clear of Everton at the top of the table and through to the FA Cup final to face a Blackburn Rovers side lying in mid-table. With eight League games to play they needed eight, possibly nine, points to be sure of the title, but only if Everton were to win all their remaining games. Few outside Goodison gave much thought that Everton might win the title, even fewer believed Dixie Dean might reach 60 goals during the course of the season. Inexplicably, Huddersfield all but collapsed during April, taking only five points and losing the cup final. Everton had whittled away their lead at the top of the table, although Huddersfield still held a slight advantage going into the games on April 28th. The story of Everton's game with Burnley was the incomparable Dean, who scored four goals to take his tally to 57, a tantalising two behind George Camsell's record and with one more game to play. Huddersfield won as well, 2–1 at Leicester; they had three games left, two of which were to be played in midweek leading up to the final weekend of League action.

1930	Huddersfield Town	A	First Division	2–1
1934	Sunderland	A	First Division	2–3
1942	Southport	A	Football League North (Second Championship)	1–2
1945	Southport	H	Football League North (Second Championship)	1–1
1948	Huddersfield Town	A	First Division	3–1
1951	Derby County	A	First Division	1–0

1958 Billy Wright born in Liverpool. An Everton fan as a schoolboy he joined the club as a junior and was upgraded to the professional ranks in August 1974. He made his debut during the 1977–78 season and seemed set for a lengthy career at Goodison Park, but on 11th December 1982 he was dropped from the side for being 8 lbs overweight! His

confidence never recovered from this blow and he left the club soon after, joining
Birmingham City and later playing for Chester.

| 1962 | Cardiff City | H | First Division | 8–3 |

1967   Earl Barrett born in Rochdale. He began his career with Manchester City but after two
years and only three first-team appearances he was sold to Oldham for £35,000. Here
he made his name and reputation and was sold to Aston Villa for £1.7 million in 1992.
Three years later a similar fee brought him to Goodison Park. He is a full England
international with three caps to his credit.

1973	Derby County	A	First Division	1–3
1979	Birmingham City	H	First Division	1–0
1980	West Bromwich Albion	H	First Division	0–0
1984	Norwich City	A	First Division	1–1
1990	Chelsea	A	First Division	1–2

APRIL 29TH

1899	Wolverhampton Wanderers	A	First Division	2–1
1911	Bristol City	A	First Division	1–0
1916	Oldham Athletic	H	Lancashire Section Southern Division Supplementary Tournament	0–2
1919	Glasgow Rangers	A	Friendly	0–4
1922	Burnley	A	First Division	0–2
1924	Huddersfield Town	H	First Division	0–2
1933	Manchester City	Wembley	FA Cup Final	3–0

As both Everton and Manchester City traditionally wore blue shirts, their meeting in the
FA Cup final prompted a change for both clubs, with City selecting the red in
preference to white. Of course, it was not the choice of colours that has marked out this
final in football's history but what was put on the back; as an experiment, both sides
were numbered for the very first time, although Everton wore the numbers 1 to 11 and
City 12 through to 22. This gave Eric Brook the distinction of becoming the first man
to wear number 12 in an FA Cup final. It also meant that City had number 13 on their
side as well, and it certainly proved unlucky as Everton ran out easy winners 3–0 thanks
to goals from Stein, Dean and Dunn, but City had been undone even before the game
kicked off, arriving at Wembley too early and allowing nerves to set in as they waited
for the kick off. Captain Dixie Dean then became the first Everton skipper to climb the
steps of Wembley Stadium to collect the FA Cup.

1939	Aston Villa	H	First Division	3–0
1944	Bury	A	Football League North (Second Championship)	0–1
1950	Sunderland	A	First Division	2–4
1954	Oldham Athletic	A	Second Division	4–0

Something of a stumble towards the end of the season had threatened to throw Everton's
promotion train off the rails, and from being almost certainties they had allowed others
to make up ground. On the last day of the season, Blackburn were top of the table with
55 points, Leicester second with 54, ahead of Everton in third place on goal average. It
was certainly to Everton's advantage that their two rivals were to meet at Filbert Street
on the same day as Everton were at Oldham Athletic, for with Oldham already relegated
Everton were expected to win to keep the pressure on the other two clubs. So it proved:

Everton 4–0 thanks to goals from John Willie Parker (two), Dave Hickson and Tommy E Jones, whilst a similar scoreline in favour of Leicester City meant promotion ahead of Blackburn. It was the last time Everton were to play Second Division football.

1961	Arsenal	H	First Division	4–1
1967	Manchester City	H	First Division	1–1
1968	Manchester City	A	First Division	0–2
1969	Arsenal	H	First Division	1–0
1978	Chelsea	H	First Division	6–0

Everton signed off the season in style with a 6–0 win over Chelsea. Bob Latchford scored twice, Martin Dobson, Mick Lyons, Neil Robinson and Billy Wright added the others as Everton pushed themselves into fourth place to earn a place in the UEFA Cup for the following season.

| 1995 | Wimbledon | H | FA Premier League | 0–0 |

APRIL 30TH

1910	Bradford City	A	First Division	0–2
1921	Burnley	A	First Division	1–1
1927	Cardiff City	A	First Division	0–1

1928 Huddersfield Town lost at home to Sheffield United and stayed three points behind Everton with just two games left.

| 1932 | Bolton Wanderers | H | First Division | 1–0 |

A 1–0 win over Bolton at Goodison Park enabled Everton to clinch the League title for the fourth time in their history and equal a feat achieved by Liverpool in 1906; champions of the Second and First Divisions in consecutive seasons. Dixie Dean scored the historic goal that secured the title. It was his 44th goal of the season, enabling him to top the individual scoring list in the division for the second time in his career.

1938	Portsmouth	H	First Division	5–2
1946	Glasgow Rangers	Windsor Park	Friendly	3–2
1955	Sunderland	A	First Division	0–3
1960	Manchester United	A	First Division	0–5

1963 Maurice Johnston born in Glasgow. He began his career with Partick Thistle before being introduced to the English game with Watford, facing Everton in the 1984 FA Cup final. Unable to settle he returned to Scotland with Celtic where he quickly became a favourite of the crowd. After a spell with French club Nantes he was believed to be back on his way to Celtic, but Rangers manager Graeme Souness nipped in first and persuaded him to go to Ibrox. The move caused a sensation, with Celtic fans furious that Johnston had let them down, and half of Rangers support upset that the club had knowingly signed a Catholic. Johnston let his goals do the talking for him at Rangers and then in 1991 joined Everton for £1.75 million. He later returned to Scotland to play for Hearts and Falkirk.

1966	Sunderland	A	First Division	0–2
1977	Norwich City	A	First Division	1–2
1983	West Ham United	H	First Division	2–0
1986	Oxford United	A	First Division	0–1
1988	Charlton Athletic	H	First Division	1–1
1989	Nottingham Forest	Wembley	Simod Cup Final	3–4

Everton met Nottingham Forest in the final of the Simod Cup at Wembley, with the day out at least attracting a crowd of 46,606 on the day. They were treated to a thrilling final, one of the best in the competition's much maligned history. It was all square after 90 minutes at 2–2, and there were a further three goals in extra time. Unfortunately, two of these were scored by Nottingham Forest, thus giving them something of a domestic double for the season, for they had already won the League/Littlewoods Cup. Still, Everton more than played their part in the entertaining 4–3 match, with their goals coming from Graeme Sharp and a double strike for Tony Cottee.

| 1994 | Leeds United | A | FA Premier League | 0–3 |

MAY 1ST

| 1902 | Glasgow Rangers | H | British League Cup Semi-Final | 1–1 |

On April 5th England had met Scotland at Ibrox, a game that had attracted a massive crowd at Rangers' stadium. Tragically part of a stand had collapsed, killing 26 people and injuring over 500 others. Almost immediately a fund was set up to raise money for the dependants of the disaster, and a British League Cup was organised, with Everton drawn at home to Rangers in the semi-final. In front of a crowd of 8,000 at Goodison Park, the two teams drew 1–1, necessitating a replay at Celtic Park.

1920	Preston North End	H	First Division	1–1
1926	Bolton Wanderers	A	First Division	2–0
1935	Sheffield Wednesday	H	First Division	2–2
1943	Tranmere Rovers	A	Football League North (Second Championship)	1–1
1948	Bolton Wanderers	A	First Division	0–0
1962	Arsenal	A	First Division	3–2
1971	Crystal Palace	A	First Division	0–2
1974	Glasgow Rangers	H	Friendly	2–1
1979	West Bromwich Albion	H	First Division	0–2
1982	Swansea City	A	First Division	3–1
1993	Arsenal	H	FA Premier League	0–0

MAY 2ND

| 1925 | Leeds United | H | First Division | 1–0 |

1928 Everton won the League title without kicking a ball; Huddersfield's 3–0 defeat at Villa Park meant Everton could not be caught at the top of the table.

| 1931 | Preston North End | A | Second Division | 1–2 |

Preston North End had been the first visitors to Goodison Park for Everton's very first Second Division League match the previous September; now Everton were to wave farewell to the division with a trip to Deepdale. Although Preston won 2–1 (George Martin scoring Everton's goal), Everton had already clinched the League title, finishing seven points ahead of West Bromwich Albion in second place. However, Martin's goal was Everton's 121st of the season, a record haul for the club.

1936	Preston North End	H	First Division	5–0
1942	West Bromwich Albion	H	Football League North (Second Championship)	1–5
1972	Nottingham Forest	H	First Division	1–1
1981	Birmingham City	A	First Division	1–1
1983	Coventry City	H	First Division	1–0
1987	Manchester City	H	First Division	0–0

| 1988 | Derby County | A | First Division | 0–0 |
| 1992 | Chelsea | H | First Division | 2–1 |

MAY 3RD

| 1902 | Glasgow Rangers | A | British League Cup Semi-Final Replay | 2–3 |

The British League Cup semi-final replay between Rangers and Everton was held at Celtic Park, Ibrox being still closed following the disaster of the previous month. Rangers won the game 3–2 in front of a crowd of 12,000 spectators.

| 1919 | Glasgow Rangers | H | Friendly | 4–3 |
| 1930 | Sunderland | H | First Division | 4–1 |

The situation at the bottom of the table going into the final game of the season couldn't have been tighter; just four points separated seven clubs who could conceivably be relegated. Everton, who were at home to Sunderland, were in a precarious position, one point behind both Burnley and Sheffield United and two adrift of Newcastle United and Grimsby Town, but all their rivals faced difficult matches; Burnley were at home to second placed Derby County, Sheffield United were at Manchester United, themselves only just safe, Grimsby had to go to Huddersfield and Newcastle were at home to West Ham. A crowd of 51,132 were at Goodison Park for the visit of Sunderland, all confident that Everton would do their part and that other results would go their way and move them away from the trapdoor. Tommy White got a hat-trick as Everton tore into their opponents, with Tommy Johnson adding another in a 4–1 win. But events elsewhere conspired against them; Burnley hammered Derby 6–2, Sheffield United trounced Manchester United at Old Trafford 5–1, Grimsby and Newcastle both registered 1–0 wins in their games. Not only was it a quite unbelievable finish to the season (Sheffield United's win enabled them to escape relegation ahead of Burnley on goal average), it also condemned Everton to the Second Division for the first time in their history, the last of the original 12 founding members of the Football League to lose their First Division status (although two of the 12, Aston Villa and Blackburn Rovers, had never actually played in the Second Division; both had been relegated and then re–elected when the First Division had been extended). Two seasons previously virtually the same team had been League champions!

1933	Sheffield United	H	First Division	1–0
1941	Burnley	H	North Regional League	0–2
1980	Brighton & Hove Albion	A	First Division	0–0
1986	Southampton	H	First Division	6–1
1989	Liverpool	H	First Division	0–0

Everton and Liverpool were due to meet in the FA Cup final at the end of the season, but the League meeting at Goodison was not seen as a trial run, for it was Liverpool's first competitive game since the Hillsborough disaster. Manager Colin Harvey pointed out in his programme notes 'Football people round the country have always marvelled at the way Everton and Liverpool supporters could gather together as both friends and rivals at derby matches. This was a special quality in happy times, and in the last two and a half weeks it has been a great strength in tragedy.' The crowd of 45,994 hushed before the game in memory of the dead and then the two teams cancelled themselves out in a 0–0 draw; the cup final clash would be a rather more entertaining affair.

1995	Chelsea	H	FA Premier League	3–3
1997	Sunderland	A	FA Premier League	0–3
1998	Arsenal	A	FA Premier League	0–4

MAY 4TH

1929	Newcastle United	A	First Division	0–2
1932	Newcastle United	A	First Division	0–0
1935	Birmingham City	A	First Division	3–2
1940	Rochdale	H	War League Cup	5–1
1946	Bury	A	Football League North	1–3
1949	Wolverhampton Wanderers	H	First Division	1–0
1955	Aston Villa	H	First Division	0–1
1963	Bolton Wanderers	H	First Division	1–0
1966	Leicester City	A	First Division	0–3
1968	Stoke City	H	First Division	3–0
1977	Leeds United	A	First Division	0–0
1981	Wolverhampton Wanderers	A	First Division	0–0
1982	Leeds United	H	First Division	1–0
1985	Sheffield Wednesday	A	First Division	1–0
1987	Norwich City	A	First Division	1–0

An uncustomary strike from Pat Van den Hauwe, his only goal of the season, was enough to beat Norwich City at Carrow Road and clinch the League title for Everton, thus pipping rivals Liverpool. It was Everton's second title in three seasons and enabled the city of Liverpool to maintain a period of domination in the English game never previously seen, for between 1982 and 1988, the League trophy resided at either Anfield or Goodison Park.

1991	Luton Town	H	First Division	1–0
1993	Sheffield United	H	FA Premier League	0–2

MAY 5TH

1923	Preston North End	A	First Division	2–2
1928	Arsenal	H	First Division	2–3

In many respects Everton were surprise champions in 1927–28, for Huddersfield had seemingly got the title wrapped up a month before and were on their way to a possible double. As we have already seen, the tension of their position and the strain of playing so many games in such a short space of time finally wrecked Huddersfield's chances in both competitions, for they finished the season empty handed. Dixie Dean's achievements in the same season are well documented, but it was perhaps only on the final day of the season that the game at large showed interest in whether he might overtake George Camsell's record. With Everton already crowned League champions, the pressure to win was off, but a crowd of 48,715 came to witness the handing over of the trophy and watch history unfold. Arsenal were the opponents, a side now managed by the great Herbert Chapman and who believed in using a solid defence as the springboard for attack (his tactics were to reach their zenith in the following decade), and it was they who took the lead after just two minutes. Dean levelled the score inside a minute to take his tally to 58 for the season, and three minutes later drew level with Camsell from the penalty spot, converting the kick after he himself had been brought down in the area. Everton's desire to assist Dean in his record attempt caused problems, for with every ball and cross seeking out him out, Arsenal were able to exploit the spaces created elsewhere, equalising ten minutes before half-time. The second half was a mixture of emotions for both the crowd and the players, for almost everyone inside the ground was willing Dean to score, but with time rapidly running out it seemed as though the chance had gone. Then, with barely eight minutes to go, Everton won a corner after George Martin had had a shot turned away by Patterson. Alec Troup took the kick, flighting the ball into the area and Dean rose above all others to head home his 60th goal of the season. The ground erupted to hail their hero, and even an Arsenal equaliser with barely seconds left could not dampen the enthusiasm. Indeed, their goal allowed the Arsenal players time to go and warmly shake Dixie Dean's hand in recognition of his feat in the lull that ensued! It was a magnificent way to end the season, for both player and club, and not surprisingly his record has not been troubled since.

1934	Aston Villa	H	First Division	2–2
1945	Accrington Stanley	A	Football League North (Second Championship)	1–1
1951	Sheffield Wednesday	A	First Division	0–6

Everton had flirted with relegation all season, with only four League wins since the New Year giving the supporters little to cheer. There was hope that they might still escape, for both Sheffield Wednesday and Chelsea had been equally erratic. Going into the final game of the season Everton had 32 points, Chelsea and Sheffield Wednesday 30, and all Everton had to do was avoid defeat at Hillsborough to ensure First Division football was welcomed at Goodison Park in 1951–52. With Wednesday needing to rely on Bolton getting a good result at Stamford Bridge against Chelsea and overcome Everton themselves, the stage was set for a dramatic finish to the season. A crowd of 41,303 were at Hillsborough to watch the drama unfold, with Wednesday hammering Everton 6–0 to condemn the visitors to a return to the Second Division. News of Chelsea's 4–0 win hushed the crowd, for it meant both Everton and Sheffield Wednesday were relegated on goal average.

1979	Tottenham Hotspur	A	First Division	1–1
1984	Manchester United	H	First Division	1–1
1986	West Ham United	H	First Division	3–1
1990	Aston Villa	H	First Division	3–3
1996	Aston Villa	H	FA Premier League	1–0

MAY 6TH

1922	Burnley	H	First Division	2–0
1933	Wolverhampton Wanderers	A	First Division	2–4
1939	Grimsby Town	A	First Division	0–3

Despite a 3–0 defeat at Grimsby Town Everton were already confirmed as League champions for the fifth time in their history, finishing four points ahead of Wolves in second place. Everton were to remain reigning champions for the next eight years, for the Football League was abandoned after only three games of the 1939–40 season owing to the Second World War. Interestingly, Everton were also League champions when the Football League was abandoned during the First World War, which must make the statesmen of the world somewhat nervous whenever the League trophy arrives at Goodison Park!

| 1950 | Manchester City | H | First Division | 3–1 |

| 1967 | Aston Villa | A | First Division | 4–2 |

1981   Gordon Lee was sacked as manager of Everton after four years in the position. He had joined in January 1977 and had taken the club to the League Cup final at the end of his first season in charge, but results since then had been disappointing, prompting the chairman to announce in April that the position of the manager and his staff were under review.

| 1985 | Queens Park Rangers | H | First Division | 2–0 |

A 2–0 win over Queens Park Rangers at Goodison confirmed Everton were to finish the season as League champions, although the matter had not been in much doubt for quite a few weeks. It was the eighth time Everton had been champions, a tally bettered only by their rivals across Stanley Park, who were the reigning champions. With the League title won, the dreamed of treble was still on course, for there were still the finals of the FA Cup and European Cup-Winners' Cup to come.

| 1989 | Norwich City | A | First Division | 0–1 |
| 1995 | Southampton | H | FA Premier League | 0–0 |

MAY 7TH

| 1905 | Tottenham Hotspur | Vienna | Friendly | 2–0 |
| 1932 | Portsmouth | H | First Division | 0–1 |

Going into the final game of the season Everton were already assured of the League title, being four points ahead of Arsenal in second place. Thus a 24,011 crowd arrived at Goodison Park expecting something of a carnival as the club celebrated its fourth championship. Visitors Portsmouth however acted as party poopers, returning to Fratton Park with a 1–0 win. Arsenal's 4–0 demolition of Blackburn ensured the final gap between the two sides would be two points.

1938	Derby County	H	First Division	1–1
1949	Bolton Wanderers	A	First Division	0–1
1963	West Bromwich Albion	A	First Division	4–0

1965   Norman Whiteside born in Belfast. Spotted by Manchester United whilst playing schools football in Belfast, he was signed as an apprentice in June 1981 and made his League debut in May 1982. That summer he was one of the stars of the Northern Ireland side that played in the World Cup finals in Spain, and his assured performances in midfield belied his tender years. His appearance made him the youngest player to have played in the World Cup finals, beating the previous record held by Pele. The following season he became the youngest player to have scored in a League Cup final (which he did against Liverpool), the youngest player to score in an FA Cup final (against Brighton) and the first player to score in the finals of both major cup competitions in the same season. Two years later he scored the winner in the FA Cup final against Everton to deprive them of a treble. A string of injuries in 1988–89 was followed by a £750,000 move to Everton in August 1989, but his time at Goodison Park was blighted as he struggled to overcome a knee injury, and in June 1991 he announced his retirement. After a brief spell as assistant manager at Northwich Victoria he resigned in order to concentrate on physiotherapy.

| 1971 | Stoke City | Selhurst Park | FA Cup 3rd/4th Place Play-Off | 3–2 |

A crowd of just 5,031 were at Selhurst Park for the FA Cup third and fourth place play-off between Everton and Stoke. The short-lived idea of having the two beaten semifinalists had been a good one for the likes of Watford the previous season, making their first appearance in the semi-final, but for the likes of Stoke and Everton, being reminded that they had lost was hardly likely to invoke much enthusiasm. Stoke won on the night 3–2, with Everton's goals coming from Alan Whittle and Alan Ball.

1977	Coventry City	H	First Division	1–1
1983	Luton Town	A	First Division	5–1
1984	Aston Villa	A	First Division	2–0
1988	Arsenal	H	First Division	1–2
1994	Wimbledon	H	FA Premier League	3–2

Twenty minutes after the start of the final game of the season, Everton were effectively dead and buried and all but relegated, 2–0 down at home to Wimbledon. It had been a depressing season, one which had seen the club go into free fall down the League. Before the game, Everton were in the final relegation position with 41 points, one behind Sheffield United, Ipswich and Southampton. A 31,233 crowd was at Goodison Park to will them on, but despite what was at stake, Wimbledon out fought and out thought them in the opening exchanges, taking a 2–0 lead thanks to Holdsworth from the penalty spot and a Gary Ablett own goal. Somehow, Everton found the will to survive and started to claw their way back, goals from Graham Stuart and Barry Horne drawing them level. The news from elsewhere wasn't good, for all three rivals were also drawing, so only a win for Everton would be enough. Nine minutes from time Graham Stuart netted again for Everton to win the game 3–2. With both Ipswich and Southampton drawing, the win was enough to take Everton out of danger, Sheffield United conceded two goals in the closing stages of their match at Chelsea and went down (four years later it would be Chelsea who again gave Everton the kiss of life, beating Bolton to send them down in Everton's place).

MAY 8TH

1972 Everton signed Stoke City midfield player Mike Bernard for a fee of £140,000, although he was later successfully converted to the defence whilst at Goodison Park.

1981 Howard Kendall was appointed manager of Everton for the first time. A former player for the club when they won the League in 1970, he had served his managerial apprenticeship with Blackburn Rovers, and after surviving a rocky period at Goodison Park went on to lead them to some of their greater glories, including two League titles, the FA Cup and the European Cup-Winners' Cup. He resigned in 1987 in order to take over at Athletico Bilbao.

| 1982 | Wolverhampton Wanderers | H | First Division | 1–1 |
| 1985 | West Ham United | H | First Division | 3–0 |

Everton beat West Ham United at Goodison thanks to goals from Derek Mountfield (two) and Andy Gray. It was Everton's tenth consecutive win in the League, a new record for the club in a single season.

| 1991 | Derby County | A | First Division | 3–2 |
| 1993 | Manchester City | A | FA Premier League | 5–2 |

MAY 9TH

1931 Jimmy Gauld born in Aberdeen. He began his career in Ireland with Waterford, subsequently being transferred to Charlton in May 1955. He joined Everton in October

1956 for £10,500, making 23 first-team appearances before leaving for Plymouth a year later. He also played for Swindon and Mansfield but is perhaps best remembered as the main link behind the betting ring of the 1960's which fixed a number of matches. A total of ten players were found guilty of fixing matches, with Tony Kay and Peter Swan, both England international players, the biggest names. Gauld had not only set up the betting ring but was also responsible for their downfall, selling his story to a national newspaper for £7,000 and then accompanying a journalist as he confronted the others involved. Gauld was sent to prison for four years, ordered to pay court costs of £5,000 and subsequently given a life ban from football by the Football Association.

| 1942 | Manchester City | A | Football League North (Second Championship) | 0–2 |
| 1945 | Tranmere Rovers | A | Football League North (Second Championship) | 3–0 |

1953 Ted Sagar made his last appearance for the club in goal for the Liverpool Senior Cup final against Tranmere Rovers at Goodison Park.

1980	Nottingham Forest	A	First Division	0–1
1987	Luton Town	H	First Division	3–1
1995	Ipswich Town	A	FA Premier League	1–0

MAY 10TH

1919	Nottingham Forest	A	Lancashire Section/Midland Section Championship Decider	0–0
1947	Wolverhampton Wanderers	A	First Division	3–2
1977	Manchester City	A	First Division	1–1
1986	Liverpool	Wembley	FA Cup Final	1–3

After having to wait over 90 years for their first pairing in a major cup final, Everton and Liverpool met in three in the 1980's, with the 1986 clash in the FA Cup at Wembley perhaps the closest clash of the three. Not in terms of the final score, which ended 3–1 to Liverpool, but in terms of the relative standing of the two clubs. Both had gone through the 1985–86 season harbouring hopes of a domestic double, with Everton at one stage looking likeliest to retain the League title. Liverpool had snatched the title at Stamford Bridge, but it was Everton who stood in their way of the double, and their own desire for some silverware at the end of a long and hard season was just as great as Liverpool's. Gary Lineker gave Everton the lead at Wembley, outpacing Alan Hansen and taking two attempts at beating Bruce Grobbelaar before seeing the ball nestle in the net. Thereafter Everton contained Liverpool superbly, cutting off the supply to the strikers and harassing the defenders constantly. The game changed however following an unforced error by Gary Stevens, driving the ball straight to Whelan from which Liverpool sprang an attack that resulted in Ian Rush rounding Bobby Mimms for the equaliser. Everton visibly wilted at that, and five minutes later Liverpool were ahead through Johnston. A final goal for Ian Rush six minutes from time wrapped up the scoring and proved the final nail in Everton's coffin, but they had more than played their part in an open final.

| 1989 | Manchester United | A | First Division | 2–1 |
| 1998 | Coventry City | H | FA Premier League | 1–1 |

An almost total collapse towards the end of the season had left Everton staring at relegation once more, and again matters were not all in the hands of the men from Goodison. They were one point behind Bolton, with Barnsley and Crystal Palace already down, in the final relegation place going into the final game of the season. They needed to win against Coventry City, who 12 months previously had gone through exactly the same traumatic end to a season, and hope that Bolton took less than the full points on offer. The only way a draw would work to Everton's advantage was if Bolton lost, and they had already shown they were more than capable of getting a result when it mattered. The days leading up to the game were particularly tense, with manager Howard Kendall publicly stating that he hoped Chelsea would field their strongest possible team, even though the Londoners were due to play in the European Cup-Winners' Cup final on the following Wednesday. In the event Chelsea did and gave their supporters a winning end to the season. Meanwhile, at Goodison Park, Everton nearly did the unthinkable and throw the game away, going ahead 1–0 through Gareth Farrelly and then being pegged back in their own half. The news that Chelsea were ahead filtered around the ground and probably affected the players, for Everton appeared to lose concentration, allowed Coventry to equalise and nearly gifted them a winner! There again, it had been that kind of season.

MAY 11TH

1940 Rochdale   A   War League Cup   2–4

1944 Andy Rankin born in Liverpool. Signed by Everton as a junior he was on the verge of quitting the game in order to become a policeman when he was persuaded to concentrate on goalkeeping by Harry Catterick. Injuries restricted his appearances for Everton to just over 100 in ten years with the club and he was sold to Watford for £20,000 in November 1971. After nearly 300 League appearances for the Vicarage Road club he was sold to Huddersfield Town.

1963 Fulham   H   First Division   4–1
Everton completed their season with a 4–1 win over Fulham at Goodison Park thanks to a Roy Vernon hat-trick and Alex Scott. This ensured Everton had been unbeaten at home throughout the campaign, with their 21 games delivering 14 wins and seven draws. At the end of the game everyone in the 60,578 waited for news of Spurs' result at Manchester City; City's 1–0 win ended the last remaining challenge to Everton and meant they were champions again for the first time since 1938–39.

1968 West Ham United   A   First Division   1–1

1985 Nottingham Forest   A   First Division   0–1
Nottingham Forest won 1–0 at the City Ground and brought to a halt a run of 10 consecutive wins in the League, a record for the club in one season.

1986 When Everton and Liverpool battled through to the FA Cup final it was decided that the two teams would parade around the city the day after, irrespective of who had actually won the cup. This, with hindsight, proved to be a wrong move, for both sides had the chance of winning the double and, should one of them end up empty handed, their players would hardly be in the mood for celebrating. As it turned out, it was Everton who were to finish the season with little to show for their efforts, and for the Everton players on the open-topped bus that drove around the city, the whole event was perhaps the biggest anti-climax of their lives. Peter Reid didn't turn up, for which he was fined by manager Howard Kendall, but probably all of the Everton squad would gladly have put their hands in their pockets rather than endure the misery of being paraded in front of a sea of red and white. That a fair few Everton fans turned out as well hardly made the day any better.

1987	Tottenham Hotspur	H	First Division	1–0
1991	Queens Park Rangers	A	First Division	1–1
1997	Chelsea	H	FA Premier League	1–2

MAY 12TH

1930 Harry Leyland born in Liverpool. He joined Everton as a junior and graduated through the ranks, signing professional forms in August 1950. He spent six years trying for a regular spot in goal but left in August 1956 for Blackburn, going on to make 166 appearances for the Ewood Park club before moving to Tranmere Rovers where he finished his career.

1945 Alan Ball born in Farnworth. He began his career with Blackpool in 1962 and made 162 appearances for the Seasiders before joining Everton for a six-figure sum in August 1966, by which time he was holder of a World Cup winner's medal. He won a League championship medal with Everton and then in December 1971 joined Arsenal for £220,000, then the biggest transfer fee in Britain. After five years with Arsenal he joined Southampton and gave them near on four years good service before landing his first managerial post with his first club, Blackpool. After he was sacked he returned briefly to playing with Southampton before trying his hand at management once again, this time with better results. He returned Portsmouth to the First Division in 1988 (although they went straight back down) and performed a financial miracle at Exeter before accepting an offer to team up with Lawrie McMenemy at Southampton in 1994, going on to Maine Road and Manchester City and finally returning to Fratton Park. In all he won 72 caps for England between 1965 and 1975.

| 1945 | Accrington Stanley | H | Football League North (Second Championship) | 0–2 |
| 1984 | Queens Park Rangers | H | First Division | 3–1 |

MAY 13TH

1937 Tony Kay born in Sheffield. He spent nine years with local club Sheffield Wednesday and had developed into one of the best wing halves in the game during his time at Hillsborough. In December 1962 he was transferred to Everton for £55,000, helping the club win the title at the end of his first season at Goodison. He also won one cap for England and seemed on the verge of greatness when he was embroiled in the greatest scandal to hit football since 1915. In April 1964 the Sunday People accused him, Peter Swan and David Layne, all of whom had been team-mates at Sheffield Wednesday, of having been bribed to throw the match against Ipswich Town on December 1st 1962 (Ipswich won 2–0 at Portman Road, although Kay was named man of the match!). Before even the FA could react to the accusations the three players, along with others involved in what transpired to be a betting syndicate, were brought before the courts and given prison sentences ranging from four months to four years. All were then banned for life from the game by the Football Association, although one of the players concerned, Brian Phillips, successfully appealed against the ban in 1971 and later led a side to the FA Vase Final. For Tony Kay, however, it was the end of his career. When Kay had served his sentence he remained in Liverpool for a while and even became a bookmaker before emigrating to Spain.

| 1967 | Burnley | A | First Division | 1–1 |
| 1989 | West Ham United | H | First Division | 3–1 |

MAY 14TH

1966　Sheffield Wednesday　　Wembley FA Cup Final　　　　　3–2

Drama hit the FA Cup final even before Everton and Sheffield Wednesday strode out at Wembley, with Harry Catterick's decision to select Mike Trebilcock in preference to Fred Pickering, having claimed that Pickering had been injured and not fully recovered. Trebilcock was relatively unknown at the time, having played only seven League and one cup match for Everton, but come the end of the game he was to have achieved national recognition. It was Wednesday who started stronger, taking the lead after only four minutes, McCalliog's shot deflecting off Ray Wilson into the net. Just short of the hour Wednesday went further ahead and Everton seemed dead and buried, but this seemed to be the signal for Mike Trebilcock to justify his selection. Two minutes after Ford's goal for Wednesday he grabbed one back for Everton when he reacted first after Temple's header had been partially saved by Ron Springett. Five minutes later Trebilcock levelled the scores with a low drive and the initiative had now passed to Everton. Ten minutes from time Derek Temple collected the ball after George Young had failed to control and tore off towards the Wednesday goal. As Springett came out to try and cover the threat, Temple slotted the ball through for a dramatic winner.

1969	Leicester City	A	First Division	1–1
1977	Birmingham City	A	First Division	1–1
1983	Ipswich Town	H	First Division	1–1
1984	West Ham United	A	First Division	1–0
1995	Coventry City	A	FA Premier League	0–0

MAY 15TH

1935　Brian Harris born in Bebbington. Discovered whilst playing for Port Sunlight and signed by Everton in January 1954 he went on to make over 350 appearances for the first team over the next 12 years. In that time he had appeared in every position bar goalkeeper, as adaptable a player as Everton have ever signed. A member of the title winning team in 1963 and the FA Cup-Winning side of 1966, he was transferred to Cardiff City for £15,000 in October 1966. He finished his playing career with Newport County.

1973　Everton were reported to be interested in Don Revie as their new manager in place of Harry Catterick. They ultimately chose former player Billy Bingham.

1982　Aston Villa　　　　　A　　　First Division　　　　　　2–1

1985　Rapid Vienna　　　　Rotterdam European Cup-Winners' Cup Final　　3–1

Everton had already won the League championship, were through to the final of the FA Cup, of which they were holders, and also through to their first European final in the European Cup-Winners' Cup. Having disposed of Bayern Munich in the semi-final the main rival for the trophy had seemingly been removed, but there was still the little matter of actually beating Rapid Vienna to ensure the glory. The Austrians were not a bad side, as their run to the final in Rotterdam had shown, but on the night Everton were simply irresistible, utilising their aerial advantage with a succession of high balls into the penalty area for Graeme Sharp and Andy Gray to wreak havoc. Everton were unlucky to have a perfectly good goal disallowed shortly before half-time, Derek Mountfield being adjudged to be offside when replays showed this might have been a mistake. The second half, however, belonged to Everton, with Gray latching on to a pass from Sharp to open the scoring after 57 minutes. Trevor Steven added a second on 72 minutes and that seemed to be it, but Rapid showed some spirit in grabbing a goal back. Then Kevin Sheedy made it all safe with a third goal and the celebrations could begin in earnest. According to Rapid's Krankl 'Everton were just too good for us. It's been a long time since we played against anyone of their class. They are possibly the best side in the whole of Europe.' Sadly, Everton would not get the chance to prove Krankl's words right, for the Heysel disaster later in the month led to a banning of English clubs from Europe, but for the time being the vast travelling army in the crowd of 50,000 were celebrating one of the greatest nights in the club's history.

1989   Derby County   H   First Division   1–0

MAY 16TH

1905   Tottenham Hotspur   Prague   Friendly   1–0
1942   Manchester City   H   Football League North (Second Championship) 6–1
Tommy Lawton grabbed a hat-trick and Frank Soo scored twice in the 6–1 win over Manchester City at Goodison Park. Everton's other goal was scored by Anderson.
1967   Sunderland   H   First Division   4–1
Johnny Morrissey waited until the final game of the season to score his only hat-trick of the campaign but it enabled Everton to sign off with a flourish. The other goal was scored by Colin Harvey in front of a crowd of 30,943.
1977   West Bromwich Albion H   First Division   1–1

MAY 17TH

1919   Nottingham Forest   H   Lancashire Section/Midland Section   0–1
                                         Championship Decider
Everton had gone through the Lancashire Section Principal Tournament with a record second to none, winning 27 games, drawing two and losing just once, against Manchester City. As a result they finished top of the League and qualified for a two legged play-off against Nottingham Forest, the winners of the Midland Section league. The first leg at the City Ground had ended a goalless draw, and a 1–0 win for Forest at Goodison enabled them to win 1–0 on aggregate.
1941   Oldham Athletic   A   North Regional League   1–1

MAY 18TH

1940   Stoke City   H   War League Cup   1–0
1962   Barry Horne born in St Asaph. He began his professional career with Wrexham and helped them win the Welsh FA Cup before moving to Portsmouth in 1987. Two years later he moved along the south coast, signing for Southampton for £700,000 and three years later switched to Goodison Park for £675,000. A member of the side that won the FA Cup in 1995 he then moved on to Birmingham City for £250,000 in 1996.
1968   West Bromwich Albion Wembley FA Cup Final   0–1
Two years after winning the FA Cup in such thrilling fashion against Sheffield Wednesday, Everton were back at Wembley to take on West Bromwich Albion. League form suggested Everton might just shade it, but West Bromwich Albion had been beaten at Wembley the previous season in the League Cup final (against Third Division Queens Park Rangers) and would therefore be going out for revenge. It turned out to be something of a dull final that rarely lived up to expectations, and it was almost a relief

when Jeff Astle scored in extra time to win the cup for West Bromwich Albion, thereby saving everyone having to sit through a replay.

1985   Manchester United   Wembley FA Cup Final   0–1

Football matches can turn on almost anything; offside decisions that result in goals being awarded or disallowed are the usual reasons why one team or another has bounced back, determined to right an injustice. The FA Cup final between Everton and Manchester United is somewhat unique, for it is probably the only major cup final to have changed as a result of a sending off. Everton's Peter Reid had knocked the ball into open space just behind the United defence when he was upended by Kevin Moran. It was not a vicious tackle, worthy of a booking at most, but the referee decided that Reid would have had a clear run on goal and for that Moran had to go. It took a while before Moran actually left the field, the very first player to be sent off in an FA Cup final, but the incident served only to galvanise United, for Everton never got a chance to make the one man advantage count. A stunning goal from Norman Whiteside settled the game in United's favour, and although Everton were a dejected side when they trooped off the field, they could still hold their heads high, for they had already won the League championship and the European Cup-Winners' Cup that season. There would be other opportunities to put the FA Cup final against Manchester United right.

MAY 19TH

1945   Stoke City   A   Football League North (Second Championship) 1–5
1977   Sunderland   H   First Division   2–0
1984   Watford   Wembley FA Cup Final   2–0

Everton's season had been heading for disaster earlier in the campaign, with only a fortunate equaliser in the Milk Cup match with Oxford supposedly having saved Howard Kendall's job at Goodison Park. The club had not looked back from there, reaching the final of the Milk Cup (which they lost against Liverpool in a replay) and now the FA Cup final. Their opponents were Watford, making their first appearance at Wembley and likely to cause an upset on the day. That said, the result was of paramount importance to Everton, more important even than the performance, and whilst the final was hardly a classic, winning the cup would provide a springboard for greater glories. So it proved, with Graeme Sharp giving Everton the lead and Andy Gray being credited with a second, although action replays of the incident showed him heading the back of the goalkeeper's hand rather than the ball. For once, victory was all.

MAY 20TH

1989   Liverpool   Wembley FA Cup Final   2–3

Back in 1953, it had been the will of the nation that Stanley Matthews collect an FA Cup winners' medal for Blackpool against Bolton, which he ultimately did. Five years later Bolton again had almost the entire country against them when they had lined up in the final against Manchester United, still recovering from the Munich disaster. And in 1989, it was Liverpool who carried all of the neutrals in their FA Cup final against Everton following the Hillsborough disaster. As Everton captain Kevin Ratcliffe said 'The final was disappointing for us because the things that went on were all Liverpool, Liverpool, Liverpool . . . it wasn't a joint day. We all felt for Hillsborough and I did my bit by raising money for them, but football's something I get paid for doing and I want to achieve as much as I can. I felt they had a goal start already – we were in a no-win situation that day.' That said, Everton more than played their part in making the final the exhibition it should be. A full house of 82,800 were present, with the barriers taken down (and one or two over-excited fans did run on to the pitch during the proceedings) in light of the Hillsborough disaster. Liverpool didn't need a goal start; they scored with their very first attack through John Aldridge, though Everton were not without chances of their own throughout the rest of the half. It was the introduction of Stuart McCall that started to change things in Everton's favour, and with barely seconds left McCall shot home a dramatic equaliser to send the game into extra time. Liverpool's Kenny Dalglish sent on his talisman Ian Rush, who carried on his love/hate relationship with Everton by putting Liverpool ahead, but McCall volleyed home a second equaliser and thus became the first substitute to have scored two goals in an FA Cup final. Unfortunately for him, Ian Rush was to equal the feat barely minutes later, and it was his strike that was to prove decisive and win the cup for Liverpool at 3–2.

1995   Manchester United   Wembley FA Cup Final   1–0
Everton had denied the public the so-called dream final between Manchester United and Spurs with their excellent performance in the semi-final; now they were out to deny United the cup. It was United's misfortune to finish the season second in both the FA Cup and Premier League, for Paul Rideout's goal on the half–hour exacted revenge for the final defeat of 1985 and won Joe Royle his first honour as Everton manager.

MAY 21ST

1944   Southport   A   Football League North (Second Championship) 1–1
1945   Tranmere Rovers   H   Football League North (Second Championship) 4–1
1968   Fulham   H   First Division   5–1
Despite finishing the season in fifth place in the First Division, Everton failed to qualify for European competition the following season. This was as a direct result of the 'one club per city' ruling then in force, which meant that Liverpool in third place kept out Everton, Chelsea in sixth position kept out Spurs and Newcastle, in tenth place 17 points behind the champions Manchester City and with a record indicative of a side in mid-table, qualified for the Inter-Cities Fairs Cup! Even though Newcastle went on to win the competition in 1968–69, it soon became apparent that the ruling was a nonsense, rewarding clubs for their geography rather than their accomplishments on the field. Despite the injustice, Everton went out in style with John Hurst scoring twice and Alan Ball, John Morrissey and Joe Royle scoring against a Fulham side already condemned to the Second Division.

MAY 22ND

1940   Wrexham   H   War Regional League, Western Division   1–2
1944   Southport   H   Liverpool Cup   0–1
1946   Howard Kendall born in Ryton-on-Tyne. One of the finest servants the club has ever had, he began his playing career with Preston North End and became the youngest player to have appeared in an FA Cup final in 1964 against West Ham (the record was subsequently broken in 1980 by Paul Allen playing for West Ham!) in a match the Hammers won 3–2. He was transferred to Everton for £80,000 in March 1967 and helped the club win the 1970 League championship, forming an excellent midfield partnership with Colin Harvey and Alan Ball. He left Everton for Birmingham City in February 1974 and then for Stoke in 1977 as well as also playing for Blackburn Rovers

before taking over as manager at Ewood Park. He first became manager of Everton in May 1981, replacing Gordon Lee, and after a hesitant start went on to guide the club to some of their finest moments, including the 1984 FA Cup and the League and European Cup-Winners' Cup the following season. After narrowly missing out on the double in 1986 he took Everton to the League title for a second time in 1987 and then sensationally agreed to become manager of Athletic Bilbao. In 1990 he became manager of Manchester City, but soon after accepted a second call to take over at Goodison Park, remaining in charge until 1993. In 1997, with the vacancy having been turned down by a number of other contenders, he was appointed for a third term, this ending at the end of the season in which Everton had only narrowly missed relegation. Although the media speculated that the board had already decided to dismiss him (which the board did not deny, thereby making his position somewhat untenable) and were attempting to lure other managers to the club, Howard Kendall kept a dignified silence. In June 1998 his contract was cancelled by mutual consent.

MAY 23RD

| 1985 | Liverpool | H | First Division | 1–0 |

The title was already won, the FA Cup lost and the European Cup-Winners' Cup had its place in the Everton trophy room, but still only 15,045 fans came out to see the Merseyside derby with Liverpool, one of three games in five days the club had to complete in order to finish the season. Paul Wilkinson scored his first goal of the season to settle one of the least remembered derby matches of the series. The three points took Everton to a points tally of 90, 13 ahead of both Liverpool and Spurs, and the first time such a tally had been recorded in the First Division since the introduction of three points for a win.

MAY 24TH

1941	Sheffield United	H	North Regional League	3–3
1947	Charlton Athletic	H	First Division	1–1
1977	Newcastle United	H	First Division	2–0

Victory over Newcastle stretched Everton's unbeaten run at the end of the season to six games and lifted them into ninth place in the table, 15 points behind champions Liverpool. It was something of an anti-climax after the cup exploits of the campaign, with the League Cup final having been reached for the first time and the semi-final of the FA Cup for a record 17th time. Goals from Martin Dobson and Duncan McKenzie at least allowed Everton to sign off on a winning note.

MAY 25TH

| 1940 | Fulham | A | War League Cup | 2–5 |

The first two rounds of the War League Cup had been decided over two legs, with Everton disposing of Preston and then Rochdale on aggregate before entering the straight knock-out phase. Victory over Stoke took Everton to the fourth round to face Fulham at Craven Cottage, but despite goals from Torry Gillick and Tommy Lawton, Fulham, scored five times to reach the semi-finals. There they were beaten by the eventual winners West Ham.

| 1984 | | | | |

Everton paid Sunderland £425,000 to bring Paul Bracewell to Goodison Park having previously tried to sign him when he moved from Stoke City in July 1983.

MAY 26TH

1945	Stoke City	H	Football League North (Second Championship)	3–2
1947	Leeds United	H	First Division	4–1
1985	Coventry City	A	First Division	1–4

Whilst Everton's title win had been achieved on the back of a run of ten straight wins and 20 matches without defeat (two draws had punctuated eight straight wins and then ten wins), Coventry had been offered a chance of First Division salvation if they were to win three straight matches, something they had proved incapable of from August through to the end of April. The corner had been turned in mid-May, and victories over already doomed Stoke and safe Luton meant they went into their final game, against Everton, needing a win and nothing else to escape relegation. The final result brought raised eyebrows in Norfolk as Coventry's 4–1 win condemned Norwich to the drop, but Everton had put the effort in when it really mattered. Paul Wilkinson scored his second goal of the season by way of consolation for Everton.

MAY 27TH

1964   Fred Pickering scored three times on his England debut as the United States were swamped 10–0, the last occasion in which an English debutant has scored as many as three goals. Pickering went on to collect a further two caps the following year, against Northern Ireland and Belgium and scored an additional two goals for his country.

MAY 28TH

1973   Former player Billy Bingham was appointed manager of Everton, replacing the retiring Harry Catterick after 12 years in the post. Bingham would remain at the club just four years before being sacked.

1985	Luton Town	A	First Division	0–2

Everton's 2–0 defeat at Kenilworth Road may have made little difference to the destination of the League title, but the club missed the chance to extend the points tally beyond the 90 mark. Still, Everton could look back at a season that had delivered the League title and European Cup-Winners' Cup and a runners-up placing in the FA Cup. There was every reason to believe that the side could go on from this success and pose a serious threat for the European Cup the following season. Sadly, the events in Belgium the following evening meant they never got the chance.

MAY 29TH

1934   Mick Meagon born in Dublin. He joined Everton in September 1952 and became a full professional 18 months later, making his debut in august 1957. He remained at Goodison for seven seasons before being part of the deal that brought Ray Wilson from Huddersfield. He made over 110 appearances for the Leeds Road club before finishing his career with Halifax. He was capped on 17 occasions by Eire.

1940	Stockport County	A	War Regional League, Western Division	2–1

1949   Brian Kidd born in Manchester. Although he served each and everyone of his five clubs with distinction, his name will forever be linked with just one: Manchester United. He was a member of the side that won the European Cup in 1968, scoring on what was his 19th birthday. He remained at Old Trafford until 1974 when he joined Arsenal, but returned to Manchester, this time with City in 1976. He joined Everton in March 1979 but by then his better days were behind him and 14 months later he was on the move again, this time to Bolton. He joined the coaching staff at Old Trafford, later being appointed assistant manager to Alex Ferguson, and has thus far resisted all attempts by other clubs to lure him away as a manager in his own right. This includes two of his former clubs, for both Manchester City and Everton have approached him with a view to taking over at either Maine Road or Goodison Park.

1985 Having won the League championship and European Cup-Winners' Cup in 1984–85 Everton were eagerly looking forward to taking on the best of Europe again in the forthcoming season, this time in the European Cup. Their performances during the campaign, especially in overcoming Bayern Munich at the semi-final stage, led many to the opinion that Everton would blaze a trail through Europe and emulate the achievements on Manchester United, Nottingham Forest, Aston Villa and Liverpool by lifting the European Cup. Sadly they never got a chance to put considered opinion into practice, for at the Heysel Stadium, Liverpool fans rioted before the European Cup final between their side and Juventus, resulting in the deaths of 39 people and an almost immediate indefinite ban on English clubs competing in Europe. By the time they were re–admitted and Everton had qualified, their great side of the mid 1980's had long since gone.

MAY 30TH

1906 The Football League meeting at the Holborn Restaurant in London rejected a proposal from Aston Villa, seconded by Everton, to abolish the maximum wage for players. The date could hardly have been more ironic, for on the same day a Football Association Commission was announcing the punishments on Manchester City for flaunting the very same rule!

1938 Glasgow Rangers   A   Empire Exhibition Cup 1st Round   2–0
Everton visited Ibrox to take on Glasgow Rangers in the Empire Exhibition Cup, winning 2–0 in front of a crowd of 47,692 to lift the trophy.

1942 Liverpool   A   Football League North (Second Championship) 1–4
A crowd of 13,761 were at Anfield for the final match of the season, a game which as well as counting towards the Football League North (Second Championship) was also staged as a Lancashire cup-tie. Tommy Lawton scored for Everton, whilst Liverpool's goals were netted by Done (two), Carney and Wharton.

MAY 31ST

1941 Liverpool   A   North Regional League   2–2
1947 Arsenal   A   First Division   1–2
1970 Claus Thomsen born in Aarhus in Denmark. First brought into the British game by Ipswich Town, he cost the Portman Road club £250,000 from his local Aarhus club in 1994. Three years later Joe Royle paid £900,000 to bring him to Goodison Park. He became a full Danish international with over 14 caps to his credit.

JUNE 1ST

1940 Manchester United   A   War Regional League, Western Division   3–0
Alex Stevenson scored a hat-trick as the curtain came down on the season, one of the most difficult in the League's history. Everton finished the season in third place in the League, three points behind the 'champions' Stoke and one behind Liverpool in second place

JUNE 2ND

1941 Liverpool   H   North Regional League   3–1
Everton closed the season with a home match against Liverpool in the Football League North. There was no proper League as such, with placings being decided by goal average. Everton won the game 3–1 in front of a crowd of 4,000.

1972 Everton's proposal for a 15 minute half-time break was rejected at the annual meeting of the Football League in London after it had failed to gain the required three quarters majority. The length of the half-time break had long been a thorny problem for the Football League; when the League began in 1888 there was no provision for a break at all, with the two teams expected to turn straight around and get on with the game. It is believed Preston were the first side to take a break, walking off the pitch in order to take refreshments and get a rub down from the trainer, and the half-time break had subsequently been introduced. Of course, by the 1990's the 15 minute break had been introduced (as well as three other items proposed at the 1972 meeting but rejected; three up and three down, Sunday football and a cup competition for Third and Fourth Division clubs).

JUNE 3RD

1970 With Everton having qualified for the following season's European Cup, the club announced that they would refuse to enter the League Cup in the coming campaign rather than risk getting caught in a fixture pile–up. At the time it was still possible for clubs to refuse to enter the competition, and although entry later became compulsory, by the late 1990's clubs which qualified for Europe were exempt from entry in the second round, joining in the third round.

JUNE 4TH

1976 Everton completed the joint transfer of John Hurst and Dave Irving to Oldham Athletic. Hurst had made 399 first-team appearances for the club since making his debut in 1965, whilst Irving had made only six appearances following his arrival from Workington and had spent some time on loan to Sheffield United the previous season.

JUNE 5TH

1909 Tottenham Hotspur   Palermo Friendly   2–2
Towards the end of the 1908–09 season both Everton and Spurs had accepted an invitation to undertake an end of season tour of Argentina to play two exhibition matches and a series of friendlies against local representative sides. The two English clubs met in Palermo and drew 2–2.

1972 Everton paid a fee of £80,000 for Huddersfield Town goalkeeper David Lawson, a record fee for a goalkeeper. He went on to make 150 appearances for the first team.

JUNE 6TH

1971 Manchester United were believed to be about to make a bid for Alan Ball, although Everton had already indicated that such a bid would be immediately rejected. In the event Ball did move on later on in the year but joined Arsenal.

1988 Derek Mountfield was sold to Aston Villa for £450,000 after making 139 first-team appearances, helping the club win two League titles, the FA Cup and the European Cup-Winners' Cup.

JUNE 7TH

1972   Huddersfield Town goalkeeper David Lawson joined Everton in a transfer deal worth £80,000. He went on to make 150 appearances for the club before being transferred to Luton Town in 1978.

JUNE 8TH

1972   Keith Newton was transferred to Burnley after just 58 first-team appearances for the club. Once he had left the club he attacked the managerial style of Harry Catterick in the press, claiming his creative style and inclination to play his way out of trouble had been criticised by the manager.

JUNE 9TH

1965   Harold Hardman died in Sale in Cheshire. Born in Manchester on 4th April 1882, Harold spent his entire playing career as an amateur, but was still good enough to have collected an FA Cup winners' medal with Everton in 1906, make four appearances for the full England team and win an Olympic Gold medal in the 1908 Games in London, where the English amateurs overcame their Danish counterparts 2–0. He had joined Everton from Blackpool in 1903 and spent five years at Goodison before leaving to join Manchester United, although he made only four appearances for the Old Trafford club. However, he served the club for over fifty years as a director and was chairman of the club from 1951 to 1965. He also served on the Football Association, Lancashire FA and the Central League, and was widely regarded as one of the finest administrators the game has ever seen.

JUNE 10TH

1950   Duncan McKenzie born in Grimsby. One of the most talented players of his age, he began his career with Nottingham Forest but made his name with Leeds United, where the fans delighted in his crowd-pleasing antics, although he was seldom a favourite with the management and coaching staff. He was sold to Anderlecht in Belgium but less than a season later returned to England to sign for Everton for £200,000 in December 1976. A change in management at Goodison saw his style at odds with the club and he was sold to Chelsea in September 1978 and later played for Blackburn before venturing over to America.

1964   Stuart McCall born in Leeds. He began his career with Bradford City, signing as an apprentice and going on to make over 200 League appearances before being sold to Everton. Here he became an extremely dependable midfield player and helped the club to the 1989 FA Cup final, where he scored twice after coming on as a substitute. He joined Glasgow Rangers in August 1991.

JUNE 11TH

1938   Bobby Laverick born in Trimdon. He began his professional career with Chelsea and joined Everton in February 1959, making 22 appearances on the wing for the club. He left in 1960 for Brighton and finished his career with Coventry City.

1971   Joe Parkinson born in Eccles. After graduating through the ranks with Wigan he was sold to Bournemouth for £35,000 in 1993 and quickly developed into an outstanding midfield player. A fee of £250,000 took him to Goodison Park in 1994 and he was a member of the side that won the FA Cup in 1995.

1979 Everton signed John Bailey from Blackburn Rovers, although as the two clubs could not agree a fee the matter would have to be referred to an independent tribunal.

JUNE 12TH

1945 Pat Jennings born in Newry. Of course, Pat never actually played for Everton, but he was signed as emergency cover just in case Bobby Mimms was injured before the 1986 FA Cup final, for Neville Southall was already ruled out of contention.

JUNE 13TH

1950 John Connolly born in Glasgow. After starring for St Johnstone John was signed by Everton in March 1972 for £75,000. He remained at Goodison for five seasons, suffering two broken legs during the process, but the appointment of Billy Bingham as manager spelt the end of his career with Everton. He joined Birmingham City in 1976 for £90,000 and in May 1978 switch to Newcastle United. He later returned to Scotland to play for Hibernian.

JUNE 14TH

1919 Joe Peacock joined Everton from non-League Atherton and went on to make 161 first-team appearances during the course of the almost eight years he spent with the club. He joined the club at right half but was also to play at centre-forward and inside-forward, switching back to wing half and going on to earn England recognition.

JUNE 15TH

1951 Everton upgraded Ken Rea to the professional ranks, the player having previously been with the club as a junior. He went on to make 46 appearances for the first team before moving into the non-League game.

JUNE 16TH

1858 Alex Parker was signed from Falkirk, even though he would not be available until nearer the end of the year as he was still completing his national service. Indeed, soon after signing for the club he was posted to Cyprus with the Royal Scots Fusiliers! Once back at Goodison he went on to make 219 first-team appearances.

JUNE 17TH

1995 Everton made a late bid to sign Nottingham Forest's Stan Collymore for £8.5 million but he decided to play on the other side of Stanley Park. As it turned out he failed to settle and was sold to Aston Villa within two years.

JUNE 18TH

1987 As Howard Kendall had already intimated to chairman Philip Carter that he was going to accept the offer to take over as manager of Athletic Bilbao, Everton appointed Colin Harvey to the position of manager. Harvey had already served the club as a player and coach to the youth, reserve and first team and his appointment was therefore seen as continuity for the club.

JUNE 19TH

1909 Tottenham Hotspur   Palermo Friendly   4–0

Everton and Spurs met again in Palermo whilst on their tour in Argentina, Everton running out 4–0 winners.

1987 Howard Kendall announced his resignation as manager of Everton after agreeing to take over as boss of Spanish side Athletic Bilbao, saying 'It has been a difficult decision to make but I feel that it is the right one. I have had six tremendous years at the club.' Everton had already appointed his successor at Goodison, his right hand man and former player Colin Harvey.

JUNE 20TH

1956 Peter Reid born in Huyton. The tough tackling midfield player was first introduced to League football by Bolton Wanderers and cost Everton £60,000 in December 1982. He was to become the engine room of the side that won the FA Cup, two League titles and the European Cup-Winners' Cup and also earned him a call-up for England, collecting 13 caps. He later linked up again with Howard Kendall at Manchester City, initially as a player and then becoming manager, and he is currently in charge at Sunderland. He was named the Professional Footballer's Association Player of the Year in 1985.

1963 Robert Warzycha born in Poland. Signed by Everton during the 1990–91 season from Gornik Zabrze, he made 72 League appearances for the club before being released at the end of the 1993–94 season. His most memorable goal for the club came at Wembley in the 1991 Zenith Data Systems Cup final.

JUNE 21ST

1996 Gary Ablett was sold to Birmingham City for £390,000 after spending four years at Goodison Park. He had made over 100 appearances for Everton during his time with the club and had spent a brief spell on loan to Sheffield United during his final season.

JUNE 22ND

1880 Alex Young born in Slamannan, Stirlingshire. He began his career with St Mirren and then Falkirk before joining Everton in 1901, winning an FA Cup winners' medal in 1906 (when he scored the winning goal in the final against Newcastle United) and a runners-up medal the following year. After ten years with Everton and having scored 110 League goals he transferred to Spurs in June 1911. After a bright opening, scoring on his debut (against Everton!) and hitting two goals in the following game, he failed to find the net in his next three games and was promptly dropped from the team. Rather than battle his way back Young demanded a transfer and was allowed to move back north with Manchester City. After his career ended he emigrated to Australia in 1914, but the following year he was charged with the wilful murder of his brother. Evidence was requested from the football authorities in England, who confirmed that during his playing career he had been prone to fits of temporary insanity! In June 1916 he was found guilty of manslaughter and sentenced to three years imprisonment, but was not released at the end of the term on the grounds of 'mental weakness'. It was therefore many years before he was able to return home to Scotland, where he died in 1959.

1924 Eddie Wainwright born in Southport. Spotted by Everton whilst playing for High Park he had to wait until the end of the Second World War before making his League debut. He went on to make over 200 appearances for the side, overcoming a broken leg along the way. He was transferred to Rochdale in 1956 and went on to make 100 appearances for them before retiring.

JUNE 23RD

1941 Keith Newton born in Manchester. He joined Blackburn Rovers as a junior and signed professional forms in October 1958, making over 300 League appearances for the Ewood Park club. He joined Everton for £80,000 in December 1969, helping the club win the League title at the end of his first season (although he played insufficient games to qualify for a medal). In June 1972 he was surprisingly sold to Burnley and went on to register over 200 games for them. An England international with 27 caps to his credit he died in June 1998.

JUNE 24TH

1909 Everton took the opportunity of watching two local sides in action whilst on tour in Argentina. A rather bigger crowd than anticipated turned up to watch as well, with the result that there was a minor pitch invasion. The response was swift: the Argentinian cavalry took to the field and set about the invaders with the flats of their swords! Not surprisingly, order was soon restored and the match was played without further incident.

JUNE 25TH

1968 Craig Short born in Bridlington. His early career at Scarborough marked him out as an exceptional defender and a transfer to Notts County in 1989 merely continued the rave reviews. Sold to Derby County for £2.5 million in 1992 he spent three years at the Baseball Ground before switching to Goodison Park for £2.7 million in 1995.

1998 After intense speculation surrounding his position, Howard Kendall's reign as manager of Everton was brought to an end by mutual consent, thus ending his third spell in charge of the club. Although he had managed to steer Everton clear of relegation it was known that some of the board were keen to replace him almost as soon as the final whistle went in the last game. There were rumours that a board meeting had voted him out of the post and that negotiations were already underway with a number of replacements, including Martin O'Neill of Leicester City, but there was no official word and Kendall kept a dignified silence until handing in his resignation.

JUNE 26TH

1923 Peter Corr born in Dundalk. He was spotted by Preston whilst playing for Irish side Dundalk and transferred to Deepdale in April 1947, although he made only three first-team appearances in a little over a year and was subsequently sold to Everton. He had 24 first-team outings whilst at Goodison Park, scoring two goals, and won four caps for the Republic of Ireland during his career.

JUNE 27TH

1986 Everton paid Manchester City £65,000 in order to bring captain Paul Power to Everton. It was a surprising transfer, since Power was 32 years of age and seemingly approaching the end of his playing career, but at the end of his first season at Goodison he helped the club win the League title, whilst his former club got relegated!

JUNE 28TH

1922 After just 55 first-team appearances for Everton, Charlie Crossley was sold to West Ham. He had certainly made an impact during his time at Goodison, netting 21 goals in the two years he spent with the club, and went on to help West Ham gain promotion from the Second Division at the end of his first season at Upton Park, although he missed out when the side played at Wembley in the first FA Cup final played there.

JUNE 29TH

1930 Cliff Britton was transferred from Bristol Rovers. He went on to make 240 appearances during the rest of the decade, although only one of these came in the 1938–39 season as Everton won the League and he therefore did not qualify for a medal. He returned to Goodison Park in September 1948 as manager, a position he held for eight years.

JUNE 30TH

1987 Kevin Langley was transferred to Manchester City after just 16 appearances for Everton and having spent a period on loan to the Maine Road club towards the end of the 1986–87 season.

1998 Slaven Bilic had an exceptional game as Croatia overcame Romania in the World Cup finals in France, progressing into the quarter-final to face Germany.

JULY 1ST

1996 Paul Gerrard signed from Oldham Athletic for a fee of £1 million. Gerrard had spent five years with Oldham and was seen as cover for veteran goalkeeper Neville Southall. On the same day Gary Speed arrived from Leeds United for £3.5 million.

JULY 2ND

1998 Everton had made a late bid to appoint the seemingly Sheffield Wednesday bound Walter Smith as manager in place of Howard Kendall, who had recently left the club by mutual agreement. Although the former Rangers manager (he had moved into an executive position at the end of the 1997–98 season) had spoken to Wednesday and agreed in principal to take over at Hillsborough, he did agree to speak to the Everton contingent and it was announced today that he would be the new manager at Goodison Park. What effectively sealed the deal in Everton's favour was an agreement that Smith could bring in Archie Knox as his assistant; at Wednesday he was expected to work with Peter Shreeves.

JULY 3RD

1956 After a year as a professional with Manchester City without having a first-team appearance, Alan Sanders moved to Goodison Park. He still had to wait until November 1957 before being given a first-team outing, but he went on to make 56 appearances for the club before moving on to Swansea.

JULY 4TH

1983 Trevor Steven was at Goodison Park undergoing a medical examination prior to his £300,000 move from Burnley to Everton. He successfully passed the test and went on to become a vital member of the side that won the FA Cup, European Cup-Winners' Cup and two League title before moving on to Glasgow Rangers.

JULY 5TH

1912 James Nat Cunliffe born in Blackrod. He began his career with Adlington FC and joined

Everton in 1930, breaking into the first team in 1932–33. He first broke into the side as a replacement for the injured Dixie Dean, but when Dean returned Cunliffe was moved to outside-right and provided countless chances for the legendary figure. Cunliffe could also be relied upon to weigh in with some vital goals of his own, scoring 76 for Everton in 187 first-team appearances. He won only one cap for England and at the end of the Second World War joined Rochdale, making two League appearances for them before retiring. His cousin Arthur was also a noted professional footballer, playing for Blackburn, Aston Villa, Middlesbrough and Rochdale during his career.

1925   John Willie Parker born in Birkenhead. Initially signed by Everton as an amateur he was upgraded to the professional ranks in December 1948 and became a regular in the side in 1951–52. He went on to make nearly 200 first-team appearances before switching to Gigg Lane with Bury in May 1956 where he finished his career. He died in August 1988.

1970   UEFA announced the draws for the forthcoming season's European competition, with Everton drawn against Icelandic champions Keflavik, a side not expected to present too many problems for Everton.

1985   Everton signed Leicester City striker Gary Lineker for a fee finally set by a tribunal at £800,000, some £425,000 less than Leicester had been asking for. As Everton sold him a year later for over £2 million, Leicester might well have had a point, if not the money!

JULY 6TH

1955   George Telfer born in Liverpool. After graduating through the ranks at Goodison Park he made his debut during the 1973–74 season and went to make nearly 100 appearances for the first team. He lost his place to Duncan McKenzie and after a spell in the reserves went to play in America, later returning to play for Scunthorpe United and Preston.

1988   Alan Harper was transferred to Sheffield Wednesday after making 147 League appearances for Everton, scoring four goals.

JULY 7TH

1954   Mickey Thomas born in Mochdre. He made his name with Wrexham and then earned a big money move to Manchester United, costing the Old Trafford club £330,000. Although an instant hit with the fans he seldom saw eye to eye with the management and in 1981 he was transferred to Everton, with John Gidman making the opposite move. He made barely 11 appearances for Everton before falling foul of the Goodison management and was placed on the transfer list. Sold to Brighton for £400,000 he went on to play for Stoke, Chelsea, West Bromwich Albion, Derby and Shrewsbury and finished his career back with his first club Wrexham.

1986   Everton signed striker Neil Adams from Stoke City.

JULY 8TH

1959   Imre Varadi born in London. Initially introduced to League football by Sheffield United, he was transferred to Everton after only a handful of games, costing the club £80,000. His stay at Goodison was only slightly longer, for he left for Newcastle United in 1981 for £125,000, and he later played for Sheffield Wednesday, West Bromwich Albion and Manchester City.

JULY 9TH

1977   After two years with Everton, during which he had made 54 first-team appearances,

Bryan Hamilton was sold to Millwall. He subsequently went on to play for Swindon and returned to Merseyside as player-manager of Tranmere Rovers in 1980 and remained at Prenton Park for five years.

JULY 10TH

1967   After over seven years and 300 appearances for the club, Jimmy Gabriel was sold to Southampton. During his time at Goodison Jimmy, who arrived in March 1960 for £8,000 helped the club win the League title in 1963 and the FA Cup three years later. He later went on to play for Bournemouth, Swindon and Brentford.

JULY 11TH

1965   Tony Cottee born in London. Signed by West Ham as an apprentice he broke into the first team whilst still a teenager and spent six years at Upton Park before a £2.3 million move to Everton in 1988. He made over 200 appearances for Everton before rejoining West Ham in 1994. Capped by England on seven occasions.

1986   Midfield player Kevin Langley joined the club from Wigan Athletic. Although he made enough appearances in his first season at Goodison Park to collect a championship medal, he was also loaned to Manchester City during the course of the campaign.

1991   Everton paid £80,000 to Bournemouth for Gerald Peyton.

JULY 12TH

1966   Goodison Park hosted the World Cup Group 3 match between the holders Brazil and Bulgaria. The Brazilian side contained Garrincha, Jairzinho and the incomparable Pele, who was singled out for some particularly rough treatment from the Bulgarian defenders but still managed to score with a free-kick. Garrincha also scored from a free-kick to give the Brazilians a winning start to their campaign.

JULY 13TH

1913   Goodison Park became the first League ground to be visited by a reigning monarch, with King George V and Queen Mary coming to inspect local school children.

1934   Gordon Lee born in Hednesford. As a player he began his career with Aston Villa, remaining at Villa Park for six years before moving on to Shrewsbury where he finished his career. He then turned to management and joined Everton in 1977 from Newcastle. After four years in charge he was sacked in May 1981.

1981   Bury goalkeeper Neville Southall joined Everton for £150,000, subsequently becoming one of the finest goalkeepers to have played for the club.

1988   Pat Nevin joined Everton from Chelsea, costing the club £925,000, almost ten times as much as he had cost the London club when joining them in 1983 from Clyde, £95,000

JULY 14TH

1991   Derby striker Dean Saunders turned down a chance to join Everton (and Nottingham Forest) in order to sign for Liverpool, although he remained with the club for a little over a year.

JULY 15TH

1966   Hungary met Brazil at Goodison Park in the World Cup Group 3 match. The presence of the Hungarians at the finals had saved the organisers from some inconsiderable embarrassment, for their qualifying group had also included East Germany; it was still not possible for East German parties to visit NATO countries and therefore visas would not have been issued had the East Germans qualified! Brazil were missing the injured Pele and went down 3–1 to a powerful Hungarian side.

1985 After helping the club win the League championship, FA Cup and European Cup-Winners' Cup, Andy Gray was sold to Aston Villa.

JULY 16TH

1926 Eric Moore born in St Helens. Initially signed as a half-back Eric was successfully converted to full-back and went on to make 184 appearances for the first team. He lost his place in 1956–57 and asked for a transfer, duly signing for Chesterfield for £10,000, but after only six games was back on Merseyside, signing for Tranmere Rovers.

1968 Stuart Barlow born in Liverpool. Signed by Everton from Sherwood Park in 1990, he spent five years at Goodison although he was unable to break into the first team on a regular basis. After a brief loan spell with Rotherham he joined Oldham in 1995 for £450,000.

1993 Peter Beardsley returned to Newcastle United, a fee of £1.4 million taking him from Goodison Park to St James' Park. He had been at Goodison for almost two years, having joined Everton in August 1991.

JULY 17TH

1966 Brazil were knocked out of the World Cup in their final Group 3 match against Portugal. The Brazilians showed nine changes from their previous game, bringing back an obviously still-injured Pele who was then given further rough treatment by Vicente and Morais. With Pele out of the way, the Portuguese then proceeded to win 3–1.

1990 Everton signed Andy Hinchcliffe from Manchester City for £800,000, with Neil Pointon making the opposite journey. Hinchcliffe was to be an integral part of the side that won the FA Cup in 1995 and broke into the England side before switching to Hillsborough with Sheffield Wednesday during the 1997–98 season.

1991 Graeme Sharp and Michael Milligan joined Oldham Athletic for £500,000 and £600,000 respectively.

JULY 18TH

1995 Everton paid Derby County £2.7 million for defender Craig Short. He had long been regarded as one of the best defenders in the game, having earned a veritable reputation whilst with Scarborough, Notts County and Derby.

JULY 19TH

1962 Paul Bracewell born in Heswall. He began his career with Stoke City in 1980 and made over 100 appearance before moving to Sunderland in 1983. Less than a year later he was signed by Everton for £425,000 and made his debut in the FA Charity Shield at Wembley against Liverpool in 1984. A member of the side that won the League title and European Cup-Winners' Cup in 1985 he suffered a serious injury on New Year's Day 1986 against Newcastle and was effectively out of the game for the next 20 months. When he finally returned he found stiff competition for places and left in August 1989 for a return to Sunderland for £250,000. Three years later he made the short hop to Newcastle and after three years at St James' Park made another return to Roker Park.

1988   Gary Stevens was sold to Glasgow Rangers for £1 million having been with Everton for the previous seven years.

1996   Barry Horne was sold to Birmingham City for a fee of £250,000 having spent four years at Goodison Park.

JULY 20TH

1980   Everton paid £250,000 to Bolton Wanderers for goalkeeper Jim McDonagh, who had also previously played for Rotherham. McDonagh played in all but two of the League games the following season but was subsequently replaced by Jim Arnold, although it was not until the arrival of Neville Southall that the goalkeeping position was adequately filled.

JULY 21ST

1995   Gary Rowett was sold to Derby County for £300,000 after just four League appearances for Everton. He had spent a brief spell on loan to Blackpool during his time at Goodison but stepped straight into the Derby first team. He was part of the deal that brought Craig Short to Goodison.

JULY 22ND

1981   After seven years with Everton striker Bob Latchford left for Swansea City for a fee of £125,000. He had originally joined the club in 1974 for £350,000 and went on to score 138 goals in 289 appearances. The goals had not dried up when he got to Swansea either as he fired 12 in his first season in the top flight.

JULY 23RD

1966   Goodison Park hosted one of the most memorable matches it had ever witnessed in the World Cup quarter-final clash between Portugal and North Korea. The North Koreans were the surprise package of the 1966 World Cup, eliminating the Italians at the group stage and proving so popular in the North East that a fair number of Sunderland and Middlesbrough fans had 'adopted' the country and made the pilgrimage to Goodison to cheer them on. After just 20 minutes the Koreans were 3–0 ahead thanks to goals from Pak Seung Jin, Yang Sung Kook and Li Dong Woon and a quite astonishing act of giant killing seemed on the cards. But then Eusebio took over, and in the remaining 70 minutes he scored four times, twice from the penalty spot, to lead Portugal towards the semi-finals and a clash with England. Jose Augusto scored Portugal's other goal in the 5–3 win.

JULY 24TH

1966   Martin Keown born in Oxford. Initially signed by Arsenal he spent a brief spell on loan with Brighton before transferring to Aston Villa. He joined Everton for £750,000 in 1989 and was capped by England during his spell with the club. He returned to Arsenal in February 1993.

1976   Gary Jones was sold to Birmingham City for £110,000 after eight years at Goodison Park.

JULY 25TH

1966   Goodison Park staged the World Cup semi-final clash between West Germany and

Russia. The Russian cause was not helped by having Chislenko sent off and another player handicapped by injury in a vicious match, with the Germans finally winning 2–1 to make the final, where they ultimately met England.

1995   Everton were reported to have reached an 'amicable' agreement for compensation to former manager Mike Walker following his dismissal from the post.

JULY 26TH

1978   Everton bought Newcastle United midfield player Geoff Nulty for £40,000.

1979   After 43 League appearances in goal for Plymouth Martin Hodge was sold to Everton. He made 31 first-team outings for the club before being sold to Sheffield Wednesday in 1983. Everton also bought defender John Bailey from Blackburn for £300,000.

1994   Peter Johnson took over as chairman of Everton in place of Dr D.M. Marsh.

JULY 27TH

1988   Alec Chamberlein was sold to Luton Town.

1989   Mike Newell joined Everton from Leicester City for a fee of £850,000 having spent just under two years at Filbert Street, with Everton striker Wayne Clarke making the opposite move as part of the deal. Newell remained with Everton for just over two years before moving on to Blackburn Rovers.

JULY 28TH

1987   Everton signed goalkeeper Alec Chamberlein from Colchester United. He was unable to break into the first team during the following season and spent a spell on loan to Tranmere Rovers.

JULY 29TH

1992   After three years at Southampton Barry Horne joined Everton in a deal worth £675,000 and went on to make 150 first-team appearances before being sold to Birmingham City for a cut price £250,000 in 1996. He looked set to return to Goodison in March 1997 but the deal was blocked following Joe Royle's resignation from the club.

JULY 30TH

1888   Nick Ross joined Everton from Preston. First spotted whilst playing for Hearts he joined Preston in July 1883 and became captain, although he was the subject of intense debate as it became obvious he was a professional at a time when such status was not allowed. He spent only one season at Everton (and thus missed out on Preston's double winning season!) but returned to Deepdale after just 19 games for Everton and collected a League championship medal as Preston retained their League title. He was only 31 when he died of consumption.

1966   Everton full-back Ray Wilson was one of the victorious England side that won the World Cup final 4–2 against West Germany at Wembley. Ray was regarded as having an exceptional tournament, making only one mistake throughout: a misplaced header that gifted the Germans their first goal! He more than made amends, however, as England stormed back to win in extra time.

JULY 31ST

1981   Alan Biley joined the club in a deal worth £350,000 from Derby County, although he made only 19 League appearances, scoring three goals, in the following season and ended it on loan to Stoke City.

AUGUST 1ST

1987   Coventry City   Wembley FA Charity Shield   1–0
Coventry City's surprise win over Spurs in the 1986–87 FA Cup final over Spurs meant a return trip to Wembley for the FA Charity Shield to face League champions Everton. Whilst the prospect of a second Wembley appearance was enough to enable Coventry to sell their entire allocation for the match, there were plenty of spaces to be found at the Everton end of the ground, where their fans were watching their team make their sixth appearance in just over three years. On the day Everton had a little bit too much know how and skill for Coventry to overcome, and a goal from Wayne Clarke was enough to secure the shield for a further 12 months, by now in almost permanent residence at Goodison.

AUGUST 2ND

1935   Alex Parker born in Irvine. He began his career with Falkirk and was transferred to Everton in June 1958, although his debut for the club was delayed whilst he completed his national service. Once in the side he went on to make over 200 first-team appearances and break into the Scottish national side, winning 15 caps. He left Everton in September 1965, joining Southport where he remained until 1968. He was later player-manager at Ballymena United and then manager at Southport,

1953   Peter Eastoe born in Tamworth. Although he was capped for England at youth level whilst with Wolves, he made only four appearances for their League side and was allowed to go to Swindon for £80,000 in 1973. He impressed whilst at the County Ground, scoring 43 goals in 91 matches and was snapped up by QPR for £100,000 in 1976. He and Mick Walsh swapped clubs in 1979 and he made over 100 appearance for Everton before joining West Bromwich Albion in 1982.

1988   Tony Cottee joined Everton from West Ham in a move costing £2.3 million.

AUGUST 3RD

1936   Micky Lill born in Romford. An England Youth international he began his professional career with Wolves and joined Everton in February 1960. He made 31 appearances for the club, scoring a healthy 11 goals from the left wing before joining Plymouth, later finishing his career with Portsmouth.

1979   Five years after joining Everton from Burnley Martin Dobson made the return journey, costing the Turf Moor club £100,000.

AUGUST 4TH

1905   The Football Association Commission looking into the events surround the matches between Manchester City and Everton on April 21st and Aston Villa versus City a week later announced their findings: Tom Booth of Everton and Sandy Turnbull of Manchester City were to be suspended for one month, the referees in both matches also suspended for a similar length of time (with the referee in the City and Everton game, Mr J.T. Howcroft being singled out for particular criticism for 'his extraordinary feebleness in a critical match', although his career recovered and he refereed the 1920 FA Cup final) and Billy Meredith was to be suspended for one season for attempting to bribe Villa captain Alec Leake. Not surprisingly, the case caused uproar and even then that wasn't the end of the matter, for later on Meredith was reported to the FA by City for attempting to claim wages from the club. Meredith showed a letter from his manager which, he claimed, showed the City officials were aware of his efforts to get Villa to throw the match. This time the FA came down like a ton of bricks: seventeen current and former players were fined a combined sum of £900, suspended for a year and forbidden to play for the club ever again, whilst the manager and chairman were banned for life, two directors for a year and the club was fined £250.

1994　Vinny Samways completed his £2.2 million transfer from Spurs to Everton. A member of the side that won the 1991 FA Cup he had become increasingly disillusioned at White Hart Lane and joined Everton in search of a fresh start. Although he made 19 League appearances during the first campaign at Goodison Park he was left out of the side for the FA Cup final against Manchester United.

AUGUST 5TH

1931　Billy Bingham born in Belfast. After starring for Irish side Glentoran he was transferred to Sunderland in November 1950 and spent eight years at Roker Park before joining Luton Town. A member of the side that reached the FA Cup final in 1959 he came to Goodison in 1960 and helped Everton win the League title in 1962–63 and left for Port Vale at the end of the season. A broken leg two years later brought his playing career to an end and he then turned to management, returning to Goodison in 1973 and remaining until he was sacked in 1977. He later managed Northern Ireland, guiding them to the World Cup finals in 1982 and 1986.

1991　Everton signed Peter Beardsley from Liverpool for a fee of £1 million, the player having been at Anfield for the previous four years.

AUGUST 6TH

1950　Jim Arnold born in Stafford. He began his career with Blackburn Rovers and was transferred to Everton in August 1981, going on to make 59 first-team appearances in goal before being replaced by Neville Southall. He was sold to Port Vale in June 1985.

1971　Glasgow Rangers　　　A　　　Friendly　　　　　　　　　1–2
A crowd of 58,000 were at the Ibrox Stadium for the pre-season friendly between Scottish League Cup winners Rangers and Everton, with the home side winning 2–1 thanks to two goals from Derek Johnstone.

AUGUST 7TH

1976　Mark Higgins was upgraded from apprentice to full professional by Everton. He went on to make a total of 181 appearance for the first team but was forced into retirement at the age of 26 owing to a serious injury. However, he later joined Manchester United and subsequently played for Bury.

AUGUST 8TH

1924　Jack Lindsay born in Auchinleck. Signed by Everton from Glasgow Rangers for £7,000 in 1951 he was an automatic first choice at full-back until he broke his leg in 1954. When he recovered he asked for a transfer and was sold to Bury, but after only one season at Gigg Lane drifted into non-League football.

1930　Tommy Ring born in Glasgow. A full Scottish international with 12 caps to his credit he joined Everton from Clyde in January 1960 and remained on the club's books until November 1961 when he was sold to Barnsley. He made 27 appearances in the club's colours, scoring six goals.

1970   Chelsea   A   FA Charity Shield   2–1

Everton won the FA Charity Shield for the fourth time in their history with a 2–1 win at Stamford Bridge, home of FA Cup winners Chelsea. Everton's goals were scored by Howard Kendall and Alan Whittle.

AUGUST 9TH

1912   Alex Stevenson born in Dublin. First spotted by Glasgow Rangers whilst playing for the Dolphin club he was transferred to Everton in 1934. He linked immediately with Jackie Coulter and helped the club win the League title in 1939. Unfortunately the Second World War cut right across his career, but he remained with Everton until 1949. He was capped 17 times for Northern Ireland and also earned seven caps for Eire.

1914   Joe Mercer born in Ellesmere Port in 1914 he joined Everton as a youngster and won a League championship medal with them before the war as well as establishing himself as a regular member of the England side. If the Second World War had not interrupted his career there might have been no end to the honours he picked up, but he resumed his career in 1946 with Everton, despite a knee injury, until December 1946, when Tom Whittaker paid £7,000 to take him to Arsenal (although Mercer was allowed to continue training with Everton and travel down to London on match days). With Mercer's experience the guiding light, Arsenal won two League championships and made one winning and one losing appearance in the FA Cup final until a broken leg in 1954 finished his career at the age of 40. He moved into management, taking over at Sheffield United, Aston Villa and then Manchester City, where, in tandem with Malcolm Allison, he led them to the League title in 1967–68, the FA Cup in 1969 (thus becoming the first man to have captained and managed an FA Cup-Winning team at Wembley) and the European Cup-Winners' Cup and League Cup in 1970. He became general manager in 1971 before retiring in 1972, although he was briefly caretaker manager of England. A former Footballer of the Year in 1950, he died in August 1990.

1969   Arsenal   A   First Division   1–0
1997   Crystal Palace   H   FA Premier League   1–2

AUGUST 10TH

1914   Norman Greenhalgh born in Bolton. Initially signed by Bolton he made his name with New Brighton, joining them in 1935. After recovering from appendix trouble and rediscovering his form he was sold to Everton, making his debut in the 1937–38 season and forming an effective partnership with Willie Cook. He helped Everton to the League title in 1939 but, like many of his generation, was unfortunate that the Second World War cut right across his career, although he remained at Goodison Park until 1949 when he was given a free transfer and joined Bangor City. He was once described by Stanley Matthews as the opponent he least enjoyed playing against.

1968   Manchester United   A   First Division   1–2
1985   Manchester United   Wembley FA Charity Shield   2–0

League champions Everton kicked off the new season in the by now traditional curtain-raiser to the new season with a 2–0 victory over FA Cup winners Manchester United in the FA Charity Shield at Wembley. They won rather more convincingly than the 2–0 scoreline suggested, thanks to goals from Trevor Steven and Adrian Heath, and gave warning that the League title would not be handed over without a fight.

AUGUST 11TH

1981   Everton and Manchester United were involved in a swap deal worth some £900,000, with Mickey Thomas moving from Old Trafford to Goodison Park and John Gidman making the opposite journey. Gidman had made 64 League appearances for Everton whilst Thomas had 90 first-team outings for United. The move turned out to work better for Gidman than it did for Thomas, for after only 11 first-team appearances he refused to play in a reserve match, claiming he should have been selected for the first team, and was placed on the transfer list, subsequently joining Brighton midway through the season.

AUGUST 12TH

1972	Norwich City	A	First Division	1–1
1995	Blackburn Rovers	Wembley	FA Charity Shield	1–0

In a change from tradition benefactor Jack Walker led the Blackburn side out for the traditional curtain-raiser to the new season at Wembley. The attendance, 40,146 was the lowest for an FA Charity Shield match since the venue was switched to Wembley, and a goal from Vinny Samways was enough to enable FA Cup holders to win the game.

AUGUST 13TH

1966	Liverpool	H	FA Charity Shield	0–1

Whilst Everton and Liverpool had met many times in the League and occasionally in the cup and could point to a vast number of trophy wins between them, they had never met in the FA Charity Shield prior to this match. A crowd of 63,329 packed into Goodison Park for the clash between the two Merseyside rivals and were treated to something special right at the very start. The two teams came out on to the pitch side by side, headed by Ray Weilson and Roger Hunt. Both had been members of the England side that had won the World Cup with England, and each had a hand on the gleaming Jules Rimet Trophy. Behind them came captains Brian Labone and Ron Yeats, and they were carrying the FA Cup and League trophy respectively. Three of the greatest prizes on offer in the game on show at the same time; the crowd were delirious! If the start was champagne, the game itself was flat beer as far as Everton were concerned, with Roger Hunt scoring the only goal of the match after nine minutes. Liverpool should have scored more, Everton didn't look as though they could score any, and the shield found its way to Anfield.

1968	Burnley	H	First Division	3–0
1969	Manchester United	A	First Division	2–0

AUGUST 14TH

1956   Andy King born in Luton. He began his career with the local side and was snapped up by Everton for £35,000 in 1976. An instant hit with the fans he spent four years at Goodison before leaving for QPR for £450,000 in 1980, but failed to settle and was on his way to West Bromwich Albion for a similar fee 12 months later. Howard Kendall rescued his career by taking him back to Everton in 1982, remaining for two seasons before going off to play in Holland.

1964   Paul Rideout born in Bournemouth. After graduating through the ranks with Swindon he was transferred to Aston Villa in 1983 for £200,000 and spent five years at Villa Park before a £430,000 move to Southampton. After a brief spell with Notts County he was surprisingly sold to Glasgow Rangers for £500,000, spending seven months in Glasgow before coming to Goodison Park for a similar fee. Scorer of the goal that won the FA Cup in 1995, he later went to play in China.

1970	Everton announced they had lifted the ban on television cameras at Goodison Park.			
1971	Ipswich Town	A	First Division	0–0
1993	Southampton	A	FA Premier League	2–0

AUGUST 15TH

1963 Ian Snodin born in Rotherham. He cost Everton £840,000 when signed from Leeds United in 1987, having started his career with Doncaster Rovers. At the end of his first season he had collected a medal for helping the club win the League title, and after a loan spell with Sunderland was released on a free transfer to join Oldham in 1995.

1970	Arsenal	H	First Division	2–2
1987	Norwich City	H	First Division	1–0
1992	Sheffield Wednesday	H	FA Premier League	1–1

AUGUST 16TH

1922 Peter Farrell born in Dublin. He developed in the same Shamrock Rovers side as Tom Eglington and was transferred with Tom for a joint fee of £10,000 in 1946. Like Tom he went on to give Everton over ten years exceptional service and was then sold to Tranmere Rovers for £2,500 in October 1957 where he became player-manager, where one of his players was Tom Eglington! He later returned to Ireland in order to continue in management, and whilst with Everton won a total of 28 caps for the Republic of Ireland and seven for Northern Ireland.

1969	Crystal Palace	H	First Division	2–1
1972	Manchester City	A	First Division	1–0
1975	Coventry City	H	First Division	1–4
1980	Sunderland	A	First Division	1–3
1986	Liverpool	Wembley	FA Charity Shield	1–1

Liverpool's double success of 1985–86, both trophies being won at the expense of Everton, meant an FA Charity Shield date with their closest rivals at Wembley. By now Wembley's capacity was down to just over 88,000, an insufficient figure given that Liverpool and Everton had struggled to accommodate all those who wished to see the game when there were 100,000 tickets available (even if not all the tickets were originally intended for sale on Merseyside). Lineker had already gone to Spain, meaning a new look Everton strike force, still built around Graeme Sharp but with the nifty Adrian Heath acting as the perfect foil. Indeed it was Heath who gave Everton the lead with just ten minutes remaining in the match, but Liverpool fought back to equalise two minutes from time through who else but Ian Rush. As a result both sides would share the shield for six months each, with the six months at Anfield the only time in four years the shield was to be found anywhere other than Goodison Park.

AUGUST 17TH

1956 Dave Jones born in Liverpool. He was signed by Everton as an apprentice and upgraded to the professional ranks in May 1974, making his debut the following November. He went on to make 86 appearances for the first team before joining Coventry. An England Youth international he also represented the country at Under-21 level.

| 1963 | Manchester United | H | FA Charity Shield | 4–0 |

It had been almost thirty years to the day since Everton had last appeared in the FA Charity Shield, when they had been beaten by Arsenal at home. This time the League champions Everton were at home to FA Cup winners Manchester United and the match went according to form, Everton registering a 4–0 win. The goals were scored by Jimmy Gabriel, Dennis Stevens, Derek Temple and Roy Vernon.

1968	Tottenham Hotspur	H	First Division	0–2
1974	Derby County	H	First Division	0–0
1985	Leicester City	A	First Division	1–3
1991	Nottingham Forest	A	First Division	1–2
1993	Manchester City	H	FA Premier League	1–0
1996	Newcastle United	H	FA Premier League	2–0

AUGUST 18TH

| 1933 | Jimmy Harris born in Birkenhead |

He joined Everton as an amateur in 1951 and made his League debut during the 1955–56 season, going on to be almost ever-present that campaign. He remained at Goodison until December 1960 when he signed for Birmingham City and later had spells with Oldham and Tranmere where he finished his playing career. In October 1958 he achieved the rare distinction of scoring a hat-trick for Everton and still finishing on the losing side – Everton were beaten 10–4 at Spurs!

| 1951 | Southampton | A | Second Division | 0–1 |

Everton kicked off only their second season in the Second Division since the addition of the League in 1892, confident that their stay would be as short and sweet as it had been in 1930–31. On the day, however, Southampton showed that the Second division would not be an easy division to climb out of, winning 1–0 at The Dell.

1956	Leeds United	A	First Division	1–5
1962	Burnley	A	First Division	3–1
1970	Burnley	H	First Division	1–1
1971	West Bromwich Albion	A	First Division	0–2
1979	Norwich City	H	First Division	2–4
1984	Liverpool	Wembley	FA Charity Shield	1–0

Liverpool and Everton met in the FA Charity Shield for the second time, this match taking place at Wembley, the second time in five months that the two great rivals had met at the national stadium. This time Everton exacted their revenge, winning 1–0 after a bizarre error from Bruce Grobbelaar gifted them a goal. To the Everton fans in the 100,000 crowd, any goal that helped them beat their traditional rivals was one to savour. It was to be the first of four consecutive wins in the FA Charity Shield.

| 1987 | Wimbledon | A | First Division | 1–1 |

AUGUST 19TH

1950	Huddersfield Town	H	First Division	3–2
1953	Nottingham Forest	A	Second Division	3–3
1961	Aston Villa	H	First Division	2–0
1967	Manchester United	H	First Division	3–1

The reigning League champions (and future European Cup winners) Manchester

United were the visitors to Goodison Park for the opening game of the season, with Alan Ball scoring twice and Alex Young grabbing the other in an impressive win.

1968	West Ham United	A	First Division	4–1
1969	Manchester United	H	First Division	2–0

Everton maintained their 100 per cent start to the season with a 2–0 win at Goodison against Manchester United in front of a crowd of 57,752. Alan Ball and John Hurst scored the goals.

1972	Manchester United	H	First Division	2–0
1975	Burnley	A	First Division	1–1
1978	Chelsea	A	First Division	1–0
1980	Leicester City	H	First Division	1–0
1989	Coventry City	A	First Division	0–2
1992	Manchester United	A	FA Premier League	3–0

1993 Everton paid £850,000 to Chelsea in order to bring Graham Stuart to Goodison Park. Stuart would go on to be a member of the side that won the FA Cup in 1995.

1995	Chelsea	A	FA Premier League	0–0

AUGUST 20TH

1949	Middlesbrough	A	First Division	1–0
1955	Preston North End	H	First Division	0–4
1960	Tottenham Hotspur	A	First Division	0–2

1961 Steve McMahon born in Liverpool. He graduated through the ranks at Everton and made over 100 appearances for the club until sold to Aston Villa for £175,000 in 1983. He returned to Merseyside, this time with Liverpool, in 1985 for £375,000 and won a host of honours and medals, including 17 caps for England. He then moved on to Manchester City in 1991 and then became player-manager at Swindon in 1994.

1966	Fulham	A	First Division	1–0

1968 Brett Angell born in Marlborough. Although signed by Portsmouth as an apprentice he began his career with non-League Cheltenham before returning to the Football League with Derby County. By the time he arrived at Goodison Park in 1994 he had also played for Stockport County and Southend, and he cost £500,000 when moving from Roots Hall to Everton. Just over a year later he was on the move again, joining Sunderland, and he has since played for West Bromwich Albion and Stockport for a second spell.

1974	Stoke City	H	First Division	2–1
1977	Nottingham Forest	H	First Division	1–3
1985	West Bromwich Albion	H	First Division	2–0
1991	Arsenal	H	First Division	3–1
1994	Aston Villa	H	FA Premier League	2–2

AUGUST 21ST

1939 Frank Wignall born in Chorley. Signed by Everton from Horwich RMI in May 1958 he found first-team opportunities at Goodison severely restricted, although he could be relied upon to give a good account of himself whenever called up for service. Indeed, he scored 14 goals in 33 League appearances and seven in the League Cup in 1960–61. Sold to Nottingham Forest in March 1963 he later went on to play for Wolves, Derby and Mansfield and won two caps for England.

1948	Newcastle United	H	First Division	3–3

1954	Sheffield United	A	First Division	5–2

After an absence of three years Everton kicked off the new season back in the First Division with an away trip to Bramall Lane to face Sheffield United. John Willie Parker and Eddie Wainwright both scored twice and Everton's other goal was netted by Tommy Eglington. Everton went on to finish the campaign in mid-table.

1965	Northampton Town	H	First Division	5–2

Newly–promoted Northampton Town made their only ever visit to Goodison Park for League points and were soundly beaten 5–2 thanks to goals from Fred Pickering (two), Derek Temple (two) and Alex Young. At the end of the season, Northampton were to be relegated back into the Second Division whilst Everton went on to win the FA Cup.

1971	Sheffield United	H	First Division	0–1
1976	Queens Park Rangers	A	First Division	4–0
1993	Sheffield United	H	FA Premier League	4–2
1996	Manchester United	A	FA Premier League	2–2

AUGUST 22ND

1881	Harry Makepeace born in Middlesbrough. His family moved to Merseyside when he was ten and he began his playing career with Bootle Amateurs, being snapped up by Everton in 1902. A regular member of the side for much of the period up to the First World War, which caused the abandonment of League football and the effective end of his career, he made over 300 first-team appearances for the club. Capped by England at both football and cricket, like team-mate Jack Sharp, he became coach at Goodison at the end of his playing career.

1951	Brentford	H	Second Division	1–0
1953	Luton Town	A	Second Division	1–1
1956	Blackpool	H	First Division	2–3
1959	Luton Town	H	First Division	2–2
1962	Manchester United	H	First Division	3–1
1964	Stoke City	A	First Division	2–0
1970	Leeds United	A	First Division	2–3
1972	Crystal Palace	H	First Division	1–1
1978	Derby County	H	First Division	2–1
1979	Leeds United	A	First Division	0–2

1986	Central defender Dave Watson signed for Everton from Norwich City, the transfer costing the Goodison Park club £900,000. Over the next 12 years Watson became one of the most consistent performers in the Everton defence.

1987	Nottingham Forest	A	First Division	0–0
1989	Tottenham Hotspur	H	First Division	2–1
1992	Norwich City	A	FA Premier League	1–1

AUGUST 23RD

1947	Blackburn Rovers	A	First Division	3–2
1950	Middlesbrough	A	First Division	0–4
1952	Hull City	H	Second Division	0–2
1958	Leicester City	A	First Division	0–2
1961	West Bromwich Albion	A	First Division	0–2
1966	Manchester United	H	First Division	1–2

1967	Tottenham Hotspur	A	First Division	1–1
1969	Manchester City	A	First Division	1–1

After an opening start of four straight wins Everton dropped their first point of the season, held to a 1–1 draw by Manchester City at Maine Road. Johnny Morrissey gave Everton the lead in the first half in front of a crowd of 43,676 but Ian Bowyer equalised for City, although Everton were still making the early running in the First division.

1975	Birmingham City	A	First Division	1–0
1977	Arsenal	A	First Division	0–1
1980	Nottingham Forest	H	First Division	0–0
1986	Nottingham Forest	H	First Division	2–0

1989 Paul Bracewell was sold back to Sunderland for £250,000. He had originally joined Everton in 1984 for £425,000 and proved a solid and reliable performer, but a bad injury sustained in 1986 had cost him 20 months of action and his place in the side.

1995	Arsenal	H	FA Premier League	0–2
1997	West Ham United	H	FA Premier League	2–1

AUGUST 24TH

1892 Goodison Park opened its doors for the first time with a crowd of 12,000, including visiting dignitaries Lord Kinnaird and Frederick Wall of the Football Association present. However, there was no match to see, instead a short athletics meeting and a selection of music were completed by a fireworks display.

1949	Newcastle United	H	First Division	2–1
1953	Hull City	A	Second Division	3–1
1955	West Bromwich Albion	A .	First Division	0–2
1957	Wolverhampton Wanderers	H	First Division	1–0
1960	Manchester United	H	First Division	4–0

Bobby Collins and Micky Lill both scored twice as Everton bounced back from their opening day defeat with a 4–0 trouncing of Manchester United in front of an enthusiastic crowd of 51,602. Everton were to finish the season in fifth place in the table, 16 points behind champions Spurs, but already a side capable of winning the major honours was being assembled at Goodison Park.

1963	Fulham	H	First Division	3–0
1968	Newcastle United	A	First Division	0–0
1971	Chelsea	H	First Division	2–0
1974	West Ham United	A	First Division	3–2
1976	Ipswich Town	H	First Division	1–1
1985	Coventry City	H	First Division	1–1
1991	Manchester United	H	First Division	0–0
1994	Tottenham Hotspur	A	FA Premier League	1–2
1996	Tottenham Hotspur	A	FA Premier League	0–0

AUGUST 25TH

1923	Nottingham Forest	H	First Division	2–1
1928	Bolton Wanderers	A	First Division	3–2

Jimmy Dunn made his first appearance for the club in the opening day match against Bolton Wanderers at Burnden Park, where a Dixie Dean hat-trick enabled Everton to record a 3–2 win. Dunn had joined the club during the summer from Hibernian and would prove to be a vital component in the side that was to win the Second and First Division championships and the FA Cup in consecutive seasons. Indeed, it was Dunn who scored the first goal in the FA Cup final against Manchester City. He stayed at Goodison until 1935 when he left to join Exeter City. One of his sons, also named Jimmy, later collected a winners' medal with Wolves in the 1949 FA Cup final.

1934	Tottenham Hotspur	A	First Division	1–1
1945	Bolton Wanderers	H	Football League North	3–2
1948	Portsmouth	A	First Division	0–4
1951	Sheffield Wednesday	H	Second Division	3–3
1952	Sheffield United	A	Second Division	0–1
1954	Arsenal	H	First Division	1–0
1956	Bolton Wanderers	H	First Division	2–2
1959	Burnley	A	First Division	2–5
1962	Sheffield Wednesday	H	First Division	4–1
1964	Nottingham Forest	H	First Division	1–0
1965	Sheffield Wednesday	A	First Division	1–3
1973	Leeds United	A	First Division	1–3
1979	Derby County	A	First Division	1–0
1984	Tottenham Hotspur	H	First Division	1–4

Everton paraded the FA Cup and FA Charity Shield to the crowd of 35,630 before the start of the game against Spurs and had a dream start when Adrian Heath gave them the lead. Spurs, the UEFA Cup holders bounced back however, and stunned the crowd with a four-goal blitz. It was hardly an auspicious start to what would be an exhilarating season.

| 1986 | Sheffield Wednesday | A | First Division | 2–2 |

After the double disappointment of 1985–86 Everton had started the new campaign with a 2–0 win over Nottingham Forest and then travelled to Hillsborough to face Sheffield Wednesday. Everton recovered from going one goal down to snatch a point thanks to goals from Graeme Sharp and Kevin Langley.

1990	Leeds United	H	First Division	2–3
1992	Aston Villa	H	FA Premier League	1–0
1993	Newcastle United	A	FA Premier League	0–1

AUGUST 26TH

1922	Newcastle United	A	First Division	0–2
1933	West Bromwich Albion	H	First Division	1–0
1939	Brentford	H	First Division	1–1

Brentford were the visitors to Goodison Park in the opening match of the season, one which Everton confidently hoped would see them retain the League title. Tommy Lawton scored Everton's goal in the 1–1 draw in what was officially manager Theo Kelly's first game in charge. Kelly had been appointed to the position, the first man to officially be named manager at Everton, at the end of the previous season and was to remain in the position until 1948 when he reverted back to secretary to make way for Cliff Britton.

| 1944 | Manchester United | H | Football League North (First Championship) | 1–2 |
| 1950 | Newcastle United | A | First Division | 1–1 |

1961	Fulham	A	First Division	1–2
1967	Sunderland	A	First Division	0–1
1969	Sheffield Wednesday	H	First Division	2–1
1970	Chelsea	A	First Division	2–2
1972	Stoke City	A	First Division	1–1
1975	Sheffield United	H	First Division	3–0
1978	Arsenal	H	First Division	1–0
1980	Blackpool	H	League Cup 2nd Round 1st Leg	3–0
1985	Tottenham Hotspur	A	First Division	1–0

Having wrecked Spurs' hopes of the League title the previous season Everton heaped further misery on the London side with a 1–0 win at White Hart Lane in the League and later on in the season a 2–1 win in the FA Cup. In both instances the vital goal was scored by Gary Lineker, an original target for Spurs some two years previously.

| 1989 | Southampton | H | First Division | 3–0 |
| 1995 | Southampton | H | FA Premier League | 2–0 |

AUGUST 27TH

| 1921 | Manchester United | H | First Division | 5–0 |

John McDonald took over as club captain. He had joined the club from Airdrie in 1920 and missed only three League matches during his first season with the club, scoring on his debut on the opening day. He proved to be an inspirational choice for captain, guiding his club to a 5–0 win over Manchester United on the opening day of the season and steering them away from relegation at the end of the campaign. After making 224 appearances for Everton he left in August 1927 to join New Brighton.

| 1923 | Burnley | A | First Division | 2–2 |
| 1927 | Sheffield Wednesday | H | First Division | 4–0 |

What was to be a championship winning and record breaking season for Dixie Dean kicked off with a 4–0 demolition of Sheffield Wednesday at Goodison Park. Dean got his first goal of the campaign, whilst the others were added by Forshaw, Troup and Weldon.

1932	West Bromwich Albion	A	First Division	1–3
1947	Manchester City	H	First Division	1–0
1949	Liverpool	H	First Division	0–0
1951	Brentford	A	Second Division	0–1
1955	Burnley	A	First Division	1–0
1956	Blackpool	A	First Division	2–5
1958	Preston North End	H	First Division	1–4
1960	Leicester City	H	First Division	3–1
1966	Liverpool	H	First Division	3–1

Two weeks after the two sides had met in the FA Charity Shield at Goodison Park, Everton and Liverpool clashed for League points at the same venue. Here Everton gained their revenge for their earlier defeat, goals from Alan Ball (two) and Sandy Brown in front of a crowd of 64,318 giving them the points.

1968	Liverpool	H	First Division	0–0
1977	Aston Villa	A	First Division	2–1
1983	Stoke City	H	First Division	1–0
1984	West Bromwich Albion	A	First Division	1–2

1988	Newcastle United	H	First Division	4–0
1994	Manchester City	A	FA Premier League	0–4
1997	Manchester United	H	FA Premier League	0–2

AUGUST 28TH

| 1920 | Bradford Park Avenue | A | First Division | 3–3 |

Charlie Crossley took his place in the starting line up for the first time in the opening day 3–3 draw at Bradford Park Avenue. He had signed for the club from Sunderland and went on to play in 35 League matches during his first season, but erratic form in the second prompted his sale to West Ham in June 1922.

| 1926 | Tottenham Hotspur | A | First Division | 1–2 |
| 1937 | Arsenal | H | First Division | 1–4 |

Everton opened the season with a home match against Arsenal and went down 4–1 in front of a crowd of 53,856. Everton's goal was scored by Dixie Dean, the last of his 349 for the club in the League.

| 1939 | Aston Villa | A | First Division | 2–1 |

For their second game of the season Everton had to visit Villa Park to play Aston Villa, and a commanding performance from the League champions saw them return home with both points thanks to a 2–1 win, with Bentham and Lawton scoring the goals.

1943	Blackburn Rovers	A	Football League North (First Championship)	3–1
1948	Middlesbrough	A	First Division	0–1
1954	Preston North End	H	First Division	1–0
1957	Manchester United	A	First Division	0–3
1965	Stoke City	A	First Division	1–1
1971	West Ham United	A	First Division	0–1
1973	Leicester City	H	First Division	1–1
1974	Stoke City	A	First Division	1–1

Everton paid Burnley £300,000 for Martin Dobson who made his debut for the club three days later in the home fixture with Arsenal.

1976	Aston Villa	H	First Division	0–2
1979	Cardiff City	H	League Cup 2nd Round 1st Leg	2–0
1982	Watford	A	First Division	0–2
1991	Sheffield Wednesday	A	First Division	1–2
1993	Arsenal	A	FA Premier League	0–2

AUGUST 29TH

1925	Sheffield United	H	First Division	2–2
1928	Sheffield Wednesday	H	First Division	0–0
1931	Birmingham City	H	First Division	3–2
1934	Leicester City	H	First Division	2–1
1936	Arsenal	A	First Division	2–3

The BBC broadcast the match between Arsenal and Everton at Highbury, the first such television showing of a football match, although as there were fewer than 10,000 television sets in the country, the viewing figures were not expected to be great! Arsenal won the match 3–2, but in scoring Everton's first goal Dixie Dean took his career tally to 352, level with the great Steve Bloomer.

| 1942 | Manchester United | H | Football League North (First Championship) | 2–2 |

1953	Oldham Athletic	H	Second Division	3–1
1953	Oldham Athletic	A	Second Division	4–0
1959	Bolton Wanderers	A	First Division	1–2
1962	Manchester United	A	First Division	1–0
1964	Tottenham Hotspur	H	First Division	4–1
1967	Tottenham Hotspur	H	First Division	0–1
1970	Manchester City	H	First Division	0–1
1972	Derby County	H	First Division	1–0
1978	Wimbledon	H	League Cup 2nd Round	8–0

Bob Latchford scored five of Everton's goals as the relative newcomers to the League Wimbledon were blitzed 8–0 at Goodison Park, with Martin Dobson also helping himself to a hat-trick. Wimbledon had only been members of the League for 12 months and were still a Fourth Division side, although they recovered from the debacle to finish the campaign promoted to the Third Division.

1981	Birmingham City	H	First Division	3–1
1983	West Ham United	H	First Division	0–1
1987	Sheffield Wednesday	H	First Division	4–0
1990	Coventry City	A	First Division	1–3
1992	Wimbledon	H	FA Premier League	0–0

AUGUST 30TH

1919	Chelsea	H	First Division	3–3
1924	Birmingham City	A	First Division	2–2
1930	Plymouth Argyle	A	Second Division	3–2

Everton took to the field at Home Park in Plymouth for their very first Second Division match. Relegation the previous season had come as a shock and the team were resolved to make their sojourn in the Second Division as short as possible. Two goals from Tommy White and one from George Martin helped them on their way to a 3–2 win and served notice that Everton were on their way back.

1933	Derby County	A	First Division	1–1
1941	Stoke City	A	Football League North (First Championship)	3–8
1947	Blackpool	H	First Division	1–2
1950	Middlesbrough	H	First Division	3–2
1952	Blackburn Rovers	A	Second Division	1–3
1958	Newcastle United	H	First Division	0–2
1961	West Bromwich Albion	H	First Division	3–1
1969	Leeds United	H	First Division	3–2

A crowd of 53,253 were at Goodison for the First Division's match of the day, the meeting between Everton and reigning League champions Leeds United. Everton had made the early running in the League, winning five and drawing the other of their opening six matches, but Leeds would provide their sternest test to date. Goals from Jimmy Husband and Joe Royle gave Everton a dream start in the first half, but not unexpectedly Leeds came back at them in the second period and scored through Billy Bremner and Allan Clarke. A second goal from Joe Royle enabled Everton to claim both points.

1975	Derby County	H	First Division	2–0
1976	Cambridge United	H	League Cup 2nd Round	3–0

Only 10,898 were at Goodison Park to see Everton kick off the League Cup trail with a 3–0 win over Cambridge United thanks to goals from Bob Latchford, Martin Dobson and Andy King, although interest would grow as Everton got closer to Wembley.

1977	Sheffield United	A	League Cup 2nd Round	3–0
1980	Ipswich Town	A	First Division	0–4
1986	Coventry City	A	First Division	1–1
1989	Sheffield Wednesday	A	First Division	1–1
1994	Nottingham Forest	H	FA Premier League	1–2
1995	Manchester City	A	FA Premier League	2–0

AUGUST 31ST

1909 The dispute between the Football Association and the Players' Union had grown over the previous few weeks to such an extent there was now a real threat that the Football League season, due to start the following day, would have to be postponed. Whilst it was Manchester United's players who had been the most resolute throughout the dispute, support for their actions had grown and players from Newcastle, Sunderland, Middlesbrough, Liverpool and Everton had soon joined with their Manchester counterparts. This forced the FA to the bargaining table and an agreement was hammered out at the eleventh hour; the players had the right to join the Union and the FA would recognise it, only if the Union in turn dropped plans to affiliate with the General Federation of Trade Unions.

1921	Newcastle United	A	First Division	0–3
1929	Bolton Wanderers	H	First Division	3–3
1932	Sheffield Wednesday	H	First Division	2–1

Both of Everton's goals were scored by Jock Thomson, his first for the club in his fourth season at Goodison. Born John Ross Thomson in Thornton he began his professional career with Dundee and joined Everton in March 1930 with the club doomed to relegation. Over the next five years he was almost ever present as the Second and First Division titles and FA Cup were won in successive seasons, a spell that also coincided with him winning his only cap for Scotland. By the time Joe Mercer had taken over his position in the side Jock had made 294 appearances for the first team, scoring five goals, and collecting a second championship medal. He retired in 1939 and served Manchester City as manager from 1947 to 1950, later running a public house. He died in 1979.

1935	Derby County	H	First Division	4–0
1938	Grimsby Town	H	First Division	3–0
1940	Manchester City	A	North Regional League	0–0
1946	Brentford	H	First Division	0–2

After a seven year break, brought about by the Second World War, normal League football was resumed, with the fixture list for 1946–47 being exactly that of 1939–40 when the League had been abandoned. That meant a home match for Everton against Brentford, with a much different line-up in 1946 to that which had taken the field in 1939. Of course, this was much the same story for every club in the land, and whilst Everton had drawn 1–1 in 1939, they now lost 2–0. A crowd of 55,338 were present to witness the return of League football to Goodison Park.

1949	Newcastle United	A	First Division	0–4
1954	Arsenal	A	First Division	0–2

1955	West Bromwich Albion	H	First Division	2–0
1957	Aston Villa	A	First Division	1–0
1960	Manchester United	A	First Division	0–4
1963	Manchester United	A	First Division	1–5
1965	Sheffield Wednesday	H	First Division	5–1
1966	Manchester United	A	First Division	0–3
1968	Nottingham Forest	H	First Division	2–1
1971	Manchester United	H	First Division	1–0
1974	Arsenal	H	First Division	2–1
1982	Aston Villa	H	First Division	5–0
1984	Chelsea	A	First Division	1–0

After two defeats in their opening matches of the season Everton finally grabbed their first points of the campaign with a 1–0 win at Stamford Bridge. Kevin Richardson got the goal that prevented Everton from being bottom of the First Division when the first table was drawn up by the media.

1985	Birmingham City	H	First Division	4–1
1991	Liverpool	A	First Division	1–3
1993	Aston Villa	H	FA Premier League	0–1

SEPTEMBER 1ST

1892 Goodison Park staged its first-ever match, a friendly against Bolton Wanderers which they won 4–2, whilst on the same night, Liverpool were playing their first match at the recently vacated Anfield, another friendly against Rotherham Town which they won 7–1. That Everton were still the premier club in the city can be gauged by the respective attendances: 10,000 were at Goodison, whilst there were 'no more than a handful of interested spectators' at Anfield, despite the fact that Liverpool had Councillor John Houlding kick off their game.

1894	Sheffield Wednesday	H	First Division	3–1
1896	Glasgow Rangers	H	Friendly	2–2
1898	Blackburn Rovers	H	First Division	2–1
1900	Preston North End	A	First Division	2–1

Tom Booth made his Everton debut in the 2–1 win at Deepdale against Preston on the opening day of the season. Born in Manchester he began his career with Blackburn Rovers and two years later had won an England cap, only transferring to Everton because the Ewood Park club needed the money. He went on to make 185 appearances for the club but had to sit out the FA Cup finals of 1906 and 1907, the first through injury and the second for tactical reasons. He remained with Everton until 1908 when he joined Preston, but before playing a single game for them moved on to Carlisle United, retiring in 1909. He added one further cap to his tally whilst at Goodison Park.

1902	West Bromwich Albion	A	First Division	1–2
1903	Blackburn Rovers	H	First Division	3–1
1906	Middlesbrough	A	First Division	2–2
1909	Sheffield Wednesday	H	First Division	1–1
1910	Tottenham Hotspur	H	First Division	2–0
1913	Burnley	H	First Division	1–1
1917	Southport	H	Lancashire Section Principal Tournament	6–1
1920	Newcastle United	H	First Division	3–1

1923	Nottingham Forest	A	First Division	0–1
1926	Bury	A	First Division	2–5
1928	Portsmouth	H	First Division	4–0

Dixie Dean scored his second hat-trick of the new season in the 4–0 win over Portsmouth, taking his tally for the campaign to six in only three games. This not unnaturally led to speculation that Dean himself might be capable of beating his own goalscoring record set the previous season, but by May Dean had to settle for a rather more modest 26 goals.

1934	Preston North End	H	First Division	4–1
1937	Manchester City	A	First Division	0–2
1945	Bolton Wanderers	A	Football League North	1–3
1948	Portsmouth	H	First Division	0–5
1951	Leeds United	A	Second Division	2–1
1956	Wolverhampton Wanderers	A	First Division	1–2
1958	Preston North End	A	First Division	1–3
1962	Fulham	A	First Division	0–1
1964	Nottingham Forest	A	First Division	1–3
1973	Ipswich Town	H	First Division	3–0
1979	Aston Villa	H	First Division	1–1
1990	Manchester City	A	First Division	0–1
1997	Bolton Wanderers	A	FA Premier League	0–0

SEPTEMBER 2ND

1893	Sheffield United	H	First Division	2–3
1895	Sheffield Wednesday	H	First Division	2–2
1899	Sheffield United	H	First Division	1–2
1901	Manchester City	H	First Division	3–1
1905	Middlesbrough	H	First Division	4–1
1907	Bristol City	A	First Division	2–3
1908	Woolwich Arsenal	A	First Division	4–0
1911	Tottenham Hotspur	H	First Division	2–2
1912	Tottenham Hotspur	A	First Division	2–0
1914	Tottenham Hotspur	A	First Division	3–1

Jimmy Galt made his first appearance for Everton having joined the club in pre-season from Glasgow Rangers. Having already won most of the honours available north of the border he was confidently expected to add to his medal tally down south, and at the end of the season he had captained the side to the First Division title. Unfortunately, his career was then wrecked by the First World War, for he rarely played for Everton again and was officially transferred to Third Lanark in 1920. He died in November 1935 at the age of 65.

1916	Bury	A	Lancashire Section Principal Tournament	3–0
1922	Newcastle United	H	First Division	3–2
1925	West Bromwich Albion	A	First Division	1–1
1929	Burnley	A	First Division	1–1
1931	Portsmouth	A	First Division	3–0
1933	Birmingham City	A	First Division	2–2

| 1936 | Sheffield Wednesday | H | First Division | 3–1 |

Dixie Dean scored Everton's first goal in the 3–1 win at home to Sheffield Wednesday, the 353rd of his career and a new individual record, surpassing the previous record set by Steve Bloomer.

| 1939 | Blackburn Rovers | A | First Division | 2–2 |

A 2–2 draw at Ewood Park enabled Everton to collect their fourth point of the season, unbeaten after three games, with Tommy Lawton scoring both of their goals against Blackburn Rovers. Unfortunately, the very next day the British government declared war on Germany and thus the Second World War was underway. The Football League was immediately abandoned, the results expunged from the records and it would be another seven years before normal League football was resumed.

1944	Manchester United	A	Football League North (First Championship)	3–1
1946	Aston Villa	A	First Division	1–0
1950	West Bromwich Albion	H	First Division	0–3
1953	Hull City	H	Second Division	2–0
1959	Burnley	H	First Division	1–2
1961	Sheffield Wednesday	H	First Division	0–4
1967	Wolverhampton Wanderers	H	First Division	4–2
1970	Manchester United	A	First Division	0–2
1972	West Bromwich Albion	H	First Division	1–0
1978	Manchester United	A	First Division	1–1
1981	Leeds United	A	First Division	1–1
1986	Oxford United	H	First Division	3–1
1987	Queens Park Rangers	A	First Division	0–1
1992	Tottenham Hotspur	A	FA Premier League	1–2

SEPTEMBER 3RD

| 1892 | Nottingham Forest | H | First Division | 2–2 |

Richard Boyle made his debut for the club in the 2–2 draw at home to Nottingham Forest on the opening day of the season. He had joined Everton from Scottish club Dumbarton but had to wait two years before given his first run out in the side, going on to make 222 League appearances for the club, his last outing coming during the 1900–01 season. This match was also the first League fixture played at Goodison Park.

1894	Small Heath	H	First Division	5–0
1898	Sheffield United	A	First Division	1–1
1904	Notts County	A	First Division	2–1

Billy Scott made his debut in goal for the club. Born in Belfast he began his professional career with Linfield and joined Everton in 1904 having already won six caps for Ireland. He made 289 appearances for Everton over the next eight seasons before leaving to join Leeds City in 1919. He recommended his brother Elisha, also a goalkeeper, to Liverpool and he was also capped by Ireland.

| 1906 | Manchester City | H | First Division | 9–1 |

Everton registered their biggest ever League win in the First Division match at home to Manchester City, 9–1. Sandy Young led the scoring with four goals, with the others being added by Settle (two), Taylor, Abbott and Bolton. Everton would equal the score against Plymouth in 1930.

1910	Middlesbrough	A	First Division	0–1
1919	Bradford Park Avenue	A	First Division	3–0
1921	Manchester United	A	First Division	1–2

Duggie Livingstone made his debut for the club in the clash with Manchester United at Old Trafford. He made his name with Celtic before moving to Everton in 1921 and went on to make exactly 100 appearances for the first team before becoming unhappy with the management and was promptly sold to Plymouth Argyle in February 1926. He spent four years at Home Park before returning to Merseyside to play for Tranmere Rovers and spent a further five years at Prenton Park. He then moved into coaching with Exeter City, Sheffield United and Sheffield Wednesday before moving to Holland. He coached Sparta and then the Belgian national side prior to taking over as manager at Newcastle on January 1st 1955. At the end of his first season he guided them to the FA Cup, their third success in five years, although he left the club early the following year after a furious row with the directors.

1923	Burnley	H	First Division	3–3
1927	Middlesbrough	A	First Division	2–4

Despite the defeat at Ayresome Park Dixie Dean netted his second goal of the season, with Ted Critchley notching the other.

1928	Sheffield Wednesday	A	First Division	0–1
1930	Preston North End	H	Second Division	2–1

Goodison Park played host to a Second Division match for the very first time, with a crowd of 29,908 welcoming the visit of Preston North End. Tom Griffiths and Tommy White scored the goals that maintained Everton's 100 per cent record to the start of the season with a 2–1 win.

1932	Birmingham City	H	First Division	4–1
1934	Leicester City	A	First Division	2–5
1938	Brentford	H	First Division	2–1
1947	Manchester City	A	First Division	1–0
1949	Huddersfield Town	H	First Division	3–0
1952	Sheffield United	H	Second Division	0–0
1955	Luton Town	H	First Division	0–1
1956	Burnley	A	First Division	1–2
1960	Aston Villa	A	First Division	2–3
1966	Stoke City	H	First Division	0–1
1968	Tranmere Rovers	H	League Cup 2nd Round	4–0
1969	Darlington	A	League Cup 2nd Round	1–0
1977	Wolverhampton Wanderers	H	First Division	0–0
1980	Blackpool	A	League Cup 2nd Round 2nd Leg	2–2
1983	Coventry City	A	First Division	1–1
1985	Sheffield Wednesday	A	First Division	5–1
1988	Coventry City	A	First Division	1–0
1991	Norwich City	H	First Division	1–1

SEPTEMBER 4TH

1893	Nottingham Forest	H	First Division	4–0
1897	Bolton Wanderers	H	First Division	2–1

1909	Tottenham Hotspur	H	First Division	4–2
1915	Bury	H	Lancashire Section Principal Tournament	5–0
1920	Bradford Park Avenue	H	First Division	1–1
1922	Tottenham Hotspur	A	First Division	0–2

David Raitt made his debut in the 2–0 defeat at White Hart Lane against Spurs. Born in Buckhaven he was first spotted by Dundee whilst playing army football during the First World War and made his debut in the 1919–20 season. Transferred to Everton in May 1922 he became the regular full-back for the club and went on to make 131 first-team appearances, although he later faced competition from first Duggie Livingstone and then John McDonald. After struggling for a place during the 1928–29 season he left for Blackburn Rovers.

1926	West Ham United	H	First Division	0–3
1935	Portsmouth	A	First Division	0–2
1937	Blackpool	A	First Division	0–1
1943	Blackburn Rovers	H	Football League North (First Championship)	0–0
1948	Birmingham City	H	First Division	0–5
1954	Burnley	A	First Division	2–0
1957	Manchester United	H	First Division	3–3
1963	Bolton Wanderers	A	First Division	1–1
1965	Burnley	H	First Division	1–0
1971	Derby County	H	First Division	0–2
1976	Leicester City	A	First Division	1–1
1982	Tottenham Hotspur	H	First Division	3–1
1984	Ipswich Town	H	First Division	1–1

Everton had still to get into their stride in the campaign, as can be witnessed by being held 1–1 at home to Ipswich. Adrian Heath netted his third goal of the season to at least avoid another defeat.

1996	Aston Villa	H	FA Premier League	0–1

SEPTEMBER 5TH

1891	West Bromwich Albion	A	Football League	0–4
1896	Sheffield Wednesday	H	First Division	2–1
1903	Notts County	H	First Division	3–1
1908	Bristol City	A	First Division	2–0
1914	Newcastle United	A	First Division	1–0
1925	Cardiff City	A	First Division	1–2
1927	Bolton Wanderers	A	First Division	1–1

Dixie Dean scored for the third consecutive game to grab a point for Everton in the 1–1 draw with Bolton.

1931	Sunderland	A	First Division	3–2
1932	Sheffield Wednesday	A	First Division	1–3
1936	Brentford	H	First Division	3–0
1938	Aston Villa	A	First Division	3–0
1942	Manchester United	A	Football League North (First Championship)	1–2
1951	Nottingham Forest	H	Second Division	1–0
1953	Bury	A	Second Division	2–2
1959	Fulham	H	First Division	0–0

1960	Blackpool	A	First Division	4–1
1962	Leyton Orient	H	First Division	3–0
1964	Burnley	A	First Division	1–1
1967	West Ham United	H	First Division	2–0
1970	West Ham United	A	First Division	2–1

The defending champions won their first match of the season 2–1 at West Ham thanks to goals from Joe Royle and Jimmy Husband. It was the seventh game of the campaign, with the opening games having garnered only three points.

1972	Arsenal	A	League Cup 2nd Round	0–1
1973	Stoke City	A	First Division	0–0
1979	Cardiff City	A	League Cup 2nd Round 2nd Leg	0–1

With Everton having already won the first leg 2–0, a 1–0 defeat at Ninian Park took them through to the next round 2–1 on aggregate. They were to face Aston Villa in the third round.

1981	Southampton	A	First Division	0–1
1987	Tottenham Hotspur	H	First Division	0–0

SEPTEMBER 6TH

1890	West Bromwich Albion	A	Football League	4–1

What was to be Everton's championship winning season kicked off with a 4–1 win at Stoney Lane, the then home of West Bromwich Albion. Fred Geary scored twice, with A. Brady and W. Campbell netting the others. Everton went on to win their opening five games of the season and dropped only one point of their opening seven on their way to the title.

1902	Middlesbrough	A	First Division	0–1
1909	Newcastle United	H	First Division	1–4
1911	Newcastle United	A	First Division	0–2
1913	Preston North End	H	First Division	2–0
1919	Chelsea	A	First Division	1–0
1924	West Bromwich Albion	H	First Division	1–0
1926	West Bromwich Albion	A	First Division	2–3
1930	Swansea Town	H	Second Division	5–1
1941	Stoke City	H	Football League North (First Championship)	3–1
1947	Derby County	A	First Division	0–1
1950	Arsenal	A	First Division	1–2
1952	Nottingham Forest	H	Second Division	3–0

1953 Ron Goodlass born in Liverpool. An Everton fan during his schooldays, he came to Goodison Park in 1971 as an apprentice and made his debut during the 1975–76 season. The arrival of Dave Thomas in 1977 restricted his first-team opportunities and he was sold to Dutch club Breda for £75,000 in October of that year. After two years he switched to Den Haag but was soon homesick for England and returned to play for Fulham. He later played for Scunthorpe and Tranmere before drifting into non-League football.

1958	Arsenal	H	First Division	1–6

The 1958–59 season had started badly and got steadily worse with Arsenal inflicting one of Everton's worst ever defeats in front of their own supporters. A crowd of 40,557 at Goodison could hardly believe their eyes as David Herd cracked home four of

Arsenal's goals that left Everton still looking for their first League point of the season after five games.

| 1961 | Manchester City | H | First Division | 0–2 |

1963 Pat Nevin born in Glasgow. After impressing in the Scottish League with Clyde he was sold to Chelsea for £95,000 in 1983 and became an integral part of the side, becoming a full Scottish international player. He cost Everton £925,000 when switching to Goodison Park in 1988 and became a firm favourite with the crowd. After a brief loan spell with Tranmere the move became permanent in 1992. He has won 28 caps for Scotland during his career.

| 1966 | Burnley | H | First Division | 1–1 |
| 1969 | Derby County | A | First Division | 1–2 |

After six wins and a draw Everton were beaten for the first time in the season, going down 2–1 at the Baseball Ground, the home of the newly promoted Derby County. John O'Hare had given Derby a first half lead which Howard Kendall cancelled in the second half, but a late winner from Kevin Hector won the game for the home side. Everton bounced back from the setback, winning nine of their next ten League matches and drawing the other as they opened up a commanding lead at the top of the First Division.

1975	Norwich City	A	First Division	2–4
1980	Wolverhampton Wanderers	H	First Division	2–0
1983	Ipswich Town	A	First Division	0–3
1986	Queens Park Rangers	H	First Division	0–0

SEPTEMBER 7TH

| 1889 | Blackburn Rovers | H | Football League | 3–2 |

Fred Geary made his League debut for the club on the opening day of the second season of the Football League. He scored twice in the 3–2 home win over Blackburn Rovers, and over the next six seasons was to become as important to his era as Dixie Dean was in his. He joined Everton from Grimsby, having previously been targeted by the club whilst playing for Notts Rangers, and went on to score 86 goals in just 98 first-team games. He was capped by England on two occasions and finished his playing career with Liverpool, joining them in 1894.

1891	Darwen	H	Football League	5–3
1895	Nottingham Forest	H	First Division	6–2
1901	Wolverhampton Wanderers	H	First Division	6–1
1907	Manchester City	H	First Division	3–3
1908	Woolwich Arsenal	H	First Division	0–3
1912	Middlesbrough	A	First Division	0–0
1914	Burnley	A	First Division	0–1

1915 Ephraim Dodds born in Grangemouth. Known universally as Jock, he had played for Sheffield United, Huddersfield and Blackpool before the Second World War, signing for Everton in November 1946. He made 56 League appearances, scoring 36 goals, and was then released to join Lincoln City in October 1948, with whom he finished his playing career. It was whilst playing for Blackpool during the Second World War that he set a record for scoring three goals within two and a half minutes, a record that lasted for nine years until equalled by Jimmy Scarth.

1918	Burnley	A	Lancashire Section Principal Tournament	6–0
1921	Newcastle United	H	First Division	2–3
1929	Liverpool	A	First Division	3–0
1935	Liverpool	A	First Division	0–6

A crowd of 48,000 were at Anfield for the opening derby of the season, with Everton starting much the brighter side in the opening exchanges. Fred Howe opened the scoring on a quarter of an hour with a glancing header, Gordon Hodgson's snap shot made it two before half an hour had passed and Hodgson added a third five minutes later. Shortly before half-time Howe made it four to Liverpool, although in fairness to Everton they had suffered two bad injuries to Dixie Dean and Williams. Everton recovered their composure in the second half and managed to hold out Liverpool for some forty minutes, but the strain of having to battle with only nine fully fit players finally told in the final four minutes as Howe netted twice to take his tally to four for the game.

1940	Manchester City	H	North Regional League	1–0
1946	Blackburn Rovers	A	First Division	1–4
1949	Manchester United	A	First Division	0–0
1955	Manchester United	A	First Division	1–2
1957	Chelsea	H	First Division	3–0
1963	Burnley	H	First Division	3–4
1965	West Bromwich Albion	H	First Division	2–3
1968	Chelsea	A	First Division	1–1
1971	Southampton	A	League Cup 2nd Round	1–2
1974	Ipswich Town	A	First Division	0–1
1985	Queens Park Rangers	A	First Division	0–3
1991	Crystal Palace	H	First Division	2–2
1996	Wimbledon	A	FA Premier League	0–4

SEPTEMBER 8TH

| 1888 | Accrington | H | Football League | 2–1 |

Everton kicked off their very first match in the newly–formed Football League with a 2–1 home win over Accrington. A crowd of 12,000, more than twice as many had been anticipated and the biggest of the day, saw Fleming score both of Everton's goals in the win.

1894	Stoke City	A	First Division	3–1
1900	Wolverhampton Wanderers	H	First Division	5–1
1906	Preston North End	H	First Division	1–0
1917	Southport	A	Lancashire Section Principal Tournament	2–0
1919	Bradford Park Avenue	H	First Division	0–0
1920	Newcastle United	A	First Division	0–2
1923	Blackburn Rovers	H	First Division	0–0
1924	Burnley	A	First Division	0–0

On the same day Jackie Grant was born in High Spen. He joined Everton during the Second World War and therefore had to wait until the end of hostilities before making his League debut. He went on to make 133 appearances for the first team, making his final appearance during the 1954–55 season and then being signed by Rochdale, where Harry Catterick was manager. He finished his playing career with Southport.

1928	Birmingham City	A	First Division	3–1
1930	Cardiff City	A	Second Division	2–1
1934	Grimsby Town	A	First Division	0–0
1937	Manchester City	H	First Division	4–1
1945	Preston North End	A	Football League North	2–0
1947	Aston Villa	A	First Division	0–3
1948	Stoke City	H	First Division	2–1
1951	Rotherham United	H	Second Division	3–3
1954	West Bromwich Albion	H	First Division	1–2
1956	Aston Villa	H	First Division	0–4
1962	Leicester City	H	First Division	3–2
1964	Manchester United	H	First Division	3–3

1966   Ray Atteveld born in Amsterdam. He joined Everton from Haarlem and made over 50 appearances for the first team.

1969   Gary Speed born in Deeside. He joined Leeds United as a trainee and was upgraded to the professional ranks in 1988. After eight years and over 300 appearances he joined Everton in 1996 for a fee of £3.5 million. He has won nearly 50 caps for Wales.

1973	Derby County	A	First Division	1–2
1979	Stoke City	A	First Division	3–2
1982	Manchester United	A	First Division	1–2
1984	Coventry City	H	First Division	2–1

Goals from Graeme Sharp and Trevor Steven enabled Everton to register only their second win of the season in front of a crowd of 20,013.

1990	Arsenal	H	First Division	1–1

SEPTEMBER 9TH

1893	Derby County	A	First Division	3–7

Jack Southworth made his debut for the club following his transfer from Blackburn Rovers. He had begun his career with Blackburn Olympic and switched to Rovers where he won two FA Cup winners' medals in 1890 and 1891. The following year he was awarded a testimonial by the club against Darwen and it cost Everton £400 to secure his signature in August 1893. Unfortunately he suffered with illness and injury whilst at Goodison and made only 32 appearances for the club, but still managed to rattle in 36 goals. He seemed to be set for a blistering goalscoring career but for injury which forced his retirement after just nine games of the 1894–95 season. He made 139 appearances for Rovers and Everton, scoring 139 goals, and also represented England on three occasions, scoring three goals! His ratio therefore is one of the best ever registered in League football. As well as his ability on the football field he was also an accomplished violinist, playing with the Halle Orchestra!

1895	Bury	H	First Division	3–2
1899	Newcastle United	A	First Division	0–2
1905	Preston North End	A	First Division	1–1
1907	Preston North End	H	First Division	2–1

John Maconnachie made his debut for the club in the 2–1 win over Preston at Goodison. Born in Aberdeen he had joined Everton from Hibernian but took a while to secure a permanent place in the side, finally slotting in at left–back and going on to make 270 appearances for the club. At the beginning of the 1920–21 he signed for Swindon Town.

1911	Manchester United	A	First Division	1–2
1916	Stoke City	H	Lancashire Section Principal Tournament	1–1
1922	Blackburn Rovers	H	First Division	2–0
1925	Birmingham City	H	First Division	2–2
1933	Sheffield Wednesday	H	First Division	2–3
1944	Bury	A	Football League North (First Championship)	2–1
1950	Stoke City	A	First Division	0–2
1958	Burnley	A	First Division	1–3
1961	Leicester City	A	First Division	0–2
1967	Fulham	A	First Division	1–2
1972	Leicester City	A	First Division	2–1
1975	Arsenal	H	League Cup 2nd Round	2–2
1978	Middlesbrough	H	First Division	2–0
1989	Manchester United	H	First Division	3–2
1995	Manchester United	H	FA Premier League	2–3

SEPTEMBER 10TH

1892	Aston Villa	A	First Division	1–4
1898	Newcastle United	H	First Division	3–0
1904	Sheffield United	H	First Division	2–0
1910	Preston North End	H	First Division	2–0
1921	Birmingham City	H	First Division	2–1
1927	Birmingham City	H	First Division	5–2

Dixie Dean and Alec Troup both scored twice for Everton in the 5–2 win over Birmingham City at Goodison, with Dick Forshaw netting the other in what was only Everton's second win of the season.

1932	Sunderland	A	First Division	1–3
1936	Sheffield Wednesday	A	First Division	4–6

A high scoring game at Hillsborough saw ten goals hitting the back of the net, with Torry Gillick (two), Willie Miller and Alex Stevenson on target for Everton.

1938	Arsenal	A	First Division	2–1
1949	Portsmouth	A	First Division	0–7

Reigning champions Portsmouth inflicted Everton's heaviest defeat of the season with a seven-goal blitz at Fratton Park. Portsmouth were to go on and retain their League title whilst Everton slid towards the bottom reaches of the table, avoiding relegation for 12 months by five points.

1952	Barnsley	A	Second Division	3–2
1953	Notts County	A	Second Division	2–0
1955	Charlton Athletic	A	First Division	2–0
1957	Arsenal	A	First Division	3–2
1960	Wolverhampton Wanderers	H	First Division	3–1
1966	Sheffield United	A	First Division	0–0
1977	Leicester City	A	First Division	5–1

Andy King scored twice and there were single efforts from Bob Latchford, Duncan McKenzie and Dave Thomas as Everton swept to their best away win of the season at Filbert Street in front of a crowd of 16,425.

1983	West Bromwich Albion	H	First Division	0–0
1988	Nottingham Forest	H	First Division	1–1
1994	Blackburn Rovers	A	FA Premier League	0–3

SEPTEMBER 11TH

1897	Derby County	A	First Division	1–5
1909	Preston North End	A	First Division	1–0
1915	Manchester United	A	Lancashire Section Principal Tournament	4–2
1920	Derby County	A	First Division	4–2
1926	Sheffield Wednesday	A	First Division	0–4
1929	Leeds United	H	First Division	1–1
1935	Portsmouth	H	First Division	3–0
1937	Brentford	A	First Division	3–0
1943	Manchester United	A	Football League North (First Championship)	1–4
1946	Arsenal	H	First Division	3–2
1948	Chelsea	A	First Division	0–6
1954	Leicester City	H	First Division	2–2
1963	Bolton Wanderers	H	First Division	2–0
1965	Chelsea	A	First Division	1–3

1968 Slaven Bilic born in Croatia. He joined West Ham from German club Karlsruhe in 1996 and switched to Goodison Park in a £4.5 million deal in 1997. A full Croatian international, he was one of the players responsible for their excellent showing in the 1998 World Cup finals in France, finishing the competition in third place, although Bilic was widely blamed for getting a French player sent off in the semi-final, thus meaning the player missed out on playing in the final. Indeed, whenever Bilic got the ball during the third and fourth place play-off against Holland he was booed by the crowd.

1971	Wolverhampton Wanderers	A	First Division	1–1
1973	Stoke City	H	First Division	1–1
1974	Aston Villa	A	League Cup 2nd Round	1–1
1976	Stoke City	H	First Division	3–0
1982	Notts County	A	First Division	0–1
1993	Oldham Athletic	A	FA Premier League	1–0

SEPTEMBER 12TH

1896	Wolverhampton Wanderers	A	First Division	1–0
1903	Sheffield United	A	First Division	1–2
1904	Aston Villa	A	First Division	0–1
1908	Preston North End	H	First Division	0–1
1914	Middlesbrough	H	First Division	2–3
1923	Aston Villa	A	First Division	1–1
1925	Tottenham Hotspur	H	First Division	1–1
1931	Manchester City	H	First Division	0–1
1936	Bolton Wanderers	A	First Division	2–1
1942	Liverpool	A	Football League North (First Championship)	0–1

1945	Liverpool	A	Football League North	1–2
1951	Nottingham Forest	A	Second Division	0–2
1953	Doncaster Rovers	H	Second Division	4–1
1956	Burnley	H	First Division	1–0
1959	Nottingham Forest	A	First Division	1–1
1962	Leyton Orient	A	First Division	0–3

Everton were visiting Brisbane Road for a League match for the first time in their history, with Leyton Orient winning the game 3–0. However, at the end of the season the respective fortunes of the two clubs couldn't have been more different; Everton won the League championship whilst Orient were relegated.

1964	Sheffield United	H	First Division	1–1
1970	Ipswich Town	H	First Division	2–0
1978	Finn Harps	A	UEFA Cup 1st Round 1st Leg	5–0

By virtue of having finished third in the League in 1977–78, Everton qualified for the UEFA Cup for the following season. In the first round they were drawn against Finn Harps, the first leg taking place in Ireland. There goals from Andy King (two), Bob Latchford, Dave Thomas and Mick Walsh earned Everton an easy 5–0 win to take into the second leg.

1981	Brighton & Hove Albion	H	First Division	1–1
1987	Luton Town	A	First Division	1–2
1992	Manchester United	H	FA Premier League	0–2

SEPTEMBER 13TH

1890	Wolverhampton Wanderers	H	Football League	5–0
1902	Newcastle United	H	First Division	0–1
1913	Newcastle United	A	First Division	1–0
1919	West Bromwich Albion	A	First Division	4–4
1924	Tottenham Hotspur	A	First Division	0–0
1930	West Bromwich Albion	A	Second Division	2–1
1941	Chester	H	Football League North (First Championship)	1–1
1947	Huddersfield Town	H	First Division	3–1
1948	Stoke City	A	First Division	0–1
1950	Arsenal	H	First Division	1–1
1952	Southampton	A	Second Division	1–1
1958	Manchester City	A	First Division	3–1
1967	Bristol City	A	League Cup 2nd Round	5–0

Everton returned to the League Cup, having played in the competition in its inaugural season of 1960–61 but then refusing to compete for the next six seasons. Although entry was still optional (and would remain so until 1969–70) only two teams failed to enter and Everton were given a potentially difficult tie away at Bristol City. Goals from Howard Kendall (two), Sandy Brown, John Hurst and Joe Royle saw them comfortably home 5–0. On the same day Warren Aspinall was born in Wigan. He joined Everton from Wigan in February 1986 for £150,000 and was loaned back immediately for the rest of the season. Unfortunately he failed to make the grade at Everton and was sold to Aston Villa in February 1987. He has since gone on to play for Portsmouth, Bournemouth, Swansea and Carlisle.

| 1969 | West Ham United | H | First Division | 2–0 |

After suffering their first defeat of the season the previous week, Everton got back on the winning trail with a 2–0 victory over West Ham thanks to goals from Alan Ball and Jimmy Husband.

1975	Newcastle United	H	First Division	3–0
1980	Aston Villa	A	First Division	2–0
1986	Wimbledon	A	First Division	2–1
1997	Derby County	A	FA Premier League	1–3

SEPTEMBER 14TH

1889	Burnley	H	Football League	2–1
1895	Bolton Wanderers	A	First Division	1–3
1901	Liverpool	A	First Division	2–2
1907	Preston North End	A	First Division	2–2
1912	Notts County	H	First Division	4–0
1918	Burnley	H	Lancashire Section Principal Tournament	6–1
1927	Bolton Wanderers	H	First Division	2–2

Dixie Dean took his tally for the season to six goals and had netted in each of the first five games of the season.

1929	Derby County	A	First Division	1–2
1935	Bolton Wanderers	A	First Division	0–2
1940	Preston North End	A	North Regional League	2–2
1946	Portsmouth	H	First Division	1–0
1955	Manchester United	H	First Division	4–2
1957	Sunderland	H	First Division	3–1
1960	Blackpool	H	First Division	1–0
1963	Ipswich Town	A	First Division	0–0
1968	Sheffield Wednesday	H	First Division	3–0
1974	Wolverhampton Wanderers	H	First Division	0–0
1985	Luton Town	H	First Division	2–0
1991	Sheffield United	A	First Division	1–2
1995	KR Reykjavik	A	European Cup-Winners' Cup 1st Round 1st Leg	3–2

English clubs had finally been re–admitted to European competition in 1990 following the ban imposed in 1985. Manchester United had made it a winning return too, winning the Cup-Winners' Cup that season. Everton had to wait five years before making their reappearance, their FA Cup win over Manchester United giving them entry into the Cup-Winners' Cup. Their opponents were KR Reykjavik and a 3–2 win, thanks to goals from John Ebbrell, David Unsworth from the penalty spot and Daniel Amokachi meant it was November 1966 since Everton had been beaten in the European Cup-Winners' Cup.

| 1996 | Middlesbrough | H | FA Premier League | 1–2 |

SEPTEMBER 15TH

1888	Notts County	H	Football League	2–1
1894	Nottingham Forest	H	First Division	6–1
1900	Aston Villa	A	First Division	2–1

1906	Newcastle United	A	First Division	0–1
1917	Burnley	H	Lancashire Section Principal Tournament	9–0

Everton took their tally of goals in the Lancashire Section Principal Tournament to 17 in just three games with this 9–0 hammering of Burnley. Gault led the scoring with four goals, with Clennell and Fleetwood both netting twice and the other goal coming from Jefferis.

1923	Blackburn Rovers	A	First Division	0–2
1926	West Bromwich Albion	H	First Division	0–0
1928	Manchester City	H	First Division	2–6

Five of City's goals were scored by T. Johnson, one of only two occasions that an opposing player has scored as many as five goals against Everton.

1934	Liverpool	H	First Division	1–0
1937	Derby County	A	First Division	1–2
1945	Preston North End	H	Football League North	1–1

On the same day Dave Clements was born in Portadown. Although he began his career with Wolves he was transferred to Coventry in 1964 for £1,000 without having made an appearance for the first team. At Coventry he was allowed to develop into a quality midfield player, later joining Sheffield Wednesday in 1971. He arrived at Goodison in September 1973 and made almost 100 appearances for the first team. In March 1975 he was appointed manager of Northern Ireland, although his subsequent decision to go and play in North America brought this position to an end.

1951	Cardiff City	A	Second Division	1–3
1954	West Bromwich Albion	A	First Division	3–3
1956	Luton Town	A	First Division	0–2
1962	Bolton Wanderers	A	First Division	2–0
1965	West Bromwich Albion	A	First Division	1–1
1973	Queens Park Rangers	H	First Division	1–0
1979	Wolverhampton Wanderers	H	First Division	2–3
1984	Newcastle United	A	First Division	3–2

After a stuttering start to the campaign Everton were at last beginning to find their form and march up the table. Goals from Andy Gray, Kevin Sheedy and Graeme Sharp brought them a 3–2 win at St James' Park against Newcastle.

1990	Sunderland	A	First Division	2–2
1992	Blackburn Rovers	A	FA Premier League	3–2

SEPTEMBER 16TH

1889	Wolverhampton Wanderers	A	Football League	1–2
1893	Aston Villa	H	First Division	4–2
1899	Aston Villa	H	First Division	1–2
1905	Newcastle United	H	First Division	1–2
1911	Liverpool	H	First Division	2–1
1916	Southport	A	Lancashire Section Principal Tournament	0–1
1922	Blackburn Rovers	A	First Division	1–5

John McIntyre of Blackburn Rovers netted the fastest hat-trick in the First Division with three goals in three minutes against Everton. McIntyre scored again two minutes later to make it four inside five minutes and Blackburn finally won 5–1.

1925	West Bromwich Albion	H	First Division	4–0
1929	Leeds United	A	First Division	1–2
1931	Derby County	A	First Division	0–3
1933	Manchester City	A	First Division	2–2
1944	Bury	H	Football League North (First Championship)	4–1
1950	Liverpool	H	First Division	1–3

1958 Neville Southall born in Llandudno. Probably one of the greatest goalkeepers to have played for Everton, he began his career with Bury, costing them £6,000 from non-League Winsford United in 1980. He cost Everton just £150,000 when transferred in July 1981 and went on to give the club exceptional service over the next 17 years. Whilst at Goodison he won two FA Cup winners' medals, two League titles, the European Cup-Winners' Cup and three FA Charity Shield medals and amassed over 90 caps for Wales. Over the years he saw off just about every challenger for his position and retained the affection of the fans throughout. He finished the 1997–98 season playing for both Southend and Stoke City after becoming Everton's most capped player and their League appearance record holder. He was named the Football Association Writers' Footballer of the Year in 1985, the first Everton player to be so honoured.

1959	Blackburn Rovers	H	First Division	2–0
1961	Ipswich Town	H	First Division	5–2

Derek Temple scored a hat-trick and Billy Bingham and Sandy Young were also on target as Everton beat newly promoted Ipswich 5–2 at Goodison. Amazingly, Ipswich went on to win the League title at the end of the season!

1964	Manchester United	A	First Division	1–2
1967	Leeds United	H	First Division	0–1
1970	IB Keflavik	H	European Cup 1st Round 1st Leg	6–2

Everton returned to the European Cup with an easy 6–2 win over the Icelandic champions Keflavik thanks to goals from Alan Ball, who scored a hat-trick, two from Joe Royle and Howard Kendall. However, one of Kefalvik's goals was an own goal from goalkeeper Gordon West, whose hand gestures to the crowd behind the goal were to cost him his place in the side for much of the rest of the season, especially as the incident was picked up on television!

1972	Southampton	H	First Division	0–1
1978	Aston Villa	A	First Division	1–1
1986	Liverpool	A	Screen Sport Super Cup final 1st Leg	1–3

In March both Everton and Liverpool had won through to the final of the Super Cup, the competition organised to give the clubs who had qualified for Europe but were banned by UEFA some form of compensation. The competition had been shambolic, unloved by the fans and players alike and the final held over to the following season. There was at last a sponsor for the tournament, Screen Sport, and a trophy to be won, with the final to be decided over two legs. At Anfield just 20,660 fans, indicative of both the esteem with which the competition was held and how frequently the two sides were being paired, saw Liverpool win 3–1 thanks to two goals from Ian Rush and one from Steve McMahon as opposed one goal from Kevin Sheedy.

1989	Charlton Athletic	A	First Division	1–0
1997	Scunthorpe United	A	Coca–Cola Cup 2nd Round 1st Leg	1–0

SEPTEMBER 17TH

1892	Blackburn Rovers	A	First Division	2–2
1898	Preston North End	A	First Division	0–0
1904	Newcastle United	A	First Division	2–3
1906	Notts County	H	First Division	2–2
1910	Notts County	A	First Division	0–0
1921	Birmingham City	A	First Division	1–1
1924	Leeds United	A	First Division	0–1
1927	Newcastle United	A	First Division	2–2

Both Everton goals were scored by Dixie Dean, his eighth goal of the season and the seventh consecutive game he had found the net.

1930	Cardiff City	H	Second Division	1–1

Everton dropped their first Second Division point as they were held to a 1–1 draw by Cardiff City at Goodison Park, Dixie Dean scoring for Everton. The team had started with five straight wins and were already top of the table, a position they were to maintain for the rest of the campaign.

1932	Manchester City	H	First Division	2–1
1938	Portsmouth	H	First Division	5–1
1947	Aston Villa	H	First Division	3–0
1949	Wolverhampton Wanderers	H	First Division	1–2
1955	Tottenham Hotspur	H	First Division	2–1
1958	Burnley	H	First Division	1–2
1960	Bolton Wanderers	A	First Division	4–3
1966	West Bromwich Albion	H	First Division	5–4
1969	Newcastle United	A	First Division	2–1

Two goals from Jimmy Husband were enough to sink Newcastle United in front of their own fans as Everton further extended their lead at the top of the table.

1975	AC Milan	H	UEFA Cup 1st Round 1st Leg	0–0

In 1971 the Inter-Cities Fairs Cup had been replaced by the UEFA Cup, with Everton's final League placing of fourth in 1974–75 enough to give them entry to the competition the following season. The opposition could not have been tougher either, for it was the ultra-defensive Italians of AC Milan who were making their first visit to Goodison Park. Here they were prepared to concede territory and possession but not a goal, and a goalless draw was always the likeliest outcome.

1977	Norwich City	H	First Division	3–0
1983	Tottenham Hotspur	A	First Division	2–1
1988	Millwall	A	First Division	1–2
1991	Manchester City	A	First Division	1–0
1994	Queens Park Rangers	H	FA Premier League	2–2
1995	Nottingham Forest	A	FA Premier League	2–3

SEPTEMBER 18TH

1897	Wolverhampton Wanderers	H	First Division	3–0
1909	Notts County	H	First Division	2–0
1912	Derby County	A	First Division	4–1

1915	Blackpool	H	Lancashire Section Principal Tournament	4–2
1920	Derby County	H	First Division	3–1
1926	Leicester City	H	First Division	3–4
1935	Preston North End	A	First Division	2–2
1937	Bolton Wanderers	A	First Division	2–1

1939 It was announced that friendly matches could be organised, a little over two weeks after the Football League had been abandoned owing to the Second World War.

| 1943 | Manchester United | H | Football League North (First Championship) | 6–1 |
| 1948 | Liverpool | H | First Division | 1–1 |

The visit of Liverpool (who else!) attracted the biggest ever crowd seen at Goodison for a League match, a total of 78,299 for a match that finished all square at 1–1, Dodds scoring for Everton.

| 1954 | Chelsea | A | First Division | 2–0 |
| 1963 | Internazionale | H | European Cup 1st Round 1st Leg | 0–0 |

Everton made their debut in the European Cup with a home match against Internazionale of Milan that ended goalless. The Italians were, of course, past masters at shutting up shop, especially away from home and frustrated all of Everton's attempts to score.

1965	Arsenal	H	First Division	3–1
1971	Arsenal	H	First Division	2–1
1973	Heart of Midlothian	H	Texaco Cup 1st Round 1st Leg	0–1

With Everton having failed to qualify for European competition since 1970–71, when they had competed in the European Cup by virtue of winning the League the previous season, Everton accepted an invitation to enter the Texaco Cup, a competition that had begun life as a pre-season tournament involving English and Scottish League sides but which had since evolved into a knock-out competition of home and away legs. Everton made their debut at Tynecastle, going down 1–0 to a strong Hearts side.

1974	Aston Villa	H	League Cup 2nd Round Replay	0–3
1976	Arsenal	A	First Division	1–3
1982	Norwich City	H	First Division	1–1
1985	Manchester United	A	Screen Sport Super Cup Group B	4–2

Immediately after UEFA announced their ban on English clubs competing in European competition, a direct result of the events at the Heysel Stadium before Liverpool's European Cup final with Juventus, the six clubs who would have qualified (League champions Everton, FA Cup winners Manchester United and the four UEFA Cup qualifiers Spurs, Norwich City, Southampton and Liverpool) had discussed how to compensate for the lack of revenue European competition would have generated. Whilst some, led by Manchester United, tried to appeal against the decision to ban English clubs through the courts, others suggested a competition exclusive to those clubs. Thus the Super Cup was born, with the six clubs being divided into two groups of three clubs, each playing the others home and away, the top two in each group then moving forward to a knock-out competition. Everton kicked off their campaign in the competition with a 4–2 win at Old Trafford, their goals coming from Kevin Sheedy (two), Gary Lineker and Graeme Sharp.

| 1993 | Liverpool | H | FA Premier League | 2–0 |
| 1996 | York City | H | Coca–Cola Cup 2nd Round 1st Leg | 1–1 |

SEPTEMBER 19TH

1891	Blackburn Rovers	H	Football League	3–1
1896	Aston Villa	H	First Division	2–3
1903	Newcastle United	H	First Division	4–1
1908	Middlesbrough	A	First Division	3–2
1914	Sheffield United	A	First Division	0–1
1923	Aston Villa	H	First Division	2–0
1925	Manchester City	A	First Division	4–4
1931	Liverpool	A	First Division	3–1

After Everton's brief sojourn in the Second Division battle against local rivals Liverpool was resumed at Anfield in the first derby of the season. In front of a crowd of 53,220 Deixie Dean scored a hat-trick to win the game for the visitors, his first hat-trick of the season.

1936	Liverpool	H	First Division	2–0

Dixie Dean scored one of Everton's goals in the 2–0 win over Liverpool (Alex Stevenson scored the other), his 19th and final goal in the derby clash and a then record. The record was finally broken by Ian Rush of Liverpool in 1994.

1942	Liverpool	H	Football League North (First Championship)	4–4
1953	Blackburn Rovers	A	Second Division	0–0
1959	Sheffield Wednesday	H	First Division	2–1
1964	Liverpool	A	First Division	4–0
1970	Blackpool	A	First Division	2–0
1979	Feyenoord	A	UEFA Cup 1st Round 1st Leg	0–1

At the end of the 1978–79 season Everton finished fourth in the League (albeit 17 points behind champions Liverpool, and this in an age when there were still only two points for a win!) and qualified for the following season's UEFA Cup. The first round paired them with Feyenoord, one of Holland's top sides, and in the first leg in Rotterdam Everton were forced to defend for much of the 90 minutes. Feyenoord scored once and should have got a couple more, but Everton were confident they could overcome the deficit in the second leg at Goodison.

1981	Tottenham Hotspur	A	First Division	0–3
1984	UC Dublin	A	European Cup-Winners' Cup 1st Round 1st Leg	0–0

Everton began their European Cup-Winners' Cup campaign with an unconvincing 0–0 draw against the University Club of Dublin. Indeed, the Irish side had chances of their own to pull off a shock win against Everton, but Everton were convinced they could score more than enough goals in the second leg to make the tie a formality.

1987	Manchester United	H	First Division	2–1
1989	Leyton Orient	A	Littlewoods Cup 2nd Round 1st Leg	2–0
1992	Crystal Palace	H	FA Premier League	0–2

SEPTEMBER 20TH

1890	Bolton Wanderers	A	Football League	5–0
1902	Wolverhampton Wanderers	A	First Division	1–1
1909	Sheffield Wednesday	A	First Division	3–1
1913	Liverpool	H	First Division	1–2

George Harrison made his debut in the League match against Liverpool at Goodison, won 2–1 by the visitors. He was born in Derbyshire in 1891 and began his career with Leicester Fosse in 1910, transferring to Everton in 1913. A powerfully built winger he went on to make 190 first-team appearances despite losing four seasons to the First World War. He was transferred to Preston midway through the 1923–24 season and finished his career with Blackpool.

1919	West Bromwich Albion	H	First Division	3–5
1924	Bolton Wanderers	H	First Division	2–2
1926	Birmingham City	A	First Division	0–1
1930	Port Vale	H	Second Division	2–3
1941	Chester	A	Football League North (First Championship)	0–2
1947	Chelsea	A	First Division	1–3
1952	Brentford	A	Second Division	4–2
1958	Leeds United	H	First Division	3–2
1961	Manchester City	A	First Division	3–1
1969	Ipswich Town	A	First Division	3–0
1975	Arsenal	A	First Division	2–2
1976	Stockport County	A	League Cup 3rd Round	1–0
1980	Crystal Palace	H	First Division	5–0

Bob Latchford hit a hat-trick for Everton, his first goals of the season as Crystal Palace were beaten 5–0 at Goodison. The other goals were scored by Peter Eastoe and John Gidman.

1994	Portsmouth	H	Coca–Cola Cup 2nd Round 1st Leg	2–3
1995	Millwall	A	Coca–Cola Cup 2nd Round 1st Leg	0–0
1997	Barnsley	H	FA Premier League	4–2

SEPTEMBER 21ST

| 1889 | Bolton Wanderers | A | Football League | 4–3 |

This win over Bolton enabled Everton to take over at the top of the table for the first time in their history, although their tenure at the top lasted only four weeks before they were replaced by champions Preston. Preston went on to win the League for a second time, but Everton's turn was soon coming.

| 1895 | Blackburn Rovers | H | First Division | 0–2 |

Blackburn Rovers were the only side to win at Goodison Park all season with this 2–0 win.

1901	Newcastle United	H	First Division	0–0
1907	Bury	H	First Division	6–1
1912	Manchester United	A	First Division	0–2
1918	Southport	A	Lancashire Section Principal Tournament	3–0
1925	Birmingham City	A	First Division	1–3
1929	Manchester City	H	First Division	2–3
1935	Huddersfield Town	H	First Division	1–3
1940	Chester	H	North Regional League	4–3
1946	Liverpool	A	First Division	0–0
1949	Peter Farrell scored for the Republic of Ireland in the international match with England. As the game was being played at Goodison Park, Farrell became the first international player to score an away goal on his own home ground! The Republic of Ireland went on to win 2–0.			

1957	Luton Town	A	First Division	1–0
1959	Blackburn Rovers	A	First Division	1–3
1963	Sheffield Wednesday	H	First Division	3–2
1968	Coventry City	A	First Division	2–2

1969   Trevor Steven born in Berwick. He began his career with Burnley and cost Everton £300,000 when signed in July 1983. A permanent fixture for the next six years until a £1.25 million move to Glasgow Rangers, he won an FA Cup, two League championship and European Cup-Winners' Cup medals at Goodison. He later had a brief spell with Marseille but returned to Ibrox when the French club were unable to pay an instalment of his transfer fee!

1974	Coventry City	A	First Division	1–1

1979   Richard Dunne born in Dublin. He is the youngest player to have played for Everton, being only 17 years and 106 days when he made his debut against Swindon in January 1997.

1985	Liverpool	H	First Division	2–3
1986	Manchester United	H	First Division	3–1
1991	Coventry City	H	First Division	3–0
1993	Lincoln City	A	Coca–Cola Cup 2nd Round 1st Leg	4–3
1996	Blackburn Rovers	A	FA Premier League	1–1

SEPTEMBER 22ND

1888	Aston Villa	A	Football League	1–2
1894	Nottingham Forest	A	First Division	3–2
1900	Liverpool	H	First Division	1–1
1906	Aston Villa	H	First Division	1–2

Villa were the only side to win at Goodison Park all season, with Everton finally finishing the campaign in third place behind Newcastle United and Bristol City.

1917	Burnley	A	Lancashire Section Principal Tournament	5–0
1920	Sheffield United	H	First Division	3–0
1923	Huddersfield Town	H	First Division	1–1
1928	Huddersfield Town	A	First Division	1–3
1934	Huddersfield Town	H	First Division	4–2
1945	Leeds United	H	Football League North	0–2
1951	Birmingham City	H	Second Division	1–3
1956	Sunderland	H	First Division	2–1
1962	Liverpool	H	First Division	2–2
1973	Wolverhampton Wanderers	A	First Division	1–1
1979	Ipswich Town	A	First Division	1–1
1981	Notts County	H	First Division	3–1
1984	Southampton	H	First Division	2–2

Although Everton dropped another two points the draw against Southampton enabled them to maintain sixth position in the League, nicely placed behind the leaders. Derek Mountfield and Graeme Sharp had enabled Everton to go in at half-time 2–1 but Steve Moran netted his second goal of the game in the second period to peg Everton back.

1987	Rotherham United	H	Littlewoods Cup 2nd Round 1st Leg	3–2
1990	Liverpool	H	First Division	2–3

SEPTEMBER 23RD

1893	Aston Villa	A	First Division	1–3
1899	Liverpool	A	First Division	2–1
1905	Aston Villa	A	First Division	0–4
1911	Aston Villa	A	First Division	0–3
1916	Blackburn Rovers	H	Lancashire Section Principal Tournament	2–5
1922	Cardiff City	A	First Division	2–0
1931	Derby County	H	First Division	2–1
1933	Arsenal	H	First Division	3–1
1944	Chester	H	Football League North (First Championship)	6–2

Tommy Lawton scored his first goals of the season, netting twice in the 6–2 win over Bury. There was also a brace for G. Makin, with Rawlings and Wainwright hitting the other two goals.

1950	Portsmouth	H	First Division	1–5
1953	Notts County	H	Second Division	3–2
1961	Burnley	A	First Division	1–2
1964	Valerengen IF	A	Inter-Cities Fairs Cup 1st Round 1st Leg	5–2

Everton's third consecutive season in European competition began with a trip to Valerengen for the Inter-Cities Fairs Cup first round, goals from Fred Pickering (two), Colin Harvey, Alex Scott and Derek Temple earning them a 5–2 victory.

1967	Liverpool	A	First Division	0–1
1972	Birmingham City	A	First Division	1–2
1975	Arsenal	A	League Cup 2nd Round Replay	1–0
1978	Wolverhampton Wanderers	H	First Division	2–0
1989	Liverpool	H	First Division	1–3
1992	Rotherham United	A	Coca–Cola Cup 2nd Round 1st Leg	0–1
1995	West Ham United	A	FA Premier League	1–2

SEPTEMBER 24TH

1892	Newton Heath	H	First Division	6–0

The first ever League meeting between Everton and the club that was ultimately to become Manchester United saw Everton register a resounding 6–0 win. Newton Heath had been elected straight into the First Division at the start of the campaign, even though the Second Division was instigated at the same time. They were obviously out of their depth at the time, finishing the season bottom of the table although they did avoid relegation by winning the Test match over Small Heath (the forerunners of Birmingham City).

1898	Liverpool	H	First Division	1–2
1904	Preston North End	H	First Division	1–0
1910	Manchester United	H	First Division	0–1
1921	Arsenal	H	First Division	1–1

Another brace for Dixie Dean meant he had scored ten goals in the opening eight games of the season, although with four of their matches having ended in draws Everton were still some way off the top of the table.

1927	Huddersfield Town	H	First Division	2–2
1932	Arsenal	A	First Division	1–2

1938	Huddersfield Town	A	First Division	0–3
1949	Aston Villa	A	First Division	2–2
1955	Portsmouth	A	First Division	0–1
1960	West Ham United	H	First Division	4–1

1965 Anders Limpar born in Solna in Sweden. He joined Arsenal from Cremonese for £1 million in 1990 and helped them win the League title in 1991. In 1994 he switched to Everton for £1.6 million and helped them win the FA Cup in 1995, subsequently going on to Birmingham City in 1997 for a cut price £100,000.

1966	Leeds United	A	First Division	1–1
1968	Luton Town	H	League Cup 3rd Round	5–1
1969	Arsenal	A	League Cup 3rd Round	0–0

With the League campaign going so well Everton took a brief diversion with the arrival of the League Cup. They were drawn against an Arsenal side that had been runners-up in both the previous two season (beaten by Leeds in 1968 and Swindon in 1969) but defended stoutly at Highbury to earn a replay at Goodison.

1974	Queens Park Rangers	A	First Division	2–2
1977	West Ham United	A	First Division	1–1
1980	West Bromwich Albion	H	League Cup 3rd Round	1–2
1983	Birmingham City	H	First Division	1–1
1986	Newport County	H	Littlewoods Cup 2nd Round 1st Leg	4–0
1988	Luton Town	H	First Division	0–2
1991	Watford	H	Rumbelows Cup 2nd Round 1st Leg	1–0
1994	Leicester City	H	FA Premier League	1–1
1996	York City	A	Coca–Cola Cup 2nd Round 2nd Leg	2–3
1997	Newcastle United	A	FA Premier League	0–1

SEPTEMBER 25TH

1897	Liverpool	A	First Division	1–3
1909	Newcastle United	A	First Division	2–1
1915	Southport	A	Lancashire Section Principal Tournament	1–2
1920	Blackburn Rovers	A	First Division	0–0
1926	Liverpool	H	First Division	1–0
1937	Huddersfield Town	H	First Division	1–2
1943	Burnley	A	Football League North (First Championship)	0–0
1948	Preston North End	H	First Division	4–1
1954	Cardiff City	H	First Division	1–1
1963	Internazionale	A	European Cup 1st Round 2nd Leg	0–1

Everton's first attempt to win the European Cup came to an end at the first hurdle. After a goalless home match with Internazionale, they lost the second leg at the San Siro Stadium in Milan 1–0. The strength of the opposition can be gauged by the fact that they went on to lift the cup, beating Real Madrid in the final and ensuring that the trophy remained in Milan following AC's victory the year before.

1965	Liverpool	A	First Division	0–5
1971	Crystal Palace	A	First Division	1–2
1976	Bristol City	H	First Division	2–0
1979	Aston Villa	A	League Cup 3rd Round	0–0
1982	Coventry City	A	First Division	2–4

| 1985 | Bournemouth | H | Milk Cup 2nd Round 1st Leg | 3–2 |
| 1990 | Wrexham | A | Rumbelows Cup 2nd Round 1st Leg | 5–0 |

Tony Cottee scored a hat-trick as Everton effectively made the second leg a formality with a 5–0 win at Wrexham. Neil McDonald and Pat Nevin scored the other Everton goals.

| 1993 | Norwich City | H | FA Premier League | 1–5 |

Everton were in fourth place in the Premier League the morning of the match; by five o'clock they had slipped to eighth place after their heaviest home defeat had been inflicted by Norwich City. Paul Rideout had even given Everton the lead in the first half, but a four-goal blitz from Efan Ekoku and one from Chris Sutton won the game for Norwich.

SEPTEMBER 26TH

1891	Accrington	A	Football League	1–1
1895	Glasgow Rangers	A	Friendly	1–3
1896	Aston Villa	A	First Division	2–1
1903	Aston Villa	A	First Division	1–3
1908	Manchester City	H	First Division	6–3
1914	Aston Villa	H	First Division	0–0
1925	Liverpool	A	First Division	1–5
1931	Arsenal	A	First Division	2–3
1936	Huddersfield Town	H	First Division	2–1
1942	Burnley	H	Football League North (First Championship)	2–1

1952 George Wood born in Douglas. He began his career in Scotland playing with East Stirling and was subsequently transferred to Blackpool in 1972. Five and a half years later he was sold to Everton for £150,000 and was ever-present for two seasons, his consistency in goal earning him a total of three caps for Scotland. Unfortunately he found it difficult to maintain that consistency and was replaced by Martin Hodge before being transferred to Arsenal for £150,000 in 1980. Three years later he moved on again to Crystal Palace.

1953	Derby County	H	Second Division	3–2
1959	Wolverhampton Wanderers	A	First Division	0–2
1964	Birmingham City	A	First Division	5–3
1970	Crystal Palace	H	First Division	3–1
1978	Finn Harps	H	UEFA Cup 1st Round 2nd Leg	5–0

Everton completed a 10–0 aggregate win, the first time they had reached double figures, in the UEFA Cup first round with a 5–0 win over Finn Harps at Goodison Park. The goals were scored by Martin Dobson, Andy King, Bob Latchford, Trevor Ross and Mick Walsh.

1981	West Bromwich Albion	H	First Division	1–0
1984	Sheffield United	A	Milk Cup 2nd Round 1st Leg	2–2
1987	Coventry City	H	First Division	1–2
1992	Leeds United	A	FA Premier League	0–2

SEPTEMBER 27TH

1884 Everton played their first match at their new ground at Anfield Road. The site was originally a field owned by club president John Houlding and the Orrell brothers, with

Houlding acting as agents for the brothers. In turning it into a football pitch, the club agreed 'That we, the Everton Football Club, keep the existing walls in good repair, pay the taxes, do not cause ourselves to be a nuisance to Mr Orrell and other tenants adjoining, and also pay a small sum of rent or substitute a donation each year to the Stanley Hospital in the name of Mr Orrell.' The visitors for the first match were Earlestown, who Everton had beaten in March to win their very first cup, the Liverpool Cup, with Everton this time winning 5–0.

1890	Accrington	A	Football League	2–1
1894	Glasgow Rangers	A	Friendly	4–1
1902	Liverpool	H	First Division	3–1
1913	Aston Villa	A	First Division	1–3
1919	Sunderland	A	First Division	3–2
1924	Notts County	A	First Division	1–3
1930	Bradford City	A	Second Division	3–0
1941	Manchester United	A	Football League North (First Championship)	3–2
1947	Liverpool	H	First Division	0–3
1952	Doncaster Rovers	H	Second Division	7–1

Doncaster Rovers were demolished 7–2 at Goodison Park, with Tom Eglington grabbing five of the goals. This would have been an exceptional performance under any circumstances, but the fact he was playing at outside-left made it even greater. Everton's other goals were scored by John Willie Parker in front of a crowd of 34,344.

1958	West Bromwich Albion	A	First Division	3–2
1969	Southampton	H	First Division	4–2
1975	Liverpool	H	First Division	0–0
1980	Coventry City	A	First Division	5–0

Everton hit five goals for the second consecutive week, this time at Coventry's Highfield Road. Bob Latchford scored twice, as did Joe McBride and Peter Eastoe grabbed the other.

1986	Tottenham Hotspur	A	First Division	0–2
1988	Bury	H	Littlewoods Cup 2nd Round 1st Leg	3–0
1997	Arsenal	H	FA Premier League	2–2

SEPTEMBER 28TH

1889	Bolton Wanderers	H	Football League	3–0
1893	Glasgow Rangers	A	Friendly	1–2
1895	Wolverhampton Wanderers	A	First Division	3–2
1901	Aston Villa	A	First Division	1–1
1907	Aston Villa	A	First Division	2–0
1912	Aston Villa	H	First Division	0–1
1918	Southport	H	Lancashire Section Principal Tournament	4–0
1929	Portsmouth	A	First Division	4–1
1935	Middlesbrough	A	First Division	1–6
1940	Leeds United	H	North Regional League	5–1
1946	Huddersfield Town	A	First Division	0–1
1963	Liverpool	A	First Division	1–2
1965	FC Nuremberg	A	Inter-Cities Fairs Cup 1st Round 1st Leg	1–1

A trip to Germany saw Everton play their first Inter-Cities Fairs Cup match of the season, drawing 1–1 with FC Nuremberg thanks to a goal from Brian Harris.

| 1966 | AB Aalborg | A | European Cup-Winners' Cup | 0–0 |
| | | | 1st Round 1st Leg | |

Everton were drawn away in the first leg of the European Cup-Winners' Cup first round with Aalborg, and a solid defensive display enabled them to register a 0–0 draw in Denmark.

1968	West Bromwich Albion	H	First Division	4–0
1974	Leeds United	H	First Division	3–2
1985	Aston Villa	A	First Division	0–0
1991	Chelsea	A	First Division	2–2
1995	KR Reykjavik	H	European Cup-Winners' Cup	3–1
			1st Round 2nd Leg	

Goodison Park staged its first European Cup-Winners' Cup match since 1985, with the visit of KR Reykjavik attracting a crowd of 18,422. With Everton already 3–2 ahead from the away leg, the visitors were not expected to pose too many problems, and goals from Graham Stuart, Tony Grant and Paul Rideout enabled Everton to win 3–1 on the night, 6–3 on aggregate.

| 1996 | Sheffield Wednesday | H | FA Premier League | 2–0 |

SEPTEMBER 29TH

| 1888 | Bolton Wanderers | A | Football League | 2–6 |

Having opened the inaugural League season with two wins Everton suffered successive defeats, including this 6–2 reverse at Bolton, their biggest defeat of the season.

1894	West Bromwich Albion	H	First Division	4–1
1900	Newcastle United	A	First Division	0–1
1906	Liverpool	A	First Division	2–1
1917	Liverpool	H	Lancashire Section Principal Tournament	2–2
1923	Huddersfield Town	A	First Division	0–2
1926	Bury	H	First Division	2–2
1928	Liverpool	H	First Division	1–0
1934	Wolverhampton Wanderers	A	First Division	2–4
1945	Leeds United	A	Football League North	3–2
1951	Leicester City	A	Second Division	2–1
1956	Charlton Athletic	A	First Division	2–1

1958 Mark Higgins born in Buxton. But for a career threatening injury Mark may well have gone on to represent England at full international level, having already collected caps for Schoolboy and Youth appearances. He had joined Everton straight from school, signing as an apprentice in 1975 and making his League debut 18 months later. He went on to make 178 appearances for the first team and was on the verge of a call-up for the England squad when his injuries were first diagnosed, a simple groin injury developing into pelvic trouble. He officially retired from the game but following revolutionary surgery made a comeback with Manchester United which cost the Old Trafford club £60,000 in insurance compensation.

| 1962 | West Bromwich Albion | H | First Division | 4–2 |
| 1973 | Arsenal | H | First Division | 1–0 |

1979	Bristol City	H	First Division	0–0
1984	Watford	A	First Division	5–4

The League meeting between the two sides that had contested the FA Cup final four months previously saw Watford crash to the bottom of the table after a 5–4 defeat by Everton. Adrian Heath scored twice and there were single efforts from Derek Mountfield, Graeme Sharp and Trevor Steven in one of the most entertaining games of the season.

1990	Southampton	H	First Division	3–0

SEPTEMBER 30TH

1889	Wolverhampton Wanderers	H	Football League	1–1
1893	Sunderland	H	First Division	7–1
1895	Aston Villa	A	First Division	3–4

Charlie Parry made the last of his 94 appearances for the club. He was spotted whilst playing in Welsh junior football and joined Everton in 1889, making his debut at the start of the second season of League football. Initially introduced as a wing half he found greater joy and more consistent performances when switched to full-back, although he did manage to score four goals in 22 appearances in his first season in the side. A member of the championship winning side of 1890–91 he left Everton for Newtown in 1895 and won a total of 13 caps for Wales, six of which he earned whilst with Everton.

1899	Burnley	H	First Division	2–0
1905	Liverpool	H	First Division	4–2
1911	Newcastle United	H	First Division	2–0
1916	Manchester City	A	Lancashire Section Principal Tournament	1–4
1922	Cardiff City	H	First Division	3–1
1933	Liverpool	A	First Division	2–3
1944	Chester	A	Football League North (First Championship)	6–2
1946				

Tommy Eglington earned his first cap for the Republic of Ireland in the match against England in Dublin, with England winning the game 1–0. Later the same year, in November, Tommy was also selected for Northern Ireland to play against Scotland, along with Peter Farrell, the only players to have won caps for more than one country whilst on Everton's books, something then permissible.

1950	Chelsea	A	First Division	1–2
1961	Arsenal	H	First Division	4–1
1967	Leicester City	A	First Division	2–0
1970	IB Keflavik	A	European Cup 1st Round 2nd Leg	3—

Everton completed a convincing 9–2 aggregate win over Keflavik with a 3–0 away win. A full house of 9,500 saw goals from Alan Whittle and two from Joe Royle win the game for Everton.

1972	Newcastle United	H	First Division	3–1
1978	Bristol City	A	First Division	2–2
1986	Liverpool	H	Screen Sport Super Cup Final 2nd Leg	1–4

Goodison Park staged the second leg of the Screen Sport Super Cup final against Liverpool, with the visitors 3–1 ahead after the first leg. A crowd of 26,068, almost six thousand more than had seen the first leg, were present to see Liverpool complete a 7–2 aggregate win. Ian Rush scored the 10th hat-trick of his career and Steve Nichol the other goal for Liverpool, whilst Everton's reply came from Graeme Sharp from the penalty spot. Liverpool thus collected the trophy in the only season it has been contested and are thus the reigning holders, although one suspects the tankards each player received for taking part have proved rather more useful over the years!

| 1989 | Crystal Palace | A | First Division | 1–2 |

OCTOBER 1ST

1891	Glasgow Rangers	A	Friendly	4–1
1892	Aston Villa	H	First Division	1–0
1898	Nottingham Forest	A	First Division	0–0
1904	Middlesbrough	A	First Division	0–1
1910	Liverpool	A	First Division	2–0
1921	Arsenal	A	First Division	0–1
1927	Tottenham Hotspur	A	First Division	3–1

Dixie Dean stretched his consecutive scoring record to eight with two goals at White Hart Lane in the 3–1 win over Spurs. Alec Troup netted Everton's other goal in front of a crowd of just 7,716, not surprisingly the lowest crowd to witness an Everton match all season.

1932	Liverpool	H	First Division	3–1
1938	Liverpool	H	First Division	2–1
1949	Charlton Athletic	H	First Division	0–1
1955	Newcastle United	A	First Division	2–1
1960	Chelsea	A	First Division	3–3
1966	Newcastle United	H	First Division	1–1
1969	Arsenal	H	League Cup 3rd Round Replay	1–0

A single strike from Howard Kendall ended Arsenal's hopes of making it three League Cup finals in as many years in the third round replay at Goodison Park. On the same day John Ebbrell was born in Bromborough. He graduated through the ranks at Goodison Park and earned England caps at Schoolboy, Youth, Under-21 and B level during his time at Everton. He was transferred to Sheffield United for £1 million in 1997 but broke a rib on his debut and was ruled out for the rest of the season!

| 1975 | AC Milan | A | UEFA Cup 1st Round 2nd Leg | 0–1 |

Everton were dumped out of the UEFA Cup in the first round, losing 1–0 at the San Siro stadium to AC Milan, the only goal in two battles between the sides.

1977	Manchester City	H	First Division	1–1
1983	Notts County	A	First Division	1–0
1988	Wimbledon	A	First Division	1–2
1994	Manchester United	A	FA Premier League	0–2
1995	Newcastle United	H	FA Premier League	1–3
1997	Scunthorpe United	H	Coca–Cola Cup 2nd Round 2nd Leg	5–0

OCTOBER 2ND

1897	Blackburn Rovers	H	First Division	1–1
1902	Nottingham Forest	A	First Division	2–2
1909	Liverpool	H	First Division	2–3
1915	Oldham Athletic	H	Lancashire Section Principal Tournament	2–3
1920	Blackburn Rovers	H	First Division	2–1

1926	Blackburn Rovers	A	First Division	3–3
1929	Sunderland	A	First Division	2–2
1937	Liverpool	A	First Division	2–1

1939 A meeting of the Football League in Crewe announced the resumption of regional league football for the rest of the season, with games to begin on October 21st. The country was effectively divided into eight regions (there was a fifty mile travel limit imposed on the nation by the government) irrespective of their League status before the outbreak of the war.

1943	Burnley	H	Football League North (First Championship)	0–0
1948	Burnley	A	First Division	0–1
1954	Manchester City	A	First Division	0–1
1963	Arsenal	H	First Division	2–1
1971	Coventry City	H	First Division	1–2
1976	Sunderland	A	First Division	1–0

1979 Michael Ball born in Liverpool. A former England Youth international Michael joined Everton as a trainee straight from school and is widely tipped for future honours

| 1982 | Brighton & Hove Albion | H | First Division | 2–2 |
| 1984 | UC Dublin | H | European Cup-Winners' Cup 1st Round 2nd Leg | 1–0 |

After a goalless first leg draw in Dublin, Everton overcame the University Club 1–0 on aggregate thanks to a goal from Graeme Sharp. In fact, Everton were made to work hard for their win and there was little sign that this was a side that could go on and frighten the rest of Europe.

| 1985 | Norwich City | H | Screen Sport Super Cup Group B | 1–0 |

Everton recorded a 1–0 win over Norwich City in their second group match of the Super Cup, the only goal coming from Gary Lineker.

OCTOBER 3RD

1891	Sunderland	A	Football League	1–2
1896	Liverpool	H	First Division	2–1
1903	Middlesbrough	H	First Division	2–0
1908	Liverpool	A	First Division	1–0
1914	Liverpool	A	First Division	5–0
1925	Huddersfield Town	H	First Division	2–3

1929 Tony McNamara born in Liverpool. He joined Everton in May 1950 and went on to make 111 appearances at outside-right, scoring 21 goals for the club. He was sold to Liverpool in December 1957 and later played for Crewe and Bury before retiring.

1931	Blackpool	H	First Division	3–2
1936	Sunderland	A	First Division	1–3
1942	Burnley	A	Football League North (First Championship)	4–1
1953	Brentford	A	Second Division	0–1
1959	Arsenal	H	First Division	3–1
1964	West Ham United	H	First Division	1–1
1970	Coventry City	A	First Division	1–3
1973	Heart of Midlothian	A	Texaco Cup 1st Round 2nd Leg	0–0

Everton's one and only home match in the Texaco Cup saw them draw 0–0 with Hearts, losing the tie 1–0 on aggregate.

| 1978 | Darlington | H | League Cup 3rd Round | 1–0 |
| 1979 | Feyenoord | H | UEFA Cup 1st Round 2nd Leg | 0–1 |

With Everton one goal behind from the first leg of the UEFA Cup first round against Feyenoord, it was vital that they scored an early goal to level the tie and give them a chance of progressing into the second round. Just as vital was the need to prevent Feyenoord scoring themselves, for a Dutch goal would mean Everton needed to find the net three times to ensure their advance. Unfortunately, Everton could not find the net on the night, got caught by a breakaway and visibly wilted as the enormity of their task sank in. Thus the 2–0 aggregate defeat was the last time Everton appeared in the UEFA Cup.

1981	Stoke City	A	First Division	1–3
1987	Southampton	A	First Division	4–0
1989	Leyton Orient	H	Littlewoods Cup 2nd Round 2nd Leg	2–2

Despite being held at home by Leyton Orient in the second leg of the Littlewoods Cup second round, Everton progressed into the next round 4–2 winners on aggregate.

| 1993 | Tottenham Hotspur | A | FA Premier League | 2–3 |

OCTOBER 4TH

1890	Derby County	H	Football League	7–0
1902	Sheffield United	A	First Division	2–0
1913	Middlesbrough	H	First Division	2–0
1919	Sunderland	H	First Division	0–3
1920	Sheffield United	A	First Division	0–2
1924	Liverpool	H	First Division	0–1
1930	Charlton Athletic	H	Second Division	7–1

Ted Critchley, Dixie Dean and Jimmy Dunn all scored twice as Everton over–powered Charlton at Goodison. The other goal was scored by Tom Griffiths.

1941	Manchester United	H	Football League North (First Championship)	1–3
1947	Wolverhampton Wanderers	H	First Division	1–1
1952	Swansea Town	A	Second Division	2–2
1958	Birmingham City	H	First Division	3–1
1969	Wolverhampton Wanderers	A	First Division	3–2

After the midweek League Cup win over Arsenal Everton returned to League action with another good away win, this time at Molineux. Goals from Colin Harvey, Johnny Morrissey and Joe Royle earned Everton both points away from home for the fifth time in the campaign.

1975	West Ham United	A	First Division	1–0
1977	West Bromwich Albion	H	First Division	3–1
1980	Southampton	H	First Division	2–1
1983	Chesterfield	A	Milk Cup 2nd Round 1st Leg	1–0
1986	Arsenal	H	First Division	0–1

A first half goal from Steve Williams eventually settled the match, the only time Everton were beaten at home during the course of the season. Everton recovered from the setback to win the League title at the end of the season.

| 1992 | Oldham Athletic | A | FA Premier League | 0–1 |

| 1995 | Millwall | H | Coca–Cola Cup 2nd Round 2nd Leg | 2–4 |

After a goalless game at the New Den, Everton seemed set for a fairly simple passage into the next round, especially after Andy Hinchcliffe from the penalty spot and Graham Stuart had given them a 2–0 lead. Millwall somehow found the inspiration to draw level inside 90 minutes to force extra time and then scored two further goals to end Everton's interest in the competition in front of their own supporters.

| 1997 | Sheffield Wednesday | A | FA Premier League | 1–3 |

OCTOBER 5TH

| 1889 | Derby County | A | Football League | 2–2 |
| 1895 | Sheffield United | H | First Division | 5–0 |

Edgar Chadwick hit a hat-trick, his only one of the season in the 5–0 win over Sheffield United. Latta and Milward added the other goals.

1901	Sheffield United	H	First Division	2–1
1907	Liverpool	H	First Division	2–4
1912	Liverpool	A	First Division	2–0
1918	Liverpool	A	Lancashire Section Principal Tournament	4–2
1929	Arsenal	H	First Division	1–1
1935	Aston Villa	H	First Division	2–2
1940	Southport	A	North Regional League	1–0
1946	Wolverhampton Wanderers	H	First Division	0–2

| 1950 | Dave Thomas born in Kirby. He made his name with Burnley and earned rave reviews and accordingly interest from the bigger clubs. He surprisingly moved to QPR in 1972, remaining at Loftus Road for five years before joining Everton for £200,000 in 1977. Two years later he was on the move again, this time to Wolves, but he was unsettled and went to play in Canada with Vancouver Whitecaps. Upon returning to England he played for Middlesbrough and then Portsmouth. |

1957	Leicester City	A	First Division	2–2
1963	Birmingham City	A	First Division	2–0
1964	Aston Villa	A	First Division	2–1
1965	Blackburn Rovers	H	First Division	2–2
1968	Manchester City	H	First Division	2–0
1974	Newcastle United	H	First Division	1–1
1976	Manchester City	H	First Division	2–2
1982	Newport County	A	Milk Cup 2nd Round 1st Leg	2–0
1985	Oxford United	H	First Division	2–0
1991	Tottenham Hotspur	H	First Division	3–1
1994	Portsmouth	A	Coca–Cola Cup 2nd Round 2nd Leg	1–1

OCTOBER 6TH

1888	Aston Villa	H	Football League	2–0
1894	Bolton Wanderers	A	First Division	3–1
1900	Sheffield United	H	First Division	3–1
1906	Bristol City	H	First Division	2–0
1917	Liverpool	A	Lancashire Section Principal Tournament	0–6

1919 Tommy Lawton born in Bolton. One of the greatest goalscorers of his or any other age, he began his career with Burnley and moved to Everton as an eventual replacement for Dixie Dean in March 1937 for £6,5000 and he soon repaid the fee by helping the club win the League title in 1939. After the Second World War he was transferred to Chelsea for £11,500 and later signed for Third Division Notts County for a then record fee of £20,000 in 1947. He then had eighteen months with Brentford before finishing his career back in the top flight with Arsenal. An England international he scored 22 goals in 23 games, although if Victory and war time matches are taken into account the tally was 46 in 45 games.

1923	Liverpool	H	First Division	1–0
1928	Arsenal	H	First Division	4–2
1934	Chelsea	H	First Division	3–2
1945	Manchester United	A	Football League North	0–0
1951	Blackburn Rovers	H	Second Division	0–2

1952 Jim McDonagh born in Rotherham. He began his career with his local club and was transferred to Bolton in 1976 after making 121 appearances in goal for Rotherham. Four years later he joined Everton and made 40 appearances in goal in 1980–81 before being replaced by Jim Arnold.

1956	Preston North End	A	First Division	0–0
1962	Wolverhampton Wanderers	A	First Division	2–0
1973	Coventry City	A	First Division	2–1
1979	Coventry City	A	First Division	1–2
1981	Coventry City	H	League Cup 2nd Round 1st Leg	1–1
1984	Arsenal	A	First Division	0–1
1987	Rotherham United	A	Littlewoods Cup 2nd Round 2nd Leg	0–0

Having already won the first leg at Goodison 3–2 Everton progressed into the third round 3–2 winners on aggregate.

1993	Lincoln City	H	Coca–Cola Cup 2nd Round 2nd Leg	4–2

Despite a plucky fight by Lincoln at Goodison Everton moved into the next round with an 8–5 aggregate win.

OCTOBER 7TH

1893	Burnley	A	First Division	1–2

Billy Stewart scored his first goal for the club following his arrival from Preston. Born in Arbroath he first came to prominence whilst playing for the Black Watch team which won the Army Cup and then, whilst stationed in Ireland with the Royal Scots Greys helped Belfast Distillery win the Irish Cup. This alerted Preston who bought him out of the army and turned him into a professional footballer. After joining Everton he helped them to the FA Cup final in 1897 and later the same year went to play for Bristol City.

1899	Preston North End	A	First Division	1–1
1905	Sheffield United	A	First Division	2–3
1911	Sheffield United	A	First Division	1–2
1916	Blackpool	H	Lancashire Section Principal Tournament	3–1
1922	Liverpool	A	First Division	1–5
1933	Middlesbrough	A	First Division	0–2
1939	Liverpool	A	Friendly	4–1

A hastily arranged friendly between the two rivals was won 4–1 by Everton, but even though there was a war on, the local press still chose to comment that the key feature of the game was 'some difference of opinion between spectators'!

1944	Tranmere Rovers	A	Football League North (First Championship)	4–1
1950	Fulham	A	First Division	5–1
1961	Nottingham Forest	H	First Division	6–0

Two goals apiece for Jimmy Fell and Roy Vernon helped Everton on their way to their biggest winning margin of the season, with Jimmy Gabriel and Sandy Young scoring the other goals. But for an 8–3 win in the penultimate game of the season this would have been Everton's best win of the season.

1963	Aston Villa	A	First Division	1–0
1967	Southampton	H	First Division	4–2
1972	Liverpool	A	First Division	0–1
1978	Southampton	H	First Division	0–0
1980	Brighton & Hove Albion	A	First Division	3–1

Everton's match at Brighton was their 3,000th First Division fixture, the first club to have reached such a milestone. In keeping with the celebrations Everton won the game 3–1 thanks to goals from Mick Lyons, Joe McBride and Steve McMahon.

1986	Newport County	A	Littlewoods Cup 2nd Round 2nd Leg	5–1
1990	Nottingham Forest	A	First Division	1–3
1992	Rotherham United	H	Coca–Cola Cup 2nd Round 2nd Leg	3–0

OCTOBER 8TH

1892	Sunderland	H	First Division	1–4
1898	Bolton Wanderers	H	First Division	1–0
1904	Wolverhampton Wanderers	H	First Division	2–1
1910	Bury	H	First Division	2–1
1921	Blackburn Rovers	H	First Division	2–0
1927	Manchester United	H	First Division	5–2

Dixie Dean scored all five of Everton's goals in the trouncing of Manchester United, his 17th goal of the season! This was to be the only occasion during the campaign that Dean hit as many as five goals, although he did net four on one occasion, five hat-tricks and a brace in 14 matches.

1932	Blackpool	H	First Division	2–0
1938	Wolverhampton Wanderers	H	First Division	1–0
1949	Arsenal	A	First Division	2–5
1955	Arsenal	H	First Division	1–1
1960	Preston North End	H	First Division	0–0
1966	West Ham United	A	First Division	3–2
1968	Liverpool	A	First Division	1–1

The 100th League meeting between Everton and Liverpool was staged at Anfield, with Everton having won 41 of the previous 99 encounters. The day finished all-square at 1–1, Alan Ball scoring for Everton.

| 1969 | Crystal Palace | A | First Division | 0–0 |

Everton dropped only their fourth point of the season with a goalless draw at Selhurst Park. Their record to date now read played 14, won 11, drawn two and lost just one.

1973	Reading	H	League Cup 2nd Round	1–0
1975	Carlisle United	H	League Cup 3rd Round	2–0
1977	Queens Park Rangers	A	First Division	5–1

Bob Latchford netted four times at Loftus Road in the 5–1 win over QPR with Everton's other goal being scored by Duncan McKenzie. The win took Everton up to third place in the League, just behind Nottingham Forest and Liverpool.

| 1985 | Bournemouth | A | Milk Cup 2nd Round 2nd Leg | 2–0 |

Everton completed a 5–2 aggregate win over Bournemouth to set up a trip to Shrewsbury in the third round.

1988	Southampton	H	First Division	4–1
1991	Watford	A	Rumbelows Cup 2nd Round 2nd Leg	2–1
1994	Southampton	A	FA Premier League	0–2

OCTOBER 9TH

1897	Wolverhampton Wanderers	A	First Division	3–2
1909	Aston Villa	A	First Division	1–3
1915	Rochdale	A	Lancashire Section Principal Tournament	2–1
1920	Huddersfield Town	A	First Division	1–0
1926	Huddersfield Town	H	First Division	0–0
1937	Wolverhampton Wanderers	A	First Division	0–2
1943	Liverpool	H	Football League North (First Championship)	4–6
1948	Blackpool	A	First Division	0–3
1954	Aston Villa	A	First Division	2–0

1957 The floodlights were switched on at Goodison Park for the first time with a visit from Liverpool in a match to celebrate the 75th anniversary of the Liverpool County FA. Everton won 2–0 on the night.

1965	Tottenham Hotspur	H	First Division	3–1
1971	Manchester City	A	First Division	0–1
1979	Aston Villa	H	League Cup 3rd Round Replay	4–1

After a goalless first meeting had brought back memories of the two sides' clashes in the final of 1977, Everton proved too good on the night for Villa, with Bob Latchford scoring twice and Brian Kidd and Andy King adding the other two goals.

| 1982 | Manchester City | H | First Division | 2–1 |
| 1990 | Wrexham | H | Rumbelows Cup 2nd Round 2nd Leg | 6–0 |

With Everton already five goals ahead from the first leg their place in the next round was hardly likely to be troubled, thus producing a crowd of just 7,415 for the second meeting at Goodison. A hat-trick from Graeme Sharp and other goals from Tony Cottee, Neil McDonald and John Ebbrell completed an 11–0 aggregate win.

OCTOBER 10TH

1891 Preston North End H Football League 1–1

The visit of Preston North End in the Football League drew a then record crowd of 30,000 to Goodison Park.

| 1896 | Burnley | A | First Division | 1–2 |
| 1903 | Liverpool | A | First Division | 2–2 |

1908	Bury	H	First Division	4–0
1914	Bradford Park Avenue	H	First Division	4–1
1925	Sunderland	A	First Division	3–7
1931	Sheffield United	A	First Division	5–1

Dixie Dean scored his second hat-trick of the season to set Everton on their way to an easy 5–1 win at Bramall Lane. The other goals were scored by Tommy Johnson and Jimmy Stein.

1936	Wolverhampton Wanderers	H	First Division	1–0
1942	Wrexham	H	Football League North (First Championship)	2–1
1953	Plymouth Argyle	A	Second Division	0–4
1959	Leeds United	A	First Division	3–3

1962 Mark Ward born in Huyton. Initially on Everton's books as an apprentice he was released and drifted into the non-League game, returning to League football with Oldham via Northwich Victoria. A £250,000 fee took him to West Ham in 1985, and after a further transfer to Manchester City he cost Everton £1.1 million to come back to Goodison Park in 1991. He then joined Birmingham City in 1994 and has since played for Huddersfield and Wigan.

1964	Sheffield Wednesday	H	First Division	1–1
1970	Derby County	H	First Division	1–1
1981	West Ham United	A	First Division	1–1
1984	Sheffield United	H	Milk Cup 2nd Round 2nd Leg	4–0

After a 2–2 draw in the first leg Everton moved into the third round with a 6–2 aggregate victory. Goals on the night from Paul Bracewell, Adrian Heath, Derek Mountfield and Graeme Sharp secured the win.

1987	Chelsea	H	First Division	4–1

OCTOBER 11TH

1890	Aston Villa	A	Football League	2–2

Fred Geary scored for the seventh consecutive League match; he had netted Everton's consolation goal in the 4–1 defeat in the last game of the 1889–90 season and had then gone on to score in the first six matches of the new campaign, netting a total of 11 goals in those games. At the end of the season, one which saw Everton lift the League title for the first time, he ended as top goalscorer, having netted 20 League goals.

1902	Grimsby Town	H	First Division	4–2
1913	Sheffield United	A	First Division	1–4
1919	Arsenal	H	First Division	2–3
1924	Sunderland	H	First Division	0–3
1930	Barnsley	A	Second Division	1–1
1941	Tranmere Rovers	H	Football League North (First Championship)	3–2
1947	Middlesbrough	A	First Division	1–0
1952	Notts County	H	Second Division	1–0
1958	Tottenham Hotspur	A	First Division	4–10

Shortly before the start of the League match at White Hart Lane between Spurs and Everton, the London club announced the appointment of new manager Bill Nicholson. His team then went out and inflicted Everton's worst ever defeat, with Spurs winning 10–4. This was despite Jimmy Harris scoring a hat-trick for Everton!

| 1966 | AB Aalborg | H | European Cup-Winners' Cup | 2–1 |
| | | | 1st Round 2nd Leg | |

Goodison Park staged its first match in the European Cup-Winners' Cup with the visit of Danish club Aalborg. Goals from John Morrissey and Alan Ball enabled Everton to win 2–1 on the night and by the same score on aggregate.

| 1967 | Sunderland | H | League Cup 3rd Round | 2–3 |

Everton suffered their first League Cup defeat in six years, going down 2–1 at home to Sunderland. This period had not seen Everton retain the trophy during that time; they had refused to enter for six seasons, only returning to the fold in 1967–68, although by 1969–70 entry was compulsory.

1969	Sunderland	H	First Division	3–1
1975	Queens Park Rangers	A	First Division	0–5
1980	Leeds United	A	First Division	0–1
1986	Charlton Athletic	A	First Division	2–3
1988	Bury	A	Littlewoods Cup 2nd Round 2nd Leg	2–2

OCTOBER 12TH

1895	Nottingham Forest	A	First Division	1–2
1901	Nottingham Forest	A	First Division	0–4
1907	Middlesbrough	A	First Division	2–0
1912	Bolton Wanderers	H	First Division	2–3

1917 Tommy G. Jones born in Connahs Quay. Discovered by Everton whilst playing for Wrexham he cost the club £3,000 when signed in March 1936. Before the Second World War broke out he managed to collect the first of his 17 caps for Wales. At the end of hostilities he became the subject of a transfer bid from Italian club Roma and a deal was agreed with the club, but this subsequently fell through when the matter got down to currency transactions. Tommy was appointed captain of Everton in 1949 but fell out with the board of directors after public comments about the way the club was being run were attributed to him. He left Everton to become player-manager of Pwllheli.

1918	Liverpool	H	Lancashire Section Principal Tournament	4–2
1929	Aston Villa	A	First Division	2–5
1932	Newcastle United	A	FA Charity Shield	5–3

It was still many years before the FA Charity Shield became a traditional curtain-raiser to the season with a meeting between the League Champions and FA Cup holders at Wembley, for this was still an age where the two clubs would meet in midweek, midway through the following season. Whilst this was hardly likely to ensure full houses there were still occasions when the match was lifted by the performances of the two sides. The meeting of FA Cup holders Newcastle United and champions Everton at St James' Park drew a crowd of only 10,000, but all those present were treated to a vintage display of attacking football by both sides. United took the lead through McMenemy, but this merely served to fire Everton, and by half-time they were 3–1 ahead with two goals from Dixie Dean and one from Tommy Johnson. Ted Hagar in the Everton goal had even saved a penalty shortly before the break. Dean completed his hat-trick soon into the second half to effectively make the game safe, and despite a United response that brought a goal from Boyd, Dean scored again two minutes from time. There was still time for one last goal, McMenemy of United taking the final score to 5–3 in Everton's favour.

1935	Wolverhampton Wanderers	A	First Division	0–4
1940	Stockport County	H	North Regional League	4–2
1946	Sunderland	A	First Division	1–4
1957	Newcastle United	A	First Division	3–2

Tony McNamara made the last of his 111 League appearances for Everton, being sold to Liverpool in December. At the end of the season he was transferred to Crewe but made just nine appearances before moving on to Bury. He thus became the first player to appear in all four divisions of the Football League within 12 months; the First with Everton, Second with Liverpool, Fourth with Crewe and Third with Bury.

| 1960 | Accrington Stanley | H | League Cup 1st Round | 3–1 |

Everton made their debut in the League Cup, beating Accrington Stanley 3–1 at Goodison Park. The introduction of the competition, instigated by Football League secretary Alan Hardaker, was not universally welcomed, with Arsenal, Spurs, Sheffield Wednesday, West Bromwich Albion and Wolves all refusing to enter, but Everton were to give a good account of themselves in the inaugural tournament, reaching the quarter-finals.

| 1963 | | | | |

Bobby Mimms born in York. After impressing for Halifax and then Rotherham he was signed by Everton for £150,000 in 1985 and proved a capable deputy for Neville Southall, appearing in the 1986 FA Cup final. After loan spells with Notts County, Sunderland, Blackburn Rovers and Manchester City he was sold to Spurs for £325,000. After being replaced by Erik Thorstvedt he was loaned to Aberdeen and then sold to Blackburn and has subsequently played for Crystal Palace and Preston.

| 1965 | FC Nuremberg | H | Inter-Cities Fairs Cup 1st Round 2nd Leg | 1–0 |

A single goal from Jimmy Gabriel was enough to overcome FC Nuremberg in the Inter-Cities Fairs Cup first round second leg, Everton progressing into the second round 2–1 on aggregate.

1968	Southampton	A	First Division	5–2
1974	Sheffield United	A	First Division	2–2
1979				

Danny Cadamarteri born in Bradford. Joined Everton as a trainee straight from school and was upgraded to the professional ranks in October 1996. He is eligible to play for any one of six countries; Nigeria, Italy, England, Ireland, Scotland and Jamaica!

| 1985 | Chelsea | A | First Division | 1–2 |
| 1996 | West Ham United | H | FA Premier League | 2–1 |

OCTOBER 13TH

| 1888 | Notts County | A | Football League | 1–3 |
| 1894 | Liverpool | H | First Division | 3–0 |

The very first in what is probably one of the most eagerly anticipated of all the country's derby matches – Everton against Liverpool. The importance of this first meeting was reflected in the preparations undertaken by the two teams; Liverpool spent the week in training at Hightown, Everton spent theirs at home but with rigorous coaching the order of the day. A crowd of 44,000 packed into Goodison Park for the historic match, with countless others climbing on to any vantage point in order to view the game. In front of the Lord Mayor of Liverpool the visitors kicked off but soon found themselves pressed back into their own half as Everton asserted authority on the field. After only ten minutes came the opening goal: an Everton free-kick was floated over by Billy Stewart and found McInnes in clear space. As a reward for scoring that historic goal McInnes found himself the recipient of some rough tackling from Liverpool which resulted in him having to leave the field for a while, but he returned and helped Everton score their second, supplying Latta with a pass from which he couldn't fail to score. Everton then had a further goal disallowed for an infringement only the referee spotted, but with time running out and the light fading, Everton got their third goal with a shot from John Bell which took a deflection and sailed past McCann in the Liverpool goal. When the referee finally called time, Everton had won the first League derby match 3–0.

1900	Manchester City	A	First Division	0–1
1906	Notts County	A	First Division	1–0
1917	Manchester United	H	Lancashire Section Principal Tournament	3–0
1923	Liverpool	A	First Division	2–1
1928	Blackburn Rovers	A	First Division	1–2

1931 Jimmy O'Neill born in Dublin. The extremely dependable goalkeeper was first spotted by Everton whilst playing local junior football in Ireland and was invited to Goodison Park for trials. Offered professional forms in May 1949 he went on to make over 200 League appearances for the side and force his way into the international set-up, winning 17 caps. He was sold to Stoke for £5,000 in July 1960 and later played for Darlington and Port Vale.

1934	Aston Villa	A	First Division	2–2
1945	Manchester United	H	Football League North	3–0
1951	Queens Park Rangers	A	Second Division	4–4
1956	Chelsea	H	First Division	0–3
1962	Aston Villa	H	First Division	1–1
1973	West Ham United	H	First Division	1–0
1979	Crystal Palace	H	First Division	3–1
1984	Aston Villa	H	First Division	2–1

OCTOBER 14TH

1893	Blackburn Rovers	H	First Division	2–2
1899	Nottingham Forest	H	First Division	2–1
1905	Notts County	H	First Division	6–2
1911	Oldham Athletic	H	First Division	1–1
1916	Rochdale	H	Lancashire Section Principal Tournament	3–0
1922	Liverpool	H	First Division	0–1
1933	Blackburn Rovers	H	First Division	7–1

Dixie Dean had scored in each of the opening five games of the season and had then been injured, forcing him out of the side until the 4th of November. Indeed, he would make only six more appearances during the course of the campaign, meaning Everton had to rely on other sources to score the goals. Against Blackburn Tommy White netted a hat-trick and there were single efforts from Jimmy Dunn, Albert Geldard, Tommy Johnson and Jimmy Stein to prove that thus far Dean wasn't being missed.

1944	Tranmere Rovers	H	Football League North (First Championship)	2–1
1950	Bolton Wanderers	H	First Division	1–1
1961	Wolverhampton Wanderers	A	First Division	3–0
1964	Valerengen IF	H	Inter-Cities Fairs Cup 1st Round 2nd Leg	4–2

Having already won the first leg away from home 5–2 Everton were expected to win by a mile in the second leg of the Inter-Cities Fairs Cup first round against Valerengen, but in the end had to settle for a 4–2 win on the night and 9–4 on aggregate.

1967	Chelsea	A	First Division	1–1
1972	Leeds United	H	First Division	1–2
1978	Ipswich Town	A	First Division	1–0
1989	Millwall	H	First Division	2–1
1995	Bolton Wanderers	A	FA Premier League	1–1

OCTOBER 15TH

| 1887 | Bolton Wanderers | A | FA Cup 1st Round | 0–1 |

Everton met Bolton Wanderers at Burnden Park in what is generally regarded as Everton's first game in the FA Cup. Everton had entered the previous year and were drawn at home to Glasgow Rangers, but unbeknown to Rangers scratched from the competition shortly before the game was played. Bolton won the game 1–0, but it was later discovered that their centre-forward Struthers was ineligible and Everton lodged a successful appeal to have the game replayed.

1892	West Bromwich Albion	A	First Division	0–3
1898	Derby County	A	First Division	5–5
1904	Bury	A	First Division	2–1
1910	Sheffield United	A	First Division	1–0
1921	Blackburn Rovers	A	First Division	2–2
1927	Liverpool	H	First Division	1–1

Alec Troup scored for Everton in the 1–1 Merseyside draw at Goodison in front of a crowd of 55,415. Liverpool had set their game plan on keeping Dixie Dean quiet throughout the game, for he had already scored in each of the opening nine games of the season, netting 17 goals in that spell. Whilst never approaching Dean's tally, Troup did at least take some of the pressure from him, getting into double figures at the end of the campaign with ten.

| 1932 | Derby County | A | First Division | 0–2 |
| 1938 | Bolton Wanderers | A | First Division | 2–4 |

1947 Jimmy Husband born in Newcastle. Joined Everton as an apprentice and graduated through the ranks to make his first-team debut in 1964–65, although it took a further two seasons or so before he became a regular. A member of the side that won the League in 1970 he left Everton in November 1973 to join Luton where he finished his career.

1949	Bolton Wanderers	H	First Division	0–0
1955	Bolton Wanderers	A	First Division	1–1
1960	Fulham	A	First Division	3–2
1963	Sheffield United	H	First Division	4–1
1966	Sheffield Wednesday	H	First Division	2–1
1969	Manchester City	A	League Cup 4th Round	0–2

Manchester City ended Everton's interest in the League Cup at Maine Road, although the cloud with the silver lining revealed that Everton could now concentrate on winning the League, unhindered by cup replays and the like.

1974	West Ham United	H	First Division	1–1
1977	Bristol City	H	First Division	1–0
1983	Luton Town	H	First Division	0–1

| 1994 | Coventry City | H | FA Premier League | 0–2 |
| 1997 | Coventry City | A | Coca–Cola Cup 3rd Round | 1–4 |

OCTOBER 16TH

1897	Liverpool	H	First Division	3–0
1909	Sheffield United	H	First Division	1–2
1915	Bolton Wanderers	A	Lancashire Section Principal Tournament	4–3
1920	Huddersfield Town	H	First Division	0–0
1926	Newcastle United	H	First Division	1–3
1937	Leeds United	H	First Division	1–1

1940 Jimmy Gabriel born in Dundee. His transfer to Everton from Dundee in 1960 for £30,000 made him the most expensive teenager in British football, and as such enormous expectations were made. He went on to make 300 appearances for the first team, helping the club win the League in 1963 and FA Cup in 1966, before switching to Southampton in July 1967, later playing for Bournemouth, Swindon and Brentford before going into coaching.

| 1943 | Liverpool | A | Football League North (First Championship) | 2–5 |

1946 Geoff Barnett born in Northwich. Signed by Everton as an apprentice he joined the professional ranks in May 1964 but proved unable to dislodge Gordon West from the Everton goal. After just ten League appearances he left for Arsenal in search of first-team football but found he was number two behind Bob Wilson, although he did appear in the 1972 FA Cup final.

1948	Derby County	H	First Division	0–1
1954	Sunderland	H	First Division	1–0
1957	Arsenal	H	First Division	2–2

1960 Graeme Sharp born in Glasgow. A relative unknown when Everton signed him from Dumbarton in 1980 for £120,000, he went on to become a feared striker during his time at the club. He helped them win the FA Cup in 1984, scoring the first goal in the final, two League titles and the European Cup-Winners' Cup and then went on to play for Oldham Athletic.

1965	Fulham	A	First Division	2–3
1968	Derby County	H	League Cup 4th Round	0–0
1971	Ipswich Town	H	First Division	1–1

1973 David Unsworth born in Chorley. Developed through the ranks at Everton and became a full professional in 1992. He went on to help the club win the FA Cup in 1995 and was also capped by England. He joined West Ham in 1997 but a year later moved on to Aston Villa. Less than a week later he announced he was homesick for Merseyside and eventually joined Everton.

| 1976 | Liverpool | A | First Division | 1–3 |
| 1982 | Swansea City | A | First Division | 3–0 |

1986 Former Everton and England goalkeeper Ted Sagar died. He had played for the club between 1929 and 1953, the longest spell any player has spent with just one club.

| 1993 | Swindon Town | A | FA Premier League | 1–1 |

OCTOBER 17TH

| 1891 | Bolton Wanderers | A | Football League | 0–1 |
| 1896 | Sheffield United | H | First Division | 1–2 |

1903	Bury	H	First Division	2–1
1908	Sheffield United	A	First Division	5–1

Bertie Freeman scored his first hat-trick of the season on his way to netting 36 goals for the season, the first Everton player to have scored as many as 30 during the course of a season. Everton's other goals were scored by Tim Coleman and Jack Sharp.

1914	Oldham Athletic	A	First Division	1–1
1925	Burnley	A	First Division	3–1
1931	Sheffield Wednesday	H	First Division	9–3

The visit of Sheffield Wednesday was to witness 12 goals scored at Goodison Park, with Everton scoring nine of them. Dixie Dean led the charge, registering five of them, with the others being scored by Ted Critchley, Tommy Johnson, Jimmy Stein and Tommy White.

1936	Leeds United	A	First Division	0–3
1942	Wrexham	A	Football League North (First Championship)	2–0
1953	Swansea Town	H	Second Division	2–2
1959	West Ham United	H	First Division	0–1
1964	Blackpool	A	First Division	1–1
1970	Arsenal	A	First Division	0–4
1981	Ipswich Town	H	First Division	2–1
1987	Newcastle United	A	First Division	1–1
1992	Coventry City	H	FA Premier League	1–1

OCTOBER 18TH

1890	Bolton Wanderers	H	Football League	2–0
1902	Aston Villa	A	First Division	1–2
1913	Derby County	H	First Division	5–0
1919	Arsenal	A	First Division	0–1
1924	Cardiff City	A	First Division	1–2
1930	Nottingham Forest	A	Second Division	2–2
1933	Arsenal	H	FA Charity Shield	0–3

Everton's reward for winning the FA Cup was a home match against League champions Arsenal for the FA Charity Shield. On the day, however, Arsenal showed why they had become the dominant force in the English game with a 3–0 win at Goodison Park thanks to two goals from Birkett and one from Bowden.

1941	Tranmere Rovers	A	Football League North (First Championship)	4–0
1947	Charlton Athletic	H	First Division	0–1
1952	Leicester City	A	Second Division	2–4
1958	Manchester United	H	First Division	3–2
1964	Michael Branch born in Liverpool. Signed by Everton as a trainee he has represented England at Schoolboy, Youth and Under-21 level and seems set for a promising future, although a broken leg brought his career to a temporary halt.			

1969	Stoke City	H	First Division	6–2
1975	Aston Villa	H	First Division	2–1
1978	Dukla Prague	H	UEFA Cup 2nd Round 1st Leg	2–1

Czechoslovakian club Dukla Prague were the visitors to Goodison Park in the UEFA Cup second round first leg, with Andy King and Bob Latchford getting on the scoresheet for Everton in the 2–1 win. Unfortunately, Dukla's goal was to prove costly to Everton in the second leg.

1980	Liverpool	H	First Division	2–2
1986	Southampton	A	First Division	2–0
1997	Liverpool	H	FA Premier League	2–0

OCTOBER 19TH

| 1889 | Notts County | A | Football League | 3–4 |
| 1892 | Newton Heath | A | First Division | 4–3 |

Alex Latta equalled T. Wylie's goalscoring record, netting all four goals in the win over Newtown Heath at North Road. This was the first season of League action for the Heathens, who later changed their name to Manchester United, with Everton recording the 'double' having already won 6–0 at Goodison Park.

1895	West Bromwich Albion	H	First Division	1–1
1901	Bury	H	First Division	1–1
1907	Sheffield United	H	First Division	2–1
1912	Sheffield United	A	First Division	1–4
1918	Manchester United	A	Lancashire Section Principal Tournament	1–1
1929	Middlesbrough	H	First Division	3–2
1935	Chelsea	H	First Division	5–1

1936 George Thomson born in Edinburgh. He began his career with the local Hearts side and joined Everton in November 1960. He spent three years at Goodison Park, making 73 appearances and scoring one goal for the club, later joining Brentford.

1940	Chester	A	North Regional League	0–1
1946	Bolton Wanderers	H	First Division	2–1
1957	Burnley	H	First Division	1–1
1963	West Ham United	A	First Division	2–4
1968	Stoke City	H	First Division	2–1
1974	Chelsea	H	First Division	1–1
1985	Watford	H	First Division	4–1
1991	Aston Villa	H	First Division	0–2
1995	Feyenoord	H	European Cup-Winners' Cup	0–0
			2nd Round 1st Leg	

After disposing of the relatively unknown KR Reykjavik in the first round, Everton's reward was something of a plum tie against the crack Dutch side Feyenoord. Feyenoord had previously played Everton in the UEFA Cup in 1979 and ended their interest with victories both home and away, and they were to frustrate Everton once again in the match at Goodison Park. A sturdy defensive display enabled Feyenoord to take the upper hand in a goalless draw in front of a crowd of 27,526.

OCTOBER 20TH

| 1888 | Derby County | A | Football League | 4–2 |
| 1894 | Blackburn Rovers | A | First Division | 3–4 |

Blackburn Rovers won 4–3 in a League match at Ewood Park, thus ending a run of 12 consecutive League wins for Everton. The run had started on March 24th the previous season and continued through the first eight matches of the current campaign. The eight match run was the best start to the season enjoyed by any club in both the First and Second Divisions.

| 1906 | Sheffield United | H | First Division | 4–2 |

1917	Manchester United	A	Lancashire Section Principal Tournament	0–0
1923	Notts County	A	First Division	1–1
1928	West Ham United	A	First Division	4–2
1934	Leeds United	A	First Division	0–2
1945	Sunderland	H	Football League North	4–0
1951	Notts County	H	Second Division	1–5
1956	Manchester United	A	First Division	5–2

Everton went to Old Trafford and ended Manchester United's run of 31 League matches without defeat at home, a run that had begun in March 1955 following defeat by Everton! This time around Everton recorded a 5–2 win thanks to goals from George Kirby (two), Donal Donovan, Tommy Eglington and Tony McNamara.

1973	Burnley	H	First Division	1–0
1979	Liverpool	A	First Division	2–2
1984	Liverpool	A	First Division	1–0
1990	Crystal Palace	H	First Division	0–0

OCTOBER 21ST

| 1893 | Darwen | H | First Division | 8–1 |
| 1899 | Glossop | A | First Division | 1–1 |

Everton paid their only ever visit to North Road, Glossop for a League match, drawing 1–1 in what was to be Glossop's only ever season in the First Division. The ground was not difficult to find either, for Glossop is the smallest town ever to have hosted First Division football.

1905	Stoke City	A	First Division	2–2
1911	Bolton Wanderers	A	First Division	2–1
1916	Bolton Wanderers	A	Lancashire Section Principal Tournament	3–1
1922	Nottingham Forest	A	First Division	1–2

On the same day Dave Falder was born in Liverpool. He joined the club from Wigan Athletic during the Second World War but had to wait for the end of hostilities before making his League debut, finally breaking into the side in 1949–50. He made 25 first-team appearances before going into the non-League game.

| 1933 | Tottenham Hotspur | H | First Division | 1–1 |
| 1939 | Stoke City | H | War Regional League, Western Division | 4–4 |

When the Football League was abandoned after just three games of the 1939–40 season following the outbreak of the Second World War there followed a period of uncertainty, with players contracts being paid up to September 6th, signing-on bonuses and removal expenses to be cleared immediately and there was at yet no provision for the refunding of season ticket sales. When it became apparent that the country was unlikely to be invaded regional leagues were organised, the object being to lift public morale. Thus Everton made their debut appearance in the Western Division and battled their way to a 4–4 draw with Stoke.

| 1944 | Liverpool | H | Football League North (First Championship) | 0–2 |

On the same day Tommy Wright was born in Liverpool. He spent his entire career with Everton, joining the club in March 1963 and going on to make 370 appearances for the first team. A member of the side that won the 1966 FA Cup and the 1970 League title, he was also capped by England and was a member of the World Cup squad for 1970. He finished his career at the end of the 19772–73 season.

1950	Charlton Athletic	A	First Division	1–2

1959 Kevin Sheedy born in Builth Wells. After beginning his career with Hereford United he was sold to Liverpool for £70,000 in June 1978. After making only two appearances in four years Sheedy asked for a transfer and was sold, reluctantly, to Everton for £100,000, the first player to have crossed Stanley Park in almost 20 years. His undoubted talents were allowed to blossom at Goodison and he helped the club win two League titles, the FA Cup and European Cup-Winners' Cup during his time with the club.

1961	Sheffield United	H	First Division	1–0
1970	Borussia Moenchengladbach	A	European Cup 2nd Round 1st Leg	1–1

Having seen off the Icelandic champions in the first round of the European Cup, there was rather stiffer opposition to face in the second round, with a crowd of 32,000 present in Germany for the clash with Borussia. A Howard Kendall equaliser in the second half enabled Everton to draw 1–1.

1972	Sheffield United	A	First Division	1–0
1978	Queens Park Rangers	A	First Division	1–1
1980	West Bromwich Albion	H	First Division	1–1
1989	Arsenal	H	First Division	3–0

OCTOBER 22ND

1892	Accrington	H	First Division	1–1
1898	West Bromwich Albion	H	First Division	1–0
1904	Aston Villa	H	First Division	3–2
1910	Aston Villa	H	First Division	0–1

1920 Harry Potts born in Hetton. He joined Burnley as an apprentice and made a number of war time appearances for the club, going on to make 165 League appearances before being transferred to Everton in October 1950. During his five year spell at Goodison Park he made 59 appearances, scoring 15 goals.

1921	Oldham Athletic	H	First Division	2–2
1927	West Ham United	H	First Division	7–0

Tommy White made his debut, deputising for the absent Dixie Dean and proved a worthy replacement, scoring twice in the 7–0 rout over West Ham. He had joined Everton from Southport earlier in the year as a centre-forward although he originally played at centre-half, a position he was later to return to during his Everton career (and even won a cap for England at centre-half!). This was his only game of the season but he went on to make 202 appearances for the first team, scoring 66 goals and collecting winners' medals for the First Division championship and the FA Cup. He left Everton for Northampton in October 1937.

1932	Leicester City	A	First Division	2–2
1938	Leeds United	H	First Division	4–0
1949	Birmingham City	A	First Division	0–0
1955	Aston Villa	H	First Division	2–1
1977	Liverpool	A	First Division	0–0
1983	Watford	H	First Division	1–0
1988	Aston Villa	A	First Division	0–2
1994	Crystal Palace	A	FA Premier League	0–1
1995	Tottenham Hotspur	H	FA Premier League	1–1

OCTOBER 23RD

1897	Bury	A	First Division	1–0
1909	Woolwich Arsenal	A	First Division	0–1
1915	Manchester City	H	Lancashire Section Principal Tournament	4–2
1920	Liverpool	A	First Division	0–1
1926	Leeds United	A	First Division	3–1

Dixie Dean had been involved in a bad motor–cycle accident in June of the year, fracturing his skull and jaw and being forced to miss the first 13 games of the season. He returned to the side for the 3–1 win at Leeds United, his importance to the side being reflected by the fact that this was only Everton's second win of the season. Not surprisingly, Dean himself got on the scoresheet, with the other goals being added by Dominy and Irvine.

1933				

Eddie Thomas born in Newton-le-Willows. A product of Everton's youth scheme he signed professional forms in October 1951 and went on to make 86 League appearances and scored 39 goals in nine years with the club. He left for Blackburn in 1960 and subsequently played for Swansea, Derby and Orient.

1937	Grimsby Town	A	First Division	1–2
1943	Wrexham	A	Football League North (First Championship)	3–1
1948	Arsenal	A	First Division	0–5

1951				

David Johnson born in Liverpool. He spent two spells with Everton, first joining the club in 1969 having risen through the ranks. He was then transferred to Ipswich Town and arrived back at Everton after a highly successful spell with Liverpool. Unfortunately his second sojourn at Goodison was unsuccessful and he was loaned out to Barnsley and then sold to Manchester City.

1954	Huddersfield Town	A	First Division	1–2
1965	Blackpool	H	First Division	0–0
1968	Derby County	A	League Cup 4th Round Replay	0–1
1971	Leeds United	A	First Division	2–3
1976	West Ham United	H	First Division	3–2
1982	Sunderland	H	First Division	3–1
1985	Norwich City	A	Screen Sport Super Cup Group B	0–1

Everton suffered their only defeat in the group matches of the Super Cup, being beaten 1–0 at home to Norwich City. Despite the competition's name, the cup was anything but super, for there was already apathy from the fans who were showing little or no interest in the event, with only 12,196 at Carrow Road.

1993	Manchester United	H	FA Premier League	0–1

OCTOBER 24TH

1891	Derby County	A	Football League	3–0
1896	Sheffield Wednesday	A	First Division	1–4
1903	Blackburn Rovers	A	First Division	2–0
1908	Aston Villa	H	First Division	3–1
1914	Manchester United	H	First Division	4–2
1925	Leeds United	H	First Division	4–2
1928	Blackburn Rovers	Old Trafford	FA Charity Shield	2–1

Everton made their first appearance in the FA Charity Shield, meeting FA Cup holders

Blackburn Rovers at Old Trafford. Dixie Dean might have been finding the goals harder to come by than in the previous season (then he had scored 60; this time he struggled to 24) but still managed to score twice to enable Everton to lift the trophy 2–1.

1931	Aston Villa	A	First Division	3–2
1936	Birmingham City	H	First Division	3–3
1942	Bury	H	Football League North (First Championship)	9–2

1950 Asa Hartford born in Clydebank. After beginning his career with West Bromwich Albion he developed into one of the outstanding midfield players in the country and later moved to Manchester City for £250,000 in 1974. Five years later he was on the move again, joining Nottingham Forest in preference to Everton, but after only three games he was on his way again, this time switching to Goodison Park in a deal worth £500,000. He made nearly 100 appearances for Everton before setting off on his travels again and went on to play for Manchester City, Norwich City, Bolton and Stockport County. However, for all of his transfers he is perhaps best known for the one that didn't happen; in 1971 he was expected to be transferred from West Bromwich to Leeds for £170,000, but one day later the deal was called off when it was discovered he had a hole in the heart.

1959	Chelsea	A	First Division	0–1
1960	Manchester City	H	First Division	4–2
1962	Dunfermline Athletic	H	Inter-Cities Fairs Cup 1st Round 1st Leg	1–0

Dunfermline Athletic were the first visitors in European competition to Goodison Park, going down 1–0 in the Inter-Cities Fairs Cup first round first leg. The only goal of the game was scored by Dennis Stevens.

1964	Blackburn Rovers	H	First Division	2–3
1967	West Bromwich Albion	H	First Division	2–1
1970	Newcastle United	H	First Division	3–1

On the same day Graham Stuart was born in Tooting. Signed by Chelsea as a schoolboy he graduated through the ranks at Stamford Bridge and went on to make over 100 first-team appearances for the club. He was sold to Everton for £850,000 in 1993 and was a member of the side that won the FA Cup in 1995. He represented England at both Youth and Under-21 level.

1981	Middlesbrough	A	First Division	2–0
1984	Slovan Bratislava	A	European Cup-Winners' Cup 2nd Round 1st Leg	1–0

After two unconvincing displays against UC Dublin in the first round of the European Cup-Winners' Cup, Everton at last found their feet with a well merited 1–0 win in Bratislava, Paul Bracewell scoring the only goal of the game.

1987	Watford	H	First Division	2–0
1989	Luton Town	H	Littlewoods Cup 3rd Round	3–0
1992	Arsenal	A	FA Premier League	0–2

OCTOBER 25TH

1890	West Bromwich Albion	H	Football League	2–3

Everton were beaten at home by West Bromwich Albion, their eighth game of the season and the best start of any of the clubs in the League.

1902	Nottingham Forest	H	First Division	1–1
1913	Manchester City	A	First Division	1–1

1919	Blackburn Rovers	H	First Division	1–0
1924	Nottingham Forest	A	First Division	1–0
1930	Tottenham Hotspur	H	Second Division	4–2

Cliff Britton made his debut in the 4–2 home win over Spurs. He first burst on to the scene with Bristol Rovers in 1926 and four years later was transferred to Everton. By 1932–33 he was on his way to becoming a regular in the side and his performances at the club were recognised at international level, earning him his first cap in 1934 and nine in total during his career. He made only one appearance in the side that won the League title in 1938–39 but by then had already begun to switch to coaching and management. He spent three years with Burnley, guiding them to the FA Cup final in 1947 and returned to Goodison Park in September the following year as manager. He remained in the position until 1956, having restored the club to the First Division, his decision to quit influenced by the fact the directors wanted to appoint an acting manager whilst he was overseas with the team.

1941	Liverpool	A	Football League North (First Championship)	2–3
1947	Arsenal	A	First Division	1–1
1952	West Ham United	H	Second Division	2–0
1953	Rotherham United	A	Second Division	2–1
1958	Blackpool	A	First Division	1–1
1966	Southampton	A	First Division	3–1

1968 David Burrows born in Dudley. He first made his name with West Bromwich Albion before joining Liverpool for £550,000 in 1988. In 1993 he joined West Ham but a little less than a year later returned to the city of Liverpool, signing for Everton. Six months later he was sold to Coventry for £1.1 million.

1969	Coventry City	A	First Division	1–0
1975	Wolverhampton Wanderers	A	First Division	2–1
1977	Middlesbrough	H	League Cup 3rd Round	2–2
1980	Manchester United	A	First Division	0–2
1986	Watford	H	First Division	3–2
1997	Coventry City	A	FA Premier League	0–0

OCTOBER 26TH

1889	Accrington	H	Football League	2–2
1895	Burnley	A	First Division	1–1
1901	Blackburn Rovers	A	First Division	1–3
1907	Chelsea	A	First Division	1–2
1912	Newcastle United	H	First Division	0–6
1918	Manchester United	H	Lancashire Section Principal Tournament	6–2
1929	Blackburn Rovers	A	First Division	1–3
1935	Blackburn Rovers	A	First Division	1–1
1940	Bury	H	North Regional League	3–1
1946	Charlton Athletic	A	First Division	1–4
1957	Preston North End	A	First Division	1–3
1963	Tottenham Hotspur	H	First Division	1–0
1968	Wolverhampton Wanderers	A	First Division	2–1

1974	Burnley	A	First Division	1–1
1976	Coventry City	H	League Cup 4th Round	3–0
1983	Chesterfield	H	Milk Cup 2nd Round 2nd Leg	2–2

Everton had already won the first leg at Chesterfield 1–0 and should have had little trouble in disposing of the lower division side at Goodison. Instead they were made to sweat before goals from Adrian Heath and Trevor Steven took them through 3–2 winners on aggregate.

1985	Manchester City	A	First Division	1–1
1991	Queens Park Rangers	A	First Division	1–3
1993	Crystal Palace	H	Coca–Cola Cup 3rd Round	2–2

Everton were surprisingly held at home by Crystal Palace in the Coca–Cola Cup third round despite goals from Peter Beagrie and Dave Watson. More worrying was the crowd figure, just 11,537 for the clash at Goodison Park.

OCTOBER 27TH

| 1888 | Derby County | H | Football League | 6–2 |

A. McKinnon scored Everton's first ever League hat-trick in the 6–2 win over Derby County. He made only six League appearances for the club, all in the inaugural season of the League and made his debut at centre-half! Everton's other goals were scored by Nick Ross (two) and R. Watson.

1894	Sunderland	H	First Division	2–2
1900	Nottingham Forest	A	First Division	1–2
1906	Bolton Wanderers	A	First Division	3–1
1917	Stockport County	A	Lancashire Section Principal Tournament	0–0
1923	Notts County	H	First Division	3–0
1928	Leeds United	H	First Division	0–1
1934	West Bromwich Albion	H	First Division	4–0
1945	Sunderland	A	Football League North	4–0
1951	Luton Town	A	Second Division	1–1
1956	Arsenal	H	First Division	4–0

A week after ending Manchester United's unbeaten home run Everton were in impressive form in front of their own fans with a 4–0 demolition of Arsenal at Goodison thanks to gaols from Peter Farrell, Wally Fielding, Tommy Jones and George Kirby.

1962	Ipswich Town	H	First Division	3–1
1973	Birmingham City	A	First Division	2–0
1979	Manchester United	H	First Division	0–0
1981	Coventry City	A	League Cup 2nd Round 2nd Leg	1–0
1982	Newport County	H	Milk Cup 2nd Round 2nd Leg	2–2
1984	Manchester United	H	First Division	5–0

Manchester United were hailed by many as the side most likely to succeed Liverpool as League champions, and manager Ron Atkinson had certainly spent big in an attempt to end a run of seventeen years without the League trophy having been seen at Old Trafford. Everton's performance on the day was highly polished and gave notice of their own title aspirations as United were torn apart from the first minute to the last. They might have taken the lead after only two minutes, Mountfield firing just over, but the miss only served to inspire Everton to greater heights and after five minutes they were ahead, Kevin Sheedy heading home, and the same player recovered from a nasty head injury to make it 2–0 after 23 minutes. Just after half an hour it was 3–0, Adrian Heath converting a chance from short range, and half-time came as a welcome relief to United. They were in for more of the same in the second half as Everton looked to press home their advantage, Albiston clearing off the line and Gary Stevens extending the lead with a shot that went in off the post. Four minutes from time Graeme Sharp rounded off an impressive afternoon with the fifth goal and a performance claimed by former player Joe Mercer, watching in the stands, as the finest he had seen from any Everton side. Praise indeed, but there were more of the same to come in a delightful season.

| 1990 | Luton Town | A | First Division | 1–1 |

OCTOBER 28TH

1893	Preston North End	H	First Division	2–3
1899	Stoke City	A	First Division	1–1
1905	Bolton Wanderers	H	First Division	3–1
1911	Bradford City	H	First Division	1–0
1916	Port Vale	H	Lancashire Section Principal Tournament	3–1
1922	Nottingham Forest	H	First Division	4–2

1924 Ted Buckle born in Southwark. He began his career with Manchester United and was transferred to Everton in November 1949, making his debut for the club against Manchester United 18 hours later! He remained at the club until 1955 when he joined Exeter City, later becoming player-manager for Prestatyn. Less than 12 months later he resigned owing to business commitments.

| 1933 | Leicester City | A | First Division | 1–3 |

1935 Edward O'Hara born in Glasgow. He joined Everton in June 1958 from Falkirk and made 29 appearances in the League for the club before moving on to Rotherham. He later played for Barnsley and won three Scottish Under–23 caps.

1939	New Brighton	A	War Regional League, Western Division	1–0
1944	Liverpool	A	Football League North (First Championship)	0–0
1950	Manchester United	H	First Division	1–4
1961	Chelsea	A	First Division	1–1
1967	Newcastle United	A	First Division	0–1
1972	Ipswich Town	H	First Division	2–2
1978	Liverpool	H	First Division	1–0
1986	Sheffield Wednesday	H	Littlewoods Cup 3rd Round	4–0
1987	Liverpool	A	Littlewoods Cup 3rd Round	1–0

The previous season Liverpool had ended Everton's hopes of the Littlewoods Cup with a 1–0 win at Goodison. Everton exacted their revenge with a similar scoreline at Anfield in front of a crowd of 44,071. Defender Gary Stevens scored the vital goal in the second half and Neville Southall pulled off a string of saves to thwart Liverpool throughout.

1989	Norwich City	A	First Division	1–1
1992	Wimbledon	H	Coca–Cola Cup 3rd Round	0–0
1995	Aston Villa	A	FA Premier League	0–1
1996	Nottingham Forest	A	FA Premier League	1–0

OCTOBER 29TH

| 1887 | Bolton Wanderers | H | FA Cup 1st Round Replay | 2–2 |

Everton and Bolton Wanderers met for a second time in the FA Cup following Everton's successful appeal after the first game at Bolton. This time around the two sides drew 2–2, necessitating a replay.

1892	Bolton Wanderers	A	First Division	1–4
1898	Blackburn Rovers	A	First Division	3–1
1904	Blackburn Rovers	A	First Division	0–1
1910	Sunderland	A	First Division	0–4
1921	Oldham Athletic	A	First Division	0–0
1924	Manchester City	H	First Division	3–1
1927	Portsmouth	A	First Division	3–1

Dixie Dean returned to the side after missing the match against West Ham and blasted a hat-trick at Fratton Park to reach the 20 mark for the season with only 12 games played.

1932	Portsmouth	H	First Division	1–1
1938	Leicester City	A	First Division	0–3
1949	Derby County	H	First Division	1–2
1955	Sunderland	A	First Division	0–0
1960	Nottingham Forest	A	First Division	2–1
1966	Leicester City	H	First Division	2–0
1977	Newcastle United	H	First Division	4–4

Despite a 4–4 draw Everton moved up a place in the League table to second, behind early leaders (and eventual champions) Nottingham Forest. The game against Newcastle was a topsy turvy affair, with Everton having to come from behind in order to snatch their point. The goals were scored by Mike Pejic, Mick Lyons and two from Bob Latchford.

1983	Leicester City	A	First Division	0–2
1985	Shrewsbury Town	A	Milk Cup 3rd Round	4–1
1994	Arsenal	H	FA Premier League	1–1

A first half goal by Arsenal's Stefan Schwarz at Goodison Park turned out to be the last goal Everton conceded for 12 hours 15 minutes, a run that covered seven League games. The run ended against Sheffield Wednesday, who scored four times!

OCTOBER 30TH

| 1886 | Glasgow Rangers | H | FA Cup 1st Round | 0–1 |

Everton played their first match in the FA Cup, being drawn against Scottish side Glasgow Rangers! It was, coincidentally, the first and only season that Rangers entered the English FA Cup, and they journeyed down to Liverpool the day before the game and were due to stay in a local hotel, but shortly after midnight the proprietor took exception to the revelry of the Rangers side and turfed them out of the hotel! Despite this slipshod preparation, Rangers proved too good for Everton, winning 1–0 with a goal from Charlie Heggie in front of a crowd of 6,000. However, Everton had already scratched from the competition as they believed they would not have won unless they fielded players ineligible (professionals in other words), and so whilst Everton are certain that the game was little more than a friendly, Rangers and most reference books show this game as an FA Cup tie!

| 1897 | Sheffield United | H | First Division | 1–4 |

Sheffield United were on their way to winning the League title and in the process were the only side to register a League victory at Goodison. Everton meanwhile finished in fourth place, seven points behind United.

1909	Bolton Wanderers	H	First Division	3–1
1915	Stoke City	A	Lancashire Section Principal Tournament	2–3
1920	Liverpool	H	First Division	0–3
1926	Arsenal	H	First Division	3–1

1929 Dave Hickson born in Ellesmere Port. Signed by Everton in May 1948 from Ellesmere Port he remained at Goodison until September 1955. He was sold to Aston Villa for £17,500 but remained only two months before switching to Huddersfield for £16,000 and then returned to Everton in August 1957 for £7,500. Just over two years later he was on the move again, making the relatively short trip across Stanley Park to sign for Liverpool, and he later finished his playing career with Bury and Tranmere. On the same day Tony McNamara was born in Liverpool. He joined the club as a junior and rose through the ranks to make 111 League appearances for the first team, scoring 21 goals. Like Hickson he also moved to Liverpool, joining them in December 1957, but after only a handful of games moved on to Crewe Alexandra, finishing his career with Bury.

1937	Preston North End	H	First Division	3–0
1943	Wrexham	H	Football League North (First Championship)	4–2
1948	Huddersfield Town	H	First Division	2–0

1953 Paul Power born in Manchester. Signed by Manchester City as a trainee and then offered full professional forms in July 1975 he was a permanent fixture of the side for the next 12 years or so. He was surprisingly sold to Everton for £65,000 in 1986, making his debut in the FA Charity Shield and then helping the club win the League title.

1954	Manchester United	H	First Division	4–2

1964 Paul Wilkinson born in Louth. After developing through the ranks at Grimsby Town Paul was sold to Everton for £250,000 in 1985 and won a winners' medal in the FA Charity Shield in 1986 and a League championship medal the following season, although he had been sold to Nottingham Forest before the end of the campaign. He has since gone on to play for Watford, Middlesbrough, Luton and Barnsley.

1965	Blackburn Rovers	A	First Division	2–1
1971	Newcastle United	H	First Division	1–0
1973	Norwich City	H	League Cup 3rd Round	0–1
1976	Tottenham Hotspur	A	First Division	3–3
1979	Grimsby Town	A	League Cup 4th Round	1–2
1982	Southampton	A	First Division	2–3
1984	Manchester United	A	Milk Cup 3rd Round	2–1
1988	Manchester United	H	First Division	1–1
1990	Sheffield United	A	Rumbelows Cup 3rd Round	1–2
1991	Wolverhampton Wanderers	H	Rumbelows Cup 3rd Round	4–1
1993	Ipswich Town	A	FA Premier League	2–0

OCTOBER 31ST

1891	Preston North End	A	Football League	0–4
1896	Wolverhampton Wanderers	H	First Division	0–0
1903	Nottingham Forest	H	First Division	0–2

1908	Birmingham City	A	First Division	2–1
1914	Bolton Wanderers	A	First Division	0–0
1925	Arsenal	A	First Division	1–4
1931	Newcastle United	H	First Division	8–1

Everton were in a rich vein of goalscoring form, having netted 35 in just eight games. Their eight in the demolition of Newcastle were scored by Dixie Dean (two), Tommy Johnson (two), Tommy White (two) Ted Critchley and Jimmy Stein. The bubble deflated somewhat in the next game, a goalless draw, before Everton got back in their stride with 34 in eight games!

1936	Middlesbrough	A	First Division	0–2
1942	Bury	A	Football League North (First Championship)	1–4
1953	Leicester City	H	Second Division	1–2
1959	Leicester City	H	First Division	6–1
1960	Walsall	H	League Cup 2nd Round	3–1
1962	Dunfermline Athletic	A	Inter-Cities Fairs Cup 1st Round 2nd Leg	0–2

Dunfermline Athletic ended Everton's interest in the Inter-Cities Fairs Cup with a 2–0 win at East End Park, thus eliminating Everton 2–1 on aggregate. This had been the first season Everton had competed in Europe.

1964	Arsenal	A	First Division	1–3
1970	West Bromwich Albion	A	First Division	0–3
1977	Middlesbrough	A	League Cup 3rd Round Replay	2–1
1981	Manchester City	H	First Division	0–1
1981	Manchester City	H	First Division	0–1
1990	Everton manager Colin Harvey was sacked from his position after two and half years in charge. He was not to leave the club however, for with the subsequent return of Howard Kendall he was appointed coach.			
1992	Manchester City	H	FA Premier League	1–3

NOVEMBER 1ST

1890	Notts County	A	Football League	1–3
1902	Bolton Wanderers	A	First Division	3–1
1913	Bradford City	H	First Division	1–1
1919	Blackburn Rovers	A	First Division	0–3
1924	Bury	H	First Division	0–0
1930	Reading	A	Second Division	2–0

The only occasion Everton have visited Elm Park in a League match saw them win 2–0 in front of a crowd of 11,919.

1941	Liverpool	H	Football League North (First Championship)	5–3
1947	Sheffield United	H	First Division	2–0
1952	Fulham	A	Second Division	0–3
1958	Blackburn Rovers	H	First Division	2–2
1960	Alan Harper born in Liverpool. Originally on the books of Liverpool as an apprentice he left the club without making a single appearance and joined Everton. After 127 League appearances he was sold to Sheffield Wednesday, but later returned to Goodison for a second spell with the club after playing for Manchester City.			
1969	Nottingham Forest	H	First Division	1–0

Tommy Wright scored the only goal of the game in front of a crowd of 49,610 at

SLEIVE MOYNE

FanFare
(the ESCNI Travel Newsletter)

Issue No. 7 //=   August 2001

Everton
SUPPORTERS CLUB
NORTHERN IRELAND

ESCNI
the Everton
Supporters Club
Northern Ireland

Monthly Meetings:

* **August Meeting:**
  Monday, 27th Aug
  @ 8.00pm

* **September Meeting:**
  Monday, 24th Sept
  @ 8.00pm

Introduction

In this edition of *FanFare* (yes, I've finally decided to give it a name!), we have news on our forthcoming *Middlesbrough* boat trip (the first Saturday game of the new season).

As more travel options become available to us, it has become noticeable that trips are becoming less of a social event; with travellers to a match often not meeting each other during the day. Consequently, we would remind you that many of the travelling *ESCNI* contingent, travel connections permitting, often meet up in the *Elm Tree* public house (near Goodison) before and/or after the match. Furthermore, many of the early arrivals also meet up first thing in the morning in Margie Boden's *Lucy in the Sky* café (located in the *Cavern Shopping Centre* in Liverpool city-centre) for coffee/tea and toast. All *ESCNI* members and their guests are welcome to join us at either venue.

Finally, please note that from this forthcoming season, I will also accept match ticket bookings **via e-mail** providing that the necessary information is given. By this I mean **not only the area of the ground required** but also the **members' names** and the **adult/child breakdown for any guests;** furthermore (in accordance with *ESCNI* rules), for the *Big Games* (probably Liverpool and Man Utd), a list of the matches you have attended within the preceding twelve months. Finally, you should also ensure that your e-mail has been acknowledged by a reply.

Peter Cross
028 9049 2059
(7pm to 9pm)
escni.peter@btinternet.com

Peter

easyJet Prices Update

By utilising easyJet's Belfast / Liverpool air service, **day-return** flights are available *from £25 return* (tax included). However, the number of places at this price is somewhat limited and the price steadily rises as the planes fill up. The forthcoming home matches (with *easyJet* day-return prices as at 30th July) are: -

Date	v Opposition (Day-Return Cost)	Outward Flights (**Cost**) / Inbound Flights (**Cost**)
<u>Mon 20th</u>Aug (**Sky: 8pm**) v **Tottenham** (£40 to £60)	[06.30 (£15) or 08.05 (£30) or 10.55 (£35) or 15.00 (£30) or 17.45 (£30) / 22.45 (£15)]
Sat 25th Aug v **Middlesbrough** (£70)	[07.20 (£40) or 11.25 (£40) / 22.10 (£20)]
Sat 15th Sep (PpV: 12pm?) v **Liverpool** (£55)	[07.20 (£30) / 16.20 (£15) or 22.10 (£15)]
Sat 29th Sep v **West Ham** (£40)	[07.20 (£15) or 11.25 (£15) / 22.10 (£15)]
*Sat 20th Oct (UEFA?) v **Aston Villa** (£70)	[07.20 (£30) or 11.25 (£30) / 22.10 (£30)]
*Sat 27th Oct (PpV?) v **Newcastle** (£65 to £75)	[07.20 (£50) or 11.25 (£40) / 22.10 (£15)]
*Sat 17th Nov (PpV?) v **Chelsea** (£50 to £65)	[07.10 (£30) or 09.10 (£30) or 10.40 (£20) / 19.00 (£20) or 21.05 (£25)]
Sun 2nd Dec (**Sky: 4pm**) v **Southampton** (£65 to £75)	[07.30 (£15) or 10.40 (£15) / 19.55 (£50) or 22.10 (£40)]
Sat 15th Dec (PpV/Sky?) v **Derby** (£45 to £50)	[07.10 (£15) or 09.10 (£20) or 10.40 (£20) / 19.00 (£20) or 21.05 (£20)]
Wed 26th Dec (PpV?) v **Man Utd** (£40 to £45)	[09.10 (£20) or 10.40 (£15) / 20.15 (£15) or 22.30 (£15)]
Sat 29th Dec (PpV/Sky?) v **Charlton** (£60 to £70)	[07.10 (£30) or 09.10 (£35) or 10.40 (£35) / 19.00 (£20) or 21.05 (£20)]
Sat 12th Jan (PpV/Sky?) v **Sunderland** (£60 to £70)	[07.10 (£20) or 09.10 (£20) or 10.40 (£20) / 19.00 (£15) or 21.05 (£15)]

*indicates matches which currently clash with Man Utd home games

Please note that **£5 can be saved** on these return fares by booking via the internet. The return fare comprises the single fares detailed above **plus £10** government tax. This tax is due on **each** single flight booked. Updated versions of these prices will also be regularly e-mailed to our membership.

For your assistance, we have indicated fixtures (?) which we still believe to be liable to alteration (*Sky, UEFA, Pay-per-View* etc). However, we stress this is for your guidance only and *ESCN/* cannot accept responsibility for any mistakes or unforeseen circumstances.

How to Book:-

As *easyJet* doesn't deal directly with group travel (or, indeed, travel agents), we would advise our members to contact *easyJet* **direct** (with a credit card to hand).

If the flight departs more than **one** month from the day of booking, seats must be purchased over the *Internet (easyjet.com)*. If the flight departs within **one month** of the day of booking, it can be purchased by telephone (**0870 6 000 000**) as well as over the *Internet*. However, you will save £5 on each return fare by booking on the *Internet*.

> *easyJet*
> **easyjet.com**
> **0870 6 000 000**

[Please note that names of passengers and flight times can be subsequently changed but at a cost of £10.00 per alteration **plus** any difference in the cost of the flight(s)].

easyJet Timetables

easyJet's Summer Timetable (25th Mar to 27th Oct): -

	Ex Belfast	Ex Liverpool
Sat:	**07.20**, **11.25**, 15.05, 17.25	10.15, 14.00, 16.20, **22.10**
Sun:	**07.20**, **11.40**, 19.35, 21.55	10.35, 18.25, **20.50**, **22.45**
Mon to Fri:	**06.30**, **08.05**, **10.55**, **15.00**, **17.45**, 22.05	07.00, 09.45, 13.50, 16.40, 20.55, **22.45**

easyJet's Winter Timetable (28th Oct to 30th Mar): -

	Ex Belfast	Ex Liverpool
Sat:	**07.10**, **09.10**, **10.40**, 19.00	07.00, 10.25, **19.00**, **21.05**
Sun:	**07.30**, **10.40**, 17.10, 21.55	08.40, 18.25, **19.55**, **22.10**
Mon to Fri:	**07.10**, **09.10**, **10.40**, **14.15**, 19.00, 21.20	07.00, 10.25, 15.35, 17.35, 20.15, **22.30**

Aldergrove daily car-parking costs are:
>   **Main Car Park: £5.50, Private (eg Boal's): £4.50**

Liverpool Taxi costs are:
>   **Speke/City: ~£10.00, City/Goodison: ~£5.00, Goodison/Speke: ~£14.00**

easyJet's new Winter Timetable seems to be generally good news for footie fans. For the first time, there will be **three** suitable flights out on the Saturday morning (**07.10**, **09.10** and **10.40**). Furthermore, there will again be **two** suitable flights home on a Saturday night (at **19.00** and **21.05**).

For Sunday matches (which, with the arrival of pay-per-view games, should be more common this season), there will be **two** suitable flights out (at **07.30** and **10.40**); with **three** potential suitable return flights (at **18.25**, **19.55** and **22.10**). Unfortunately, for any midweek matches (which kick-off at 7.45pm this season), the last flight has been brought forward by fifteen minutes to **22.30**.

07718928890

Norse Merchant Ferries Trip

NorseMerchant
Ferries

v MIDDLESBROUGH

3.00pm on Saturday, 25th August 2001;
at Goodison Park

Included in the cost: -

**Belfast/Liverpool Return Ferry
(incl. berths, dinners and breakfasts)
Match Ticket (*Top Balcony*)**

In conjunction with Everton FC, *ESCNI* will
be running a trip to the above game. Outline details of the trip are as follows: -

Friday 19.30: meet at Belfast Harbour Victoria Terminal (free car parking available adjacent to the terminal); a four-course dinner will be served before sailing.

Saturday 07.30 (approx.): following breakfast, arrive at Liverpool (transport to city centre provided).

Saturday 20.00 after the match, board transport outside the *Elm Tree* to return to the ferry for the return sailing to Belfast; again, dinner will be served on-board.

Sunday 08.00 (approx.): after breakfast, arrive Belfast Harbour.

Return Fares (including match ticket):	
Adult (ESCNI member): £90	Child (under 16): £79
Adult (non-member): £95	Child (under 15): £62

Please note the following points:-

- The match tickets have been guaranteed by Everton FC to *ESCNI*.
- A limited number of other tickets are also available.
- Please note that in the event of your non-attendance, travel costs are non-refundable.
- Fares are based on sharing a four-berth cabin (with en-suite facilities) and includes evening meals and breakfasts.
- Providing advance notice is given, an optional Sunday night return is available at no additional charge.

How to Book:-

<u>Places on this trip are limited.</u> If you are interested in the above trip, please phone **Billy Johnston** on **028 9336 6437 (between 7pm and 9pm)** and then forward a cheque or postal order (<u>made payable to *ESCNI*</u>) for full payment to the *Club Travel Secretary* for this match: -

Billy Johnston
028 9336 6437
(7pm to 9pm)
billy-johnston@supanet.com

Billy Johnston, 3 Fairview Park, CARRICKFERGUS, BT38 7JG

NMF's New Colours

Not only Everton will be wearing a new kit on their travels this season. *Norse Merchant's **Mersey Viking** has recently* returned from her refit in Falmouth sporting new colours; the ship is now wearing the livery which has been depicted in the promotional material issued by *Norse Merchant Ferries* this year.

The new livery is striking and will appeal to those who like traditional ship colours. The web name "norsemerchant.com" is probably more controversial but may well prove to be a valuable advertisement when the *Twelve Quays* terminal opens (due to be during March 2002) in Birkenhead and the vessels berth **on** the River Mersey.

ESCNI Polo Shirts

In heavier material than our previous version and with an improved multi-colour badge, our new *ESCNI* polo shirts are selling well.

They are available in the following sizes and colours at **£15 each**, plus **£1 p&p per order:** -

      XL: white & royal

      Large: white, royal & navy

      Medium: white, royal & navy

      Small: royal

Club member, **Billy Latta**, modelling *a little white number*.

If you are interested in obtaining one, please contact **Ian Hutchinson** on **028 9335 5853** (7pm to 9pm please) and then post a cheque (made payable to *ESCNI*) to:-

Ian Hutchinson
028 9335 5853
(7pm to 9pm)

16 Windslow Close, CARRICKFERGUS, BT38 9BD

The Secretary's AGM Report

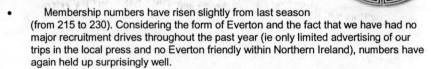

Reproduced from the Secretary's Report at our 2001 AGM:-

Membership:

- Membership numbers have risen slightly from last season (from 215 to 230). Considering the form of Everton and the fact that we have had no major recruitment drives throughout the past year (ie only limited advertising of our trips in the local press and no Everton friendly within Northern Ireland), numbers have again held up surprisingly well.

- The profile of the club has again been chiefly maintained through the usual methods of our calling cards and by word-of-mouth; this has been achieved without the substantial expense of a local advertising campaign. However, it is planned that another inexpensive mailshot of local newspapers (which proved quite successful several years ago) will be undertaken this summer. Last summer's launch of our new *website* has also helped us to raise our profile.

- Our *Membership Secretary*, John McAllister, has also advised me that, as well as contacting our existing members for their renewals, he will also be writing out to over two hundred people who either have been members or have contacted us over recent years. The renewal forms will be out with members towards the end of July.

- Incidentally, we are still the only official branch in Northern Ireland and, indeed, remain the biggest branch on the island.

Travel:

- With the arrival of *easyJet* two years ago, and in particular their availability of *day-return* trips, it has become evident that approximately 80% of our travellers prefer to travel by this method. However, it is also apparent that a significant number of our members still, on occasions, want to sail with *Norse Merchant Ferries* and so we have continued to organise some of these trips throughout the past two seasons. It remains our intention to continue to utilise *Norse Merchant Ferries* during the forthcoming season.

- At the start of last season, we ran a *day-return* trip to the game against Derby utilising the Belfast/Heysham *Seacat* service. However, the trip was poorly supported by our existing membership and we were only rescued from a financial disaster by a last-minute influx of new members hastily recruited from plugs in the *Belfast Telegraph* and the *Sunday Life*. From this, I would conclude that generally our members are no longer willing to tolerate a long day travelling through England or Scotland and would much prefer the convenience of the *easyJet* and *Norse Merchant Ferries* direct services. Consequently, it is our intention to continue to concentrate our travel advice on these two services, albeit with occasional advice on other services available.

- Once again, and on behalf of the Committee, I would like to thank all of our travellers for their exemplary behaviour on the various trips throughout the season.

Match Tickets:

- Our status as an *Official Branch* has continued to prove invaluable this season, as we were able to gain significant ticket allocations for all *home* games (including the Liverpool and Man Utd games). The situation for *away* matches remains good with tickets (albeit in small numbers) having been obtained on every occasion that we applied for them.

- From this season, I will also accept match ticket bookings via e-mail providing, where applicable, that the necessary information is also given. However, members must ensure that their e-mail has been acknowledged by a reply from myself.

Correspondence:

- As usual, during the past season considerable effort, not to mention expense, has gone into keeping our members informed of the various efforts of *ESCNI* in organising trips, meetings, social events, etc. and this again constitutes the bulk of the club's costs.

- Halfway through last season it was agreed that *ESCNI* should purchase a laser printer and hopefully our *Treasurer* can confirm a drop in printing costs (without any drop in the quality of our correspondence). On a personal note, it has made our printing times much quicker and I would like to thank the club committee and membership for their support in its purchase.

- Hopefully the club's latest venture our *Travel Newsletter (FanFare)*, which was launched last summer, has succeeded in providing members with more detailed and regular information on the various travel methods available and I intend to continue its production (new wife permitting) during the forthcoming season.

- Our other regular publication *Blueprint* will continue on an intermittent basis next season, as and when the availability of articles dictate.

- Thanks to the sterling work of Hugh McKillop, we also launched our own website last summer. However, problems with the updating of the site have meant that its impressive start has been somewhat undermined and its use has been a little disappointing. However, we will investigate this matter further and hope to improve the situation in the near future.

- On a more optimistic note, our e-mail distribution service has proved a lot more effective. On an almost daily basis, the 36% of our membership who have submitted an address are bombarded with club information (including the latest fixture news and travel information). Consequently, I would again urge all of our members to gain access to an e-mail address. [NB This will be particularly advantageous this season, as six of our home games currently coincide with Man Utd home games.]

- Correspondence from Everton FC's own *Official Supporters Club* (into which we enrol all of our members) is currently undergoing another review, under yet another new management team. Although their magazine tends to be aimed largely at the younger market, we would still consider the overall benefits of being an "*Official Supporters Club Branch*" to merit our continued perseverance.

Badges:

- The practice of issuing all new *ESCNI* members with a complimentary enamel club lapel badge has continued. It has been agreed to retain this practice for the forthcoming season.

Peter Cross

(*ESCNI Secretary*)

25th June 2001

Everton v Liverpool (12.00pm, Saturday, 15th or 3.00pm, Sunday, 16th September)

Although still subject to possible rearrangement, we have decided to allocate our tickets for this season's *derby* game at Goodison. Unfortunately, we won't know the exact date of the Liverpool game until they have played the second leg of their *Champions League* qualifying game on **22nd August**.

If Liverpool fail to qualify for the group stage of the *Champions League* and go into the *Uefa Cup*, this game will be played on **Sunday 16th September** and will **not** be a featured match on *pay-per-view* TV), otherwise the game will proceed as a *pay-per-view game* on **Saturday 15th September** at **12.00pm**.

> *Peter Cross*
> **028 9049 2059**
> (7pm to 9pm)

Our initial allocation of match tickets will be made available to our club members and, in accordance with *ESCNI* club rules, these will be allocated according to the number of match tickets ordered through *ESCNI* within the preceding twelve months.

Consequently, please phone the *Secretary*, **Peter Cross**, on **028 9049 2059 (between 7pm and 9pm please)** [quoting the matches (home or away) that you have attended since the 15th September 2000] from the following dates: -

Four (or more):	**Sunday, 12th August (3 to 5pm)**
Three matches:	**Sunday, 12th August (7 to 9pm)**
Two matches:	**Monday, 13th August**
One match:	**Tuesday, 14th August**
No matches:	**Wednesday, 15th August**
Guests:	**Thursday, 16th August**

ESCNI 2001 Charity Evening

The *Chairman* of our *Social Committee,* Billy Johnston, has advised that so far **over £1,000** was raised for the **Northern Ireland Childrens' Hospice** at this year's *ESCNI Charity Social Evening.*

Northern Ireland Hospice Children's Service

Congratulations to all of those involved in organising the evening and a big thank you to all of you who attended it (particularly our big bidders **Jeff Quigg** and **Tony Haren**). Also a big thank you to **Paul Graham** who made and very generously donated a child's rocking chair for auction.

Due to their recent well-publicised management problems, it was agreed (at our *AGM*) to delay the presentation of the cheque to the *Hospice* until **after** their forthcoming EGM. Consequently, our *Treasurer* (Tony Haren) has **temporarily** lodged the money in a separate *ring-fenced* bank account. We will advise you of future developments.

Hotel Accommodation

ESCNI have been able to negotiate a special deal of **£25.00** per person (sharing) for *B&B* per night (weekends only) with the excellent *four-star **Atlantic Tower Thistle Hotel*** (situated near Pier Head); single rooms also available at **£45.00** per person.

However, please note that this rate is only available for Everton *home weekends* and that their normal midweek rate is **£82.00** per person (room only)!

> *Atlantic Tower Thistle Hotel*
> **0151 227 4444**
> *Stephanie Lewis*

Anyone interested should telephone **Stephanie Lewis** (Revenue Manager) on **0151 227 4444** and, in order to obtain these rates, please quote *"Everton Supporters Club Northern Ireland"* when making a reservation.

For a more basic hotel, there is the ***Lord Nelson Hotel*** (situated in Lime Street).

Their very economical rates, based on two people sharing, for *B&B* are **£20.00** per person (**£24.00** en-suite) per night; **£24.00** for a single room (**£29.00** en-suite).

> *Lord Nelson Hotel*
> **0151 709 4362**

These rates apply **throughout** the week.

If neither of the above are suitable, then anyone requiring a hotel room (at very reasonable rates) should contact the *Merseyside Tourism Reservation Service* on *0345 585291*.

> *Merseyside Tourism Reservation Service*
> **0345 585291**

Sad Loss of Mike Morgan

It is with deep regret that we have to announce the sad loss of *ESCNI* member **Mike Morgan**.

Mike, who was originally from Liverpool but was living near Lisburn, passed away on Thursday, 17th May while working out in Cyprus.

He had just turned forty-five in March and will be sorely missed by his family and all his fellow Evertonians; particularly those in *ESCNI*.

ESCNI News Snippets

The *Mersey Docks & Harbour Company* aim to have the *Norse Merchant Ferries* Belfast-service transferred to the new Wirral terminal by **mid March 2002**. The number of **daytime** sailings will increase from **three** to **five** per week (Dublin sailings are expected to transfer three months later).

With the opening of its new terminal in March 2002, *Liverpool Airport* is to officially change its name to **Liverpool John Lennon Airport.**

Next season, child reductions will be available **throughout** Goodison; prices will be as follows:-
> **£11:** Top Balcony, Family Enclosure, Upper Gwladys, Lower Gwladys, Lower Bullens & Paddock
> **£15:** Upper Bullens & Park Stand
> **£17:** Main Stand

Adult seat prices at Goodison are to remain **unchanged** (and are, as usual, detailed on the back page of this publication). There will be only **two** *premium* priced games; the *Liverpool* and *Man Utd* games.

Following our recent *Charity Night*, we have a number of sets of car blinds left over from the event. They are available at **£3 per pair** (with all of the proceeds going to the charity). If you are interested please e-mail or telephone Peter on **028 9049 2059** (between **7pm** and **9pm** please).

2000/01 *ESCNI* Player of the Season Trophy

Following the election at our *AGM*, the final result for our *Player of the Season 2000-01* is: -

Michael Ball:	107 points
David Weir:	104 points
Steve Watson:	26 points
David Unsworth:	17 points

It is anticipated that the presentation of the *Tyrone Crystal* trophy will be made to **Michael Ball** at one of the matches early in the new season. As usual, one adult and one child (drawn from those *ESCNI* members attending the relevant match) will make the presentation.

This is of course assuming that our usual *kiss-of-death* has not been enforced and that he hasn't moved on (not entirely impossible at the time of writing!).

Twenty (Almost Completely Useless) Statistics About *ESCNI* Members

Everton
SUPPORTERS CLUB
NORTHERN IRELAND

At the risk of appearing to have nothing better to do over the summer, I have analysed our membership list of 230 people and have come up with the following *Twenty Things You Didn't Know (or Probably Didn't Want to Know) About ESCNI Members*:-

Oldest: our oldest member is **77** (06/04/34)

Youngest: our youngest member is **8** (12/03/93)

Average: the average age of our membership is **34**

Females: **7%** (ie 16) are female

Under 18s: **15%** (34) are under 18

Over 65s: **2%** (4) are over 65

Most Popular Post Code: **BT15** is the most popular post code (12)

Most Popular Post Town: **Belfast** (75); followed by Newtownabbey (16)

Most Popular House Number: No. **1** (16) is the most popular house number

Most Popular Birth Year: **1975** (14); followed by 1956 (12)

Most Popular Birth Month: September (25)

Least Popular Birth Month: July (14)

Most Popular Birth Decade: **28%** during the **70's** (65)

Shared DoB: only one date is shared; by two of our members **(10/09/57)**

e-mail address: **36%** (83) have e-mail addresses

Most Popular e-mail Provider: **hotmail.com** (16)

Mobile Phone: **41%** (95) admit to having a mobile phone

Most Popular Forename: **David** (11)

Most Popular Surname: **Boyd, Hamilton, O'Hara & Simpson** (with 4 each)

Most Members at One Address: **3** (by 4 different families)

Speke Coach Service

LIVERPOOL AIRPORT

The coach (**Number 500**) departs every 30 minutes (from **outside the Terminal Building**) with the first coach departing at 05.15 and the last service departing at 00.15. On the return journey the coach leaves (from **Lime Street**) with the first coach departing at 05.57 and the last service departing at 00.57.

The coach service takes approximately **30 minutes** and calls at the major city centre hotels en route. The service runs every day, seven days a week (except for Christmas Day). The cost of a single journey is **£2 for an adult** and **£1 for a child**.

Merseytravel
0151 236 7676

ESCNI

17 Greer Park Drive
BELFAST
BT8 7YQ

Phone: **028 9049 2059**
Email:
escni.peter@btinternet.com

**Northern Ireland's
only official
Everton Supporters Club**

www.escni.co.uk

Match Ticket Prices (2001/02)

	Adult	Junior	OAP
Main Stand	26.00	17.00	~
Upper Bullens	24.00	15.00	~
Park Stand	23.00	15.00	~
Top Balcony	22.00	11.00	~
Lower Bullens	22.00	11.00	13.00
Upper Gwladys	22.00	11.00	~
Family Enclosure	22.00	11.00	13.00
Paddock Stand	22.00	11.00	~
Lower Gwladys	18.50	11.00	~
Disabled Enclosure	23.00	~	~

**(Adult tickets £3 extra for two *premium* games:-
Man U & Liverpool)**

Booking Match Tickets (exc *Club Trips*)

Having booked your travel, by whatever method, you should then telephone the *ESCNI Secretary*, Peter Cross on **028 9049 2059 (between 7pm and 9pm please)** or e-mail via **escni.peter@btinternet.com** to book your match ticket(s).

[N.B. Match tickets for **non-members** will be surcharged at the rate of **£2.00 for adults** and **£1.00 for children**; this surcharge is to make a contribution towards the *ESCNI* administration costs.]

> *Peter Cross*
> **028 9049 2059**
> (7pm to 9pm)
> escni.peter@btinternet.com

Cheques or POs (made payable to ***ESCNI***) for match ticket payments should then be forwarded, as soon as possible please, to: -

Peter Cross, 17 Greer Park Drive, Belfast, BT8 7YQ

Please note that monies **must** be received **at least seven days** before the game; otherwise, tickets ordered may be reallocated or returned to Everton FC.

Away Match Tickets

Anyone interested in *away* tickets should submit their application to the *ESCNI Secretary*, Peter Cross, at least **one month before** the date of the game. Last season's last *away* travellers (losers again, I'm afraid!) were:-

Chelsea: David Lavery, Paul Graham & Karen McCabe

Goodison to stretch Everton's lead at the top of the table. They had already posted 32 points out of a possible 36 so far in the season.

1975	Leicester City	H	First Division		1–1
1978	Dukla Prague	A	UEFA Cup 2nd Round 2nd Leg		0–1

Everton slipped out of the UEFA Cup at the second round stage, beaten 1–0 on the night by Dukla Prague and thus eliminated on the away goals rule.

1980	Tottenham Hotspur	H	First Division		2–2
1987	Liverpool	A	First Division		0–2
1994	West Ham United	H	FA Premier League		1–0

NOVEMBER 2ND

1889	Stoke City	H	Football League		8–0

Fred Geary scored his first hat-trick for the club in the 8–0 win over Stoke, with Brady (two), Latta (two) and Milward adding the other goals. The win took Everton back to the top of the table ahead of Preston, although they were themselves overtaken two weeks later.

1895	Wolverhampton Wanderers	H	First Division		2–0

Alex Latta made his 148th and final appearance for the club in the 2–0 win over Wolves at Goodison. Born in Dumbarton in 1867 he began his career with Dumbarton and joined Everton in 1889, making his debut in the opening game of the 1889–90 season. During his time with the club he won a League championship medal and a runners-up medal in the FA Cup to go with the two caps he had already won for Scotland. He left Goodison in 1896 to cross Stanley Park for Liverpool and upon his retirement as a player joined a yacht–making company. He died in August 1928.

1901	Stoke City	H	First Division		1–0
1907	Nottingham Forest	H	First Division		1–0
1912	Oldham Athletic	A	First Division		0–2
1918	Stoke City	H	Lancashire Section Principal Tournament		5–1
1929	Newcastle United	H	First Division		5–2

Despite the fact that Everton finished the season being relegated into the Second Division for the first time in their history, there were still results and performances to savour, with the 5–2 win over Newcastle one of the best seen at Goodison during the campaign. George Martin scored twice and Ted Critchley, Dixie Dean and Tommy White all added one apiece.

1935	Stoke City	H	First Division		5–1
1940	Bury	A	North Regional League		1–2
1946	Grimsby Town	H	First Division		3–3
1957	West Bromwich Albion	H	First Division		1–1
1962	Derek Mountfield born in Liverpool. An Everton fan as a schoolboy he began his career with Tranmere Rovers before winning a dream move to Goodison Park for £30,000 in June 1982. Injuries to Mark Higgins finally enabled him to claim a regular place in the side and he helped Everton win the League, FA Cup and European Cup-Winners' Cup. The arrival of Dave Watson restricted his first-team opportunities with Everton and in 1988 he joined Aston Villa.					
1963	Blackpool	A	First Division		1–1
1965	Neil McDonald born in Wallsend. A graduate of Newcastle's youth scheme he made				

over 150 appearances for the Magpies before a £525,000 transfer to Everton in 1988. In three years at Goodison he made over 100 appearances for the club before a move to Oldham, later playing for Bolton and Preston.

1968	Sunderland	H	First Division	2–0
1974	Manchester City	H	First Division	2–0
1985	West Ham United	A	First Division	1–2
1986	West Ham United	A	First Division	0–1
1991	Luton Town	A	First Division	1–0
1995	Feyenoord	A	European Cup-Winners' Cup 2nd Round 2nd Leg	0–1

Feyenoord ended Everton's dream of reclaiming the European Cup-Winners' Cup with a 1–0 win in Rotterdam, thereby winning the tie 1–0 on aggregate. It was the first match Everton had lost in the competition since 1966 when Real Zaragoza had beaten them in Spain 2–0.

1996 Middlesbrough's Nick Barmby became Everton's record signing when he joined the club in a transfer deal worth £5.75 million. Barmby had joined Middlesbrough the previous year from Spurs but had failed to settle in the North East, thus prompting a move to Everton. At the time he joined the club he was something of a regular in the England side, although he was later to lose his place.

1997	Southampton	H	FA Premier League	0–2

NOVEMBER 3RD

1888	Bolton Wanderers	H	Football League	2–1
1894	Small Heath	A	First Division	4–4
1900	Blackburn Rovers	H	First Division	0–0
1906	Manchester United	H	First Division	3–0
1917	Stockport County	H	Lancashire Section Principal Tournament	2–3
1923	Sheffield United	A	First Division	0–4
1928	Burnley	A	First Division	0–2
1934	Arsenal	A	First Division	0–2
1945	Sheffield United	A	Football League North	0–4
1951	Bury	H	Second Division	2–2
1956	West Bromwich Albion	A	First Division	0–3
1962	Manchester City	A	First Division	1–1
1965	Ujpest Dozsa	A	Inter-Cities Fairs Cup 2nd Round 1st Leg	0–3

Ujpest Dozsa were the opposition for the Inter-Cities Fairs Cup second round, with the Hungarians at home in the first leg. There they effectively ended Everton's interest in the competition, winning 3–0 in something of a canter.

1973	Tottenham Hotspur	H	First Division	1–1
1979	Norwich City	A	First Division	0–0
1984	Leicester City	H	First Division	3–0

A 3–0 win over Leicester at Goodison enabled Everton to take over at the top of the table for the first time in the campaign, with a run of four straight victories having taken them above Manchester United and Liverpool on their way. The goals were scored by Adrian Heath, Kevin Sheedy and Trevor Steven in an exemplary second half performance.

1990	Queens Park Rangers	H	First Division	3–0

NOVEMBER 4TH

1893	Sheffield Wednesday	A	First Division	1–1
1899	Sunderland	A	First Division	0–1
1905	Woolwich Arsenal	A	First Division	2–1
1911	Woolwich Arsenal	A	First Division	1–0
1916	Oldham Athletic	A	Lancashire Section Principal Tournament	3–2
1922	Arsenal	H	First Division	1–0
1933	Huddersfield Town	H	First Division	0–1

1939 Goodison Park staged the first representative match of the Second World War, with a Football League XI drawing 3–3 with an all–British side in front of a crowd of 15,000 (the crowd size was restricted on government orders in case of air attack from the Germans) who paid £1,244 towards the Red Cross.

1944	Manchester City	A	Football League North (First Championship)	3–1
1950	Blackpool	A	First Division	0–4

1953 Mike Buckley born in Manchester. Despite obvious overtures from both City and United in Manchester, Mike opted to begin his career with Everton, signing for the club in 1971. He broke into the first team in 1971–72 and remained something of a permanent fixture until sidelined by injury in 1976. When he returned to full fitness he had lost his place to Trevor Ross, and after a loan spell with QPR was transferred to Sunderland in 1978. He later joined Carlisle United.

1961	Tottenham Hotspur	H	First Division	3–0
1967	Manchester City	H	First Division	1–1
1970	Borussia Moenchengladbach	H	European Cup 2nd Round 2nd Leg	1–1

Goodison Park was packed with 42,744 fans for the visit of Borussia in the second round second leg match. The first leg had finished all square at 1–1, and the second leg was destined to finish the same, a goal from John Morrissey being cancelled out by Lauman. Extra time failed to separate the two sides either, so it was a penalty shoot out to decide who would progress into the third round, the first time it had been used in European competition. Everton duly won 4–3 to go on to meet Panathinaikos.

1972	Crystal Palace	A	First Division	0–1
1978	Nottingham Forest	A	First Division	0–0
1996	Coventry City	H	FA Premier League	1–1

NOVEMBER 5TH

1892	Derby County	A	First Division	6–1

Fred Geary and Alex Latta both scored hat-tricks as Derby were overwhelmed at the Racecourse Ground, the first time two Everton players had both registered as many as three goals apiece. At the end of the season Geary had 19 goals to his credit with Latta registering one less.

1898	Sheffield Wednesday	H	First Division	2–0
1904	Nottingham Forest	H	First Division	5–1

Alex Young scored four of Everton's five goals in the 5–1 win over Forest, with Jack Taylor notching the other.

1910	Woolwich Arsenal	H	First Division	2–0
1921	Liverpool	H	First Division	1–1
1927	Leicester City	H	First Division	7–1

Everton hit seven goals for the second time in a fortnight, this time crushing Leicester City in front of an enthusiastic Goodison crowd of 30,392. Dixie Dean again led the scoring, firing home three goals for his third hat-trick of the campaign (and his second in successive weeks), with Weldon (two), Critchley and Troup adding the others.

1932	Newcastle United	A	First Division	2–1
1938	Middlesbrough	H	First Division	4–0
1949	West Bromwich Albion	A	First Division	0–4
1955	Huddersfield Town	H	First Division	5–2
1960	West Bromwich Albion	H	First Division	1–1
1966	Sheffield Wednesday	A	First Division	2–1
1977	Derby County	A	First Division	1–0
1988	Sheffield Wednesday	A	First Division	1–1
1989	Aston Villa	A	First Division	2–6

1990 Howard Kendall returned to Everton as manager for the second time, joining them from Manchester City, and immediately appointing previous manager Colin Harvey as coach! Kendall was to spend three years at Everton the second time around and returned once again in 1997 for a further year.

1994	Norwich City	A	FA Premier League	0–0
1995	Blackburn Rovers	H	FA Premier League	1–0

NOVEMBER 6TH

1897 West Bromwich Albion A First Division 2–2
Walter Balmer made his debut for the club in the 2–2 draw with West Bromwich Albion at The Hawthorns. The older of the two Balmer brothers to play for Everton by four years (his younger brother Robert joined the club in 1902) he joined the club in 1897 and went on to make over 300 appearances for the first team, partnering first Jack Crelley and then his own brother at full-back. In 1905 he won his only cap for England and the following year collected a winners' medal in the FA Cup. He remained at Everton until 1908 when he went to join Croydon Common, later serving Huddersfield Town as coach.

1909	Chelsea	A	First Division	1–0
1915	Burnley	H	Lancashire Section Principal Tournament	1–2
1920	Bradford City	A	First Division	2–2
1926	Sheffield United	A	First Division	3–3
1937	Middlesbrough	A	First Division	2–1
1943	Tranmere Rovers	H	Football League North (First Championship)	9–2

Tommy Lawton fired home five goals in the thrashing of local rivals Tranmere in the regional league, with Bentham adding two and McIntosh and Stevenson completing the scoring.

1948	Manchester United	A	First Division	0–2
1954	Portsmouth	A	First Division	0–5
1965	Leicester City	H	First Division	1–2
1971	Tottenham Hotspur	A	First Division	0–3
1976	Leeds United	H	First Division	0–2
1982	Liverpool	H	First Division	0–5

Ian Rush equalled the individual goalscoring record for the Merseyside derby with a four goal blast at Goodison, with Mark Lawrenson adding the other in a complete rout by Liverpool. Everton's cause was not helped by having Glenn Keeley sent off for a professional foul on Kenny Dalglish, but they recovered to finish the season in seventh place and managed a creditable 0–0 draw at Anfield against the eventual champions later in the season.

| 1983 | Liverpool | A | First Division | 0–3 |
| 1993 | Coventry City | A | FA Premier League | 1–2 |

NOVEMBER 7TH

1891	West Bromwich Albion	H	Football League	4–3
1898	West Bromwich Albion	A	First Division	0–3
1903	Sheffield Wednesday	A	First Division	0–1
1908	Sunderland	H	First Division	4–0
1914	Blackburn Rovers	H	First Division	1–3
1925	Manchester United	H	First Division	1–3
1931	Huddersfield Town	A	First Division	0–0
1936	West Bromwich Albion	H	First Division	4–2

Dixie Dean scored the 37th and last hat-trick of his career in the 4–2 win over West Bromwich Albion at Goodison Park.

1942	Tranmere Rovers	A	Football League North (First Championship)	3–1
1953	Stoke City	A	Second Division	4–2
1959	Newcastle United	A	First Division	2–8
1964	Leeds United	H	First Division	0–1

1967 Marc Hottiger born in Lausanne in Switzerland. He began his English career with Newcastle United in 1994 and switched to Everton for £700,000 in 1996, although the transfer was initially held up over acquiring a work permit.

1970	Nottingham Forest	H	First Division	1–0
1978	Nottingham Forest	H	League Cup 4th Round	2–3
1981	Liverpool	A	First Division	1–3
1984	Slovan Bratislava	H	European Cup-Winners' Cup 2nd Round 2nd Leg	3–0

Goals from Adrian Heath, Graeme Sharp and Kevin Sheedy enabled Everton to beat Bratislava 3–0 in the European Cup-Winners' Cup second round second leg match at Goodison Park for a 4–0 aggregate victory.

| 1992 | Nottingham Forest | A | FA Premier League | 1–0 |

NOVEMBER 8TH

1890	Blackburn Rovers	A	Football League	1–2
1902	Blackburn Rovers	A	First Division	2–3
1913	Blackburn Rovers	A	First Division	0–6
1919	Bradford City	H	First Division	0–1
1924	Manchester City	A	First Division	2–2
1930	Wolverhampton Wanderers	H	Second Division	4–0

Everton beat Wolves 4–0 at Goodison in front of a crowd of 32,228. Their first goal was scored by Dixie Dean, his 200th senior goal and which made him the youngest player ever to have reached such a tally; he was 23 years and 290 days old at the time. The record has never been bettered but it has been equalled: Jimmy Greaves was exactly the same age when he netted the 200th goal of his career over thirty years later.

1941	Wrexham	H	Football League North (First Championship)	3–1
1947	Stoke City	A	First Division	1–1
1952	Rotherham United	H	Second Division	0–1
1958	Aston Villa	A	First Division	4–2
1969	West Bromwich Albion	A	First Division	0–2

West Bromwich inflicted Everton's second League defeat of the season with a 2–0 win at the Hawthorns. Despite the defeat, Everton remained on top of the table.

1975	Stoke City	A	First Division	2–3
1980	Norwich City	A	First Division	1–2
1986	Chelsea	H	First Division	2–2
1988	Oldham Athletic	H	Littlewoods Cup 3rd Round	1–1
1994				

After less than a year in the job Mike Walker was sacked as manager of Everton. An abysmal start to the season, with only one win in the opening 13 games of the season (the 13th proving lucky on this occasion) had seen the club rooted to the bottom of the table and the manager's position in jeopardy.

| 1997 | Blackburn Rovers | A | FA Premier League | 2–3 |

NOVEMBER 9TH

1889	Stoke City	A	Football League	2–1
1895	Sheffield United	A	First Division	2–1
1901	Grimsby Town	A	First Division	2–0
1907	Manchester United	A	First Division	3–4
1912	Chelsea	H	First Division	1–0
1918	Stoke City	A	Lancashire Section Principal Tournament	2–0
1929	West Ham United	A	First Division	1–3
1935	Manchester City	A	First Division	0–1
1940	Manchester United	H	North Regional League	5–2
1946	Leeds United	A	First Division	1–2
1957	Tottenham Hotspur	A	First Division	1–3
1963	Blackburn Rovers	H	First Division	2–4
1966	Real Zaragoza	A	European Cup-Winners' Cup	0–2
			2nd Round 1st Leg	

Having dismissed Danish cup holders Aalborg in the first round of the European Cup-Winners' Cup Everton were rewarded with a trip to Spain to face Real Zaragoza. It was expected Everton would soak up any pressure from the Spaniards and look to finish them off in the home leg at Goodison, but things didn't go according to plan, with Zaragoza winning 2–0 on the night.

1968	Ipswich Town	A	First Division	2–2
1974	Tottenham Hotspur	A	First Division	1–1
1982	Arsenal	H	Milk Cup 3rd Round	1–1
1983	Coventry City	H	Milk Cup 3rd Round	2–1

After making hard work of beating Chesterfield over two legs in the previous round Everton proved too good for an ordinary Coventry side, with goals from Adrian Heath and Graeme Sharp easing them into the next round to face West Ham.

| 1985 | Arsenal | H | First Division | 6–1 |

Arsenal arrived at Goodison in fifth place in the League table, one place above Everton, and with an impressive record thus far. Everton's own title aspirations received the perfect boost with an impressive display in front of a crowd of 28,620 as Gary Lineker and Adrian Heath both scored twice, and Trevor Steven from the penalty spot and Graeme Sharp completed the scoring. Everton still remained in sixth place but caught up three points with the teams above them.

NOVEMBER 10TH

| 1888 | Blackburn Rovers | A | Football League | 0–3 |

Alfred Milward made his debut in the 3–0 defeat at Leamington Road against Blackburn. Born in Great Marlow he first made his name with Old Borlasians and Marlow and joined Everton in 1888 and spent nine seasons with the club, making 224 appearances and scoring 96 goals. A more than able goalscorer in his own right, he linked especially well with Edgar Chadwick and went on to collect four caps for England. He left Everton to join New Brighton Tower in 1897 and subsequently switched to Southampton, earning a Southern League championship medal and a runners-up medal in the FA Cup before finishing his career with New Brompton. He died in June 1941 at the age of 70.

1900	Stoke City	A	First Division	2–0
1906	Stoke City	A	First Division	0–2
1917	Oldham Athletic	A	Lancashire Section Principal Tournament	3–1
1923	Sheffield United	H	First Division	2–0
1928	Cardiff City	H	First Division	1–0
1934	Portsmouth	H	First Division	3–2
1945	Sheffield United	H	Football League North	1–0
1951	Swansea Town	A	Second Division	2–0
1956	Portsmouth	H	First Division	2–2
1962	Blackpool	H	First Division	5–0
1973	Chelsea	A	First Division	1–3
1979	Middlesbrough	H	First Division	0–2
1984	West Ham United	A	First Division	1–0
1990	Sheffield United	A	First Division	0–0
1992	Wimbledon	A	Coca–Cola Cup 3rd Round Replay	1–0
1993	Crystal Palace	A	Coca–Cola Cup 3rd Round Replay	4–1

| 1994 | Former Everton player Joe Royle returned to Goodison Park, this time in the capacity of manager. He had long been a target for several big clubs, his success at Oldham not having gone unnoticed, and he would go on to save the club from relegation and lift the FA Cup at the end of his first season in charge.

NOVEMBER 11TH

1893	Derby County	H	First Division	1–2
1899	West Bromwich Albion	H	First Division	1–3
1905	Blackburn Rovers	H	First Division	3–2
1911	Manchester City	H	First Division	1–0
1916	Preston North End	H	Lancashire Section Principal Tournament	3–1
1922	Arsenal	A	First Division	2–1
1933	Sheffield United	A	First Division	1–1
1939	Manchester City	H	War Regional League, Western Division	3–1
1944	Manchester City	H	Football League North (First Championship)	4–1

1950	Tottenham Hotspur	H	First Division	1–2
1961	Blackpool	A	First Division	1–1
1964	Kilmarnock	A	Inter-Cities Fairs Cup 2nd Round 1st Leg	2–0

One of the major appeals of European football, especially among the fans, was that it gave them a chance to witness at first hand different styles of playing the game: the flamboyant Dutch, the methodical Germans, the defensive minded Italians and so on. So Everton's reward for disposing of Valerengen in the first round of the Inter-Cities Fairs Cup was a trip to . . . Scotland to face Kilmarnock! Goals from Derek Temple and John Morrissey gave Everton a commanding 2–0 lead to take back to Goodison Park for the second leg.

1967	Arsenal	A	First Division	2–2
1972	Manchester City	H	First Division	2–3
1975	Notts County	H	League Cup 4th Round	2–2
1978	Chelsea	H	First Division	3–2
1981	Oxford United	H	League Cup 3rd Round	1–0
1989	Chelsea	H	First Division	0–1

NOVEMBER 12TH

| 1887 | Bolton Wanderers | A | FA Cup 1st Round 2nd Replay | 0–0 |

Everton and Bolton Wanderers met for a third time in the FA Cup first round and there was still nothing between the two sides as they drew again 0–0.

1892	Stoke City	H	First Division	2–2
1898	Sunderland	A	First Division	1–2
1904	Sheffield Wednesday	A	First Division	5–5
1910	Bradford City	A	First Division	1–3
1921	Liverpool	A	First Division	1–1

Bobby Irvine was pitched into the cauldron of a Merseyside derby for his debut, playing at centre-forward in the 1–1 draw although he failed to find the net. Signed from Dunmurry in September 1921 he enjoyed a whirlwind start to his career at Everton, earning his first Irish cap in March 1922 and going on to collect 15 in total. He made 199 League appearances for Everton before being transferred to Portsmouth in March 1928 and finished his career back in Ireland.

| 1927 | Derby County | A | First Division | 3–0 |

Another pair of goals for Dixie Dean took his tally to 25 goals from 14 games, with Weldon netting Everton's other in the 3–0 win.

1932	Aston Villa	H	First Division	3–3
1938	Birmingham City	A	First Division	0–1
1949	Manchester United	H	First Division	0–0
1955	Cardiff City	A	First Division	1–3
1960	Cardiff City	A	First Division	1–1

On the same day Kevin Ratcliffe was born in Mancot. Signed by Everton as an apprentice he went on to become captain and led the side to their greatest triumphs in recent times, including two League titles, the FA Cup and European Cup-Winners' Cup, as well as collecting 58 caps for Wales. He picked up one further cap whilst playing for Cardiff City and at the end of his playing career switched to management and is currently in charge at Chester.

| 1966 | Arsenal | H | First Division | 0–0 |
| 1977 | Birmingham City | H | First Division | 2–1 |

1980	Leicester City	A	First Division	1–0
1983	Nottingham Forest	H	First Division	1–0
1988	Charlton Athletic	A	First Division	2–1

NOVEMBER 13TH

1897	Aston Villa	A	First Division	0–3
1909	Blackburn Rovers	H	First Division	0–2
1915	Preston North End	A	Lancashire Section Principal Tournament	2–0
1920	Bradford City	H	First Division	2–2
1926	Derby County	H	First Division	3–2
1937	Chelsea	H	First Division	4–1

1938 Derek Temple born in Liverpool. Introduced into the Everton first team in March 1957 he went to make nearly 300 appearances for the first team, helping them win the League title in 1963 and the FA Cup in 1966, scoring the winning goal in the final against Sheffield Wednesday. He was transferred to Preston in September 1967 for £35,000 and later played non-League football with Wigan Athletic. He won one cap for England, against West Germany in 1965.

1943	Tranmere Rovers	A	Football League North (First Championship)	6–2
1948	Sheffield United	H	First Division	2–1
1954	Blackpool	H	First Division	0–1
1962	Nottingham Forest	A	First Division	4–3
1965	Sheffield United	A	First Division	0–2
1971	Liverpool	H	First Division	1–0
1979	Leeds United	H	First Division	5–1

Bob Latchford netted his first hat-trick of the season in the 5–1 win over Leeds at Goodison, a day after Leeds manager Jimmy Adamson was given two months by his board of directors to improve results! Everton's other goals were scored by Brian Kidd and an own goal.

| 1982 | Arsenal | A | First Division | 1–1 |

NOVEMBER 14TH

1891	Darwen	A	Football League	1–3
1896	Bolton Wanderers	H	First Division	2–3
1903	Sunderland	H	First Division	0–1
1908	Chelsea	A	First Division	3–3
1914	Notts County	A	First Division	0–0
1925	Notts County	A	First Division	3–0
1931	Chelsea	H	First Division	7–2

After a goalless draw the previous week Everton found their scoring boots once more with Dixie Dean hitting five of their tally of seven against luckless Chelsea at Goodison. The other two goals were scored by Tommy Johnson and Jimmy Stein.

1936	Manchester City	A	First Division	1–4
1942	Tranmere Rovers	H	Football League North (First Championship)	3–5
1953	Fulham	H	Second Division	2–2
1959	Birmingham City	H	First Division	4–0
1964	Chelsea	A	First Division	1–5
1970	Stoke City	A	First Division	1–1

1974   Tony Grant born in Liverpool. He graduated through the Everton ranks and made the professional ranks in 1993. A member of the side that won the FA Charity Shield in 1995, he spent a brief spell on loan to Swindon in 1996.

1987   West Ham United   H   First Division   3–1

NOVEMBER 15TH

1890   Sunderland   H   Football League   1–0
1895   Neil McBain born in Campbeltown. He is assured of his place in the history books for becoming the oldest player to have appeared in the Football League; in 1947, at the age of 51 years and four months, he was forced to select himself as emergency goalkeeper for New Brighton, where he was manager, conceding three goals as Hartlepools United won 3–0. He began his career with Manchester United in November 1921 shortly after his £6,250 transfer from Ayr United. He requested a transfer in January 1923 and was sold to Everton, spending four seasons at Goodison, later playing for St Johnstone, Liverpool and Watford before moving into management. His last position was back at Ayr United in 1963. He died on 13th May 1974.

1902   Sunderland   A   First Division   1–2
1913   Sunderland   H   First Division   1–5
1919   Bradford City   A   First Division   0–3
1924   Arsenal   H   First Division   2–3
1930   Millwall   A   Second Division   3–1
1941   Wrexham   A   Football League North (First Championship)   4–0
1947   Burnley   H   First Division   0–3
1952   Plymouth Argyle   A   Second Division   0–1
1958   West Ham United   H   First Division   2–2
1969   Chelsea   A   First Division   1–1
1975   Manchester City   H   First Division   1–1
1980   Sunderland   H   First Division   2–1
1981   Glasgow Rangers   A   Colin Jackson Testimonial Match   1–1
       Everton provided the opposition for Rangers defender Colin Jackson's testimonial match at Ibrox, with a crowd of 25,000 turning out in his honour. After the game had finished 1–1 Rangers won 3–1 on penalties!

1986   Leicester City   A   First Division   2–0

NOVEMBER 16TH

1889   Preston North End   H   Football League   1–5
       The game that effectively cost Everton the League title in 1890–91, with reigning champions Preston inflicting Everton's only home defeat of the campaign. Before the game kicked off, Everton were top of the table, ahead of Preston, but the pair swapped places after the game and remained in that order for the rest of the campaign. At the end of the season, Preston retained the title, two points ahead of Everton.

1895   Sunderland   H   First Division   1–0
1901   Sunderland   A   First Division   4–2
1907   Blackburn Rovers   H   First Division   4–1
1912   Woolwich Arsenal   A   First Division   0–0
1918   Bury   H   Lancashire Section Principal Tournament   5–1
1929   Huddersfield Town   H   First Division   0–2

| 1935 | Arsenal | H | First Division | 0–2 |
| 1940 | Manchester United | A | North Regional League | 0–0 |

1944 Colin Harvey born in Liverpool. One of the finest servants the club has ever had, he signed as an apprentice and was upgraded to the professional ranks in October 1962. He went on to make almost 400 appearances for the first team, helping them to win the League title and the FA Cup in that time. He was transferred to Sheffield Wednesday in 1974 but was plagued by injuries and retired as a player in 1976. He then returned to Goodison, where he has filled just about every position on the coaching and management staff.

1946	Manchester United	H	First Division	2–2
1957	Birmingham City	H	First Division	0–2
1963	Nottingham Forest	A	First Division	2–2
1965	Ujpest Dozsa	H	Inter-Cities Fairs Cup 2nd Round 2nd Leg	2–1

Everton made their final appearance in the Inter-Cities Fairs Cup with a 2–1 win over Ujpest Dozsa at Goodison Park. A goal from Brian Harris and an own goal enabled Everton to win on the night, but Ujpest's 3–0 win in the first leg enabled them to progress 4–2 on aggregate.

1968	Queens Park Rangers	H	First Division	4–0
1974	Liverpool	H	First Division	0–0
1985	Ipswich Town	A	First Division	4–3
1991	Wimbledon	H	First Division	2–0
1996	Southampton	H	FA Premier League	7–1

A superb first half performance in the match against Southampton at Goodison had left Everton 5–1 ahead at the break, which prompted goalkeeper Neville Southall to suggest giving Paul Gerrard his League debut in the second half! Everton went on to win 7–1 with Gary Speed scoring a hat-trick, Andrei Kanchelskis netting twice and Graham Stuart and Nick Barmby adding the other two goals. Paul Gerrard kept a clean sheet during his 45 minutes of action.

NOVEMBER 17TH

| 1888 | Burnley | A | Football League | 2–2 |
| 1894 | Liverpool | A | First Division | 2–2 |

Everton's first visit to Anfield for League points came in a season they were to finish as runners-up to Sunderland in the First Division, whilst Liverpool's battles were all at the other end of the table; they were relegated! Everton should have won the match, taking a 2–1 lead thanks to goals from Kelso and Latta, but a moment of madness in the last minute resulted in a penalty which was duly converted by Ross. It would be another two years before Everton would again have to go to Anfield for the battle for League points.

1900	West Bromwich Albion	H	First Division	1–0
1906	Blackburn Rovers	H	First Division	2–0
1917	Oldham Athletic	H	Lancashire Section Principal Tournament	4–2
1923	West Bromwich Albion	H	First Division	2–0
1928	Sheffield United	A	First Division	1–2
1934	Stoke City	A	First Division	2–3
1945	Middlesbrough	H	Football League North	1–1
1951	Coventry City	H	Second Division	4–1
1956	Newcastle United	A	First Division	0–0

1962	Blackburn Rovers	A	First Division	2–3
1973	Norwich City	A	First Division	3–1
1979	Arsenal	A	First Division	0–2
1984	Stoke City	H	First Division	4–0

A 4–0 home win over a poor Stoke side ensured Everton remained on top of the First Division thanks to goals from Adrian Heath (two), Peter Reid (his first of the season) and Trevor Steven.

| 1987 | Oldham Athletic | H | Littlewoods Cup 4th Round | 2–1 |

Goals from Dave Watson and Neil Adams took Everton into the quarter-finals of the Littlewoods Cup at Oldham's expense, where they would meet Manchester City at Goodison Park.

• NOVEMBER 18TH

1905	Sunderland	A	First Division	1–2
1911	Preston North End	A	First Division	1–2
1916	Burnley	A	Lancashire Section Principal Tournament	2–2
1922	West Bromwich Albion	A	First Division	0–0

1931 Charlie Gee won his first cap for England in the match against Wales at Anfield, England winning 3–1. Less than 12 months previously he had made his League debut for Everton, having begun his career with Stockport County and switching to Goodison in July 1930. Initially he was put into the Central League team but got his chance at first-team action when called in for the injured Tommy Griffiths and made the position his own. Indeed, for his international debut his opposite number on the Welsh side was the same Tommy Griffiths! A cartilage operation in 1932 kept him out of the side for much of the year and he played his last game for the club in 1940.

1933	Wolverhampton Wanderers	H	First Division	1–2
1939	Chester	A	War Regional League, Western Division	2–3
1944	Crewe Alexandra	H	Football League North (First Championship)	3–5
1950	Wolverhampton Wanderers	A	First Division	0–4
1961	Blackburn Rovers	H	First Division	1–0
1967	Sheffield United	H	First Division	1–0
1972	Arsenal	A	First Division	0–1
1978	Arsenal	A	First Division	2–2
1989	Wimbledon	H	First Division	1–1
1990	Tottenham Hotspur	H	First Division	1–1
1995	Liverpool	A	FA Premier League	2–1

Everton registered their first win at Anfield for ten years thanks to two goals from Andrei Kanchelskis.

NOVEMBER 19TH

| 1887 | Bolton Wanderers | H | FA Cup 1st Round 3rd Replay | 2–1 |

Everton finally beat Bolton Wanderers in their FA Cup first round tie that had run to four matches; Bolton had won the first game 1–0 but had been found to have played an ineligible player and two replays had been drawn. This time Everton won 2–1 thanks to goals from Goodie and Watson and earned the right to meet Preston in the next round, but even this wasn't the end of the matter, for Bolton subsequently discovered that seven of the Everton team were ineligible, lodged an appeal and were successful, even though Everton had already met Preston in the second round!

| 1898 | Wolverhampton Wanderers | H | First Division | 2–1 |
| 1904 | Sunderland | H | First Division | 0–1 |

This was the only home defeat Everton suffered all season, but it was one they could well have done without, for at the end of the campaign they finished second behind Newcastle United in the League by just one point.

1910	Blackburn Rovers	H	First Division	6–1
1921	Cardiff City	A	First Division	1–2
1927	Sunderland	H	First Division	0–1
1932	Middlesbrough	A	First Division	2–0
1938	Manchester United	H	First Division	3–0
1949	Chelsea	A	First Division	2–3
1955	Manchester City	H	First Division	1–1
1960	Newcastle United	H	First Division	5–0

Bobby Collins scored a hat-trick as Newcastle were thrashed 5–0 at Goodison. Roy Vernon and Frank Wignall added the other goals.

1965 Gary Ablett born in Liverpool. He joined Liverpool as an apprentice in 1983 and made over 100 appearances for the first team, subsequently spending loan spells with Derby and Hull. Signed by Everton for £750,000 in 1992 he spent four years at Goodison Park before joining Birmingham City for £390,000 in 1996.

1966	Manchester City	A	First Division	0–1
1977	Ipswich Town	A	First Division	3–3
1983	Arsenal	A	First Division	1–2
1986	Norwich City	A	Littlewoods Cup 4th Round	4–1

A 4–1 win over Norwich set up a clash with Liverpool in the quarter-finals of the Littlewoods Cup. Kevin Sheedy, Graeme Sharp, Trevor Steven and Adrian Heath all found the net on the night.

| 1988 | Norwich City | H | First Division | 1–1 |

NOVEMBER 20TH

1897	Preston North End	A	First Division	1–1
1909	Nottingham Forest	A	First Division	0–1
1915	Stockport County	H	Lancashire Section Principal Tournament	2–5
1920	Sunderland	H	First Division	1–1
1926	Manchester United	A	First Division	1–2
1937	West Bromwich Albion	A	First Division	1–3
1943	Crewe Alexandra	A	Football League North (First Championship)	8–0

Everton's fifth straight win in the regional league was accomplished with their best away win of the campaign, 8–0 at Crewe. Tommy Lawton scored three, McIntosh and Stevenson two and T.G. Jones added the other. In the second championship, Everton registered 9–1 and 6–2 wins over Crewe, and even the other game in the first championship against the same opposition provided ten goals; the pair drew 5–5!

| 1948 | Aston Villa | A | First Division | 1–0 |
| 1954 | Charlton Athletic | A | First Division | 0–5 |

| 1957 | Blackpool | H | First Division | 0–0 |

1961 Dave Watson born in Liverpool. He first signed professional forms with Liverpool in 1979 but was sold to Norwich City for £100,000 without having played for the first team in 1980. After helping the Canaries to the League Cup in 1985 he returned to Merseyside in 1986, costing Everton £900,000. He collected a League championship medal in 1987, n FA Cup winners' medal in 1995 and FA Charity Shield medals twice as well as 12 caps for England. In 1997 he was appointed caretaker manager following the departure of Joe Royle.

| 1965 | Leeds united | H | First Division | 0–0 |
| 1971 | Southampton | H | First Division | 8–0 |

Everton turned on the style, thumping luckless Southampton for eight at Goodison Park. David Johnson scored a hat-trick, Joe Royle went one better and Alan Ball grabbed the other in the 8–0 win, Everton's biggest League victory for years.

1976	Derby County	H	First Division	2–0
1982	West Bromwich Albion	H	First Division	0–0
1984	Grimsby Town	H	Milk Cup 4th Round	0–1
1993	Queens Park Rangers	H	FA Premier League	0–3
1996	Liverpool	A	FA Premier League	1–1

NOVEMBER 21ST

1891	Wolverhampton Wanderers	A	Football League	1–5
1896	Liverpool	A	First Division	0–0
1903	West Bromwich Albion	A	First Division	0–0
1908	Blackburn Rovers	H	First Division	4–4
1914	Sunderland	H	First Division	7–1

Bobby Parker kept on course to equal Bertie Freeman's individual goalscoring record for a single season with a hat-trick against Sunderland at Goodison that pushed Everton up to fifth place in the table. Joe Clennell added two goals, whilst Harrison and Jefferis completed the scoring. At the end of the season, Parker had netted 36 goals, exactly the same tally Freeman had scored six years previously.

1925	Aston Villa	H	First Division	1–1
1931	Grimsby Town	A	First Division	2–1
1936	Portsmouth	H	First Division	4–0
1942	Crewe Alexandra	H	Football League North (First Championship)	4–0
1953	West Ham United	A	Second Division	1–1
1959	Tottenham Hotspur	A	First Division	0–3
1964	Leicester City	H	First Division	2–2
1970	Liverpool	A	First Division	2–3
1978	Manchester United	H	First Division	3–0
1981	Sunderland	H	First Division	1–2
1987	Portsmouth	A	First Division	1–0
1992	Chelsea	H	FA Premier League	0–1
1994	Liverpool	H	FA Premier League	2–0

Joe Royle's first match in charge of Everton couldn't have been any tougher: a visit from Liverpool! Goals from Duncan Ferguson (on loan from Rangers but later to move permanently) and Paul Rideout made it a good start for Royle in the 2–0 win.

NOVEMBER 22ND

1890	Preston North End	A	Football League	0–2
1902	Stoke City	H	First Division	0–1
1913	Tottenham Hotspur	A	First Division	1–4
1919	Bolton Wanderers	H	First Division	2–3
1924	Aston Villa	A	First Division	1–3
1930	Stoke City	H	Second Division	5–0

Dixie Dean scored his first hat-trick of the season with Tommy Johnson also netting twice in the 5–0 win over Stoke. At the end of the season Dean had scored 39 goals in the League and a further nine in the FA Cup to head the Everton goalscoring list once again.

1936   Alex Scott born in Falkirk. An integral part of the Glasgow Rangers side of the early 1960's he was sold to Everton for £40,000 in February 1963. He helped the club win the title at the end of his first season and later the FA Cup in 1966. In September 1967 he was sold to Hibernian for £15,000.

1941	Manchester City	A	Football League North (First Championship)	4–3
1947	Manchester United	A	First Division	2–2
1952	Leeds United	H	Second Division	2–2
1958	Nottingham Forest	A	First Division	1–2
1969	Burnley	H	First Division	2–1
1975	Aston Villa	A	First Division	1–3
1980	Arsenal	A	First Division	1–2
1989	Nottingham Forest	A	Littlewoods Cup 4th Round	0–1
1995	Queens Park Rangers	H	FA Premier League	2–0
1997	Aston Villa	A	FA Premier League	1–2

NOVEMBER 23RD

1889	Aston Villa	A	Football League	2–1
1895	West Bromwich Albion	A	First Division	3–0
1901	Small Heath	H	First Division	1–0
1907	Bolton Wanderers	A	First Division	0–3
1912	Bradford City	H	First Division	2–1
1918	Bury	A	Lancashire Section Principal Tournament	3–0
1929	Birmingham City	A	First Division	0–0
1935	Grimsby Town	A	First Division	4–0
1940	Tranmere Rovers	A	North Regional League	9–0

Tommy Lawton and Alex Stevenson both scored hat-tricks against local rivals Tranmere at Prenton Park, with Simmons netting twice and Arthur the other goal in the 9–0 win.

1946	Stoke City	A	First Division	1–2
1957	Portsmouth	A	First Division	2–3
1960	Bury	H	League Cup 3rd Round	3–1
1963	Stoke City	H	First Division	2–0
1964	Kilmarnock	H	Inter-Cities Fairs Cup 2nd Round 2nd Leg	4–1

Kilmarnock were the visitors for the second leg of the Inter-Cities Fairs Cup second round, with Everton already 2–0 ahead from the first leg. There was to be no way back for the Scottish side, Fred Pickering (two), Colin Harvey and Alex Young scoring the goals in a 4–1 win, Everton progressing 6–1 on aggregate.

| 1966 | Real Zaragoza | H | European Cup-Winners' Cup | 1–0 |
| | | | 2nd Round 2nd Leg | |

Everton had lost their first leg match in Spain against Real Zaragoza 2–0 and so were committed to almost non stop attack in an effort to rescue the tie. Sandy Brown gave them a glimmer of hope when he scored to bring Real within sight, but despite numerous chances Everton failed to add a second and so went out of the cup 2–1 on aggregate.

1968	Leeds United	A	First Division	1–2
1982	Arsenal	A	Milk Cup 3rd Round Replay	0–3
1985	Nottingham Forest	H	First Division	1–1
1986	Liverpool	H	First Division	0–0
1991	Notts County	H	First Division	1–0
1993	Leeds United	H	FA Premier League	1–1
1996	Leicester City	A	FA Premier League	2–1

NOVEMBER 24TH

1888	Burnley	H	Football League	3–2
1894	Blackburn Rovers	H	First Division	2–1
1900	Sheffield Wednesday	H	First Division	1–1
1906	Sunderland	A	First Division	0–1
1917	Bury	A	Lancashire Section Principal Tournament	5–2
1923	West Bromwich Albion	A	First Division	0–5
1928	Bury	H	First Division	1–0
1934	Manchester City	H	First Division	1–2
1945	Middlesbrough	A	Football League North	0–0
1951	West Ham United	A	Second Division	3–3
1956	Sheffield Wednesday	H	First Division	1–0
1962	Sheffield United	H	First Division	3–0

Everton moved two points clear of Spurs at the top of the table with a 3–0 win over Sheffield United at Goodison, with Roy Vernon scoring twice and Dennis Stevens netting the other. With Everton due at Spurs the following week, this was seen as a perfect rehearsal.

1973	Newcastle United	H	First Division	1–1
1976	Newcastle United	A	First Division	1–4
1979	Tottenham Hotspur	H	First Division	1–1
1981	Notts County	A	First Division	2–2
1984	Norwich City	A	First Division	2–4
1990	Wimbledon	A	First Division	1–2

Just 6,411 fans witnessed Everton's 2–1 defeat at Wimbledon as they slid to 18th place in the First Division. Not surprisingly, this was the lowest crowd to watch Everton during the course of the campaign, although for Wimbledon it seemed to be an occupational hazard; they ended the season with an average gate of 7,631, a 1.6 per cent drop on the previous season.

NOVEMBER 25TH

| 1893 | Burnley | H | First Division | 4–3 |
| 1899 | Blackburn Rovers | A | First Division | 1–3 |

1905	Birmingham City	H	First Division	1–2
1911	West Bromwich Albion	A	First Division	0–1
1916	Manchester United	H	Lancashire Section Principal Tournament	3–2
1922	West Bromwich Albion	H	First Division	0–1
1933	Stoke City	A	First Division	2–1
1939	Crewe Alexandra	H	War Regional League, Western Division	6–2
1944	Crewe Alexandra	A	Football League North (First Championship)	5–1
1950	Sunderland	H	First Division	3–1
1961	West Ham United	A	First Division	1–3
1967	Coventry City	A	First Division	2–0
1972	West Ham United	H	First Division	1–2
1975	Notts County	A	League Cup 4th Round Replay	0–2
1978	Norwich City	A	First Division	1–0
1987	Bayern Munich	H	Football League Centenary Match	3–1

With English clubs still effectively under house arrest from European competition, the approaching centenary of the Football League would have to be marked in some way other than their representatives cutting a sway through Europe. Thus West German League champions Bayern Munich were invited to play their English counterparts Everton in a centenary match at Goodison, with the game being afforded sponsorship from Mercantile Credit. Despite all of the activity behind the scenes, just over 13,000 attended the game in which Everton repeated their European Cup-Winners' Cup score of three years previously, winning 3–1. Two goals from Graeme Sharp and one from Adrian Heath only served to show how much English football was missing European competition and vice versa.

1989	Nottingham Forest	A	First Division	0–1
1995	Sheffield Wednesday	H	FA Premier League	2–2

NOVEMBER 26TH

1887	Preston North End	A	FA Cup 2nd Round	0–6

Having finally beaten Bolton Wanderers in the FA Cup first round at the fourth attempt, Everton met Preston North End at Deepdale in the second round. Preston won 6–0, but already a Bolton appeal was underway, for they had discovered that seven of the Everton side had been ineligible for their last meeting on November 19th, an appeal that would subsequently be upheld. Everton were therefore thrown out of the competition (after they'd already been knocked out!), suspended for a month and Preston had to play Bolton in a second round match! For the record, Preston beat Bolton too, winning 9–0 on their way to the final.

1892	Sheffield Wednesday	H	First Division	3–5
1898	Bury	H	First Division	0–1
1905	Woolwich Arsenal	A	First Division	3–1

Everton had emerged as one of the early season favourites to win the League title, along with Newcastle United, but November was effectively to become the month in which the title was lost. A solitary win over Nottingham Forest had been followed by a draw against Sheffield Wednesday and defeat by Sunderland, but at Woolwich Arsenal Everton seemed to be back on the right track, powering their way into a 3–1 lead. Then, after 78 minutes, disaster struck as fog rolled in and caused the game to be abandoned. When it was replayed the following April, Everton lost 2–1 and were pipped to the title by Newcastle by a single point!

1910	Nottingham Forest	A	First Division	1–1

1919 Wally Fielding born in London. Although he had signed amateur forms for Charlton during the Second World War, he joined Everton as a professional at the end of hostilities, a decision that caused a furious row between Charlton, who believed they had first option on the player, and Everton. He broke into the Everton first team in 1945–46 and went on to make over 400 appearances for the first team, later spending a season with Southport before retiring. The closest he came to representative honours was playing for England against Scotland in 1946 in a match to raise funds for the victims of the Bolton disaster, although this match was not classified as a full international and therefore no caps were awarded. On the same day Harry Catterick was born in Darlington.

1921	Cardiff City	H	First Division	0–1
1927	Bury	A	First Division	3–2

After a blank week at home to Sunderland, Dixie Dean got back on the goal trail with a pair against Bury with Ted Critchley notching the other.

1932	Bolton Wanderers	H	First Division	2–2
1938	Stoke City	A	First Division	0–0
1949	Stoke City	H	First Division	2–1
1955	Wolverhampton Wanderers	A	First Division	0–1
1960	Arsenal	A	First Division	2–3
1966	Blackpool	H	First Division	0–1
1977	Coventry City	H	First Division	6–0

Bob Latchford hit a hat-trick to take his tally for the season to 14 in the 6–0 win over Coventry. Everton's other goals were scored by Martin Dobson, Andy King and Jim Pearson.

1983	Norwich City	H	First Division	0–2
1985	Chelsea	A	Milk Cup 4th Round	2–2
1988	West Ham United	A	First Division	1–0
1994	Chelsea	A	FA Premier League	1–0
1997	Chelsea	A	FA Premier League	0–2

NOVEMBER 27TH

1897	West Bromwich Albion	H	First Division	6–1
1909	Sunderland	H	First Division	2–1
1915	Liverpool	A	Lancashire Section Principal Tournament	1–4
1920	Sunderland	A	First Division	2–0
1926	Bolton Wanderers	H	First Division	1–1
1937	Stoke City	H	First Division	2–0
1943	Crewe Alexandra	H	Football League North (First Championship)	5–5

1946 Tommy Eglington was capped by Northern Ireland against Scotland at Hampden Park to become the first Everton player to have represented two countries, having earned a cap for the Republic of Ireland earlier in the year. The game finished all square at 0–0. Only Peter Farrell, also making his debut for Northern Ireland on the day, went on to emulate the feat, earning his first Republic cap the following year against Spain.

1948	Sunderland	H	First Division	1–0
1954	Bolton Wanderers	H	First Division	0–0
1963	Glasgow Rangers	A	British Championship 1st Leg	3–1

League champions Everton travelled to Glasgow to take on Rangers in the first leg of what was to be billed 'The British Championship'. Goals from Alex Scott, Derek Temple and Sandy Young gave them a 3–1 win in front of a crowd of 64,006, with Rangers' goal being scored by John Greig.

1965	West Ham United	A	First Division	0–3
1971	Leicester City	A	First Division	0–0
1976	West Bromwich Albion	A	First Division	0–3
1982	West Ham United	A	First Division	0–2
1991	Leicester City	A	Zenith Data Systems Cup Quarter-Final	1–2

Everton played their last ever match in the Zenith Data Systems Cup, going down 2–1 at Leicester City. With English clubs having been restored to European competition, the cup, previously the Full Members' and Simod Cup, was viewed to have run its course and was abandoned at the end of the season.

| 1993 | Wimbledon | A | FA Premier League | 1–1 |

NOVEMBER 28TH

| 1891 | Aston Villa | H | Football League | 5–1 |
| 1896 | Burnley | H | First Division | 6–0 |

John Cameron scored a hat-trick, the only one of his Everton career, in the 6–0 win over Burnley. The other goals were added by Bell, Chadwick and Milward.

1903	Small Heath	H	First Division	5–1
1908	Bradford City	A	First Division	1–1
1914	Sheffield Wednesday	A	First Division	4–1
1925	Leicester City	A	First Division	1–1
1931	Leicester City	H	First Division	9–2
1936	Chelsea	A	First Division	0–4
1942	Crewe Alexandra	A	Football League North (First Championship)	2–4
1953	Leeds United	H	Second Division	2–1
1959	Manchester United	H	First Division	2–1
1964	Sunderland	A	First Division	0–4

1965 Peter Beagrie born in Middlesbrough. He began his career with his local club and later moved on to Sheffield United, costing £35,000 in 1986. Two years later he joined Stoke City and soon attracted interest from other clubs, finally joining Everton for £750,000 in 1989. After a loan spell with Sunderland he was sold to Manchester City for £1.1 million in 1994.

1970	Tottenham Hotspur	H	First Division	0–0
1981	Arsenal	A	First Division	0–1
1987	Oxford United	H	First Division	0–0
1992	Ipswich Town	A	FA Premier League	0–1

NOVEMBER 29TH

1890	Blackburn Rovers	H	Football League	3–1
1902	Derby County	H	First Division	2–1
1913	West Bromwich Albion	A	First Division	1–1
1919	Bolton Wanderers	A	First Division	2–0
1930	Bradford Park Avenue	A	Second Division	1–4
1941	Manchester City	H	Football League North (First Championship)	9–0

A week after winning 4–3 at Maine Road Everton thumped Manchester City 9–0 at Goodison Park thanks to goals from H. Jones (two), Stevenson (two), Bentham, Cook, Lyon, Mutch and an own goal.

1944 Mike Trebilcock born in Gunnislake. He began his career with Plymouth and was transferred to Everton for £20,000 in December 1965. Although he made only 14 appearances for the club and scored five goals, one of those games and two of the goals came in the 1966 FA Cup final when he was surprisingly picked ahead of Fred Pickering. In January 1968 he was transferred to Portsmouth and finished his playing career with Torquay United.

1947	Preston North End	H	First Division	2–1
1952	Luton Town	A	Second Division	2–4
1958	Chelsea	H	First Division	3–1
1975	Leeds United	A	First Division	2–5
1977	Sheffield Wednesday	A	League Cup 4th Round	3–1

Goals from Martin Dobson, Mick Lyons and Jim Pearson saw off the challenge of Sheffield Wednesday in the League Cup and eased Everton into the quarter-finals to face Leeds United at Elland Road.

1980	Birmingham City	H	First Division	1–1
1986	Manchester City	A	First Division	3–1
1988	Oldham Athletic	A	Littlewoods Cup 3rd Round Replay	2–0
1997	Tottenham Hotspur	H	FA Premier League	0–2

NOVEMBER 30TH

1895	Burnley	H	First Division	2–1
1901	Derby County	A	First Division	1–3
1912	Manchester City	A	First Division	0–1
1918	Blackpool	H	Lancashire Section Principal Tournament	6–0
1929	Leicester City	H	First Division	4–5

1933 Dennis Stevens born in Dudley. He began his career with Bolton Wanderers and helped them win the FA Cup in 1958 before signing for Everton in March 1962, collecting a League championship medal at the end of his first full season. In December 1965 he was sold to Oldham for £20,000 and finished his playing career back on Merseyside with Tranmere Rovers.

1935	Sunderland	H	First Division	0–3
1940	New Brighton	H	North Regional League	2–1
1946	Middlesbrough	H	First Division	2–1

1955 Andy Gray born in Glasgow. He begun his career with Dundee United but really made his name when he switched to the English game with Aston Villa in October 1975 for £100,000. He cost 15 times that amount when transferred to Wolves in 1979, the £1.5 million fee being a then British record. Both the record and Wolves' severe financial problems seemed to affect his game, and his switch to Goodison for £250,000 in 1983 was something of a surprise. However, his arrival galvanised and transformed Everton, and within two years they were champions, FA Cup and European Cup-Winners' Cup winners. He moved back to Aston Villa for £150,000 in July 1985, later signing for West Bromwich Albion. After a brief spell on the coaching staff of Aston Villa he left to concentrate on a career as a broadcaster for Sky, and turned down the chance to return to Goodison Park as manager in 1997 in favour of continuing with Sky.

| 1957 | Sheffield Wednesday | H | First Division | 1–1 |

1960 | Gary Lineker born in Leicester. An all–round sportsman he had an opportunity to become a cricketer but chose football instead, graduating through the ranks at Leicester City. His exceptional goalscoring talents soon made him a target for the bigger clubs and a tribunal fixed fee of £800,000 took him to Everton in 1985. In his only season at Goodison he scored 30 League goals and six in the FA Cup, although Everton were destined to finish second in both competitions behind Liverpool. Top scorer in the World Cup finals in Mexico in 1986 he was then targeted by Barcelona, signing for £2.5 million shortly after returning from England duty. In 1989 he was sold to Spurs for a cut price £1 million and finished his career with a season in Japan. He scored 48 goals for England in 80 internationals, one goal short of the record held by Sir Bobby Charlton. When his playing career ended he became a broadcaster. He was named Football Writers' Association and PFA Player of the Year in 1985, the first Everton player to win both awards in the same season.

| 1963 | Wolverhampton Wanderers | A | First Division | 0–0 |
| 1968 | Leicester City | H | First Division | 7–1 |

Joe Royle netted a hat-trick in the 7–1 win over Leicester City at Goodison, with Alan Ball, Gerry Humphreys, John Hurst and Jimmy Husband scoring the other goals. The win lifted Everton to second place in the table, two points behind Liverpool.

1974	Birmingham City	H	First Division	4–1
1983	West Ham United	A	Milk Cup 4th Round	2–2
1985	Southampton	A	First Division	3–2
1991	Leeds United	A	First Division	0–1
1993	Manchester United	H	Coca–Cola Cup 4th Round	0–2
1996	Sunderland	H	FA Premier League	1–3

DECEMBER 1ST

1888	West Bromwich Albion	A	Football League	1–4
1894	West Bromwich Albion	A	First Division	4–1
1900	Sunderland	A	First Division	0–2
1906	Birmingham City	H	First Division	3–0
1917	Bury	H	Lancashire Section Principal Tournament	7–1

Joe Clennell led the scoring with four in this regional league against Bury, with Wareing scoring twice and Murray adding the other. It meant Everton had scored 21 goals in just five games, of which Clennell had netted 11! Despite this phenomenal goalscoring record, Everton still finished no higher than third in the end of season league table.

1923	Birmingham City	H	First Division	2–0
1928	Aston Villa	A	First Division	0–2
1934	Middlesbrough	A	First Division	2–3
1945	Stoke City	A	Football League North	3–2
1951	Sheffield United	H	Second Division	1–0
1956	Cardiff City	A	First Division	0–1
1962	Tottenham Hotspur	A	First Division	0–0

The First Division's match of the day with top placed Everton visiting White Hart Lane, home of second placed Spurs. A crowd of 60,626 saw a tense struggle between the two sides, with Everton's defence earning most of the plaudits.

1973	Southampton	A	First Division	0–2
1976	Manchester United	A	League Cup 5th Round	3–0
1979	West Bromwich Albion	A	First Division	1–1
1984	Sheffield Wednesday	H	First Division	1–1
1990	Manchester United	H	First Division	0–1

DECEMBER 2ND

1893	Newton Heath	A	First Division	3–0
1899	Derby County	H	First Division	3–0
1905	Wolverhampton Wanderers	A	First Division	5–2
1911	Sunderland	H	First Division	1–0
1916	Liverpool	A	Lancashire Section Principal Tournament	1–2
1922	Sunderland	A	First Division	1–3
1933	Chelsea	H	First Division	2–1
1939	Liverpool	A	War Regional League, Western Division	2–2
1944	Wrexham	A	Football League North (First Championship)	0–1
1950	Aston Villa	A	First Division	3–3
1961	Manchester United	H	First Division	5–1

United may well have been a team in transition, but theirs was still a prized scalp, and a scintillating performance by Everton ensured both points as they kept up the challenge on the sides above them in the table. Roy Vernon scored twice, whilst there were single strikes from Bobby Collins, Jimmy Fell and Alex Young in front of a crowd of 48,099.

1963	Glasgow Rangers	H	British Championship 2nd Leg	1–1

Everton scored twice on the night, with Sandy Brown turning the ball past Andy Rankin to register one for Rangers and Alex Young netting at the right end to win Everton the unofficial British championship 4–2 on aggregate. A crowd of 42,000 were at Ibrox for the game.

1967	Nottingham Forest	H	First Division	1–0
1972	Coventry City	A	First Division	0–1
1989	Coventry City	H	First Division	2–0
1992	Chelsea	H	Coca–Cola Cup 4th Round	2–2
1995	Tottenham Hotspur	A	FA Premier League	0–0

DECEMBER 3RD

1892	Preston North End	A	First Division	0–5
1898	Notts County	A	First Division	1–0
1904	Derby County	H	First Division	0–0
1910	Manchester City	H	First Division	1–0
1921	West Bromwich Albion	H	First Division	1–2
1927	Sheffield United	H	First Division	0–0
1932	Chelsea	A	First Division	0–1
1938	Chelsea	H	First Division	4–1

Chelsea were struggling at the wrong end of the table whilst Everton were on their way to winning the championship, and the gulf between the two sides was shown at Goodison Park. Goals from Tommy Lawton (two), Torry Gillick and Alex Stevenson wrapped up the points for Everton.

1949	Burnley	A	First Division	1–5
1955	Chelsea	H	First Division	3–3
1960	Sheffield Wednesday	H	First Division	4–2
1966	Chelsea	A	First Division	1–1
1977	Chelsea	A	First Division	1–0
1983	Manchester United	A	First Division	1–0
1986	Newcastle United	H	Full Members Cup	5–2

When the six English clubs banned from European competition organised their own competition, what became the Screen Sport Super Cup, there were those at other clubs who believed they should have a competition of their own. Thus, spurred on by the likes of Ken Bates at Chelsea, the Full Member's Cup was born. Even though the Super Cup was abandoned after only one season, the Full Member's Cup limped along for considerably longer, with Everton making their debut in the competition with a 5–2 win over Newcastle United at Goodison Park. Everton's goals were scored by Graeme Sharp (three), Adrian Heath and Kevin Sheedy in front of a crowd of just 7,530.

1988	Tottenham Hotspur	H	First Division	1–0

DECEMBER 4TH

1893	Wolverhampton Wanderers	A	First Division	0–2
1909	Middlesbrough	A	First Division	1–1
1915	Bury	A	Lancashire Section Principal Tournament	3–0
1920	Middlesbrough	A	First Division	1–3
1926	Aston Villa	A	First Division	3–5
1937	Charlton Athletic	A	First Division	1–3
1943	Chester	A	Football League North (First Championship)	0–1
1948	Wolverhampton Wanderers	A	First Division	0–1
1954	Tottenham Hotspur	A	First Division	3–1

1962 Kevin Richardson born in Newcastle. He came through the ranks at Everton and was a member of the side that won the FA Cup in 1984, the League in 1985 and the European Cup-Winners' Cup the same year before being sold to Watford for £225,000 in 1986. He returned to the top flight with Arsenal in 1987 following a £200,000 transfer, earning a second League championship medal in 1989. He then went to Real Sociedad for £750,000 in 1990 and returned in 1991 to Aston Villa for £450,000 and completed his set of domestic medals with the League Cup in 1994. A move to Coventry followed in 1995 for £300,000. He won one cap for England.

1965	Sunderland	H	First Division	2–0
1971	Stoke City	H	First Division	0–0
1982	Birmingham City	H	First Division	0–0
1985	Manchester United	H	Screen Sport Super Cup Group B	1–0

A 1–0 win over Manchester United, courtesy of a Frank Stapleton own goal, confirmed that Everton would progress from the group stage of the Super Cup, along with Norwich City. In the other group both Liverpool and Spurs had advanced at the expense of Southampton, and the subsequent draw kept the two Merseyside clubs apart, Everton drawing Spurs.

1991	Leeds United	H	Rumbelows Cup 4th Round	1–4

1993   Southampton   H   FA Premier League   1–0
Shortly after the 1–0 home win over Southampton, Everton's first home win in ten weeks, manager Howard Kendall resigned, thus ending his second spell in charge of the club. He had returned to the fold in 1990 but had been unable to repeat his earlier success.

DECEMBER 5TH

1887   For fielding seven professionals in an FA Cup tie against Bolton Wanderers Everton were suspended for a month by the Football Association. They were also punished by the Liverpool FA, who duly confiscated the Liverpool Cup which had been won in the two previous years. The combined punishments disheartened Everton, who refused to enter the FA Cup in 1888–89.

1891	Blackburn Rovers	A	Football League	2–2
1903	Wolverhampton Wanderers	A	First Division	2–2
1908	Manchester United	H	First Division	3–2
1914	West Bromwich Albion	H	First Division	2–1

1915   Billy Lindley born in Keighley. He first appeared for Everton during the 1939–40 season in the War Regional League and had to wait until the end of hostilities before making his League debut. He made 51 appearances after war had ended.

1925	West Ham United	H	First Division	2–0
1931	West Ham United	A	First Division	2–4
1936	Stoke City	H	First Division	1–1
1942	Chester	H	Football League North (First Championship)	3–1
1953	Birmingham City	A	Second Division	1–5
1959	Preston North End	A	First Division	0–0
1964	Wolverhampton Wanderers	H	First Division	5–0

Two goals apiece for Fred Pickering and Derek Temple and a single effort from Sandy Brown took Everton to their biggest win of the season in front of a crowd of 27,533.

1970	Huddersfield Town	A	First Division	1–1
1981	Swansea City	H	First Division	3–1
1987	Charlton Athletic	A	First Division	0–0
1994	Leeds United	H	FA Premier League	3–0

DECEMBER 6TH

1890	Wolverhampton Wanderers	A	Football League	1–0
1902	Sheffield Wednesday	A	First Division	1–4
1913	Sheffield Wednesday	H	First Division	1–1

Tom Fern made his first appearance in goal for Everton in the 1–1 home draw with Sheffield Wednesday, Bobby Parker scoring Everton's goal on what was his debut game for the club. With Billy Scott having left for Leeds City the previous year, the goalkeeping berth had been a difficult position to fill with a number of players tried but none possessing the required ability to successfully make the position theirs. Tom Fern proved to be that man, making 231 appearances for the club until his departure to Port Vale in June 1924.

1919	Notts County	H	First Division	1–2
1924	Blackburn Rovers	A	First Division	0–3
1930	Oldham Athletic	H	Second Division	6–4

Dixie Dean scored four times in a thrilling match against Oldham at Goodison. Additional goals from Ted Critchley and Jimmy Dunn finally enabled Everton to see off Oldham.

1941	New Brighton	H	Football League North (First Championship)	4–0
1947	Portsmouth	A	First Division	0–3

1950 Terry Darracott born in Liverpool. He joined Everton as an apprentice and made his debut before signing professional forms, appearing in the side against Arsenal in April 1968. He went on to make 166 appearances for the first team and was then offered the position of youth team coach, turning it down in favour of continuing his playing career in America. He returned in September 1979 to sign for Wrexham and returned to Goodison in February 1984 as reserve team coach. After a brief spell as assistant manager at Grimsby he returned once again to Goodison as assistant manager to Colin Harvey.

1952	Birmingham City	H	Second Division	1–1
1958	Wolverhampton Wanderers	A	First Division	0–1
1969	Liverpool	H	First Division	0–3

A crowd of 57,370 were at Goodison for the first derby match of the season, with Everton sitting at the top of the table having lost only one League game in the last 13. Everton started the stronger but were unable to convert their superiority into goals, meaning the game arrived at the break still goalless. Liverpool recovered in the second period, scoring three times thanks to Hughes, a Sandy Brown own goal and Graham, thus inflicting on Everton their only home defeat of the campaign. But Everton got their revenge, winning 2–0 at Anfield later in the season and going on to win the title by nine points from Leeds.

1975	Ipswich Town	H	First Division	3–3
1980	Stoke City	A	First Division	2–2
1983	West Ham United	H	Milk Cup 4th Round Replay	2–0
1986	Norwich City	H	First Division	4–0
1997	Leeds United	A	FA Premier League	0–0

DECEMBER 7TH

1889	Notts County	H	Football League	5–3

Alex Latta scored his first hat-trick for the club, one of six he was to net in the club's colours.

1895	Small Heath	A	First Division	3–0
1896	Bolton Wanderers	A	First Division	0–2
1901	Sheffield Wednesday	H	First Division	5–0

Jimmy Settle and Jack Sharp both scored twice and Alex Young got the other goal in the 5–0 win that kept Everton on top of the First Division just ahead of Sunderland. At the end of the season however the two clubs had swapped places; Sunderland finished as champions with Everton as runners-up.

1907	Newcastle United	A	First Division	1–2
1912	West Bromwich Albion	H	First Division	1–3

1918	Blackpool	A	Lancashire Section Principal Tournament	3–1
1929	Grimsby Town	A	First Division	3–0
1935	West Bromwich Albion	A	First Division	1–6
1940	Southport	H	North Regional League	2–1
1946	Chelsea	A	First Division	1–1
1957	Manchester City	A	First Division	2–6

Ken Barnes of Manchester City scored a hat-trick of penalties against Everton, with Jimmy Harris grabbing both of Everton's goals.

1963	Chelsea	H	First Division	1–1
1968	Arsenal	A	First Division	1–3
1974	Leicester City	A	First Division	2–0
1985	West Bromwich Albion	A	First Division	3–0

Whilst Albion had hit the bottom of the table in the second week of League action and remained there for nine months, they still pulled off a shock or two during the course of the season, even if it amounted to taking a point off a side expected to win handsomely. Everton never gave them a chance at the Hawthorns, taking an early lead through Kevin Sheedy and creating a number of chances thereafter, with Pat Van Den Hauwe extending the lead before half-time. Although Albion fought back in the second half, Everton's defence held firm and Gary Lineker finished off the scoring to register a 3–0 win.

1991	West Ham United	H	First Division	4–0
1992	Liverpool	H	FA Premier League	2–1
1996	Chelsea	A	FA Premier League	2–2

DECEMBER 8TH

1894	Bolton Wanderers	H	First Division	3–1
1900	Derby County	H	First Division	2–0

Sam Wolstenholme scored his first goal for the club. Born in Little Lever he joined Everton in 1897 and made one appearance in the 1897–98 season, but thereafter established himself as a regular in the side and soon won England recognition, making his debut in April 1904. Everton surprisingly sold him to Blackburn soon after, even though he was still only 25 years of age, and he went on to add to his tally of caps at Ewood Park. He had made 170 appearances for Everton at the time of his transfer, scoring eight goals. In 1908 he joined Croydon Common and later switched to Norwich City before retiring in 1913. He then turned to coaching and had the misfortune to be in Germany when the First World War broke out, being interned along with Steve Bloomer and Fred Spikesley, although the three persuaded the camp commandant to allow them to organise a league among the other prisoners!

1906	Derby County	H	First Division	2–0
1917	Stoke City	A	Lancashire Section Principal Tournament	0–3
1923	Birmingham City	A	First Division	1–0
1928	Leicester City	H	First Division	3–1
1934	Blackburn Rovers	H	First Division	5–2
1945	Stoke City	H	Football League North	6–1
1951	Barnsley	A	Second Division	0–1

On the same day Mick Lyons was born in Liverpool. A stalwart of the Everton defence for over ten years, he had the misfortune to play for the club during a period they failed to win any major honours, although that never stopped him giving his all on the club's behalf. Signed by the club in July 1969 he went on to make over 430 appearances for the first team, finally leaving in August 1982 when he signed for Sheffield Wednesday. He later had a spell as player coach at Grimsby Town but was sacked when they were relegated to Division Three in 1987. He then returned to Everton, his first love, as reserve team coach.

1956	Birmingham City	H	First Division	2–0
1962	West Ham United	H	First Division	1–1
1973	Liverpool	H	First Division	0–1
1979	Brighton & Hove Albion	H	First Division	2–0
1984	Queens Park Rangers	A	First Division	0–0
1987	Glasgow Rangers	Dubai	Dubai Champions' Cup	2–2

With English clubs still banned from European competition, League champions Everton were invited to play against their Scottish counterparts in a one-off challenge match in Dubai for the Dubai Champions' Cup. A crowd of 8,000 were at the game which ended a 2–2 draw, Rangers then winning 8–7 on penalties.

| 1990 | Coventry City | H | First Division | 1–0 |
| 1993 | Manchester City | A | FA Premier League | 0–1 |

DECEMBER 9TH

1893	Sheffield United	A	First Division	3–0
1899	Bury	A	First Division	1–4
1905	Derby County	A	First Division	0–0
1911	Blackburn Rovers	A	First Division	1–2
1916	Stockport County	H	Lancashire Section Principal Tournament	0–1
1922	Sunderland	H	First Division	1–1
1933	Portsmouth	A	First Division	0–0
1939	Port Vale	H	War Regional League, Western Division	3–1
1944	Wrexham	H	Football League North (First Championship)	2–2
1950	Derby County	H	First Division	1–2
1961	Cardiff City	A	First Division	0–0
1967	Stoke City	A	First Division	0–1
1972	Wolverhampton Wanderers	H	First Division	0–1
1978	Birmingham City	A	First Division	3–1

Everton stretched their unbeaten start to the season to 18 games with a 3–1 win at St Andrews thanks to goals from Bob Latchford, Trevor Ross and Colin Todd in front of a crowd of 23,391.

| 1989 | Tottenham Hotspur | A | First Division | 1–2 |

DECEMBER 10TH

1892	Wolverhampton Wanderers	H	First Division	3–2
1898	Stoke City	H	First Division	2–0
1904	Stoke City	H	First Division	4–1
1910	Oldham Athletic	H	First Division	1–0
1921	West Bromwich Albion	A	First Division	1–1
1927	Aston Villa	A	First Division	3–2

Dixie Dean hit the 30 goal mark for the season after just 18 games (although he had missed one of these) with all three of Everton's goals in the 3–2 win over Villa in front of a crowd of 40,353 at Villa Park.

1932	Huddersfield Town	H	First Division	2–0
1938	Preston North End	A	First Division	1–0
1949	Sunderland	H	First Division	0–2
1955	Blackpool	A	First Division	0–4
1960	Birmingham City	A	First Division	4–2
1963	Arsenal	A	First Division	0–6

Everton were to finish the season in third place in the League, unable to retain their title which went to Liverpool. Their cause was not helped by this defeat at Highbury, the heaviest inflicted during the course of the campaign with Joe Baker and George Eastham both scoring twice.

1975	Tottenham Hotspur	A	First Division	2–2
1977	Middlesbrough	H	First Division	3–0
1983	Aston Villa .	H	First Division	1–1
1985	Chelsea	H	Milk Cup 4th Round Replay	1–2
1994	Aston Villa	A	FA Premier League	0–0

DECEMBER 11TH

1897	Notts County	H	First Division	1–0
1915	Manchester United	H	Lancashire Section Principal Tournament	2–0
1920	Middlesbrough	H	First Division	2–1

1923 Jack Hedley born in Wellington Quay. He joined Everton from North Shields during the Second World War and made 54 post war League appearances before being sold to Sunderland, where he made over 250 League appearances. He finished his career with Gateshead.

| 1926 | Cardiff City | H | First Division | 0–1 |
| 1937 | Birmingham City | H | First Division | 1–1 |

Dixie Dean made his 399th and final appearance for the club in the League in the match against Birmingham City which was drawn 1–1, joining Notts County early the following year. Everton's goal in the game was scored by Albert Geldard.

1943	Chester	H	Football League North (First Championship)	0–1
1948	Bolton Wanderers	H	First Division	1–0
1954	Sheffield Wednesday	H	First Division	3–1
1965	Aston Villa	A	First Division	2–3
1971	Nottingham Forest	A	First Division	0–1
1976	Coventry City	A	First Division	2–4
1982	Ipswich Town	A	First Division	2–0
1988	Liverpool	A	First Division	1–1
1993	Sheffield United	A	FA Premier League	0–0
1995	West Ham United	H	FA Premier League	3–0

DECEMBER 12TH

| 1891 | Wolverhampton Wanderers | H | Football League | 2–1 |
| 1896 | Sunderland | A | First Division | 1–1 |

1903	Stoke city	A	First Division	3–2
1908	Sheffield United	H	First Division	1–0
1914	Manchester City	H	First Division	4–1

William Brown made his debut for Everton in the 4–1 win at home to Manchester City. It was a difficult time to be making your first appearance for the club, for with the First World War being raged this was to be the last Football League season until 1919–20, but Brown had time on his side, for he was only 17 when first brought into the team. He remained at Goodison until May 1928 when he was sold to Nottingham Forest, having made 170 appearances in the League.

1925	Newcastle United	A	First Division	3–3
1931	Middlesbrough	H	First Division	5–1
1936	Charlton Athletic	A	First Division	0–2
1942	Chester	A	Football League North (First Championship)	3–2

1948 Colin Todd born in Chester-le-Street. An immensely talented defender he began his career with Sunderland and cost Derby County £170,000 when transferred in 1971. During his seven years at the Baseball Ground he won two League titles and was then sold to Everton for £300,000 in September 1978. He fell out with manager Gordon Lee a year later and was sold to Birmingham City for £275,000 and later played for Nottingham Forest before going into management. He is currently manager of Bolton Wanderers.

1953	Nottingham Forest	H	Second Division	3–3
1959	West Bromwich Albion	H	First Division	2–2
1964	Stoke City	H	First Division	1–1
1970	Southampton	H	First Division	4–1
1987	Derby County	H	First Division	3–0
1992	Sheffield United	A	FA Premier League	0–1

DECEMBER 13TH

| 1890 | Derby County | A | Football League | 6–2 |

T. Wylie became the first Everton player to score as many as four goals in one League match in this clash at the Racecourse Ground. It was Wylie's second game for the club, and he went on to make only 20 appearances, scoring five goals! Everton's goals were scored by Brady and Geary.

1902	West Bromwich Albion	H	First Division	3–1
1913	Bolton Wanderers	A	First Division	0–0
1919	Notts County	A	First Division	2–1
1924	West Ham United	H	First Division	1–0
1930	Burnley	A	Second Division	2–5
1941	New Brighton	A	Football League North (First Championship)	5–1
1947	Bolton Wanderers	H	First Division	2–0
1952	Bury	A	Second Division	5–0
1958	Portsmouth	H	First Division	2–1
1969	West Ham United	A	First Division	1–0
1975	Birmingham City	H	First Division	5–2

Five different players got on the scoresheet for Everton; Bob Latchford, Garry Jones, Martin Dobson, Bryan Hamilton and George Telfer as Birmingham were swept aside 5–2 at Goodison in front of a crowd of 20,188.

| 1980 | Brighton & Hove Albion | H | First Division | 4–3 |

1986	Luton Town	A	First Division	0–1
1997	Wimbledon	H	FA Premier League	0–0

DECEMBER 14TH

1895	Stoke City	H	First Division	7–2
1901	Notts County	A	First Division	2–0
1907	Sunderland	A	First Division	2–1
1912	Sunderland	H	First Division	0–4
1918	Stockport County	H	Lancashire Section Principal Tournament	2–1
1929	Manchester United	H	First Division	0–0
1935	Leeds United	H	First Division	0–0

Torry Gillick made his League debut for Everton shortly after his arrival from Glasgow Rangers, having cost the club £8,000. An adventurous winger able to play on either flank he took great delight in entertaining the crowd and but for the Second World War might have become one of the legends of Goodison. His debut kicked off with a 0–0 draw at home to Leeds United, but in his final League season he had a championship medal to his credit. He returned to Rangers in November 1945 and died in 1971.

1940	Tranmere Rovers	A	North Regional League	8–2

Stan Bentham led the scoring with a hat-trick whilst Tommy Lawton hit two and there were single strikes from Boyes, Cook and Stevenson. Everton had beaten Tranmere 9–0 earlier in the season!

1946	Sheffield United	H	First Division	2–3
1957	Nottingham Forest	H	First Division	1–1
1963	Fulham	A	First Division	2–2
1968	Southampton	H	First Division	1–0
1974	Derby County	A	First Division	1–0
1985	Leicester City	H	First Division	1–2
1988	Bradford City	A	Littlewoods Cup 4th Round	1–3
1991	Oldham Athletic	A	First Division	2–2

DECEMBER 15TH

1888	Stoke City	A	Football League	0–0
1894	Preston North End	A	First Division	2–1
1900	Bolton Wanderers	A	First Division	0–1
1906	Woolwich Arsenal	A	First Division	1–3
1917	Stoke City	H	Lancashire Section Principal Tournament	3–2
1923	Manchester City	A	First Division	1–2
1928	Manchester United	A	First Division	1–1
1934	Sheffield Wednesday	A	First Division	0–0
1945	Grimsby Town	H	Football League North	2–1
1951	Southampton	H	Second Division	3–0
1956	Leeds United	H	First Division	2–1
1962	Burnley	H	First Division	3–1

After two successive draws Everton got back on the winning trail and opened up a three point lead over Spurs at the top of the table with a 3–1 win over Burnley. Goals from Dennis Stevens, Roy Vernon and Alex Young secured the points in front of a crowd of 48,443.

1973	Sheffield United	H	First Division	1–1
1979	Southampton	A	First Division	0–1
1981	Ipswich Town	H	League Cup 4th Round	2–3
1984	Nottingham Forest	H	First Division	5–0

Everton kept on top of the First Division with an impressive 5–0 win against Nottingham Forest thanks to goals from Peter Reid, Graeme Sharp (two), Kevin Sheedy and Trevor Steven. The result made up for the news that Adrian Heath, injured in the start of the month clash with Sheffield Wednesday, would be out for the rest of the season with severe knee ligament trouble.

DECEMBER 16TH

1893	Blackburn Rovers	A	First Division	3–4
1899	Notts County	H	First Division	0–2
1905	Sheffield Wednesday	H	First Division	2–0
1911	Sheffield Wednesday	H	First Division	1–0
1916	Bury	H	Lancashire Section Principal Tournament	5–0
1922	Birmingham City	A	First Division	1–1
1933	Sunderland	H	First Division	1–0
1944	Stockport County	H	Football League North (First Championship)	6–1
1950	Huddersfield Town	A	First Division	2–1

1960 Pat Van den Hauwe born in Belgium. An uncompromising defender he began his career with Birmingham City and was transferred to Everton for £100,000 in 1984. A member of the side that won the League title in 1985 and 1987 (he scored the goal that clinched the title in the latter season) he opted to play for Wales and won a total of 13 caps. After struggling to retain his place in the side he was transferred to Spurs, where he won an FA Cup winners' medal, and later played for Millwall.

1961	Aston Villa	A	First Division	1–1
1965	Manchester United	A	First Division	0–3
1967	Manchester United	A	First Division	1–3
1972	Tottenham Hotspur	H	First Division	3–1
1978	Leeds United	H	First Division	1–1
1990	Leeds United	A	First Division	0–2
1992	Chelsea	A	Coca–Cola Cup 4th Round Replay	0–1
1995	Newcastle United	A	FA Premier League	0–1
1996	Derby County	A	FA Premier League	1–0

DECEMBER 17TH

1892	Notts County	A	First Division	2–1
1898	Aston Villa	A	First Division	0–3
1904	Small Heath	A	First Division	2–1
1910	Sheffield Wednesday	A	First Division	2–0
1921	Manchester City	A	First Division	1–2
1927	Burnley	H	First Division	4–1
1932	Sheffield United	A	First Division	2–3

1934 Ramon Wilson born in Shirebrook. Known throughout his career as Ray he was given his first taste of League football with Huddersfield and spent a total of 13 years at Leeds Road before being transferred to Everton in 1964. The 1965–66 season probably represented the pinnacle of his career, for in May he helped Everton win the FA Cup and two months later was a member of the England team that won the World Cup. He remained at Goodison Park until 1969 when he joined Oldham Athletic and finished his career with Bradford City. Upon retiring as a player he joined the family business and became an undertaker. He won a total of 63 caps for England.

| 1938 | Charlton Athletic | H | First Division | 1–4 |

This was the only home defeat suffered all season but despite the setback Everton went on to win the League title, four points clear of Wolves in second place.

1949	Middlesbrough	H	First Division	3–1
1955	Preston North End	A	First Division	1–0
1960	Tottenham Hotspur	H	First Division	1–3
1966	Fulham	H	First Division	3–2
1977	Birmingham City	A	First Division	0–0
1983	Queens Park Rangers	A	First Division	0–2
1988	Queens Park Rangers	A	First Division	0–0
1989	Manchester City	H	First Division	0–0
1994	Tottenham Hotspur	H	FA Premier League	0–0

DECEMBER 18TH

1897	Sunderland	A	First Division	0–0
1909	Bradford City	H	First Division	1–1
1915	Blackpool	A	Lancashire Section Principal Tournament	4–1
1920	West Bromwich Albion	A	First Division	2–1
1926	Burnley	A	First Division	1–5
1937	Portsmouth	A	First Division	1–3
1943	Manchester City	H	Football League North (First Championship)	4–0
1948	Newcastle United	A	First Division	0–1
1954	Sheffield United	H	First Division	2–3
1965	Fulham	H	First Division	2–0
1971	Derby County	A	First Division	0–2
1976	Birmingham City	H	First Division	2–2
1982	Luton Town	H	First Division	5–0
1990	Blackburn Rovers	A	Zenith Data Systems Cup 2nd Round	4–1

Despite having reached the final of the Simod Cup in 1989, Everton did not compete in the following year's competition, by which time the sponsors had changed and the trophy was now the Zenith Data Systems Cup. They returned in 1990–91, winning their opening match with Blackburn Rovers at Ewood Park 4–1 thanks to goals from Mike Newell, Tony Cottee and two from Dave Watson.

| 1993 | Newcastle United | H | FA Premier League | 0–2 |

DECEMBER 19TH

1896	Stoke City	H	First Division	4–2
1903	Derby County	H	First Division	0–1
1908	Leicester City	A	First Division	2–0
1914	Chelsea	A	First Division	0–2
1925	Bolton Wanderers	H	First Division	2–1
1931	Bolton Wanderers	A	First Division	1–2

| 1936 | Grimsby Town | H | First Division | 3–0 |
| 1942 | Manchester City | A | Football League North (First Championship) | 1–7 |

1952 Former Everton player Harry Makepeace died in Bebington. One of the few men to have been capped by England at both football and cricket he played for the club between 1902 and 1915 in the League and later became team coach.

1953	Luton Town	H	Second Division	2–1
1959	Luton Town	A	First Division	1–2
1964	Tottenham Hotspur	A	First Division	2–2
1970	Leeds United	H	First Division	0–1
1975	Coventry City	A	First Division	2–1
1981	Aston Villa	H	First Division	2–0
1987	Arsenal	A	First Division	1–1
1992	Southampton	H	FA Premier League	2–1

DECEMBER 20TH

1879 Everton played their very first match, a friendly against local club St Peter's in Stanley Park and won 6–0. As the game was little more than the type of kick–about that can be seen on any public park (the Everton players had to carry their own posts out on to the pitch, which they also marked), the local paper reported the score of the game only – we have no way of knowing who played or scored.

1890	Sunderland	A	Football League	0–1
1902	Notts County	A	First Division	0–2
1913	Chelsea	H	First Division	0–0
1919	Liverpool	H	First Division	1–0
1924	Sheffield United	A	First Division	1–1
1930	Southampton	H	Second Division	2–1

1933 George Kirby born in Liverpool. He joined Everton as a junior and graduated through the ranks, going on to make 26 League appearances at centre-forward and scoring nine goals. He then joined Sheffield Wednesday and later played for Plymouth, Southampton, Coventry, Swansea, Walsall and Brentford.

1941	Stockport County	A	Football League North (First Championship)	1–1
1947	Blackburn Rovers	H	First Division	4–1
1952	Hull City	A	Second Division	0–1
1958	Leicester City	H	First Division	0–1

1960 Brian Borrows born in Liverpool. After graduating through the ranks at Everton he seemed set for a lengthy career at Goodison when he was surprisingly sold to Bolton in 1983 for £10,000. He returned to the top flight with Coventry in 1985 and earned a cap for the England B side. He has since made over 400 League appearances for Coventry.

1969	Derby County	H	First Division	1–0
1986	Wimbledon	H	First Division	3–0
1988	Millwall	H	Simod Cup 3rd Round	2–0

Everton entered the Simod Cup at the third round stage and registered a 2–0 win over Millwall at Goodison thanks to an own goal by Terry Hurlock and a strike from Tony Cottee. There was still little interest from the fans, with just 3,703 paying customers on the night.

| 1997 | Leicester City | A | FA Premier League | 1–0 |

DECEMBER 21ST

1889	Preston North End	A	Football League	2–1
1895	Aston Villa	H	First Division	2–0
1901	Bolton Wanderers	H	First Division	1–0
1907	Woolwich Arsenal	H	First Division	1–1
1912	Sheffield Wednesday	A	First Division	2–1
1918	Stockport County	A	Lancashire Section Principal Tournament	0–0
1929	Sheffield United	A	First Division	0–2
1935	Birmingham City	A	First Division	2–4
1940	Preston North End	H	North Regional League	0–3
1946	Preston North End	A	First Division	1–2

On the same day Bryan Hamilton was born in Belfast. After being spotted whilst playing for Linfield he was brought to England by Ipswich Town, signing with them in 1971. Four years later he cost Everton £40,000 and spent less than two years at Goodison Park, although they were action packed to say the least. He left Everton for Millwall in 1977 and later played for Swindon and Tranmere and then went into management. He has managed Tranmere, Wigan and Northern Ireland, for whom he won 50 caps as a player.

1957	Wolverhampton	A	First Division	0–2
1960	Tranmere Rovers	A	League Cup 4th Round	4–0

Frank Wignall took his tally of League Cup goals to seven for the season with a hat-trick in the local derby with Tranmere Rovers. Billy Bingham scored Everton's other goal in the 4–0 win at Prenton Park.

1963	Manchester United	H	First Division	4–0
1968	Stoke City	A	First Division	0–0
1974	Carlisle United	H	First Division	2–3
1985	Coventry City	A	First Division	3–1
1991	Arsenal	A	First Division	2–4
1996	Leeds United	H	FA Premier League	0–0

DECEMBER 22ND

1888	Preston North End	A	Football League	0–3
1900	Notts County	H	First Division	0–1
1906	Sheffield Wednesday	H	First Division	2–0
1917	Preston North End	A	Lancashire Section Principal Tournament	1–0
1923	Manchester City	H	First Division	6–1
1928	Newcastle United	H	First Division	5–2

Whilst Dixie Dean was always unlikely to get even close to his goal tally for the previous season, he did rattle in a healthy 26 goals in just 29 appearances during the campaign, including his third hat-trick of the season in this 5–2 win. Everton's other goals were scored by Martin and Ritchie.

1934	Birmingham	H	First Division	2–0
1945	Grimsby Town	A	Football League North	2–1
1947	David Lawson born in Wallsend. After spells on the books of Newcastle, Shrewsbury and Bradford Park Avenue, where he made his League debut, he made his name at Huddersfield Town. He joined Everton in 1972 and was virtually ever present in goal for the next two seasons, but sadly injury cost him his place and he was transferred to Luton for £15,000 in 1978. He later played for Stockport County.			

| 1951 | Sheffield Wednesday | A | Second Division | 0–4 |
| 1962 | Sheffield Wednesday | A | First Division | 2–2 |

1971   Alan Ball was transferred to Arsenal for a fee of £220,000 after five years with the club. Later the player's father was reported as stating 'Alan didn't want to move South but Arsenal guaranteed him £12,500 a year.'

1973	Arsenal	A	First Division	0–1
1979	Manchester City	H	First Division	1–2
1984	Chelsea	H	First Division	3–4

Everton lost a thrilling match at home to Chelsea and with it the leadership of the First Division. Paul Bracewell and Graeme Sharp with two goals (one from the penalty spot) scored for Everton but Chelsea replied through a Gordon Davies hat-trick and Colin Pates. Spurs won 2–1 at Norwich on the same day to take over at the top of the table (with Manchester United moving up to second spot), and most of the media reflected on how the team on top of the table at Christmas time usually went on to win the League title. Everton had other ideas; they did not lose another match until May 11th by which time the title was already won.

| 1990 | Norwich City | A | First Division | 0–1 |

DECEMBER 23RD

| 1893 | Sheffield Wednesday | H | First Division | 8–1 |

Jack Southworth equalled the record previously set by Alex Latta and Fred Geary by scoring four of Everton's goals in the 8–1 win, with Bell (two), Chadwick and Latta himself netting the other goals. A week later Southworth set a new record with six goals in one game.

1899	Manchester City	A	First Division	2–1
1905	Nottingham Forest	A	First Division	3–4
1911	Bury	A	First Division	2–1
1916	Stoke City	A	Lancashire Section Principal Tournament	2–0
1922	Birmingham City	H	First Division	2–1

1929   Donal Donovan born in Cork. Spotted by Everton whilst playing for Maymount Rovers (Everton were on tour in Eire at the time) he was invited to come to England and take up professional football. He signed in May 1949 and first broke into the first team in season 1951–52, going on to make 187 first-team appearances. He then switched to Grimsby Town, for whom he made over 200 League appearances before retiring as a player. He won 5 caps for the Republic of Ireland.

1933	Aston Villa	A	First Division	1–2
1939	Tranmere Rovers	A	War Regional League, Western Division	9–2
1944	Stockport County	A	Football League North (First Championship)	7–0
1950	Newcastle United	H	First Division	3–1
1961	Fulham	H	First Division	3–0
1966	Nottingham Forest	H	First Division	0–1
1967	Sunderland	H	First Division	3–0
1969	Manchester City	H	First Division	1–0
1972	Chelsea	A	First Division	1–1
1975	Manchester United	H	First Division	1–1
1978	Coventry City	A	First Division	2–3

Everton began the season unbeaten in their first 19 matches, the best record in the entire

League, and lost the record in a 3–2 defeat at Coventry. Despite the run they never once headed the League table, second place for some three months the best they could manage. They briefly went top in February but later slipped to fourth place.

| 1995 | Coventry City | A | FA Premier League | 1–2 |

DECEMBER 24TH

1892	Burnley	H	First Division	0–1
1898	Burnley	H	First Division	4–0
1904	Manchester City	H	First Division	0–0
1910	Bristol City	H	First Division	4–3
1927	Arsenal	A	First Division	2–3

Dixie Dean scored one of Everton's goals in the 3–2 defeat, with Alec Troup netting the other, Dean's 31st goal of the season.

| 1932 | Wolverhampton Wanderers | H | First Division | 5–1 |

After the drama of the League title win of the previous season, 1932–33 started disappointingly for Everton, with a mid-table placing being the best that could be achieved, although the FA Cup was to provide more than adequate compensation later on in the season. Meanwhile, Everton demolished Wolves in this League game thanks to two goals from Dixie Dean and single strikes from Jimmy Dunn, Tommy Johnson and Jimmy Stein.

1938	Blackpool	H	First Division	4–0
1949	Liverpool	A	First Division	1–3
1955	Burnley	H	First Division	1–1

DECEMBER 25TH

1891	Sunderland	H	Football League	0–4
1893	Glasgow Rangers	H	Friendly	1–2
1895	Glasgow Rangers	H	Friendly	5–1

Everton's FA Cup tie with Glasgow Rangers in 1886 had started a relationship between the two clubs that often saw Rangers visiting Goodison Park and Everton playing at Ibrox. Perhaps it was because it was Christmas Day, only 5,000 fans ventured out of their homes for the friendly, won 5–1 by Everton.

1897	Aston Villa	H	First Division	2–1
1899	Stoke City	H	First Division	2–0
1900	Sheffield United	A	First Division	1–2
1901	Aston Villa	H	First Division	2–3
1902	Grimsby Town	A	First Division	0–0
1905	Bury	A	First Division	2–3
1906	Bury	A	First Division	2–1
1907	Notts County	A	First Division	1–2
1908	Notts County	H	First Division	0–1
1909	Bristol City	A	First Division	1–3
1911	Middlesbrough	A	First Division	0–0
1912	Blackburn Rovers	H	First Division	2–1
1913	Manchester United	A	First Division	1–0
1914	Bradford City	H	First Division	1–1

1915	Southport	H	Lancashire Section Principal Tournament	2–0
1919	Manchester City	A	First Division	2–1
1920	Arsenal	H	First Division	2–4
1921	Manchester City	H	First Division	2–2
1922	Manchester City	H	First Division	0–0
1924	Newcastle United	H	First Division	0–1
1925	Blackburn Rovers	A	First Division	2–2
1926	Sunderland	H	First Division	5–4

Ted Critchley made his debut for the club in the thrilling 5–4 home win over Sunderland at Goodison Park where Dixie Dean scored four of the goals. Indeed, it was Critchley who was to become chief provider for Dean and a more than adequate replacement for Sam Chedgzov on the right wing. He made over 200 appearances for the club but is perhaps best remembered for one he didn't appear in; in 1933 he was a late replacement for the injured Albert Geldard in the FA Cup semi-final against West Ham and was responsible for forcing a defender into conceding an own goal which took Everton into the final against Manchester City. By then Geldard had recovered and took his place at Wembley.

1928	Sunderland	H	First Division	0–0
1929	Sheffield Wednesday	H	First Division	1–4
1930	Bury	A	Second Division	2–2
1931	Blackburn Rovers	A	First Division	3–5
1933	Newcastle United	A	First Division	2–1
1934	Sunderland	H	First Division	6–2

A Christmas Day crowd of 37,931 were treated to an eight goal feat, with Everton's goals being netted by Jimmy Cunliffe (two), Jackie Coulter, Dixie Dean, Albert Geldard and Alex Stevenson. Sunderland didn't long to wait before gaining their revenge, for the two sides were scheduled to meet the following day, Boxing Day, at Roker Park.

1936	Derby County	H	First Division	7–0

For once Dixie Dean was put in the shade by the achievements of another member of the strike force, with Jimmy Cunliffe netting a hat-trick, Dean and Alex Stevenson two apiece in the 7–0 win at Goodison in front of a crowd of 32,349.

1937	Leicester City	A	First Division	1–3
1940	Liverpool	A	North Regional League	1–3
1941	Stockport County	H	Football League North (First Championship)	6–0
1942	Manchester City	H	Football League North (First Championship)	6–3
1943	Manchester City	A	Football League North (First Championship)	5–3
1944	Tranmere Rovers	H	Football League North (Second Championship)	2–4
1945	Blackpool	A	Football League North	2–5
1946	Derby County	H	First Division	4–1
1947	Sunderland	A	First Division	0–2
1948	Manchester City	H	First Division	0–0
1950	Burnley	H	First Division	1–0
1951	Doncaster Rovers	A	Second Division	1–3
1953	Bristol Rovers	H	Second Division	4–0
1954	Wolverhampton Wanderers	A	First Division	3–1
1956	Tottenham Hotspur	A	First Division	0–6
1957	Bolton Wanderers	H	First Division	1–1

The last time Everton had to play on Christmas Day, with 29,584 present to see the 1–1 draw with Bolton Wanderers, George Kirby scoring for the home side.

1981 Tom Griffiths died in Wrexham. He had begun his career with Wrexham and was transferred to Everton in 1926, developing into a powerful centre-half and earning the first of his 21 caps for Wales whilst at the club. He lost his place at Goodison to Charlie Gee and moved on to Bolton, later serving Middlesbrough and Aston Villa before retiring to become a publican in his home town.

DECEMBER 26TH

1890	Accrington	H	Football League	3–2
1896	Sunderland	H	First Division	5–2
1899	West Bromwich Albion	A	First Division	0–0
1900	Bury	H	First Division	3–3
1901	Wolverhampton Wanderers	A	First Division	1–2
1902	Glasgow Rangers	H	Friendly	1–2
1903	Manchester City	A	First Division	3–1
1904	Wolverhampton Wanderers	A	First Division	3–0
1905	Bury	H	First Division	1–2
1906	Manchester City	A	First Division	1–3
1907	Bristol City	H	First Division	0–0
1908	Notts County	A	First Division	0–0
1910	Newcastle United	A	First Division	0–1

Sam Chedgzov made his debut for the club in the 1–0 defeat at Newcastle United. Born in Ellesmere Port in 1890 he is best remembered for a goal he scored against Spurs in 1924; he dribbled the ball in from the corner spot past bemused defenders and attackers alike and poked the ball home, the rule about goals being scored direct from a corner making no mention that the player taking the corner could only touch the ball once! He remained with Everton until 1926, having collected a League championship medal in 1914–15 and retired to Canada where he died in 1967.

1911	Middlesbrough	H	First Division	1–0
1912	Blackburn Rovers	A	First Division	2–1
1913	Manchester United	H	First Division	5–0

Bobby Parker scored the first hat-trick of his Everton career in the 5–0 win over Manchester United, the other goals being scored by T. Nuttall. Parker had joined from Glasgow Rangers in November 1913 and proved a sensation at Goodison Park, netting 71 goals in just 92 appearances and leading the First Division scoring charts in 1914–15 as Everton won the League. He was surprisingly sold to Nottingham Forest in May 1921.

1914	Bradford City	A	First Division	1–0
1919	Manchester city	H	First Division	2–0
1921	Sunderland	A	First Division	2–1
1922	Manchester City	A	First Division	1–2
1923	Sunderland	H	First Division	2–3

Sunderland became the only side to win at Goodison Park during the season, one of ten away victories they achieved, the best in the division.

1924	Newcastle United	A	First Division	1–1

1925	Blackburn Rovers	H	First Division	3–0
1927	Cardiff City	H	First Division	2–1

Both of Everton's goals were scored by Dixie Dean, his 32nd and 33rd goals of the season after only 20 League appearances during the campaign.

1929	Sheffield Wednesday	A	First Division	0–4
1931	Blackburn Rovers	H	First Division	5–0
1932	Blackburn Rovers	A	First Division	1–3
1933	Newcastle United	H	First Division	3–7
1934	Sunderland	A	First Division	0–7

There has probably never been a greater turn–around of fortunes than that experienced by Sunderland against Everton; the previous day Everton had won 6–2 at Goodison, the two games therefore producing 15 goals! Not only did Sunderland go one better than Everton they also managed to keep Dixie Dean and the rest of the Everton strike force quiet throughout the game.

1935	Sheffield Wednesday	H	First Division	4–3
1936	Arsenal	H	First Division	1–1
1938	Derby County	H	First Division	2–2
1942	Tranmere Rovers	A	Football League North (Second Championship)	1–2
1944	Liverpool	H	Football League North (Second Championship)	2–2
1945	Blackpool	H	Football League North	7–1
1946	Derby County	A	First Division	1–5
1947	Sunderland	H	First Division	3–0
1949	Fulham	H	First Division	1–1
1950	Burnley	A	First Division	1–1
1951	Doncaster Rovers	H	Second Division	1–1
1952	Lincoln City	A	Second Division	1–1
1955	Birmingham City	A	First Division	2–6
1956	Tottenham Hotspur	H	First Division	1–1
1957	Bolton Wanderers	A	First Division	5–1

Just 24 hours after being held 1–1 at home by Bolton, Everton travelled to Burnden Park and recorded a 5–1 win! Their goals were scored by Brian Harris (two), Jimmy Harris, Dave Hickson and Jack Keeley.

1958	Bolton Wanderers	H	First Division	1–0
1959	Manchester City	H	First Division	2–1
1960	Burnley	A	First Division	3–1
1961	Bolton Wanderers	H	First Division	1–0
1963	Leicester City	A	First Division	0–2
1964	West Bromwich Albion	H	First Division	3–2
1966	Nottingham Forest	A	First Division	0–1
1967	Burnley	H	First Division	2–0
1968	Manchester City	A	First Division	3–1
1970	Wolverhampton Wanderers	A	First Division	0–2
1972	Birmingham City	H	First Division	1–1
1973	Manchester City	H	First Division	2–0
1974	Wolverhampton Wanderers	A	First Division	0–2

1977	Manchester United	H	First Division	2–6
1978	Manchester City	H	First Division	1–0
1979	Bolton Wanderers	A	First Division	1–1
1980	Manchester City	H	First Division	0–2
1983	Sunderland	H	First Division	0–0
1984	Sunderland	A	First Division	2–1

Derek Mountfield scored twice in the first half to put Everton firmly in control of the game, and although Sunderland pulled one back in the second half Everton held on to move back up to second place in the League.

1985	Manchester United	H	First Division	3–1
1986	Newcastle United	A	First Division	4–0

With Arsenal only able to draw at Leicester City, Everton moved two points closer to the top of the table with a majestic performance at St James' Park in front of a crowd of 35,079. Paul Power gave Everton a first half lead and Trevor Steven added two and Adrian Heath one in a blistering second half performance.

1987	Luton Town	H	First Division	2–0
1988	Middlesbrough	H	First Division	2–1
1989	Derby County	A	First Division	1–0
1990	Aston Villa	H	First Division	1–0
1991	Sheffield Wednesday	H	First Division	0–1
1992	Middlesbrough	H	FA Premier League	2–2
1994	Sheffield Wednesday	H	FA Premier League	1–4
1995	Middlesbrough	H	FA Premier League	4–0

Everton's improvement continued with a 4–0 win over mid-table Middlesbrough at Goodison. The goals were scored by Craig Short, Graham Stuart (two) and Andrei Kanchelskis.

1996	Middlesbrough	A	FA Premier League	2–4
1997	Manchester United	A	FA Premier League	0–2

DECEMBER 27TH

1890	Burnley	H	Football League	7–3

Edgar Chadwick hit a hat-trick and Alex Latta contributed two as Everton swamped Burnley on their way to the League title. The other goals were scored by Brady and Milward.

1902	Bolton Wanderers	H	First Division	3–1
1904	Derby County	A	First Division	2–1
1909	Bristol City	H	First Division	1–0
1910	Liverpool	H	First Division	0–1
1913	Preston North End	A	First Division	0–1
1919	Liverpool	A	First Division	2–3
1920	Arsenal	A	First Division	1–1
1924	Birmingham City	H	First Division	2–1
1926	Sunderland	A	First Division	2–3
1927	Cardiff City	A	First Division	0–2
1930	Plymouth Argyle	H	Second Division	9–1

The Second Division match against Plymouth Argyle saw Everton equal their record League score with a 9–1 victory at Goodison Park. Dixie Dean scored four times, as did

Jimmy Stein, with Tommy Johnson adding the ninth. Everton had previously scored nine in a League match against Manchester City in 1906.

1932	Blackburn Rovers	H	First Division	6–1
1937	Leicester City	H	First Division	3–0
1938	Derby County	A	First Division	1–2
1941	Sheffield Wednesday	A	Football League North (Second Championship)	3–0
1943	Chester	A	Football League North (Second Championship)	5–3
1948	Manchester City	A	First Division	0–0
1949	Fulham	A	First Division	0–0
1954	Wolverhampton Wanderers	H	First Division	3–2
1955	Birmingham City	H	First Division	5–1
1958	Bolton Wanderers	A	First Division	3–0
1960	Burnley	H	First Division	0–3
1965	Nottingham Forest	A	First Division	0–1
1969	Leeds United	A	First Division	1–2
1971	Huddersfield Town	H	First Division	2–2

On the same day Duncan Ferguson was born in Stirling. He began his career with Carse Thistle and was subsequently signed by Dundee United, developing into a highly feared striker. A £4 million transfer fee took him to Glasgow Rangers in 1993, but a series of highly publicised bookings and sendings off, culminating in a court case which led to him being jailed, prompted Rangers to sell him to Everton for £4.4 million in 1994, just before Rangers were due to make additional payments for appearances. His time at Goodison has been equally volatile, but on his day he is one of the best strikers in the game. A full Scottish international he asked not to be considered for the 1998 World Cup finals; Scotland missed his aerial threat.

1975	Middlesbrough	A	First Division	1–1
1976	Manchester United	A	First Division	0–4
1977	Leeds United	A	First Division	1–3
1980	Middlesbrough	A	First Division	0–1
1982	Stoke City	A	First Division	0–1
1983	Wolverhampton Wanderers	A	First Division	0–3
1993	Sheffield Wednesday	H	FA Premier League	0–2

DECEMBER 28TH

1889	Blackburn Rovers	A	Football League	4–2
1891	Aston Villa	A	Football League	4–3
1907	Sheffield Wednesday	A	First Division	2–1
1912	Middlesbrough	H	First Division	1–0
1918	Blackburn Rovers	A	Lancashire Section Principal Tournament	4–1
1929	Bolton Wanderers	A	First Division	0–5
1935	Derby County	A	First Division	3–3
1936	Derby County	A	First Division	1–3
1946	Brentford	A	First Division	1–1
1953	Bristol Rovers	A	Second Division	0–0

Everton made their only ever visit to Eastville for League points, drawing 0–0 with

Bristol Rovers three days after Rovers had made their only League trip to Goodison Park.

1957	Aston Villa	H	First Division	1–2
1959	Manchester City	A	First Division	0–4
1963	Leicester City	H	First Division	0–3
1974	Middlesbrough	H	First Division	1–1
1981	Coventry City	H	First Division	3–2
1982	Nottingham Forest	H	First Division	3–1
1985	Sheffield Wednesday	H	First Division	3–1
1986	Leicester City	H	First Division	5–1

Two days after winning at Newcastle, Everton turned on the same kind of display for their own fans at Goodison with a 5–1 win over Leicester City. Goals from Adrian Heath (two), Paul Wilkinson, Kevin Sheedy and an own goal wrapped up the points to bring Arsenal in sight again.

1987	Manchester United	A	First Division	1–2
1991	Liverpool	H	First Division	1–1
1992	Queens Park Rangers	A	FA Premier League	2–4
1996	Wimbledon	H	FA Premier League	1–3
1997	Bolton Wanderers	H	FA Premier League	3–2

DECEMBER 29TH

1888	Accrington	A	Football League	1–3
1900	Preston North End	H	First Division	4–1
1906	Middlesbrough	H	First Division	5–1
1917	Preston North End	H	Lancashire Section Principal Tournament	6–0
1923	Bolton Wanderers	A	First Division	0–2
1928	Bolton Wanderers	H	First Division	3–0

Jimmy Stein made his debut in the 3–0 win over Bolton, helping Dixie Dean claim a hat-trick. Born in Coatbridge Stein first came to prominence with Dunfermline before switching to Everton in 1928 and went on to collect winners' medals from the Second Division, First Division and FA Cup in consecutive seasons. He made 215 appearances for the club, scoring 65 goals, including one in the 1933 FA Cup final, before leaving for Burnley in October 1936. He later played for New Brighton before his retirement.

1934	Tottenham Hotspur	H	First Division	5–2

Everton recovered from their 7–0 hammering against Sunderland three days earlier with a blast for Spurs, with Dixie Dean scoring a hat-trick and Coulter and Cunliffe adding the other two goals.

1945	Liverpool	H	Football League North	2–2
1951	Leeds United	H	Second Division	2–0
1956	Wolverhampton Wanderers	H	First Division	3–1
1973	Derby County	H	First Division	2–1
1976	Middlesbrough	H	First Division	2–2
1979	Derby County	H	First Division	1–1
1984	Ipswich Town	A	First Division	2–0
1990	Derby County	H	First Division	2–0
1993	Blackburn Rovers	A	FA Premier League	0–2

DECEMBER 30TH

1893	West Bromwich Albion	H	First Division	7–1

Jack Southworth scored six of Everton's seven goals by which they beat West Bromwich Albion at Goodison Park. A crowd of 25,000 were present, although the match itself had been in some doubt owing to fog, but their patience was rewarded with a fine 7–1 win in which Southworth excelled. The other Everton goal was scored by John Bell. Southworth's achievement was the first time any player had managed to score a double hat-trick in one League match.

1899	Sheffield united	A	First Division	0–5
1905	Middlesbrough	A	First Division	0–0
1911	Tottenham Hotspur	A	First Division	1–0
1916	Southport	H	Lancashire Section Principal Tournament	1–1
1922	Huddersfield Town	H	First Division	0–3
1933	West Bromwich Albion	A	First Division	3–3
1944	Tranmere Rovers	A	Football League North (Second Championship)	4–0
1950	West Bromwich Albion	A	First Division	1–0
1967	Burnley	A	First Division	1–2

1972 Daniel Amokachi born in Nigeria. Signed by Everton from FC Brugge he exploded on to the English game in 1994–95, his two goals in the FA Cup semi-final against Spurs the highlight of his brief stay with the club.

1978	Tottenham Hotspur	H	First Division	1–1
1989	Queens Park Rangers	A	First Division	0–1
1995	Leeds United	H	FA Premier League	2–0

DECEMBER 31ST

1898	Sheffield United	H	First Division	1–0
1904	Notts County	H	First Division	5–1
1910	Middlesbrough	H	First Division	2–0
1921	Bolton Wanderers	H	First Division	1–0
1927	Sheffield Wednesday	A	First Division	2–1

Another pair of goals from Dixie Dean took him to 35 goals for the season, on course to beat George Camsell's record set the previous year.

1932	West Bromwich Albion	H	First Division	1–2

Billy Cook made his debut for the club in the 2–1 home defeat by West Bromwich Albion. Signed from Celtic for £3,000 earlier in the month, he remained an almost permanent fixture in the side until the 1938–39 season, helping the club win the League championship that season. At the end of the Second World War he signed for Wrexham and after a spell as player-manager at Rhyl joined the Sunderland coaching staff. He then became coach to the Peruvian FA and had a spell in Norway before returning to England to take over as manager of Wigan Athletic in 1966.

1933 Ken Birch born in Birkenhead. He joined Everton as a junior and signed professional forms in August 1951, going on to make 43 League appearances before joining Southampton in March 1958. He made 33 first-team outings with the Saints before slipping into the non-League game.

1936 Graham Williams born in Wrexham. He began his career with Bradford City and joined Everton in March 1956, going on to make 31 appearances for the club. He later signed for Swansea, Wrexham, Tranmere and Port Vale, and represented Wales on five occasions.

1938	Brentford	A	First Division	0–2
1949	Huddersfield Town	A	First Division	2–1
1955	Luton Town	A	First Division	2–2
1960	Leicester City	A	First Division	1–4
1966	Liverpool	A	First Division	0–0
1977	Arsenal	H	First Division	2–0
1983	Coventry City	H	First Division	0–0
1988	Coventry City	H	First Division	3–1
1994	Ipswich Town	H	FA Premier League	4–1